Windows® NT®/2000 Network Security

E. Eugene Schultz

MTP
MACMILLAN
TECHNICAL
PUBLISHING
U·S·A

Windows® NT®/2000 Network Security

FIRST EDITION: *August, 2000*

International Standard Book Number: 1-57870-253-4

Library of Congress Catalog Card Number: 00-102979

04 03 02 01 00 7 6 5 4 3 2 1

Interpretation of the printing code: The rightmost double-digit number is the year of the book's printing; the rightmost single-digit number is the number of the book's printing. For example, the printing code 00-1 shows that the first printing of the book occurred in 2000.

Composed in Sabon and MCPdigital by MTP

Printed in the United States of America

Trademarks

All terms mentioned in this book that are known to be trademarks or service marks have been appropriately capitalized. MTP cannot attest to the accuracy of this information. Use of a term in this book should not be regarded as affecting the validity of any trademark or service mark. Windows is a registered trademark of Microsoft Corporation. Tivoli is a registered trademark of IBM.

Warning and Disclaimer

This book is designed to provide information about Windows network security. Every effort has been made to make this book as complete and as accurate as possible, but no warranty or fitness is implied.

The information is provided on an as-is basis. The authors and MTP shall have neither liability nor responsibility to any person or entity with respect to any loss or damages arising from the information contained in this book or from the use of the discs or programs that may accompany it.

Publisher
David Dwyer

Executive Editor
Al Valvano

Managing Editor
Gina Brown

Product Marketing Manager
Stephanie Layton

Manager of Publicity
Susan Petro

Acquisitions Editor
Theresa Gheen

Development Editor
Katherine Pendergast

Project Editor
Kristy Knoop

Copy Editor
Keith Cline

Indexer
Lisa Stumpf

Manufacturing
Jim Conway
Chris Moos

Book Designer
Louisa Klucznik

Cover Designer
Aren Howell

Proofreaders
Debbie Williams
Chrissy Andry
Sarah Cisco

Composition
Amy Parker
Suzanne Pettypiece
Gina Rexrode

Table of Contents

About the Author

Eugene Schultz, Ph.D., CISSP, is the Research Director and Trusted Security Advisor for Global Integrity Corporation (an SAIC Company) and is also an adjunct professor at Purdue University. Prior to joining Global Integrity, Dr. Schultz was Principal Consultant at SRI Consulting. An expert in NT, Unix, LAN, network security, and security administration and management, Dr. Schultz has co-authored several books and published over 80 journal articles. He is Editor of *Information Security Bulletin* and a consulting editor of *Network Security*. He was voted one of the Top Presenters at the SANS Conferences, was co-recipient of the Best Paper Award at the 1995 National Information Systems Security Conference, and received the Information Systems Security Association (ISSA) Professional Contribution Award in 1998. Dr. Schultz is also the founder and former manager of the Computer Incident Advisory Capability (CIAC) for the U.S. Department of Energy. He has provided expert testimony in the U.S. Senate and House of Representatives.

About the Technical Reviewers

Jesper M. Johansson is an Assistant Professor in the MIS Department at Boston University. He holds a Ph.D. from the University of Minnesota, a Masters of Science in Information Systems, and a Masters of Business Administration, from the University of Maryland. His primary research interests are in the areas of information systems security and administration and IT infrastructure design, especially the underlying networking and database designs. He teaches networking and telecommunications at Boston University. He also teaches System Administration and Security on the Windows NT and 2000 Platforms and edits the SANS (System Administration, Networking and Security) Windows Security Digest. He has 11 years of experience in system administration and holds several professional certifications on Microsoft products, including the Microsoft Certified Systems Engineer and Microsoft Certified Professional + Internet certifications.

Dedication

This book is dedicated to a special individual who has always encouraged and inspired me, Cathy Brown Schultz.

Acknowledgments

Several individuals were instrumental in the effort to write and produce this book. Dan Woolley and Bill Marlow, of Global Integrity Corporation, generously allowed me the time to finish this writing effort. Janice Hughes of Global Integrity Corporation helped format each chapter properly and pasted in screen shots for most of the chapters. Phil Cox of System Experts not only wrote Chapter 9 of this book, but revised portions of Chapters 7 and 8, provided a generous amount of advice, and also contributed to making many screen shots. Ariel Silverstone, formerly of Global Integrity Corporation and now with KPMG Consulting, helped rewrite Chapter 11. Jesper Johannson of Boston Univerity, Ian Cook of Citibank, Andrew Stewart of Internet Security Systems, Paul Boyer of Global Integrity Corporation, and Rik Farrow provided considerable helpful feedback.

My wife, Cathy Brown Schultz, not only tolerated my going into "hibernation" mode to write this book, but also continued to lovingly help me achieve a reasonable balance between my work life and home life. My youngest daughter, Leah Brown Schultz, the only daughter still living in our household, was also more patient and understanding than I deserved!

Finally, I would like to thank Al Valvano, Katie Pendergast, Kristy Knoop, Gina Brown, and Theresa Gheen of New Riders Publishing for providing so much guidance and support.

Tell Us What You Think

As the reader of this book, you are the most important critic and commentator. We value your opinion and want to know what we're doing right, what we could do better, what areas you'd like to see us publish in, and any other words of wisdom you're willing to pass our way.

As the Executive Editor for the Networking team at MTP, I welcome your comments. You can fax, email, or write me directly to let me know what you did or didn't like about this book—as well as what we can do to make our books stronger.

Please note that I cannot help you with technical problems related to the topic of this book, and that due to the high volume of mail I receive, I might not be able to reply to every message.

When you write, please be sure to include this book's title and author as well as your name and phone or fax number. I will carefully review your comments and share them with the author and editors who worked on the book.

Fax: 317-581-4663
Email: nrfeedback@newriders.com
Mail: Al Valvano
Executive Editor
New Riders Publishing
201 West 103rd Street
Indianapolis, IN 46290 USA

Introduction

Windows NT is an enormously popular operating system that some people claim is the most secure system commercially available today. Windows NT does, in fact, offer an extensive set of security features, ranging from password controls to access control lists (ACLs), to various types of network security measures. But the system also poses a wide range of vulnerabilities, many of them related to Windows NT's network capabilities.

Windows NT is a network integrated operating system. Many systems (Windows NT among them) can be highly secure in standalone mode yet extremely vulnerable as a network entity. Unfortunately, that is particularly true in the case of Windows NT, which utilizes a number of networking mechanisms and protocols potentially weak from a security perspective.

Too many Windows NT security books focus heavily on standalone system security. Readers may conclude that in order to secure Windows NT, they need only to set up accounts with the proper levels of privilege, create groups appropriately, assign access levels, choose appropriate policy settings, and so forth. Readers are too often lulled into thinking that clicking the right settings in the right dialog boxes will almost magically make their systems secure. This approach is potentially dangerous—and it's far removed from reality! Although system security is important, it is only part of a reasonable security strategy. *A successful security strategy is one in which both host- and network-level control mechanisms are properly designed and implemented.* In this book, I strongly advocate such a combined strategy.

About this Book

I wrote this book to share with you the lessons I've learned while trying to understand the many Windows NT-related security issues and secure Windows NT environments in my own and other organizations' networks. Although I am an educator in a computer science department at a university, I am first and foremost a consultant. In the latter role, I must go to client organizations, study each client's needs, and offer solutions. Certain solutions work; others fail. One of the many advantages of my job as a consultant is that I constantly obtain feedback concerning the benefits (and sometimes otherwise) of the solutions I recommend across a large number of organizations. This book incorporates this feedback from the first page to the last. My fear, in fact, is that too many authors become locked into the operating environment in which they live from day-to-day, basing their view of security and technology on this environment alone.

Windows NT is a complex product with many features, most of which affect security in one way or another—and in many cases their features interact with each other. This interaction often complicates the task of choosing the particular settings and configurations needed to achieve the desired level of security. Although the actual user actions ("picking and clicking") you need to enable a particular feature or choose a setting are usually not too much of a challenge, obtaining sufficient information about what really happens when the feature is enabled or a setting is chosen is quite a challenge. Implementing and maintaining Windows NT is not as easy as it may seem; the same is true for Windows NT security. But in this book I try to ease your burden by providing advice concerning how to achieve good security. One book on this topic even consists of multiple volumes! Unfortunately, a great deal of this security advice is superfluous. It is, in fact, exceptionally easy to fall into the trap of viewing Windows NT security in a reductionistic manner, assuming that if you simply adopt control measure one, then control measure two, then control measure three, and so forth, your Windows NT systems will be secure. You need to learn what is *really important* in securing Windows NT systems—and especially, what is really important about network capabilities and vulnerabilities in Windows NT.

My main goals in this book are to:

- Provide a framework that will promote genuine understanding and provide a big picture of the Windows NT (both Windows NT Workstation and Windows NT Server) security model and its relationship to network security.
- Elevate your understanding of security-related exposures that exist in Windows NT networking protocols and services, and then help you understand the relative severity of each of these exposures. *Windows NT/2000 Network Security*, in fact, attempts to balance the need for checklists (which are so often necessary for system administrators who are occupied with a myriad of daily activities) with the need to comprehend the intrinsic nature of vulnerabilities and the relative value of each possible solution.
- Acquaint you with the special security risks resulting from using Windows NT in heterogeneous computing environments (Windows NT domains that integrate other platforms in addition to hetero geneous TCP/IP environments which include Windows NT platforms) and how to maximize security in each.

- Acquaint you with Windows NT network security control measures and assist you in choosing among them and implementing them correctly.
- Counter the bad advice and misconceptions about Windows NT security, which, unfortunately, appear too often in net postings and in the work of consultants.
- Understand and effectively deal with the additional security issues resulting from introducing Windows NT machines on the Internet.
- Provide recent coverage of Windows NT security issues. One of the major intended advantages of this book is that it provides current and up-to-date information. It is easy for a book released a year or so earlier to become out-of-date because of the rapid changes in the technology arena. This book will be the resource you need *now* in securing your Windows NT 4.0 systems.
- Guide you in planning and implementing network infrastructures to accommodate Windows NT security-related requirements and capabilities. In particular, the last chapter of this book, Chapter 11, "Security Considerations for Windows 2000," looks at the security features of Windows 2000, the most recent release of this operating system.

Audience

This book is intended primarily for system and network administrators, application and system programmers, information security staff, and advanced users. Although the main focus of the book is technical, many facets of Windows NT security also involve practicing sound security control *procedures* and *administrative measures* (establishing a good security policy). Therefore, much of the book's discussion is pertinent to all of these audiences.

What Windows Version is Applicable?

As I'm completing this book, Windows NT 4.0 is in use at most sites, and the new version, Windows 2000, has just been released. Although this book touches on important security-related Windows 2000 features throughout the text and devotes the final chapter, Chapter 11, to this new version, the bulk of the book focuses on Windows NT 4.0. Despite the fact that Windows 2000 has now been released, it will take some time for organizations to deploy this new system and get up to speed with the myriad of new features included in this release. Moreover, it's doubtful that many organizations will want to entrust their security to a brand new and largely untested version. Consequently, I emphasize reliable 4.0 security features, while providing information about Windows 2000 that will allow users to plan for its later deployment. I intend to publish a Windows 2000-specific edition of this book once Windows 2000 has been installed at a substantial number of sites and organizations make themselves ready to use this version in security-critical situations.

A few organizations still use Windows NT 3.51. Although various considerations may influence their decision to not upgrade to Windows 4.0, at this point in time it is safe to say that security cannot be one of them. Upgrading from Windows NT 3.51 to Windows NT 4.0 is an important step in improving security of Windows NT systems and networks. The default permissions on Windows NT 4.0 are, for example, considerably better in protecting against unauthorized write and delete access by the universal user than are the default permissions on Windows NT 3.51. The Windows NT 4.0 Service Packs also contain a number of features that can elevate security considerably. The best advise I can offer to users of Windows NT 3.51 is to upgrade to Windows NT 4.0 if security is a major consideration.

Please refer any comments and/or questions to:

Eugene Schultz, Ph.D.,
3314 Crawford St.
West Lafayette, IN 47906-1182
gene.schultz@globalintegrity.com

Organization of this Book

Windows NT Network Security thoroughly covers security-relevant technical issues, such as maintaining integrity of the Registry and controlling potentially dangerous processes such as SMB- and NetBIOS-related processes, and emphasizes network security risks. How to implement the solutions is also carefully explained in increasing detail with each chapter. If you are a relative beginner in the Windows NT arena, you should undoubtedly start at the beginning of the book. If you are advanced in your knowledge of Windows NT, you may want to skip the first two or three chapters.

The book is organized to provide a logical progression between topics. It contains eleven chapters and six appendices.

Chapter 1, "Introduction and Overview," presents an overview of Windows NT and the implementations of this product (Windows NT Workstation, Windows NT Server, Windows NT, Enterprise Edition, and Windows NT Terminal Server). It describes system advantages and disadvantages, takes a look at the potential conflict between functionality and security, and briefly examines some basic information security concepts and considerations.

Chapter 2, "The Structure of Windows NT Security," explains the basic security model and architecture of Windows NT and the effect both have upon Windows NT security capabilities. This chapter will leave you with a better understanding of basic security mechanisms, such as access tokens, security descriptors, and the many modules implemented in the Windows NT architecture. This chapter also describes how password encryption occurs in Windows NT, how passwords are stored, and how both local and remote authentication occur.

Chapter 3, "The Windows NT Network Environment," starts with the basics of networking then proceeds rapidly to Windows NT networking. You learn about the network protocols used in the Windows NT network environment and how they relate to the Open Systems Interconnect (OSI) model. You also learn the security-related vulnerabilities associated with many of these protocols and how they affect ability to obtain unauthorized access to Windows NT systems as well as result in denial of service. Chapter 3 devotes considerable coverage to Microsoft's implementation of both the Server Message Block (SMB) and NetBIOS, and specific features of both, which make the Windows NT network environment difficult to secure.

Chapter 4, "Basic Windows NT Security Exposures" takes a detailed look at the types of system and network vulnerabilities in Windows NT. This chapter presents a basic vulnerability taxonomy with associated solutions (if they exist) and analyzes selected vulnerabilities in detail.

Chapters 5, "Configuring Windows NT Server for Security," maintains that it is impossible to implement suitable network security unless the hosts within a network are secure at some baseline level. The starting point of system security is installing system properly.

Chapter 6, "Maintaining Windows NT Security," complements Chapter 5 by describing how to maintain systems in a manner that maximizes the likelihood that they will *stay* secure (assuming they have been set up to be secure). Together, Chapters 5 and 6 provide a wide range of suggestions for specific control measures and the tradeoffs involved in implementing each.

Chapter 7, "Basic Network Security Measures," deals with network security, an especially difficult challenge in the Windows NT arena. It explain how measures, such as firewalls, packet filters, and intrusion detection tools can help in the battle to achieve network security.

Chapter 8, "Securing Network Services and Protocols," presents major security-related vulnerabilities in network services that run in the Windows NT environment and suggests possible solutions to minimize the risks these vulnerabilities create. The major emphasis is on Web- and FTP-based services, although a reasonably wide range of services is covered. Chapter 8 covers challenges in securing the transmission of traffic over the network in addition to vulnerabilities due to interoperability of Windows NT and other platforms.

Chapter 9, "Virtual Private Networks," covers the problem of protecting against unauthorized capture of network transmissions and how to use data that traverse networks to determine whether or not attacks are transpiring.

Chapter 10, "Workstation Security," examines the role of clients in the Windows NT arena and the baggage they bring as far as security goes. Viruses are a major problem in this arena. Chapter 10 explains how viruses work, why they are a special problem in the Windows NT systems, and the types of solutions most appropriate. This chapter also provides coverage of the threat of malicious programs that can be downloaded into browsers. With the growing popularity of Java, JavaScript, and ActiveX, these types of programs are becoming of increasing concern. The final topic is vulnerabilities in clients themselves—ways clients can be misused to attack Windows NT servers, as well as solutions to the types of vulnerabilities that exist in these clients.

Chapter 11, "Security Considerations for Windows 2000," deals with Windows 2000, the newest release of Windows NT. This chapter covers the basic functionality of Windows 2000 and provides an analysis of the security features included in this release. The goal of this chapter is to help you, the reader, plan for the security of Windows 2000 well before you actually deploy this product. The complexity of Windows 2000 leaves no other alternatives. It may take awhile for sites to entrust their security to this new release, but this chapter will help you plan ahead using Windows 2000 in the most secure fashion possible.

Appendix A, "Port Assignment Conventions," lists all major Windows NT ports and the functions of each.

Appendix B, "RFCs Supported by the Windows NT Implementation of TCP/IP," lists the major Windows NT network services and the relevant Request for Comments (RFCs) for each.

Appendix C, "Significant Security-Related Features of Service Packs 3-6a for Windows NT 4.0," lists the major EventIDs for Windows NT auditing and the meaning of each.

Appendix D, "Useful Security-Related Tools from the Windows NT 4.0 Resource Kit," lists the security-related features in Windows NT 4.0 Service Packs 3 through 6.

Appendix E, "A Script for Securing Windows NT Systems," lists a script (written by Mad Dog) that can be used as is or modified to tighten the security of Windows NT systems.

Appendix F, "Manual Clean-Up Procedures for Tightening Security after Script Execution," describes steps that can be taken after the security script is run to tighten security even more.

Conventions Used in this Book

This book uses the following conventions:

- **Italics.** Used for the names of files, directories, host names, domain names, URLs, and to emphasize new terms and important ideas when they are first introduced.
- **Constant Width.** Represents display text, error messages, examples, and in-text references to syntax models.
- **Constant Width Italics.** In some code examples, indicates an element (for example, a parameter) you supply.
- [ ]. In syntax examples, square brackets enclose optional items.

Windows 95 and Windows 98 are collectively referred to as Win9X. Abbreviations and acronyms are used freely throughout, but each is written out when it is first introduced—for example, Server Management Block (SMB).

1

Introduction and Overview

"But the UNIX revolution isn't over yet."
–An anonymous information technology manager

Not too many years ago, the UNIX operating system had firm control over the hearts and minds of people within the information technology arena. Mail servers were implemented on UNIX platforms, as were FTP servers, DNS servers, firewalls, and almost every other kind of imaginable server in the TCP/IP environment. At the same time, Novell NetWare was the predominant product when it came to *local area networks* (LANs). A little-known Microsoft product named LAN Manager (a predecessor to Windows NT) was on the market, but it was anything but a bestseller. Microsoft LAN Manager (LanMan) offered mechanisms called "shares" to enable users to remotely access files, directories, and printers.

LanMan was in several respects a big step forward in that it introduced network logons in which users were authenticated to a network of machines. LanMan was a major improvement over typical LAN logons of the time. After LanMan users were authenticated to the network, they could reach different servers without having to reauthenticate. In contrast, most LAN products at that time required users to authenticate to each individual server to access the files stored on each server. LanMan worked fairly well within the context of token-ring networking and could also be deployed in Ethernet environments. The first release of LanMan unfortunately had a bug of such Herculean proportions that if a user entered a particular set of keystrokes, the server not only crashed, but had to be reinstalled. News of this bug circulated widely, causing negative publicity that hurt LanMan's popularity. Ironically, however, LanMan had reasonably good security potential. Security in LanMan depended on a number of critical settings, many of which were within the LANMAN.INI file. A system administrator could set security-related parameters (for example, **ENCRYPT = YES**) to provide an encrypted link between LanMan clients and servers to increase security control considerably.

IBM OS/2, another predecessor to Windows NT, was in many ways a better product than LanMan. It offered similar (and, in many ways, better) kinds of functionality but, unfortunately, suffered (among other ailments) from an underwhelming marketing effort. It therefore also did less to capture the hearts and minds of the user community than a technologically superior product of its time should have. Unfortunately, technology too often plays a secondary role to marketing considerations.

Windows NT emerged shortly afterward as the logical successor to the previous LAN products. With the promise of delivering "new technology," its sales statistics were initially less than impressive. UNIX and NetWare still ruled. New releases of Windows NT with new features emerged. Sales improved. Slowly but surely, Windows NT emerged from the proverbial operating system heap as an increasingly dominant product. People who were justifiably concerned with UNIX (and, to a lesser degree, NetWare) security and its limitations quickly shifted their focus to the upstart Windows NT operating system. Used initially more as a desktop platform than anything else, Windows NT made inroads into the server area.

The UNIX revolution is indeed not yet over. Despite the extensive marketing hype afforded Windows NT, the popularity of the UNIX operating system has not really suffered. Meanwhile, Linux, a "near-relative" of UNIX, is growing rapidly in popularity. Many of the variations ("flavors") of UNIX still continue to provide a high degree of functionality and operational reliability seldom realized with many other operating systems. In contrast, however, over the years a very large number of security-related vulnerabilities in UNIX have emerged. Perhaps predictably, vulnerabilities in the various flavors of UNIX continue to surface at a rapid rate.

Windows NT is by no means the answer to all of today's information technology needs. But "prime time" in today's information technology environment no longer belongs exclusively to UNIX. Whether or not you like the Windows NT operating system, Windows NT has lodged itself in almost every current operating environment in major countries throughout the world. As in UNIX and Linux, security in Windows NT is a major concern. What are the major issues in the Windows NT security arena? Is Windows NT really the "most secure operating system product that is commercially available," as some marketing hype claims? Is Windows NT as full of security-related vulnerabilities as its detractors claim? These and the many other security-related issues surrounding Windows NT must be resolved if one is to deploy this product in accordance with business and operational needs.

Overview of Windows NT

What are the major features and properties of this product? What is the difference between Windows NT Workstation and the Windows NT Server products? What tradeoffs between security and functionality should one consider when deciding among measures to implement to elevate Windows NT security? This section addresses these and other critical questions.

What Is Windows NT?

Windows NT is Microsoft's 32-bit, multitasking *network operating system* (NOS) product. An NOS is a type of operating system built to provide an environment that supports networking by providing the ability to connect to remote devices (disks, for example) in addition to local devices. Windows NT supports mail, file transfers, remote printing, fax modems, and many other network-related services that require connections to remote as well as local devices. Windows NT, furthermore, is not merely a *networking application* loaded on top of an operating system. Examples of networking applications include LanMan and Novell NetWare 3.x and earlier versions. All these products required that you first install an operating system (for example, IBM's OS/2 operating system), and then install LanMan or NetWare. Both of these older products provided networking functionality, but depended on an underlying operating system for functionality, such as scheduling. Networking functionality is (in contrast) intrinsic to the Windows NT operating system. Windows NT is therefore part of a new generation of products that supercede what have traditionally been called LAN products. Windows NT can provide a LAN environment, although it is not by any means limited to a local area environment. Windows NT can also participate in and support wide area networking. Sales hype even includes references to the kind of network functionality that Windows NT can provide as "enterprise networking."

> ***Distinguishing between NOS and NIOS***
>
> *I find it useful to distinguish between a NOS and a NIOS (Network Integrated Operating System). Novell Netware is a true NOS. It performs only network functions and cannot be used as a regular operating system. By contrast, NT and UNIX are NIOSs, where the Networking functionality is an integral part of the overall network functionality. This enables them to also be used for other aspects of computing than just networking.* ◆

Windows NT incorporates many vestiges from both the older Microsoft LAN Manager and IBM OS/2 products. These vestiges include:

- Domain authentication
- Redirectors (functions that create and move network sessions between machines, as appropriate)
- Auditing
- The Network Basic Input Output System (NetBIOS[1]) layer of networking
- The Server Message Block (SMB[2]) protocol for file, directory, and printer access
- Fault-tolerance features

But Windows NT is also in many ways considerably more advanced than IBM OS/2 and LAN Manager. Windows NT, for example, incorporates extensive support for TCP/IP-based networking, making it much more suitable for today's networking (especially *wide area networking*) needs. This product also includes a considerable number of popular network services, supports interdomain trust, offers advanced security features, and has a more sophisticated and usable *graphical user interface* (GUI).

Advantages of Windows NT

The wide use of Windows NT within industry, government, and academic computing environments attests to the fact that many organizations have found this product to be useful. Windows NT has numerous shortcomings, too; gaining a basic understanding of the advantages and limitations of this product is important in making sound decisions concerning how this product should be used and configured. Putting appropriate security measures in place in particular requires pitting the advantages of security control measures against the costs associated with implementing them. One of the most important types of potential advantages is the ability to control avenues of unauthorized access that can be exploited by perpetrators, whereas one of the typical disadvantages is reduction or loss of some of the functionality that Windows NT provides.

Before considering security-related tradeoffs, let's first take a look at Windows NT itself to discover some of its advantages, including the following:

- **32-bit operating system.** Windows NT's 32-bit operating system allows applications to run more efficiently than in a 16-bit operating system environment. The 32-bit operating system provides more memory space, allowing more instructions to be loaded at any given point in time. Note, however, that a number of competing operating systems offer far more than 32 bits of memory space.

[1] *The NETBIOS Application Programming Interface (API), Chapters 3, "The Windows NT Network Environment" and beyond cover this protocol extensively.*

[2] *The SMB protocol API is also covered in subsequent chapters of this book.*

- **Multitasking.** Windows NT allows multiple processes and threads to time share, which increases the efficiency of processing considerably.
- **Symmetric load balancing.** Windows NT distributes processing load among multiple processors. The Workstation version of Windows NT currently supports up to two processors, the Server version supports up to four, and the Enterprise Server version supports up to eight.
- **Efficient file system.** The *NT File System* (NTFS) is in a number of respects more advanced than many other, competing file systems such as *File Allocation Table* (FAT) and *High Performance File System* (HPFS), the file system for IBM OS/2. NTFS offers a reasonable compromise between the best features of other file systems, namely between instant recoverability, fast writes, and "lazy writes" (for example, from a cache when the system is not too busy). NTFS also features a granular set of access permissions, protection against scavenging for deleted files, and other advantageous capabilities.
- **Usability.** Windows NT's GUI facilitates learning how to use this product (although it can impede advanced users by requiring multiple user actions to enter a single command).
- **Interoperability.** Windows NT provides network interoperability with Microsoft Workgroup products such as Windows 95 or Windows 98, (Win9x) and even the older Microsoft *Windows for Workgroups* (WFW) 3.11. It can also interface with other platforms such as UNIX, Novell NetWare, Apple Macintosh, and mainframe platforms.
- **Single logon capability.** Windows NT allows a user to logon once to access a large number of servers. If configured appropriately, Windows NT also allows a single logon to provide access to networks other than the user's home network.
- **Central system and network administration.** With access to the network, an administrator can from a single machine configure and maintain machines within that network as well as in other networks.
- **Fault tolerance.** Strong fault-tolerance capability is another advantage of Windows NT, which provides an interface to support disk mirroring or *redundant array of independent drives* (RAID). The latter efficiently writes information necessary to rebuild files to multiple disk drives.
- **Security features.** As will be discussed extensively in this book, Windows NT offers a large set of security features. Because many of these features are flexible, the security level of this product can be modified as needed to meet most organizations' requirements.

Disadvantages and Limitations of Windows NT

Like any other computing product, Windows NT also has a number disadvantages and limitations. The following are among the most frequently mentioned disadvantages of Windows NT:

- **Lack of product maturity.** Windows NT was first released in 1993. Although several versions of Windows NT have been developed, the list of "lessons learned" for this product is not yet very long. New releases too often have introduced new features in favor of correcting what was wrong with current releases. This might seem to be a minor problem, but it is in fact a major one. Many Windows NT critics would rather see one stable Windows NT release than a new one that involves additional features but requires additional hot fixes and services.
- **Limited development environment.** Windows NT has many *Application Programming Interfaces* (APIs) for running applications, but the set of system calls, debugging tools, compilers, and other resources that greatly facilitate the task of the application programmer are still to a large degree undocumented.
- **Backward compatibility.** Windows NT attempts to be backward compatible with many older releases of client and server products. As explained in later chapters, this causes a range of problems including the necessity for supporting older network protocol implementations. Many of these problems are directly linked to security-related vulnerabilities.
- **Limitations in networking.** The Windows NT network environment is "chatty," with many broadcasts and elections constantly occurring by default. Network services, such as the NetLogon service, tend to be relatively slow and inefficient, causing sluggishness and sometimes even anomalies in areas, such as handling network authentication requests.
- **Instability.** Although no software product runs perfectly under all conditions of use, newer products tend to have more bugs—unexpected crashes, errors that cause anomalous behavior, and other problems. Windows NT has not been exempt from these problems—the number of Microsoft service packs and hot fixes that incorporate fixes for bugs discovered since each release of Windows NT provide more than ample evidence. Perhaps more noteworthy is that some of the Windows NT service packs have been so problem prone that Microsoft has on more than one occasion had to release a new service pack to correct the bugs in previous service packs.
- **Limited availability of certain network services.** Although Microsoft and third-party vendors have increased the number of network service-

providing programs for the Windows NT environment, the number of network services available, as well as the functionality of certain services that exist in the NT environment, are deficient compared to UNIX. Network services I'd like to see would include built-in NFS mounts and different built-in shell environment options.

- **Lack of information or, sometimes, lack of accurate information.** Many aspects of Windows NT are not documented; or, if they are, they are not sufficiently documented for the needs of the user community. Critics of Windows NT are quick to point out that most of the documentation used to configure and modify this product originates from Microsoft. Microsoft understandably does not want to "air its dirty laundry" by documenting to any degree of detail problems and limitations with this product. Source code and adequate documentation are, furthermore, nearly impossible to obtain. The user community as well as others, consequently, too often do not get the full story when it comes to Windows NT, its capabilities, and its limitations.
- **Problems with hot fixes and service packs.** Microsoft has been reasonably responsive when new, potentially serious security-related vulnerabilities have been posted to newsgroups. Like most other vendors, Microsoft often recommends a workaround (a "makeshift" solution, such as changing permissions) until it develops a hot fix. Unfortunately, not all hot fixes work as intended right away; Microsoft then goes back to the proverbial drawing board and modifies each faulty hot fix until it works correctly. The list of hot fixes to be applied grows, but now another important consideration comes into play. The order in which hot fixes are installed is generally (but not always) critical. If a system administrator installs only one hot fix out of order in a given system, the consequences are potentially catastrophic. Additionally, the service packs that incorporate the hot fixes later seldom work correctly right after they are initially released. Consider Service Pack 2 for Windows NT 4.0, which critics have labeled a denial-of-service attack by Microsoft! Service Pack 4 for the same release also caused many problems. In both cases, Microsoft had to develop still another service pack, mostly to correct these problems. In noncritical computing environments in which disruption of service, problems with hot fixes and service packs may not make much difference; in critical computing environments, however, potential and real unreliability of hot fixes and service packs are a major concern. Making source code available to individuals and groups who can spot and fix potential security and other vulnerabilities would provide the most effective remedy for the problems that hot fixes and services packs have created for the user community.

- **Security limitations.** A fairly high proportion of the known bugs in Windows NT are security-related. As discussed more fully in subsequent chapters, certain of these security-related bugs are extremely serious but still have no clear-cut, acceptable control solution. Additional security-related bugs result from using Windows NT and other platforms, such as Win9x, DOS together, and still others result from how disks are partitioned and other factors that Windows NT itself cannot control. As people have gained more experience with Windows NT, they have discovered more security exposures, making achieving the desired level of security more difficult than people had envisioned when this product first emerged.

Types of Windows NT Products

Windows NT is actually four related, yet somewhat different types of products: Windows NT Workstation; Windows NT Server; Windows NT Server, Enterprise Edition; and Windows NT Server, Terminal Server Edition. The primary difference between these products is in terms of the role they typically play in networking environments. Windows NT Server (as its name implies) is intended to be a network server, providing services such as file sharing, mail handling, and central authentication services to clients. After a server has authenticated a user, the user can access information resources and services in other services and possibly workstations. Most of the attention that Windows NT receives is focused on Windows NT Server (either Windows NT Server itself or Windows NT Server, Enterprise Edition). This product potentially allows somewhat more sophisticated network functionality than does Windows NT Workstation, although the latter offers more than one might imagine. Perhaps more importantly, Windows NT Server is most frequently deployed in its intended use: as a file, application, or network server. Not surprisingly, the majority of the more difficult security issues typically relate to the *server* side of Windows NT. In many cases, the issues relating to servers also apply to workstations. However, the nature of the deployment of servers makes them a more attractive target, and therefore a more natural focus for security.

Windows NT Workstation

Windows NT Workstation can be deployed in a peer-to-peer environment, or as a client in a Windows NT domain (as discussed in the following section, "Windows NT Server"), or as an independent workstation (on or off the network).

The first context of usage for Windows NT Workstation is the peer-to-peer environment. In this environment, each Windows NT Workstation performs its own authentication of users; has its own rules for making directories, files, printers, and services available to local and remote users; and allows users and processes the privileges assigned to them on that individual machine. Each peer machine is an entity unto itself in terms of controlling what occurs within the machine and how the network and remote users communicate with it. Each machine is, therefore, rather autonomous; in actuality, it is potentially both a client and a server. The main advantage of this configuration is simplicity; setting up a peer-to-peer network to allow the exchange of mail, file sharing, printer sharing, and other functions is generally not as large a task as in a client/server networking environment. Furthermore, other Microsoft Workgroup products such as Win9x are interoperable in the peer-to-peer setting. The main disadvantage is administration; the lack of central administration capability inherent in the client/server environment is missing in the peer-to-peer environment. Maintenance, creation of uniform environments, setting configurations to enforce a uniform set of operational practices and security policies, and similar considerations are therefore more difficult.

The second context of usage for Windows NT Workstation is as a client machine within a Windows NT domain. In this environment, one or more Windows NT Servers participate in a domain (a network of machines that share and can access a common authentication database). Windows NT Workstation can be used as a client from which users can obtain access to one or more domains.

A third context of usage for Windows NT Workstation is as an independent platform (standalone or networked). In the context of standalone deployment, Windows NT Workstation serves in the same role as a standalone PC. Compared to the standalone platforms that run DOS or the Macintosh operating system, however, Windows NT Workstation in this environment offers considerably more functionality and can attain a considerably higher level of security. The standalone environment for Windows NT platforms is not, however, a focus of this book.

Windows NT Server

Windows NT Server is intended to run primarily in the context of a Windows NT domain (although it does not have to). A domain consists of one or more servers and typically numerous workstations deployed for the purpose of remotely accessing the server(s).

The Primary Domain Controller

Exactly one *primary domain controller* (PDC) exists in a Windows NT domain. The PDC is always the first machine installed during a domain installation. The PDC, and only the PDC, can update the authentication database, the *Security Accounts Manager* (SAM) database in Windows NT domains. Another way of saying this is that only the PDC is authoritative with respect to changes in the SAM database. The SAM database defines all user accounts and contains information needed for authenticating users to domains and allowing access to domain resources.[3]

Backup Domain Controllers

A domain may have one or more additional domain controllers called *backup domain controllers* (BDCs). All domain controllers, BDCs included, hold a copy of their domain's SAM database. The PDC will, however, hold the *master* copy of this database, and then update it as needed. At a consistent interval (in Windows NT 4.0, the default interval is 15 minutes), the NetLogon service on the PDC distributes changes in the SAM database to other domain controllers throughout the domain.

If the PDC goes down, you can promote one BDC in the same domain to take the role of the PDC until the PDC comes back up. The PDC regularly polls the BDCs to determine the current processing load within each; the BDC with the lowest load at the moment the PDC fails is the best candidate for promotion. In some computing environments, continuity of operations is sufficiently important to warrant the purchase and deployment of commercial software (see `http://www.octopus.com` and `http://www.vinca.com`) that provides for automatic promotion of one BDC in case of PDC failure. You should not, however, impulsively promote a BDC every time the PDC crashes. If you promote a BDC but the PDC comes back, you now have an undesirable situation due to the conflict between the promoted BDC (which now acts like the PDC) and the PDC itself. It is generally better, therefore, to devote one's efforts to bringing the PDC back up if the expected downtime is reasonably short (that is, an hour or so).

BDCs perform another, very important function, namely authenticating users and services during the logon process. Although authentication is discussed in detail in Chapter 2, "The Structure of Windows NT Security." suffice it to say at this point that this second function of BDCs frees the PDC to engage in other tasks with less likelihood of becoming overloaded. Needless to say, having at least one BDC (normally organizations deploy

[3] *Resources are objects available to users. Examples of resources include files, directories/folders, and printers*

somewhere between two or three and several dozen BDCs) is extremely advantageous in computing environments in which continuity of operations is critical.

The PDC uses the NetLogon service to distribute changes in domain authentication and other databases to the BDCs. BDCs, in contrast, do not update security and other databases stored in the BDC. Individual clients within the domain pass data to the PDC. An example is password changes; when a user changes a password, redirectors set up a session between the client and the PDC to send the password change. The PDC then sends this and other updated information to the BDCs at the designated time (which by default is every 15 minutes). Alternatively, the Windows NT Server Manager on every domain controller enables system administrators to synchronize the domain SAM database immediately, ensuring that each BDC has the identical copy to the one that the PDC holds. In this latter case, the NetLogon service sends the entire database, not merely the changes, across the network to every BDC.

If the PDC goes down, the system administrator can promote one BDC to temporarily serve as the PDC until the PDC comes back up. If no BDC is promoted, disruption in areas, such as authentication services, invariably occurs in time because the only authoritative server with respect to making changes is down.

After users have logged on to a Windows NT domain[4], they can access resources and services throughout the domain (depending on the particular privileges and access permissions assigned). Services include database access (through Microsoft's SQL Server, Oracle, or a number of other database servers that run in the Windows NT environment), Web services, browser services that locate objects[5] which users can reach on remote servers, and many others. One file may reside on one server and a second within another server within the same domain, but the user need only to log on once to be able to access both files. The same is true of other resources and services.

Access is not necessarily limited to one domain at a time, however. Windows NT domains also support trust relationships between domains. Trust means that users and groups from one domain may be allowed access to some or all of the resources and services on another domain. Trust functionally extends the authentication of a single logon to the network to different networks, requiring a user to enter only one password for access to

[4] *In special cases, a user may also be given the right to perform a special type of logon, such as a local logon to an individual server.*

[5] *In the most basic sense, an "object" is an entity that possesses certain characteristics. A file provides an intuitive example, although many types of objects exist in Windows NT.*

resources and services in both domains. Trust will be one of the major focuses of Chapter 6, "Maintaining Windows NT Security."

There are three sever types that need to be identified at this point:

- **Member Servers.** Member servers are servers that are part of a domain. They are, however, not domain controllers. They do not store copies of the domain's SAM database, nor do they have any role in authenticating users to the domain in which they are located. The purpose of member servers is to provide remote file and service access to users.
- **Individual Servers.** Windows NT does not require that all users who access resources and services on Windows NT Servers be domain users. Individual servers are machines that are network connected, but are not part of any domain.
- **Non-Networked Servers.** Non-networked servers are similar to individual servers. They are not, however, connected to the network.

Windows NT Server, Enterprise Edition

Windows NT Server, Enterprise Edition is a high-end version of Windows NT Server. The Enterprise Edition version, for example, offers increased performance capabilities through support for eight concurrent processors (as opposed to four in Windows NT Server), capability to tune memory for high-volume applications, and clustering services for availability. The same security-related issues that apply to Windows NT Server also apply to the Enterprise Edition, so from now on the term "Windows NT Server" refers to both products.

Windows NT Server, Terminal Server Edition

Windows NT Server *Terminal Server Edition* (TSE) is essentially NT Server with the additional capability to function as a terminal server to remote clients. Using Terminal Server, clients can run the Terminal Services Client on a low-end workstation or handheld device, and have a fully functional NT environment. Terminal Services introduce their own peculiar set of vulnerabilities in some instances, but for the most part TSE is vulnerable to the same problems as Windows NT Server. Therefore, for the remainder of this book, we will take NT Server to include TSE, except where it is fruitful to explicitly consider the two as separate products.[6]

[6] *Note that Windows 2000, the next version of Windows NT, includes the Terminal Services in all the server versions, thus eliminating the need for a distinction between TSE and the remainder of the server family.*

Functionality Versus Security

Functionality is almost always a two-edged sword. High functionality increases the value of computing resources and operations but also generally introduces a greater number of security-related vulnerabilities. Increasing the number of functions available almost invariably entails more files and programs that require access control. The result is increased opportunity for mistakes in assigning permissions and the likelihood of coding or other errors that cause programs to behave in a manner that a perpetrator could exploit.

Resolution of the functionality versus security issue is often extremely difficult. One extreme is to obtain as much functionality as possible without worrying about security. In some operational contexts, such as university settings where the educational philosophy dictates open and free access to computing resources, this approach may be acceptable. The opposite extreme is to implement Windows NT security features to the degree that functionality is severely restricted.

In other operational contexts, such as military computing environments, this approach can be suitable. Conforming to the U.S. *National Computer Security Center's* (NCSC's) criteria for evaluating systems and networks can result in severely restricted functionality, especially at the higher levels of evaluation. In most computing contexts, however, neither extreme represents the optimal approach to security. *Analyzing the tradeoffs between cost and benefits is the key*. Some Windows NT services, such as Web-based services, introduce a sufficient amount of security risk to preclude their introduction into environments in which an organization cannot afford the prospect of unauthorized access because of the extreme value or sensitivity of data (for example, lease bid data), or potential for business loss resulting from disruption of services or loss of network availability. In this case, placing stringent restrictions on parameters, such as minimum password length, the number of failed logons within a criterion time period, the number of privileged users in a domain, and the particular files and directories that can be accessed is a wise move.

Windows NT Server also permits a great deal of centralized control over user accounts and groups; availability and functionality of services; access to files, directories, and printers; and user environments. As mentioned previously, however, a given Windows NT Server does not have to be part of a domain. This platform can also run as an independent node within a heterogeneous network environment, such as a TCP/IP environment that includes UNIX, Digital VMS, and Windows NT Server hosts. In this role, a Windows NT platform can perform one or more of a number of functions, including a firewall, DNS server, router, file server, authentication server, and others. The many tradeoffs involved in implementing Windows NT in this manner are discussed in detail in Chapter 7, "Basic Network Security Measures," and Chapter 8 "Securing Network Services and Protocols." Before we go any further, we need to lay the foundation for information security.

About Information Security

This book focuses on one of the most fascinating and important topics in computing today: information security (formerly known as computer security). At a minimum, *information security* (InfoSec) involves protecting systems against unauthorized loss of confidentiality of data and network communications; integrity of data, systems, and networks; and availability of services and data. Confidentiality of data, such as pending patent data, marketing data, and personnel medical records, is a major concern for most organizations today. Integrity of data and applications is also of paramount importance. Consider, for example, the impact of sending corrupted data to a billing application or scientific application. The disruption and resulting financial loss can be gargantuan. And, finally, availability has become increasingly important to the point that in many organizations it is a more critical requirement than either confidentiality or integrity. "Just keep the systems and networks running, and I'll find out what's wrong later" is not too uncommon a quote in today's information technology arena. Consider also the needs of those involved with information warfare, in which the side that can disrupt the other side's computing operations gains a huge advantage in today's electronic battlefield scenarios.

Not all InfoSec practitioners agree that security is as simple as protecting confidentiality, integrity, and accessibility. Some, for example, argue that protecting confidentiality actually involves protecting against unauthorized disclosure of data, as well as unauthorized possession (whether intentional or not) of data. Similarly, certain professionals propound that there is a large difference between data being available (that is, stored on one or more systems) and being accessible. One of the things that plagues the InfoSec profession, in fact, is the imprecise definition of terms.

To genuinely understand and solve Windows NT security issues, it is important to first understand what difference security makes and the major approaches to security. This understanding will in turn facilitate your ability to determine the real impact of security vulnerabilities inherent in the Windows NT environment and to control the ones worth controlling.

Why Information Security Is Important

InfoSec, although hardly a mature discipline, has evolved from a hardly noticed issue during the early days of computing (exception: within U.S. military and intelligence circles) to a major focus in the computing world of the 21st century. The primary causes are differences in the way computers are used today. Computers control, or at least in many cases, keep track of most aspects of our lives in one way or another to the point where they are now dominant in all major arenas: business, government, military, academia, and so forth. Stock transactions and banking have become electronic, making them major targets for perpetrators motivated by greed and dishonesty. The 1999 Computer Security Institute Computer Crime Survey indicated that approximately half of all respondents to the survey had experienced a major security-related incident; the cumulative loss among those who responded was $265.5 million, more then doubling the losses reported in 1998 (see `http://www.gocsi.com/prelea_000321.htm`).

Consider also that the disruption of key computers and networks could potentially leave a nation's economy and military capabilities in disarray. Furthermore, today's computers are not the computers of yesterday. Yesterday's computers were largely intended to be standalone machines. Unless modems were attached to these machines, these machines were not remotely accessible. Although unauthorized local access is a major InfoSec concern, unauthorized remote access is at least in some respects as great (if not in some instances greater) a threat. A major problem with the threat of remote access is the sheer number of users who could conceivably attack in this manner.

Defending Networks: Mission Impossible?

Securing systems is a difficult challenge. If anything, however, securing networks is an even greater challenge. The reason that networks are even more difficult to deal with include the following:

- **Operating systems are sophisticated.** The complexity of today's networks has required increasingly complex operating systems that support access to resources and services over the network. As operating systems have increased in complexity (consider Windows NT), they have generally concurrently introduced more flaws that can be exploited by an attacker.
- **Networks are designed for widespread access.** By design, networks allow remote users access. The easier and more efficient the access, the better the network design is. The problem in terms of security is that good networking makes thus security control more difficult; the ideal

network from a security perspective would be one that makes free and easy access available to only a few users.

- **Individual machine security is complex.** Securing individual machines is a complex problem. However, securing a network and the machines attached to it is exponentially more complex. Consider the following: If any machine has *n* potential vulnerabilities, the interaction between two machines means that each of those vulnerabilities could potentially interact with every vulnerability on the other machine. This results in n^2 vulnerabilities. Three machines result in n^3 vulnerabilities, and so on. Clearly this problem is of exponential complexity.
- **Network boundaries are nebulous.** The boundaries that have in the past so readily characterized networks have for the most part disappeared. From a security perspective, boundaries are necessary barriers in security enforcement. Where does one draw the line to lock out unauthorized users but allow in legitimate users in today's network environments?
- **Many potential targets exist.** Current network environments provide an ideal set of targets for intruders. Not only are the servers that hold files and applications tempting targets, the network infrastructure itself is a target. Many of today's attackers first probe to discover the nature of the infrastructure to determine whether a firewall is in place, how many routers exist and how they are configured, how the *domain name service* (DNS) is implemented, whether network information servers provide data about the hosts within the network, and so forth. Then these attackers proceed to attack critical components of this infrastructure, especially firewalls, routers, and DNS servers before targeting other servers. Therefore, the range of potential targets is very large.
- **Attackers can initiate attacks with a low probability of being identified.** Many network services (Web, anonymous FTP, Gopher, DNS, for example) are anonymous in nature. Unless special logging capabilities are enabled, any user can connect to a server that supports these services without being identified. The possibility of connecting to victim and other systems without being identified not only emboldens attackers, but also makes identifying and tracing attacks more difficult.
- **Networking is controlled chaos.** Anyone who thinks that networks are fundamentally orderly in nature is likely to be sorely disappointed after examining the output of a packet capture device (a device used to capture network traffic) over a period of time. Events such as packet collisions, broadcast floods, crashes of critical servers, and others are all too familiar to network administrators. The controlled chaos that surrounds networking makes achieving security control even more difficult.

The Insider Versus Outsider Threat

Statistics relevant to computer crime and its sources abound. The insider (an employee, contractor, consultant, or third-party business affiliate) is without a doubt one of the greatest sources of security-related threats to computers and networks. Outsiders "hackers", employees and consultants for competing organizations, for example with no direct connection to a target organization also comprise a major source of threat. Although suspicions concerning the data itself and the methods used to gather the data are well founded, considering the origin of any threat is wise indeed. Is the insider or the outsider the greater threat in Windows NT, and, given that one can adequately answer this question, what difference does this make in Windows NT security?

A Comparison of the Relative Occurrence of Insider and Outsider Attacks

The relative susceptibility to insider- and outsider-originated attacks depends on many factors, some of which are well beyond the scope of this book. Among the relevant factors are the following:

- **Personnel security.** Some organizations carefully screen all personnel (not only actual employees, but also contract personnel and consultants) before they are allowed access to computing systems, to determine whether their background is sufficiently unblemished to merit trust in them. Better yet, some organizations conduct personnel-screening activities not once, but regularly throughout each person's career. Good personnel security substantially diminishes the threat of an insider attack.
- **Policy.** Having a policy that allows free, unrestricted access to network services generally elevates the proportion of outsider attacks. Policies that call for tighter security (especially network-based security) and that result in restrictions for dissemination of information about networks and the servers therein help reduce outsider attacks in particular.
- **Type and extent of connectivity.** Organizations that do not allow Internet connectivity are, for example, less susceptible to outsider attacks than those that do. The same principle applies to modem dial-ins. Extensive internal connectivity (that is, numerous internal networks connected together), in contrast, increases the probability of internally initiated attacks.
- **Network architecture.** Networks that have traffic screening and security management barriers generally provide less opportunity for outsider attacks than do those that do not. Multiple entry points (as opposed to a single entry point) into a network are more conducive to outsider attacks.

- **Intrusion-detection capabilities.** Deploying intrusion-detection tools appropriately and taking the time to carefully investigate the data they provide can also affect the relative proportion of insider versus outsider attacks. Most of today's commercial intrusion-detection tools are better at discovering outsider attacks. Most current attacks on networks and the systems therein do not occur at a single point in time; they often occur over a period of days, weeks, and even months. Intrusion-detection tools can help shut these attacks off by enabling an organization to discover an attack early, thereby enabling network and security administrators to change packet-filtering rules, disconnect target machines from the network, and take other evasive measures to prevent further, successful attacks. The overall result is less likelihood of outsider attacks (although insider attacks can also be reduced in a similar manner).

Insider Versus Outsider Attacks: Which Causes Greater Loss?

Although the issue of the relative proportion of insider versus outsider attacks will continue to be debated, one fact remains virtually indisputable: The financial and other losses due to insider attacks far exceeds the loss attributable to outsider-initiated attacks. Hundreds of outsider attacks may cause considerable financial loss, but a single insider attack can produce devastating results. Consider, for example, the case of Nick Leeson of Baring's Bank. Mr. Leeson, a trusted employee, discovered how to circumvent the "two-man rule" in Bering's trading systems to initiate new trades (Parker, 1998). The motive was to reverse losses from previous trades. Leeson's new trades incurred even greater and greater losses, to the point that they became so massive that Baring's Bank became bankrupt. Although possible, it is unlikely that an outsider could have produced massive losses of these proportions. Many (but not all) externally initiated attacks are called "ankle-biter" attacks by those who must respond to them. These attacks can be expensive and disruptive, but they generally do not create the same kind of potential for loss that internally initiated attacks do.

The Trust Element with Insiders

It goes without saying that it makes no sense whatsoever to trust people you do not know. If insider attacks are by far the more serious threat, however, shouldn't an organization quit trusting insiders? System administrators and system programmers, after all, own the proverbial "keys to the shop." They could, in connection with a corrupt business or other manager, financially devastate the organization for which they work. Consider, furthermore, that major motives for insider attacks include financial greed, revenge, political motivations, and competition from within. Wouldn't it be a wise move to revoke trust normally afforded to individuals?

Two major problems with revoking trust extended to insiders exist. The first is that if you revoke trust to people, such as system administrators, work that needs to get done just will not get done. Second, and perhaps most importantly, insider-initiated attacks do not comprise the major source of loss associated with computing systems. Human error is by far the greatest source of loss! Therefore, revoking trust but not dealing with the human-error problem hardly solves the problem. That said, of course, any sensible security administrator would take care not to assign people any more rights than what they need to do their job, in accordance with the principle of least privilege.

One More Look at the Insiders Versus Outsiders Issue

A final consideration in the insiders versus outsiders issue is that the distinction between insiders and outsiders is breaking down. Today's corporations, for example, are increasingly turning to outsourcing to fill their needs in areas such as system administration and security. Additionally, these same corporations form third-party business alliances with other entities that may also have alliances with the corporations' competitors! The distinction between insiders and outsiders that could be so nicely defined back in the days when mainframe platforms reigned supreme and remote connectivity was rare has at least to some degree broken down in today's computing and business environments.

InfoSec and Windows NT

When Windows NT was first released, many people accepted the marketing hype that it was the most secure operating system commercially available. Not only did Windows NT have a large number of security-related features, but controlling these feature through the GUI was (as least from the viewpoint of a less-experienced system administrator) more straightforward and intuitive than it was for other, competing products. Talk of Windows NT as the "C2-hardened Rock of Gibraltar" started to circulate. Certainly no commercial, off-the-shelf operating system could potentially be more secure than Windows NT, right?

Intentions were good, but the effort to make Windows NT into the most secure commercial, off-the-shelf operating system that money could buy ran into a number of obstacles. The growing number of security-related vulnerabilities that have surfaced in Windows NT have, for example, increased the potential for loss and disruption due to the potential for widespread, unauthorized access to files, services, and networks as well as disruption that Windows NT vulnerabilities allow. Equally alarming is the potential for exploitation of existing vulnerabilities. Automated tools (sometimes referred to as "kiddie scripts") that enable even the most naive of users to perpetrate powerful attacks on systems and networks thousands of miles away or (perhaps worse yet) locally are now freely available on the Internet. InfoSec considerations in fact loom as one of the most important issues in the Windows NT arena.

The Current Picture for Windows NT

With capabilities, such as symmetric multiprocessing, a sophisticated file system, network access capability, support for a single logon capability, compatibility with a wide range of computing platforms and protocols, fault-tolerance features, and many security-related capabilities, Windows NT has steadily increased its share of the operating systems market since its inception in 1993. With an eye for decreasing operating expenses (particularly with respect to system and network administration), the business world has also recently shifted increasingly toward deploying Windows NT. Windows NT is now being widely used as a network server for Internet connectivity and enterprisewide networking in addition to as a distributed application server platform. Sales statistics are anything but reliable; nevertheless, most current statistics point to the fact that at the time this book is being written, Windows NT is among the best-selling server software products in the world. The point here is not to speculate on the reason for the success of Windows NT in the marketplace—the reason could be superior technology, or it could be superior marketing. The point instead is that Windows NT is deployed so widely that it has become a reality and necessity to learn to deal with it and its many security quirks!

Although the sales picture for Windows NT has been a source of exhilaration for Microsoft, the challenge of securing Windows NT has, if anything, caused an increasing sense of concern within a large part of the user community. Problems in Windows NT security that have surfaced have not for the most part resulted from faulty design; Windows NT security from the time of its original release has been based on a logical security model. Windows NT has, furthermore, passed several evaluations based on formal security criteria. At the time this book was being written, for example, the U.S. NCSC had long determined that several 4.0 versions of Windows NT were compliant[7] with C2 security requirements. Although meeting these

[7] *The term "certification" does not apply to Trusted Computer System Evaluation Criteria (TCSEC) product evaluations (that is, evaluations conducted by the U.S. National Computer Security Center) but applies only to environments in which products are deployed.*

requirements would to the uninitiated seem to imply that Windows NT is virtually foolproof in terms of its security capabilities, this is far from the case. One of the greatest limitations of the C2 requirements, however, is that they apply only to standalone systems. Few systems in today's computing world are not networked! Windows NT Server 4.0 more recently passed the European *Information Technology Security* (ITSEC) E3 requirements. This is almost certainly a more meaningful achievement; the ITSEC requirements apply to networked systems.

Interestingly, the Microsoft Knowledge Base site currently states that no commercially available operating system more secure than Windows NT is currently available. Cynics scoff at this statement. At the same time, the user community has increased its scrutiny of the security merits of this product. A week seldom goes by before new Internet postings about yet another security-related vulnerability in Windows NT appear in public Web sites such as WIN2KSECADVICE (`http://www.win2ksecadvice.com`). Furthermore, as stated previously, a disconcertingly high proportion of the fixes Microsoft has created and distributed either have not completely controlled the security-related vulnerabilities they were supposed to eliminate, or they have initially caused other, negative side-effects such as unexpected crashes or interference with one or more functions. Perhaps most disconcerting of all
is that Windows NT is not the only source of security-related exposures. Numerous vulnerabilities in applications, such as Internet Explorer and Outlook 97 and 98, that run in the Windows NT environment have also surfaced, making security in the Windows NT environment ever more challenging.

A Look at What's New in Windows 2000

Windows 2000 has recently been released. In many respects this release represents a radical departure from the versions that Microsoft has released so far. Many of the changes are for the sake of security; others enhance functionality. Some of the major new features and capabilities in Windows 2000 include the following:

- **Active Directory (AD).** This provides a sophisticated set of directory services for locating and accessing resources over the network.
- **Kerberos.** Software that authenticates users, and then issues tickets for all users access to files, applications, and services.
- **Microsoft Management Console (MMC).** Provides a more effective and efficient means of administering systems than is currently available with an out-of-the-box Windows NT installation. Included is an improved version of the *Security Configuration Manager* (SCM).

- **Terminal Services.** Terminal Services supports the capability for thin clients running on a reasonably wide range of different hardware platforms.
- **Distributed File System (DFS).** DFS provides mechanisms that support remote access to files; these mechanisms work in connection with Windows 2000 directory services.
- **Clustering Services.** This Microsoft product, which supports clustering to obtain better performance with complex applications, is integrated into the Advanced Server and Datacenter Server versions of Windows 2000.
- **Windows Driver Model.** Windows 2000 uses a new driver model, designed to provide greater availability of third-party drivers for the NT platform. The original intent was that all Win9x drivers would work on Windows 2000, but that has not materialized completely. In fact, lack of hardware support may continue for some time because many Windows NT drivers are not compatible with Windows 2000.
- **Disk quotas.** In Windows 2000, you can establish disk quotas on a per-partition/per-user basis.
- **Dynamic disks.** The days of fixed disk space allocation, which is currently the mechanism, will be gone. Using dynamic disks, partitions can be resized on-the-fly.
- **Plug and Play.** This enables users to start services just by inserting the appropriate hardware.
- **Universal Serial Bus.** A *Universal Serial Bus* (USB) is a new peripheral bus type that has previously been used on the Macintosh and Windows 98 platforms. USB provides full Plug and Play capability, enabling users to plug in and unplug peripherals without restarting the computer.
- **IntelliMirror.** This feature provides a type of steady-state environment in which workstation-specific settings and files are cached on domain controllers.
- **Power management.** On computers that support either *Advanced Power Management* (APM) or the newer *Advanced Configuration and Power Interface* (ACPI), Windows 2000 can manage power usage of the computer and certain peripherals.

Preparing for deploying (let alone securing) Windows 2000 will require major planning and effort. Chapter 11, "Security Considerations for Windows 2000," prepares you by discussing the most important issues you need to consider and resolve.

Conclusion

This chapter has provided an initial look at Windows NT 4.0, delving into what it is, where it came from, and some of the many advantages, as well as limitations of this Network Integrated Operating System. Each of the versions of Windows NT, Windows NT Workstation, Windows NT Server, Windows NT Enterprise Server, and Windows NT Terminal Sever, provide somewhat different contexts of usage and functionality. Securing systems and networks is not easy, regardless of the particular operating system and version in question. The more functionality, the greater the number of vulnerabilities that can allow unauthorized access, denial of service, and other undesirable outcomes. Evaluating tradeoffs between functionality and security is thus a difficult task. Whatever the outcome of functionality-security tradeoffs, information security is too important to neglect. The cost of a single security-related incident is now so high that failing to adopt at least a minimum of security measures constitutes irresponsibility. Windows 2000 is now available. It will offer many features (including security-related features) that are not currently available in Windows NT 4.0. Windows NT 4.0 is, however, currently much more widely deployed; securing Windows NT 4.0 now and planning for a secure migration to Windows 2000 later is thus a sound strategy.

Reference

Parker, Donn B. 1998. *Fighting Computer Crime: A New Framework for Protecting Information*. New York: John Wiley & Sons.

2

The Structure of Windows NT Security

"To NT or not to NT, that is the question"
–Panel Session at JCSC2000 conference, Orlando, Florida

Although this book contains a wealth of detailed information about specific Windows NT settings and configurations and their effect on security, delving into all the solutions without first presenting an idea of the design and structure that supports the various security-related features and settings would lead to piecemeal knowledge rather than a comprehensive understanding. This chapter, therefore, describes the *fabric* of Windows NT security. Discussion topics include:

- The Windows NT architecture and the components that most affect security
- The Windows NT security model
- The types of NT security features that Windows NT offers
- The structure of privileges in Windows NT
- How object access authorization occurs
- The overall security level that Windows NT provides

The questions you should keep in mind as you read this chapter are how the Windows NT security model and architecture affect the ability to control security and how you can use your knowledge of both to your advantage in securing your network environment.

Architecture

The architecture of an operating system is an embodiment of its design. The design, in turn, affects the various security capabilities. Figure 2.1 presents an overview of the Windows NT architecture.

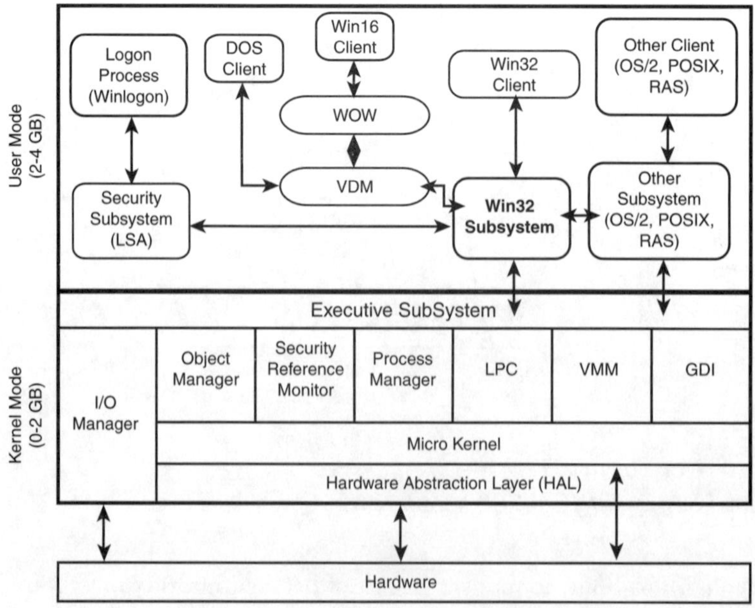

Figure 2.1 *The Windows NT architecture.*

Legend: LSA = Local Security Authority, WOW = Windows on Windows, NTVDM = NT Virtual DOS Machine, RAS = Remote Access Service, LPC = Local Procedure Call, VMM = Virtual Memory Manager, GDI = Graphics Driver Interface

Figure 2.1 provides a good indication of the complexity of the Windows NT architecture. It is also a very modular architecture, however, making identifying the various components and their functionality relatively easy. Note also that the architecture for Windows NT Workstation, Windows NT Server, and Windows NT Server, Enterprise Edition is identical. This architecture is divided into two parts: User mode and Kernel mode.[1]

User Mode

User mode consists of a number of memory-independent subsystems that provide much of the functionality of Windows NT but are not part of the kernel itself. Not all these subsystems affect security equally, however. The User mode subsystems that affect security the most are as follows:

- **The logon process.** The logon process, also called WinLogon, initiates all logon requests. It requests the Windows32 subsystem to generate the logon screen in which users enter their usernames and passwords, and then sends these entries to the security subsystem.

[1] *User mode is constrained with respect to access to components of the Windows NT architecture, memory, and so forth; Kernel mode is not. User mode processes and programs, for example, cannot directly access hardware.*

- **The security subsystem.** The security subsystem is often also called the *Local Security Authority* (LSA). The security subsystem plays an especially key role in user logons to any NT domain or workstation by taking the logon request data passed to it by the logon process[2] and sending this information to the *Security Accounts Manager* (SAM). As discussed in Chapter 1, "Introduction and Overview," the SAM has its own database of authentication-related information (including logon IDs and password representations) necessary to authenticate logon requests; it compares data in the logon request to information contained in its database to determine whether logon requests are valid. If the username and password are not correct, the security subsystem notifies the Windows32 subsystem to generate a failed logon screen (see Figure 2.2). The security subsystem also controls security logging to determine which events will and will not be captured in the Security (Audit) log (according to the Audit Policy) during every logon session.

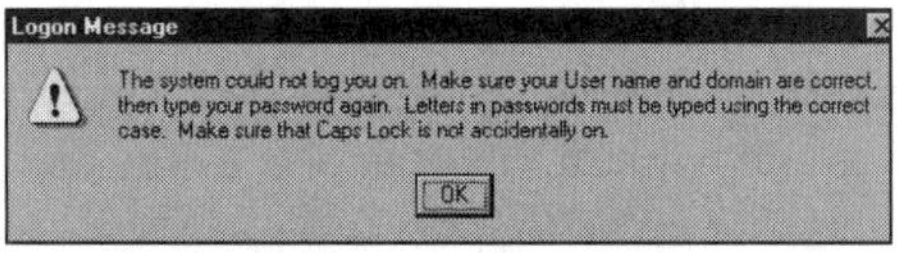

Figure 2.2 *Screen displayed when a failed logon attempt occurs.*

- **The Windows32 subsystem.** The "heart" of Windows NT in many respects is the *Windows32* (Win32) subsystem. This subsystem interacts with virtually all other subsystems in User mode to receive and pass on inputs for other subsystems and to control and coordinate messages sent throughout the system. The Win32 subsystem also enables applications to read Windows-style data structures.
- **Windows on Windows (WOW).** WOW is the subsystem that interacts with other systems when 16-bit applications (that is, applications written to run on platforms that support 16-bit addressing, as in the case of MS-DOS and OS/2 applications) are run. This part of the architecture thus provides support for older, lower-end applications.

[2] *Users must press Ctrl+Alt+Del during the logon sequence. Microsoft calls this keystroke combination the "Secure Attention Sequence" because it is captured by the desktop object (which handles all input and output) to ensure that the logon process communicates directly with the LSA. The goal is to prevent other programs or processes from intervening (that is, to prevent trojan-horse programs from being executed during the authentication process).*

- **The environment (emulation) subsystems.** The various *Application Programming Interfaces* (APIs)—particularly the *NT Virtual DOS Machine* (NTVDM), OS/2, and POSIX[3] APIs (sometimes called "virtual machines") shown in Figure 2.1—are also critical parts of the User mode architecture. These APIs interface with the environment subsystems, one for DOS, one for OS/2, and one for POSIX. The environment subsystems emulate other operating systems to make it possible to run applications written for other platforms within the NT environment. Instead of having to create a separate, dedicated DOS partition, for example, you may be able to run DOS applications using the NTVDM (sometimes also called the DOS subsystem). This subsystem is a Win32 application that emulates the Intel 386, architecture with its software. This application supports the DOS BIOS and disk interrupts and includes support for a set of virtual device drivers that enable many DOS applications to run within Windows NT. Likewise, 16-bit emulation exists to support running 16-bit applications on character-based OS/2 applications using NT's OS/2 subsystem. POSIX[4]-compliant applications can run using NT's POSIX subsystem, although these applications cannot obtain direct access to the facilities of the Win32 subsystem such as networking and graphics facilities, but must instead pipe commands to and from these facilities. Each subsystem has its own client interface.

User mode also contains an API for *Remote Access Service* (RAS) and a RAS subsystem for managing dial-in and other connections. These applications run within User mode for an important reason, namely to (among other reasons) enable RAS to run as efficiently as possible. If they were to run in Kernel mode, the Windows NT operating system would intervene to a greater extent because of Kernel mode's extra level of protection.

Kernel Mode

The Windows NT Kernel mode, sometimes called the Executive mode, differs from User mode in that in the former, programs or processes have a sufficient level of privilege to be able to perform any operation that

[3] *Portable Operating System Interface*

[4] *Windows NT 4.0, however, does not support the OS/2 file system, High Performance File System (HPFS); if OS/2 applications require HPFS, therefore, you may need to create an OS/2 partition instead of running these applications using the OS/2 subsystem. In addition, Windows NT does not support the OS/2 subsystem on RISC-based systems. Interestingly, both POSIX and OS/2 subsystems are part of Windows 2000. Note that the OS/2 subsystem will run only Character-mode OS/2 applications. It cannot be used to run GUI OS/2 applications.*

Windows NT can perform. A Kernel mode process can, for example, overwrite any memory location or kill other processes. User-initiated processes can directly affect events that occur in User mode but cannot directly affect events in Kernel mode. User-initiated processes that might possibly affect Kernel mode events are analyzed by the *Security Reference Monitor* (SRM) (discussed in more detail throughout this chapter).

Each processor in Windows NT's multiprocessor configuration can run in the NT Kernel mode when the need arises for a user process to invoke a special group of services called the *Executive Services* available to all Windows NT processes. These services include the I/O Manager, Object Manager, Security Reference Monitor, Process Manager, Local Procedure Call, Virtual Memory Manager, and Graphics Driver Interface. A short description of each follows:

- **I/O Manager.** This service manages all input and output for the operating system and also controls interdriver communications. It includes and supports a cache manager, hardware device drivers, file system drivers, and network drivers.
- **Object Manager.** An object is a named entity. Windows NT has many types of objects, including files, directories ("folders"), printers, and so forth. The Object Manager provides conventions for creating, naming, retaining, using, and securing these objects. To support efficient access to objects, this service creates object handles (pointers to objects and the access control data associated with each), as explained in detail in Chapter 7, "Basic Network Security Measures." The Object Manager also assigns a unique *object ID* (OID) to every object within a Windows NT system and deletes the object's OID if the object is deleted.
- **Security Reference Monitor (SRM).** The SRM controls whether a user or process is allowed access to Kernel mode. It also controls the following two extremely important functions:
    1. The SRM checks information contained in security descriptors against information in *access control lists* (ACLs) to validate access requests—the SRM thus allows or denies attempted accesses to an object by a subject (that is, a user and/or a process that runs on behalf of the user). This is discussed in more detail later in this chapter.
    2. The SRM controls the audit-generation policy, ensuring that the Security log captures information specified by the Audit Policy and that appropriate audit messages are generated.
- **Process Manager.** When Windows NT runs, process threads (that is, pointers to processes) are constantly created and killed. The Process Manager manages all processes by creating, tracking, feeding, and

starving threads in accordance with the kernel's scheduling constraints. It also assigns a unique *process ID* (PID) to each process and deletes this ID when the process is killed.

- **Local Procedure Call (LPC).** The LPC service enables messaging between applications and environment subsystems as well as other User mode modules when the client and server reside on the same host.
- **Virtual Memory Manager (VMM).** The VMM controls virtual memory by defining page structure and determining how pages are swapped in and out of memory. If processes that use system memory had to deal with memory's physical organization, these processes would be terribly slow and inefficient. The VMM therefore hides the physical organization of system memory from each process that uses it.
- **Graphics Driver Interface (GDI).** The GDI provides a direct interface between graphics drivers and the kernel itself.

In addition to the executive services, Kernel mode includes the kernel itself and a *Hardware Abstraction Layer* (HAL).

- **Kernel.** The Windows NT kernel, the true "heart" of Windows NT, is the final part of Kernel mode. It controls critical functions such as interrupts, exception handling, process scheduling, low-level virtual memory management, and coordination of threads that run on different processors.
- **Hardware Abstraction Layer (HAL).** An operating system faces challenges when dealing with different types of hardware. One approach is to attempt to hide any differences between different types of hardware from the rest of the operating system by making a wide variety of hardware platforms look like a single machine. This is exactly what Windows NT does through its HAL, which attempts to interface with all hardware through what some people describe as a single device driver (although others prefer to view the HAL as a single API). The Windows NT kernel and device drivers call HAL routines. Although some modification may be required to accommodate certain hardware architectures, the HAL allows Windows NT to install and run on a variety of platforms, including Intel, Alpha, MIPS, and PowerPC[5].

[5] *Note that starting with Service Pack 3 for NT 4.0, the MIPS and PowerPC platforms are no longer supported. Microsoft also provides no updates for those platforms. The Alpha platform is supported on all versions and service packs of NT 4.0, but not on Windows 2000.*

In conclusion, Windows NT's architecture is reasonable not only from the standpoint of design, but also from the perspective of security. First, an integrated architecture, such as Windows NT's, is conducive to security. Second, the division of its architecture into User and Kernel modes helps ensure that only certain processes can obtain access to certain parts of the system, including hardware devices. Finally, the architecture includes all the critical subsystems needed to support the Windows NT security model, the next topic of this chapter.

The Windows NT Security Model

One of the primary strengths of the Windows NT security design is that it is based on a security model. A security model is an overall scheme or approach for enforcing security constraints. A product that is not based on a cohesive security framework at best offers a number of security-related features that exist in isolation to each other. The result is increased difficulty in achieving security control. Windows NT security, on the other hand, is *potentially* easier to manage because it is based on a coherent security framework. The Windows NT security framework is thoroughly integrated into nearly all aspects of Windows NT's architecture and functionality, both in Windows NT Workstation and Server. The four essential components of this framework are the security subsystem, logon process, SRM and the C2 security requirements. Before we address these issues, a review of Security Identifiers (SIDs) is in order.

How User Security Identifiers Are Created and Used

Three types of SIDs can be found in Windows NT: previously discussed individual account SIDs, group SIDs, and computer SIDs. Individual account and host SIDs are assigned automatically and are unique within every domain, server, and workstation (although it is possible to use a utility such as Ghost to clone workstations with the same SIDs). Consider, for example, the individual account SIDs. Each serves as Windows NT's primary reference for each user. In the case of domain accounts, the SID actually consists of several parts:

- **Revision number.** This is always S-1.
- **Authority value.** Parameters that refer to the properties of the SID. (For example, the value of SECURITY_NT_AUTHORITY is 5; the next value of 21 designates that the SID is not a built-in SID.)
- **Subauthority values.** This is a set of three numbers generated on the basis of variables such as the time of day the account was created and domain name.
- **Relative ID (RID).** The last part.

Therefore if a SID of a domain account is S-1-5-21-1054487329-2137791366-30482200-500, for example, the first part, S-1-5-21, indicates the revision number; 5-21 indicates the authority value. A RID of 500 indicates that this account is either the default Administrator account or an account that has been copied from this account. A RID of 501 means that the account is either the default Guest account or an account cloned from this account. RIDs of nondefault accounts begin at 1000 and are incremented from this value as each new account is created with the exception that copied accounts retain the RID of the account from which they are copied.

Account SIDs have some important properties. Besides having to be unique within domains or individual computers, they remain the same if the name of an account is changed. If an account is deleted, however, the SID is forever deleted and cannot be used again. Even if a new account with the same name of the previously deleted account is created, the SID for the new account differs.

Providing that you have Administrator-level privileges, you can look at the SIDs on any domain controller or individual Windows NT box by reading them out of the Registry. SID data is available in several different parts of the Registry. One path that works is `\HKLM\Software\Microsoft\WindowsNT\CurrentVersion\Profile List`. (Chapter 6, "Maintaining Windows NT Security," explains how to use a Registry editor to read and edit the Registry.)

Security Subsystem (Local Security Authority)

As discussed earlier in this chapter, the security subsystem (also called the Local Security Authority, or [LSA] not only is responsible for authentication, but also creates access tokens. Access tokens are one of the fundamental elements of the Windows NT security model. For every logon to Windows NT, the LSA creates an access token on behalf of the user ID that has been authenticated.

What Is an Access Token?

An *access token* is a data structure held in the Server Service User Table. Some machine (a domain controller or workstation, depending on whether a user logs on to a domain or directly to the workstation) will hold an access token for that user. The same is true of processes. Access tokens are Windows NT's way of establishing that a user or process has been authenticated; as discussed shortly, they are used to determine whether users and programs are eligible for access to objects, such as files and Registry keys.

Primary Access Tokens

A primary access token is associated with a user when the user interactively logs on to a Windows NT machine. Figure 2.3 shows what a typical primary access token looks like. This access token contains the following:

- The name and numeric identifier for the domain.
- A SID for the account as well as the SID of each group to which the user/account belongs.
- Security attributes for that account (that is, privileges that may be enabled under certain conditions if particular values are present). The following example illustrates the Windows NT security attribute `SeMachineAccountPrivilege`. When the attribute value for this descriptor is 0, the person or process for whom this access token has been created cannot assign privileges to any account on the particular machine for which the value has been assigned. When the value is 1, that person or process can assign privileges on that machine if the need arises during a session. (Note that some security attributes have maximum values greater than 1.)

```
Domain: NTUR.COM34556790-2310972344-1052
SID:  S-1-5-21-161845891022
Member of this group:  S-1-5-21-114678463-1555678966-15384451103-1030
Member of this group:  S-1-1-0
Member of this group:  S-1-5-21-193553911-3786542993-12227545091-1053
Holds a SeTcbPrivilege with attributes:  0
Holds a SeMachineAccountPrivilege with attributes:  0
Holds a SeCreateTokenPrivilege with attributes:  0
Holds a SeCreatePermanentPrivilege with attributes:  0
Holds a SeAuditPrivilege with attributes:  0
Holds a SeLockMemoryPrivilege with attributes:  0
Holds a SeAssignPrimaryTokenPrivilege with attributes:  0
Holds a SeChangeNotifyPrivilege with attributes:  0
Holds a SeShutdownPrivilege with attributes:  0
Default information:
Owner:  Administrators from ONEDER domain
Access 0x100000000 allowed to:  Administrators from ONEDER domain
Access 0x100000000 allowed to:  Administrators from NTDOM domain
```

- The SID of the primary group to which the user belongs. (This is used only by POSIX-compliant applications, which require this parameter.)
- Data related to object ownership (so that if a new child object is created, a SID for the default owner of the new object can be assigned).
- The default ACL, which specifies the particular accesses and actions performed on a given object that will be captured by Windows NT's auditing.

Process and Impersonation Tokens

Windows NT contains several additional types of access tokens besides the primary access tokens already discussed. A user or process typically needs to switch to a new usage context (that is, to gain access to objects on a different computer or to a new service that the user or process does not own). A member server obtains data from the authenticating machine to determine whether the user or process is eligible for access (and, if so, also at which particular *level* of access—read, write, delete, and so forth) to a given object on that server. The basis for determining eligibility is the user's SID, group SIDs, and other data. The LSA of the member server then builds an access token for the user or process authorized for access to the object if the user or process credentials are sufficient. Therefore, *multiple* access tokens that persist for the life of the logon session are typically created for each user; these access tokens are usually held by multiple machines throughout a domain. Logging off of a Windows NT domain results in deletion of the access tokens for the logged-off user or process from every machine in which a token is held.

Additional types of access tokens are called *process tokens* and *impersonation tokens*. As implied by the name, *process tokens* are created only on behalf of processes. Process tokens are also held in the Server Service User Table of a particular machine as long as its threads run within that machine. Sometimes a program needs to run a thread with a different level of privileges than the user who has started the program has. In this case, an *impersonation token* is created. This type of token allows an application to run using the security profile of another user so that the application can execute with the needed level of privileges. Users cannot freely impersonate other users, however, but must have the requisite rights, abilities, and/or permissions before they are allowed to do so. It is not at all uncommon for the Server Service User Tables within many machines in a domain to hold many access tokens on behalf of a user who invokes multiple programs that run on these machines.

Logon Process

Windows NT's logon process helps ensure the proper authentication of every user and process. For details of the logon process please see the "Types of Security Features" section later in this chapter.

Security Reference Monitor

The SRM ensures that every initial access to every object by every user and process is checked according to a set of access restrictions. These restrictions are implemented as *access control entries* (ACEs) within ACLs that determine the necessary set of security descriptors for user access to objects after each user has been authenticated. *Security descriptors* are collections of attributes used in determining whether processes and threads can access objects. Every named object in Windows NT (every directory, file, synchronization object, mailslot, process, thread, pipe, access token, desktop, Registry key, and so forth) has a security descriptor. Figure 2.3 shows the general structure of security descriptors. Note that Discretionary Access Control Lists (DACLs)(discussed later in this chapter) are discretionary access control lists (ACLs) that determine qualifications needed for access to objects.

Figure 2.3 *How security descriptors are structured. (Note that SACL refers to system access control list.)*

C2 Security

Microsoft's implementations of Windows NT (Workstation and Server) are geared toward compliance with C2-level requirements. These requirements are based on military standards (specifically, MIL-STD 5200, "Trusted Computer System Evaluation Criteria" [The Orange Book]) for computing systems developed by the U.S. *National Computer Security Center* (NCSC). The C2-compliant security features in Windows NT supplement the basic Windows NT security model; all the elements of the Windows NT security model previously discussed coincide with requirements for C2 security. These requirements include the following:

- **Discretionary access control.** A C2 system must have access controls that govern subjects' (for example, users and processes that run on behalf of users) access to objects (for example, files and directories). In C2 systems, the access controls are set at the discretion of each object's owner. Windows NT's object security functionality (which allows, for example, a file or folder's creator/owner to change permissions) and security descriptors fulfill this requirement.
- **Object reuse protection.** Object reuse means the capability to recover objects even though these objects have been deleted. In the DOS operating system, for example, when a user uses the **delete** command with a

filename as an argument, the file itself is not really deleted—only the pointer to the file in the File Allocation Table is deleted. Someone can use the **undelete** command to recover the file. Object reuse *protection* does not allow DOS's file deletion method, but rather requires that a deleted object cannot be recovered through conventional file access and recovery methods.

From a security perspective, object reuse is *un*desirable; it can allow a perpetrator to obtain copies of sensitive and/or proprietary files which the owners assume are not accessible by anyone because they have deleted unnecessary copies. The Windows *NT File System* (NTFS) attempts to overwrite deleted files and directories and the VDM does not support the **undelete** command. You are undoubtedly familiar with the variety of data-recovery utilities that enable recovery of previously deleted DOS files; several such utilities may also work in the Windows NT environment. From the standpoint of C2 compliance, therefore, complete object reuse protection has been a problem with a number of Windows NT releases. Microsoft has in response made several modifications to NTFS to address these problems.

- **Mandatory authentication.** Mandatory authentication means that access to a system can occur only as the result of authentication to that system. Windows NT meets this condition by requiring a logon before *all* accesses when Windows NT systems are running as standalone systems. In addition, a networked Windows NT system can be set to severely restrict access by unauthenticated users.
- **Auditing.** C2 compliance requirements dictate (among other things) that all events which involve access to objects or that affect the capability to access objects be continuously captured in an Audit log. If configured appropriately, the Windows NT Security (Audit) log (discussed in detail in Chapter 6) records virtually every such event and thus meets the C2 auditing requirement.

Unfortunately, C2 security is one of the most widely misunderstood concepts in the entire field of information security for the following several reasons:

- Products per se are not certified according to C2 criteria—only environments in which products are implemented. Yet one doesn't have to read or listen to very much information about Windows NT before hearing another vendor claiming to have "C2-certified" products.

- C2 compliance is not a particularly high level of security compliance. This level of compliance does not by any means imply either that a state of "perfect" security exists or that no security-related vulnerabilities could be exploited by perpetrators.
- In addition, C2 applies only to standalone systems. The minute a network wire is connected to a Windows NT Workstation or Server platform, C2 security per the "Orange Book" no longer applies. Undoubtedly, it is better to have the option of having C2-level security features than to not have such an option. You should, however, avoid developing a false sense of confidence about Windows NT security based on any C2 security label. C2 security requirements were developed when computing systems and networks were considerably more rudimentary than they are now; these requirements address the need for confidentiality of information at the expense of other, now sometimes even more important requirements, such as availability and integrity.
- C2 as well as the entire TCSEC is becoming obsolete, as discussed earlier.

The NCSC has determined that several environments in which Windows NT 4.0 is deployed as well as one prior version (3.5 Workstation) are C2 compliant.

If you install the C2-rated versions of Windows NT, they will not be C2 compliant right out of the box. The Resource Kit for Windows NT 3.51 and 4.0 provides a tool called the C2 Configuration Manager to help you evaluate what features of Windows NT 3.51 and 4.0 systems are compliant with C2 requirements. You can also use this tool to change settings to conform with C2 requirements. Remember that the minute you connect any machine (Windows NT or any other type) to the network, however, it cannot be C2 compliant according to MIL-STD 5200. Be careful, too: Changes you make using the C2 Configuration Manager can be downright disruptive to system functionality. Consider, for example, the result of deleting the *Virtual DOS Machine* (VDM), something that the C2 Configuration Manager says must be done to achieve C2 compliance. Deleting the VDM also deletes both the Command Prompt and the Run menu. You will not be able to run DOS applications anymore.

Types of Security Features

Table 2.1 summarizes the major groups of security-related features in Windows NT. These features are covered in more detail in the following sections. Understanding these features helps in conceptualizing the structure of Windows NT security.

Table 2.1 Major Windows NT Security Features

Area	Feature(s)
Authentication	Secure logon attention sequence
	Mandatory logon
	Encryption of logon request
Account security	NT security policies
	Logon scripts
File protection	Access based on both rights/abilities and permissions
	NTFS permissions
	Share permissions
	Server access restrictions
	Object reuse protection
System integrity	Rights and abilities
	File permissions
Privilege control	Granularity of privileges
	Rights and abilities
Remote access	Group memberships
	RAS authentication features
Printer access	Rights and abilities
	Printer access permissions
User accountability	Three logs
Real-time notification	Alerts

Authentication

Of all the security-related features in any operating system, none is more critical to security than the authentication capabilities. This section explains how the Windows NT authentication works and how the passwords used during authentication are created and stored.

The Windows NT Authentication Process

As discussed previously in this chapter, logging on to Windows NT is mandatory; even noninteractive access such as a service or network logon system still requires logon-based authentication. Additionally, Windows NT at a minimum provides password encryption for logons during most contexts of authentication. The Windows NT authentication process begins with a secure attention sequence, during which the user presses the Ctrl+Alt+Del key sequence, the logon process communicates *directly* with the LSA to preclude the possibility of a trojan horse program being inserted between the two. The LSA uses an API, LsaLogonUser, that calls an authentication package. The default authentication package is MSV1_0. Data used during the authentication process is stored in the SAM database.

The MSV1_0 Package

Although Windows NT features several different types of logon contexts, a network logon from a Microsoft client (Win9x or Windows NT Workstation) to a Windows NT Server by default features a challenge-response mechanism that involves two different parts of a client/server dialog box whenever a user attempts to log on (see Figure 2.4). The upper part (the authentication server) runs on the machine (that is, a server within a domain or, in the case of a local logon to an NT Workstation, the workstation itself) that has a copy of the authentication database to be used. The bottom part (the client) runs on the client machine.

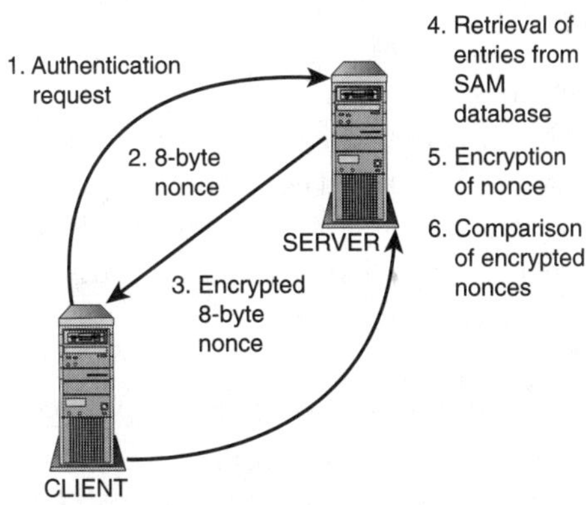

Figure 2.4 *MSV1-0 challenge-response authentication in domains.*

MSV1-0 Challeng-Response Authentication Sequence

The client sends a request for authentication to a domain controller, which sends a random challenge string (a "nonce") back to the client. The client encrypts the nonce with the appropriate password representation (LM or NT), and then sends the encrypted nonce back. ◆

Data passed between the upper and lower parts of the MSV1_0 package include the logon ID.

During remote logon attempts, the client and the server are (in contrast to local logons) always on different machines. The lower part (client) of the MSV1_0 package encrypts the password that the user has entered. The upper part of the MSV1_0 package by default sends an 8-byte, random challenge string, a nonce, to the lower half. Using a version of the Data

Encryption Standard (DES) algorithm, the lower half encrypts the nonce with the password hash three times:

1. First with the first 7 bytes of the password representation or hash (that is, the NT hash and LAN Manager (LM) password representation in the case of NT clients and the LM password representation only in the case of LM or Win9x clients.)
2. Second (independent of the results of the first encryption) with the next 7 bytes of the password representation or hash
3. A third time (independent of the results of the first and second encryptions) with the remaining 2 bytes of the password representation or hash with an added 5-byte block of filler (null characters), once again bringing the key length to 7 bytes

Each encryption step produces 8 bytes of ciphertext, resulting in 24 total bytes of ciphertext that the client sends to the server. Meanwhile, the server encrypts a copy of the nonce it has sent to the client in exactly the same manner. If the client does not use the correct password representation or hash (for example, because the user has entered the wrong one), the encrypted nonce it sends will not match the encrypted nonce that the server derives. LsaLogonUser will consequently abort the logon. If the encrypted nonce sent by the client is identical to the encrypted nonce derived by the server, LsaLogonUser logs the user on and then proceeds to create an access token on behalf of the user.

The series of events differs somewhat for an interactive logon. Whenever a *remote*, interactive logon attempt transpires, the upper half does not issue a challenge. The NetLogon service prompts the lower half of MSV1_0 (on the remote client) to send a password representation or hash for the to-be-authenticated user across the network. The bottom half of MSV1_0 then just pulls the appropriate entry out of the SAM database and compares it with the password representation or hash sent by the upper half. Whenever a *local*, interactive logon attempt occurs, the machine to which the user attempts to gain access is the same one as the one that holds the user's account information. In this case, the MSV1_0 package does *not* use the NetLogon service to call both parts, but rather has the top part directly call the bottom part, again without issuing a challenge. As in the case of a remote, interactive logon, the upper part once again just checks the SAM database to verify that the password representations or hashes are identical. If so, MSV1_0 authenticates the user.

Consider the strengths of this version of the Windows NT authentication process. Clear-text passwords are not sent over the network, and Windows NT attempts to provide an additional level of protection by trying to prevent processes not connected to a primary access token from accessing the SAM database. This at least in theory makes extracting this database difficult, even if a perpetrator gains unauthorized Administrator privileges.[6] Additionally, NT passwords are case sensitive, further protecting them by making them more difficult to guess than passwords that are not case sensitive (as in the case of Microsoft LAN Manager (LM) password representations).

Authentication in Windows 2000

By default, authentication in Windows 2000 is done through Kerberos, a package that prevents passwords being sent over the network in the clear and requires the client to use a particular set of session keys to establish sessions with servers that contain data and/or services. Chapter 11, "Security Considerations for Windows 2000," discusses Kerberos in detail. Windows 2000 also has the Security Support Provider Interface (SSPI) that allows Windows 2000 systems to interface with other types of authentication. ◆

The SAM Database

The path to the SAM database in terms of Registry access is `HKEY_LOCAL_MACHINE\sam\…\…\…`. The specific path depends on the particular type of SAM data that you want to reach. Each user account entry normally contains two password representations for each account, one for Windows NT authentication (the NT password representation) and another (the LM password representation) for compatible authentication with LM and Win9x systems.

The password representations are created using two different protocols, depending on whether the representation is the LM representation or the NT hash:

- LM passwords are first converted to all uppercase. They are then padded with null characters to make them 14 characters long if they are less than 14 characters, and are truncated to the first 14 characters if they are longer than 14 characters. Each LM password is then divided into two 7-byte halves from which two 8-byte odd parity DES keys are created (each from one of the halves). A "magic value" (based on the encryption of 0x4B7532140232425) is then hashed with the first key, then the second to produce a 16-byte result.

[6] *A clever perpetrator with Local Administrator–level privileges can, however, use a variety of techniques to gain access to the SAM database. One option, for example, includes running* ***RDISK /S****. This will update the Registry hive copies stored in* `%systemroot%\repair`*, including the copy of the SAM database stored there. These files are readable by Administrators. There are also tools to get the hashes straight out of memory, as would be needed, for example, if they are encrypted.*

- In the case of NT passwords, each password is first converted to Unicode[7] characters. The string is then hashed using the MD-4 algorithm to produce a 16-byte result.[8]

Vulnerabilities in the Windows NT Password Creation Process

Despite the apparent strengths of the MSV1_0 challenge-response authentication, several serious security-related vulnerabilities concerning Windows NT authentication have surfaced. In particular, cracking Windows NT password hashes is not nearly as difficult as it initially appeared to be. An NT-based cracking tool can hash a dictionary of candidate passwords the same way Windows NT does to determine whether any result matches a hash string. If so, the dictionary password is the actual password. Windows NT's hashing algorithms produce 100% predictable outcomes; a particular password becomes a particular password representation or hash string. Windows NT password-cracking tools can thus generate a large number of candidate passwords quickly, even on low-end platforms, such as Intel 486 hosts. It is not at all unusual to crack 25% to 35% of the passwords within a given domain of a few thousand users within two or three hours. The problem is even worse with LM passwords because the case of each character is not even preserved in the LM password representation. Even so, password-cracking tools such as l0phtCrack (available from `http://www.l0pht.com`) consequently present options that include generating *every* possible permutation of permissible Windows NT password characters—a sure way to crack a shorter password (regardless of whether it is a LM password representation or NT hash) given enough time. Other tools, such as Quakenbush Password Appraiser (`http://www.quakenbush.com`) come with precomputed hashes for passwords. This significantly speeds up password cracking.

The fact that Windows NT passwords are relatively easy to crack would comprise a considerably less significant problem if no one could gain access to entries in the SAM database. However, many vulnerabilities that allow

[7] *Unicode is an international character-encoding standard in which strings are represented as 2-byte words.*

[8] *Windows NT password representations are one-way and nonreversible representations because passwords themselves are not hashed; instead, passwords are used as keys during the hashing process. Microsoft calls the NT password hash that results from application of the MD-4 algorithm a "one-way function (OWF)." The LanMan representation resulting from using the DES algorithm, however, should also technically be considered an OWF representation.*

access to these representations exist. Access to the SAM database itself to obtain password representations and hashes is in fact not even necessary. Some versions of Microsoft's *Internet Explorer* (IE) may, for example, "volunteer" a Web browser user's password when the browser contacts a Web server that supports *Server Message Block* (SMB)–based authentication. (SMB is a major focus of Chapter 3, "The Windows NT Network Environment.") Although the transmitted password is encrypted, someone could use either a packet-capturing device or program or set up a bogus Web server to obtain the password. Worse yet, several individuals have developed tools that extract the SAM database entries using a variety of techniques ranging from obtaining interactive Registry access to making API calls that result in access to the SAM database. One of these tools is PWDump2 (`razor.bindview.com/tools`). The latest versions (2.x) of L0phtCrack not only retrieve a copy of the SAM database entries, but also crack passwords.

Although passwords are an area of security weakness in Windows NT, other features are at least more conducive to security. Ability to control users' usage patterns and security-related properties of user accounts is, for example, another necessary capability in most of today's computing environments. Windows NT provides a number of *account* security capabilities that can meet these needs. Windows NT's account policies, for example, enable control over important account-related security parameters, such as minimum password length, password expiration, and account lockouts after a criterion number of logon failures. Windows NT also supports logon scripts, which can be used to put users into particular environments (for example, application environments) and thus limit the potential for unauthorized access to resources or systems themselves.

File Access Protection

Unauthorized access to data or executable files is a major threat in virtually every operational environment. Provided that appropriate settings are selected, Windows NT's extensive file-protection measures can very adequately address this type of threat. The best known of these measures (ACLs) restricts access to files, directories, and printers. Permissions that determine access rights for both local and remote access can be assigned to all NTFS-based files and directories. In addition, remote access can be further controlled through assigning share permissions. Controlling rights to log on locally to servers also helps protect files on each server. Finally, Windows NT's object reuse protection helps protect against unauthorized recovery of files that have been deleted.

Tables 2.2 and 2.3 shows the options for the NTFS directory and file permissions.

Table 2.2 NTFS Standard File Permissions

Permission	Description
No access	No access of any kind
Read	Display data in a file Display file attributes Execute file
Change	All permissions associated with READ Display file ownership and permissions Modify file Delete file
Full control	All permissions associated with CHANGE, plus Change permissions Take ownership

Table 2.3 NTFS Standard Directory Permissions

Permission	Description
No access	No access of any kind
Read	Display directory filenames and attributes Change attributes Go to a directory's subdirectories
List	Display directory filenames and attributes Go to a directory's subdirectories Display owner and permissions
Add	Display and change directory attributes Go to a directory's subdirectories Change subdirectories Add files Display owner and permissions
Add and read	Combination of ADD and READ permissions
Change	ADD AND READ access, plus delete empty subdirectory Delete the directory
Full control	Change access, plus Change permissions Take ownership

In addition to standard permissions, NTFS has special access (individual) permissions that enable you to assign permissions on a more granular level. Special Access file and directory permissions include Read, Execute, Write,

Delete, Change Permissions, and Take Ownership. If a group needs to execute but not read an executable, for example, assigning the Special Access Execute permission is more appropriate than a standard Read permission (which allows both a read and execute).

System Integrity Control

System integrity is another constant challenge. A favorite trick of those who obtain unauthorized access to systems is to subvert the target systems, planting backdoor programs that enable easy access whenever the perpetrator desires and modifying logging programs or log files. Inappropriate permissions on critical system files and/or excessive privilege allocation are frequent causes. Windows NT provides a number of features that help ensure integrity of workstations and servers. Rights and abilities that allow changes to system configuration-related settings are assigned by default only to privileged groups. Default permissions for most system files in critical directories are for the most part set appropriately in Windows NT 4.0 to provide some degree of protection against unauthorized modification. Some notable exceptions exist, however, including the `%systemroot%`[9] and `\SYSTEM32` directories, which by default allow Everyone to Add and Delete files.

Privilege Control

Privilege control is also an extremely important consideration; escalation of privileges is another common attribute of intrusions into systems. As explained more fully in the next section of this chapter, Windows NT offers a reasonably granular set of privilege levels, and allows tailoring of privileges through the ability to assign individual rights and abilities to individual users and groups.

Remote Access Security

Failure to adequately control remote access to resources, especially in Internet-connected networks, can spell big trouble. Security features that limit the potential for unauthorized remote access are therefore especially important. Windows NT share access can be set up to ensure that certain groups obtain access only at a certain level. Windows NT domains in fact support two types of groups, global and local groups (see Figure 2.5).

---

[9] `%systemroot%` *is a system variable available on all NT systems. It points to the directory that holds the operating system, typically* `C:\WINNT`*. Because the operating system can be installed anywhere, however, it is common practice to use the system variable when referring to the* `WINNT` *directory in documentation.*

Global groups are eligible for access to any server within the domain in which they have been created as well as servers within other, remote domains. Local groups can be granted access only to machines within the domain in which they have been created; they cannot be granted access to resources in other, remote domains.[10]

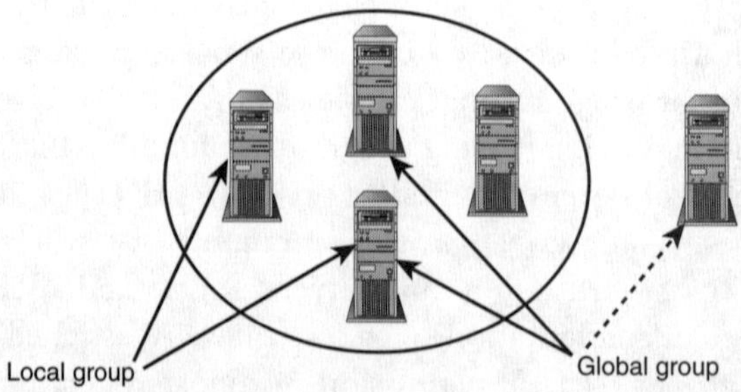

Figure 2.5 *Global and local group access in Windows NT server.*

The distinction between global and local groups in Windows NT Server is significant; placing users in local groups limits their access to only the servers within a single domain that allow access to the local groups. Figure 2.5 depicts a domain in which some servers allow access to global and/or local groups; global group membership in this case also allows access to a server (depicted as the server on the far right) in a completely different domain. Note that you can include a global group in a local group to increase the number of user SIDs within the local group, but you cannot include a global group in another global group and cannot include a local group in any other type of group.

Defining, populating both types of groups correctly, and then assigning appropriate access permissions are the responsibility of data and application owners in addition to system and security administrators. In addition, other types of Windows NT remote access mechanisms can be conducive to security. The Windows NT RAS service, for example, provides reasonable authentication features that, if set correctly, can help make remote access through this service reasonably secure. (Chapter 8, "Securing Network Services and Protocols," covers RAS security in detail.)

[10] *Membership in groups can result in access to more servers than one might imagine. The Domain Administrators group, for example, by default gets Administrator-level access to every server and client within the entire domain in which it exists.*

Printer Access Control

Printer access is a problem in some operational environments. If printer privileges are not adequately controlled, users can control whether printers are even a network resource and can kill jobs in the print queue to make their jobs run at the expense of others. Windows NT provides a set of printer permissions that, if assigned appropriately, minimize printer-related security risk. In addition, by default rights and abilities related to printer management are assigned only to certain privileged groups.

User Accountability

Some operating systems are considerably better than others with respect to establishing user accountability—recording usage patterns; then if users engage in unauthorized actions, an audit trail providing information concerning who the user was, what the action was, when it occurred, and more is accurately preserved in log files. Windows NT provides three types of logs:

- **The System Log.** This log records system-related events.
- **The Security (Audit) Log.** This log records security-related events, such as successful and failed logon attempts and accesses to resources.
- **The Application Log.** This log records errors and other conditions in applications.

If configured appropriately, in addition, Windows NT can provide alerts to inform system and security administrators as well as others if events, such as a criterion number of bad logon attempts, occur.

Privilege Structure

This section describes the Windows NT privileges for the NT Server and Workstation products.

Windows NT Server privileges are tiered into four basic levels: Administrator, Operator, User, and Guest (see Figure 2.6). The following sections describe each of the levels.

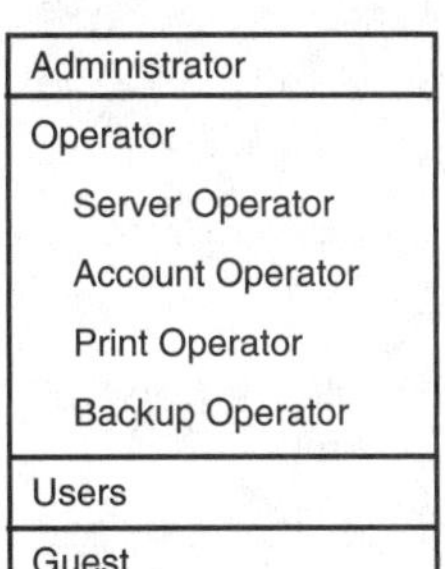

Figure 2.6 *Privilege levels in Windows NT Server Operator.*

Administrator

The highest level of privileges for anyone with interactive ("shell") access in Windows NT, amounting to "superuser" status, is Administrator. The Administrator has Full Control access to every file and directory within the system partition, but Administrator cannot necessarily by default immediately access every file and directory within any system. Permissions may, for example, allow only one user access to a particular file. The Administrator nevertheless can ultimately access any of these other files and directories because of the Take Ownership right granted to people with this level of privileges. Within a domain, Take Ownership allows anyone to take ownership, and then subsequently access *any* file or directory within that domain if access permissions for that file are not originally set to allow access to someone with Administrator privileges.

Installation of Windows NT Server results in a default Administrator account with Administrator privileges, but you can also create other accounts with this level of privilege. Only the most knowledgeable and trustworthy persons who have a bona fide, job-related reason for superuser access should be assigned Administrator privileges.

Operator

The next highest level of privileges for interactive usage in Windows NT Server is Operator-level privileges. This level consists of subsets of Administrator privileges appropriate for certain job functions. Assigning nothing but Administrator privileges to enable people to perform these functions is not likely to be wise—after all, it takes only one corrupt or disgruntled Administrator to cause a catastrophe (for example, by making a backup tape of all information stored on a domain, and then selling it to a competitor organization). The Operator level of privileges allows certain job functions that require elevated privileges to be performed without having to assign full superuser privileges. Types of Operator privileges include the following:

- **Account Operator.** An Account Operator can create and delete certain accounts and can control certain usage properties for these accounts (for example, the hours during which access is allowed).
- **Server Operator.** A Server Operator can perform tasks related to server maintenance and tuning.
- **Backup Operator.** As the name implies, a Backup Operator can back up and restore server machines.
- **Print Operator.** A Print Operator can perform tasks related to printer management.

The total set of privileges resulting from assigning a user all levels of Operator privileges does not equal the set of privileges for the Administrator. Assigning Account Operator, Server Operator, Backup Operator, and Print Operator privileges to a user, therefore, is *not* the same as assigning Administrator privileges to that user; the latter can do more with respect to accessing and controlling server and domain configuration and functionality. Only Administrators can, for example, take ownership of objects by default.

User

The next highest level of privileges for interactive usage in Windows NT Server is the User level. This privilege level is intended for users who do not need to perform system and/or network administration tasks. Users with this privilege level can potentially access any file, but only if the file permission allows. User-level privileges by default also allow use of the browser, inspection of the System log, access to a limited number of system files, and a number of other actions and prerogatives.

Guest

The lowest level of privileges is the Guest level. In theory this level of privileges should allow only very limited access to servers and domains, but in actuality the level of privileges afforded someone with Guest-level privileges is the same as with the User level. The reason is that every account is a member of a group named Everyone. Every user (even anonymous users who are remotely connected to a system via a network service), regardless of the level of assigned privileges, is a member of the Everyone group on every Windows NT machine. All users with User-level privileges are, of course, also in the Everyone group on the machine to which they have access. The default level of access to Windows NT functions is determined more by membership in the Everyone group (equivalent in some respects to "World" in other operating systems—in fact, it is even represented by a globe icon) than by User- versus Guest-level privileges. Assigning someone Guest-level privileges therefore really provides little or no advantage in the struggle to limit privileges compared to the User level of privileges when it comes to limiting access to Windows NT functions. The Guest level of privileges is therefore, for the most part, both unnecessary and even potentially misleading.

Privilege Levels in Windows NT Workstation

Figure 2.7 illustrates the various levels of privilege in Windows NT Workstation 4.0.

Administrator Level

As in the case of Windows NT Server, the highest level of privilege for interactive access is the Administrator level of privileges in Windows NT Workstation. The Administrator once again by default has access to most files (including executable files), and can exercise the Take Ownership right if denied access to a particular file.

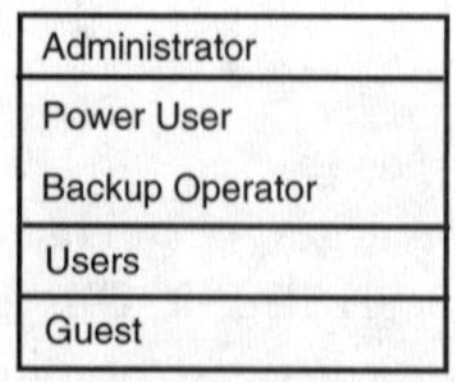

Figure 2.7 *Privilege levels in Windows NT Workstation.*

Power User

The Operator level of privileges in Windows NT Workstation is, however, somewhat different from Windows NT Server. Instead of four different types of Operator-level privileges, Windows NT Workstation has only two types of Operator-level privileges. The first, Power User, represents a combination of what in Windows NT Server is Account, Server and Print Operator privileges, allowing the Power User to perform a wide range of workstation management tasks on Windows NT Workstations.

Backup Operator, User, and Guest

The Backup Operator in Windows NT Workstation can back up and restore the workstation (similarly to how the Backup Operator in Windows NT Server can back up and restore servers). The User- and Guest-level privileges in Windows NT Workstation are parallel to the User- and Guest-level privileges in Windows NT Server.

Some Advice on Privileges

Windows NT's privilege-structuring scheme offers reasonable opportunity for controlling against the dangers of out-of-control privilege allocation. The existence of multiple levels of privilege in both Windows NT Server and Workstation allows a reasonable degree of granularity of privilege assignment. Ideally, multiple Windows NT domains might have only two persons, a primary and backup administrator, with full Administrator-level privileges. Others with lower levels of privileges might also perform other tasks, such as creating and deleting unprivileged accounts and managing servers. The most important point, however, is that adhering to the principle of least privilege is essential in protecting against unauthorized or misused privileged access. *Assign users the minimum level of privileges needed to get their jobs done!*

If a user needs only to read electronic mail, edit files, and access certain databases, do not assign anything more than User-level privileges to that user. And do not be misled by what appears to be safety in assigning only Guest-level privileges to users who do not need much access to a Windows NT Workstation or domain. The baseline of privileges for all practical purposes is User-level privileges.

Privilege assignment on the basis of individual accounts for all practical purposes becomes unmanageable when the number of users becomes greater than a few dozen. Therefore, assignment to groups is (in most Windows NT deployments) the only realistic way to assign and control privileges in anything but very small Windows NT deployments. Group-based privilege assignment has many drawbacks, however, one of the most important of which is the increased likelihood of group-inclusion errors. You might, for example, accidentally put a user in a privileged group even though you meant to place this person in another, unprivileged group. Another possibility for error arises when users resign or get moved to other organizations. In Windows NT, therefore, it is extremely important to frequently check the composition of groups, particularly privileged groups, to look for unauthorized changes and suspicious inclusion in groups.

Privilege Structuring in Windows 2000: Major Changes

In Windows 2000, "Administrator" per se is no longer a necessary privilege level to administer systems. You can assign rights to users in an extremely granular fashion. One group of users who administer systems may be assigned most or even all of these rights; another group, also created to administer systems, may be assigned only a relatively small subset of these rights. This new rights-assignment scheme will enable rights to be assigned directly on the basis of business and/or operational needs rather than on the basis of the rights of preexisting groups such as the Administrator, Server Operator, Account Operator groups in Windows NT 4.0. Alternatively, you can use the basic Windows NT 4.0 rights-assignment scheme based on the same default privileged groups that Windows NT 4.0 has. ◆

In summary, Windows NT provides a reasonably suitable structure for controlling privileges in most operational settings. You must exercise proper care in assigning privileges, however, if this structure is to be beneficial.

In some cases, the privilege assignment and control scheme in Windows NT may still not meet your security needs. In these cases, you will do better to buy a third-party tool that breaks Windows NT privileges down into smaller units. One of these tools, for example, allows a designated person to have only the right to take ownership of certain files but not others. Check out vendors such as Computer Associates (`http://www.ca.com`), Mission Critical (`http://www.missioncritical.com`), and Master Design and Development (`http://www.mdd.com`).

Object Access Authorization Architecture

This section describes Windows NT's approach to determining the authorization to access objects, such as files and system resources.

Object access authorization capabilities built in to Windows NT are some of the stronger security-related features in Windows NT. The Object Manager and SRM work closely together to authorize or deny access to resources. Any time after a user has logged on to a system or a domain, that user may want to obtain access to a particular file, directory, printer, and so forth, on the machine that logged the user on. The user initiates an action to obtain access through the user interface (for example, by clicking on the appropriate icon in the NT Explorer or entering the appropriate command in the Command Prompt). The authorization check is actually performed within the Windows NT kernel itself.

Local Access to Objects

If the desired object is on the same machine to which the user has been authenticated, the Object Manager obtains SID and other data about the requestor from the Win32 subsystem and then passes this data to the SRM. The SRM in turn checks each ACE within the DACL for the object and SID in question. The SRM checks the ACEs in serial order, starting with the topmost entry, then the next entry down, and so on until the bottommost entry is evaluated. An important exception exists: When any ACE specifically allows No Access to the SID in question, the SRM stops checking at that point. Note that a security descriptor with a null list of entries denies all access to everyone, but a security descriptor with no DACL whatsoever allows access to anyone.

The SRM allows or disallows access on the basis of the match between the SID data concerning the requestor that it obtains and the SID data in each ACE. If they are congruent with each other (for example, the requesting user's or processes' individual or group SID matches the SID in the access token), the requested access is matched with the appropriate access mask. If the requested access is to write to a particular object and this mask allows a write to the requestor's SID, the SRM notifies the Object Manager that the requested access is allowed. If the SRM finds a rule that denies the requested level of access to the SID of the account that initiated the access request, it immediately aborts its evaluation because it has sufficient data to make a decision (namely that access is not allowed), and then finally calls the Win32 subsystem to have it display an error message.

Remote Access to Objects

In the case of remote access to an object, the Server Service on the remote machine uses the access token that is stored in the Server Service User Table for that authenticated user to access the object. From this point on, the access check and process of obtaining access are the same as a local access.

Access Control Entry Structure

ACEs contain data about access rules, SIDs, and access masks, including the following:

- Rules are any or all of the following types:

  Explicit access denied (a requested access is denied)

  Implicit access denied (nothing in the list of ACEs allows access, so access is not permitted)

  Access allowed

- SIDs are the second part of ACE structure. SIDs may be for individual user accounts or groups.
- Access masks correspond to NTFS permissions (covered in detail in Chapter 5, "Configuring Windows NT Server for Security"). These masks indicate the actions that the SID in question is or is not allowed to perform on the target object. Figure 2.8 presents an example of an ACE showing its structure. Note that in this example GROUP1 is not allowed to Write and Delete, but that user ADRIAN (who is this example is not a member of GROUP1) is allowed Full Control access.

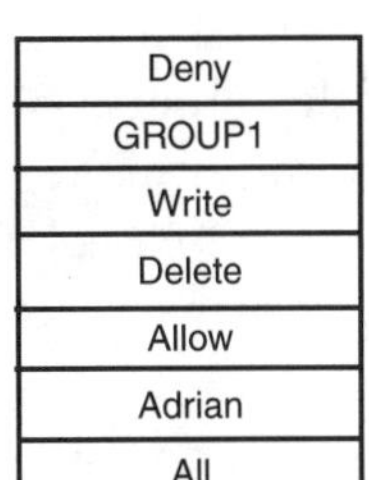

Figure 2.8 *Structure of an ACE.*

How Subsequent Access Requests Are Handled

When the SRM authorizes access, the Object Manager then creates a file handle for this access and returns it to the appropriate process. If at any time during the logon session the user wants to reaccess the same object at the same level of access, the Object Manager confirms the existence of the appropriate file handle instead of contacting the SRM once again. If the user logs off or if the object for which a file handle has been created is closed, however, the file handle is deleted. A user who wants access to that object again must therefore "start from scratch;" his access request must go through the SRM, which once again must obtain data about the requestor to compare with ACEs.

The starting point in establishing secure access in your Windows NT systems is ensuring that every partition has NTFS installed. Any non-NTFS partition (even if another file system such as the NetWare File System is installed because you converted a NetWare server to Windows NT) is as wide open as DOS—Windows NT cannot read file permissions other than NTFS file permissions.

How Secure Is Windows NT?

This chapter has looked at the Windows NT security model and architecture, the types of security-related features that Windows NT offers, and how Windows NT allows privileges to be structured and controlled. Thus far, it appears that Windows NT has much to offer with respect to establishing and maintaining security. This question is qualified somewhat, however, by a number of additional considerations. One of the most important considerations is whether we are talking about Windows NT Workstation or Windows NT Server. Some aspects of security are more difficult to manage with Windows NT Workstation (see Chapter 9, "Virtual Private Networks," for more details); others are more difficult with Windows NT Server. The Server version of this product offers centralized administration and control through domains, for example; however, at the same time, if someone gains access to an account within a domain, that person potentially has access to resources on many dozens of servers.

Is Windows NT Free of Security-Related Vulnerabilities?

An article titled "Security Expert Adds Weight to Doubts About NT Security" appeared in the *London Computer Times* in October, 1996. This article summarized interviews with a Microsoft employee from the United Kingdom and myself. I told the reporter who conducted the interviews that Windows NT, although strong in many ways from a security perspective, is by no means perfect, but has a number of security-related exposures. The article quoted the Microsoft engineer as saying that my position was "groundless," and that Windows NT has "no known security vulnerabilities." The latter statement, unfortunately, is an embodiment of a widely shared misconception about Windows NT security: Namely that this product is perfectly secure, and that an organization that uses Windows NT will just not have to worry about security. This position is not only wrong but, unfortunately, it also invites catastrophe. Good security requires a certain degree of paranoia; those who ignore security are the most likely to be victims of intrusions and other unauthorized, malicious activity. In addition, those who buy a product for the wrong reasons (that is, with the expectation that after they buy the product, they will get all the security they need) are likely to be extremely disappointed when they come to grips with reality.

All products used for computing purposes, no matter how good the security model, architecture, and security-related features, have some security vulnerabilities. Security vulnerabilities are features and flaws, such as programming errors, that can be exploited to allow unauthorized access to systems and the data or executables therein, disruption, unauthorized modification of data or executables, and/or other undesirable outcomes. The ability of users to choose their own passwords (which Windows NT provides by default) is a simple, but nevertheless a real vulnerability; a user can select an easy-to-guess password, allowing an attacker to gain unauthorized local or remote access to that account. More complex Windows NT vulnerabilities (many of which have already been exploited by unauthorized users in real operational environments) are discussed at length in Chapters 3 and 4.

Since Windows NT 4.0's initial release, Microsoft has released many service packs, sets of "patches" that fix bugs and other problems in Windows NT. One way to obtain these fixes is online at `http://www.microsoft.com/downloads/search.asp` Some service packs have corrected security vulnerabilities (although Microsoft often does not provide much information about the specific nature of problems that service packs address), and service packs released in the future will undoubtedly continue to address Windows NT security vulnerabilities.

Don't be duped into believing that Windows NT is a vulnerability-free product. You should actively investigate its security weaknesses so that you can make intelligent decisions concerning the particular weaknesses you should fix—and which you should leave alone if the cost of fixing them is not justified by the benefits.

Windows NT Security Limitations

Overall, Windows NT offers the *potential* for an operational environment with a high level of security. As stated previously, Windows NT's security model is the basis for an integrated, complete (as opposed to a piecemeal) set of security features—the best way by far to implement security into a product. Furthermore, even if dozens of security-related flaws in Windows NT do exist, the fact that Windows NT source code can hardly be found anywhere but within Microsoft facilities[11] to some degree lessens the threat of exploitation.

Despite a reasonable security model, architecture, and security features, Windows NT has some significant limitations in security capabilities. As discussed in the preceding sidebar (and in more detail in the next chapter), the fact that Windows NT has a number of exploitable security vulnerabilities should come as no surprise—all operating systems have security-related flaws. Perhaps more notable, however, is the ever-expanding functionality of the Windows NT environment, which offers an increasing number of avenues of unauthorized access.

When I first started writing this book, for example, the telnet service was not supported in the Windows NT environment. Inbound telnet access is, however, now available from third-party vendors such as Georgia Softworks (`http://www.georgiasoftworks.com`), expanding the possible ways an intruder can get to either a domain or individual workstation or server. The same is true of the remote shell service. Additionally, the more connectivity, the greater the likelihood of unauthorized access. Windows NT supports a high degree of connectivity through its support of a wide range of protocols (many of which are used for interconnectivity) and RAS. Finally, as explained in Chapter 1, Windows NT is not yet by any means a mature product; we are still discovering new, undocumented features of Windows NT and how perpetrators could exploit these features in real-life settings.

Above all, don't be lulled into the belief that Windows NT security is so perfect that nothing has to be done for the sake of security after this product has been installed. *The level of security attained after Windows NT has been installed depends completely on how this product is configured and maintained.*

Consider, for example, a worst-case scenario in which someone installs a number of servers belonging to the same Windows NT domain, and then

[11] *Windows NT source code can be purchased, but there are some legal entanglements associated with obtaining source code with which many organizations have not wanted to deal. Few organizations, therefore, have the source code for Windows NT.*

creates 50 domain accounts, all of which are members of the Domain Administrators group. Access permissions for files may be properly set throughout every system within the domain and group memberships (other than membership in the Domain Administrators group). The fact that even the most amateur user has Administrator privileges and that there are 50 superuser accounts to attack (when access to only one is necessary to have almost unlimited privileges within the entire domain) is an extremely serious liability from the standpoint of security. The critical point here is that in most cases the out-of-the-box configurations and settings for Windows NT, as in all other operating systems, are insufficient to ensure adequate levels of security. Additional work and appropriate caution are necessary to obtain the desired levels of security.

How secure is Windows NT? To a large degree, the answer is: "as secure as you are willing to make it."

Security Policy and Technology Standards: What Difference Do They Make?

If technology alone cannot solve the Windows NT security problem, what else do you need? Again, we must turn to information security policy and appropriate technology-related security standards for the answer.

Policy

An effective information security policy is the cornerstone of a successful information security effort. An information security policy is a management edict that defines in broad terms the business and operational goals of information security, establishes a framework in which to meet these goals, and defines basic elements (for example, management, responsibilities, resources) of an ongoing program to pursue and track progress toward these goals. Without a comprehensive and sound security policy backed and enforced by upper-level management, efforts to secure systems and networks are for the most part futile—the resources, strategy, and authority necessary to establish a given level of security are missing.

The information security arena abounds with books and papers on this subject, yet organizations too often have a deficient security policy or may not even have one at all. One of the most common shortcomings is to confuse a written policy statement with policy itself. The written policy statement should be the *embodiment* of the policy—just writing a policy statement in and of itself does not necessarily mean that an organization now has a meaningful information security policy. Senior management buy-in and creation of a meaningful infrastructure and process are far more essential than merely having a piece of paper labeled "Information Security Policy[12]." On the other hand, failing altogether to develop a written policy statement is also a serious mistake to which many organizations fall prey.

An effective information security policy addresses many critical issues, including the following (at a minimum):

- Who owns the systems, networks, applications, and data accessible to users?
- What ongoing programs (for example, training and awareness) must be in place and what are their objectives?
- What constitutes "acceptable use" of computing resources and data?
- What is the relationship between job function and privileges that users receive? Must privileges be limited, and, if so, how?
- What are the responsibilities of management, resource owners, and users?
- What is the baseline level of security controls to be implemented within systems and networks?
- What must be done to secure connections from third parties?
- What level of monitoring and user accountability must be in place?
- What level of privacy can users expect and how should privacy expectations be communicated to users?
- What are the consequences of violating the policy?
- When, why, and how must the policy be updated?

One of the most effective ways to "bring the policy down to the level of users" is to create a user accountability statement. A *user accountability statement* provides an encapsulation of the information security policy in wording that users can understand. In many organizations with an effective information security program, users are required to read and sign a user accountability statement once, or sometimes even twice, a year (often after a particular security training and awareness activity).

Technology-Specific Standards

Having an effective information security policy is extremely important, but, in and of itself, it is not sufficient. Security policy is broad in nature, and is therefore independent of specific technologies. Because of the complexity of securing these specific technologies, your organization should also develop

[12] *You can, in fact, pay a fee to obtain a boilerplate policy from various commercial organizations. Caveat emptor!*

technology-specific standards. These should describe specific procedures to be followed and the settings and configurations to be adopted. Although more detailed than the policy, the standards should be in conformance with the security policy itself.

Despite the abundance of security features that Windows NT offers, this product lacks several features needed to comply with many corporations' security policies and even has a number of features (for example, "Allow Blank Password") that detract from achieving the security level often needed for compliance. In this case, you need to ensure that Windows NT–specific standards specify the appropriate settings and procedures. These standards may also delineate actions in which users are or are not to engage. Suppose, for example, that to limit the possibility of virus infections or illegal DOS boots, your organization forbids anyone but Administrators to use their Windows NT machine's floppy disk drive. You could disable the floppy disk drive through software, and then reenable it whenever you needed it, or you could even disable and reenable the hardware. These procedures would be unduly cumbersome. Worse yet, Windows NT features, in and of themselves, cannot adequately address this issue. Someone with the necessary level of privileges needs to perform enabling and disabling actions in this (inefficient) scheme.

In cases such as these, in fact, the reasonable, alternative solution might be just to include in your Windows NT security standards (or possibly in your information security policy itself) a provision that no user may use a floppy disk drive on any computer owned or operated by the organization without the advance, expressed written permission of that person's line manager. It's true that some users might ignore this provision; some virus infections and illegal DOS boots might occur because of defiance or ignorance. But this provision may achieve the overall desired effect anyway—enough users may comply to drastically limit the associated security-related threats.

Managing Windows NT security requires more than just clicking on the right alternatives in dialog boxes. It also almost inevitably requires putting in place the appropriate security policy and Windows NT–related security standards. You will almost certainly have to deploy network security control measures (such as appropriately configured and maintained firewalls, for example) to compensate for some of Windows NT's network security weaknesses. You may also want to strongly consider installing additional third-party security tools, such as third-party authentication servers, password checkers, file encryption programs, and so forth. Without giving due consideration to *all* of these elements, your efforts to achieve the level of Windows NT security you need are likely to be unsuccessful.

Conclusion

In conclusion, the Windows NT security model and architecture are part of a strong framework for achieving needed levels of Windows NT security. Windows NT's security-related features and privilege structure are also potentially advantageous with respect to obtaining needed levels of security control. The important point, however, is that the work of securing Windows NT begins the minute you install this platform. All the "bells and whistles" in the world won't do you much good unless you use them correctly. No product is perfect from a security perspective; Windows NT has many security-related vulnerabilities, just like any other product. In many, if not most deployments, introducing additional measures not intrinsic to Windows NT is also necessary.

Checklist for System Administrators

1. Check to determine what your organization's security policy is. If one is in place, be sure to read it and determine its requirements before you change the configuration and settings of your Windows NT systems.
2. Ensure that all partitions are NTFS partitions. NTFS is in many respects the starting point of Windows NT security.
3. Observe the principle of least privilege. Assign only the minimum level of privileges needed to enable users to get their jobs done.

3

The Windows NT Network Environment

"The network is the computer."
–Scott McNealy

Network security is a major consideration in securing any computing system; Windows NT is by no means an exception to this principle. Before delving too deeply into the topic of security in the Windows NT network environment, however, let's first set the stage by providing an introduction to networking itself paying particular attention to principles applying to the environments in which Windows NT is typically deployed.

You need to understand the fundamentals of networking before you can comprehend many Windows NT security-related vulnerabilities. Unfortunately, Windows NT networking is anything but simple. Many of its many protocols and services are legacies from an earlier era of local area network (LAN) technology; others are part of the NT environment because of the need for interoperability between platforms; and still others are used in providing user services such as *World Wide Web* (WWW) and mail services. Securing these protocols and services is truly a challenging task.

This chapter covers the essentials of networking, including types of networks and network components, network topologies, the *Open Systems Interconnect* (OSI) model and its relationship to Windows NT network protocols and services, fundamental network services and protocols commonly found in Windows NT network environments, and other basic information about how networks operate. The chapter then concludes with a lengthy discussion of how Network Basic Input Output System (NetBIOS)- and Server Message Block (SMB)-based networking mechanisms work in the Windows NT environment. If you are very proficient with networking in general and Windows NT networking in particular, you might want to skip ahead to the final section.

Types of Network Implementations

Although there are many different definitions of networks, for purposes of this book network is defined as a collection of hosts, applications, protocols, and peripheral devices (such as printers)—all of which can communicate with each other through some combination of hardware, software, and protocols. One of the most notable changes in computing over the past decade has in fact been the proliferation of networking. The percentage of network hosts has grown steadily through the 1990s to the point that by the late 1990s, the percentage of non-network-capable ("standalone") hosts has diminished to a very small proportion.

Networks can be implemented in a number of different ways. One possible network implementation is a LAN. A LAN consists of hosts and peripheral devices that are relatively near to each other in terms of physical distance. In a *wide area network* (WAN), the hosts and peripheral devices are more physically disparate from one another.

Another consideration is the relationship of the computers within a given network to each other. In a peer-to-peer network, every network application has basically the same relationship (or at least the same *potential* relationship) to every other as all others do; no application is specialized in terms of its role in the network. Client/server networking, however, entails specialized functions—server and client. Servers provide network services (for example, the domainwide services that Windows NT domain controllers provide, the *Domain Name Service* (DNS), print services, *File Transfer Protocol* (FTP) services, and many others) and access to data stored in a database, for example. Clients provide users and applications with access to the servers through software, such as user interface routines, that translate user input and then send it to applications which reside on the server. The typical outcome is increased efficiency in resource utilization; At a minimum, each client needs enough processing power to remotely communicate with applications residing on servers. In a peer-to-peer network, in contrast, all computers are in many respects both clients and servers. They are clients because they provide an interface to applications and are servers to the degree that they run applications and provide data and services to clients.

Although peer-to-peer networks are advantageous when the need for a LAN with relatively few (perhaps fewer than a dozen) machines exists, client/server-based implementations tend to pose less security risk. In peer-to-peer networking, the security-related configuration of individual systems within the network are not generally built in. Client/server networks, on the other hand, provide support for servers used to centrally set configurations and parameters that affect the type and quantity of access to potentially every computer within the network. Exceptions to this generalization exist (for example, when client/server networks are poorly configured); but all things considered, client/server networking is more conducive to security than are peer-to-peer implementations.

Some Basic Terminology

The following basic terminology is essential in understanding networking and the many mechanisms involved. Terms covered here include the following:

- Network interface card
- MAC address
- Internet protocol
- Packet
- Networking protocol
- Ethernet
- Source host
- Destination host
- Broadcast
- Multicast
- Sniffer
- Protocol Analyzer
- Socket
- Firewall

Network Interface Card

The *network interface adapter* or *card* (NIC) connects the computer on which it is installed to the cable medium, converting the output that the computer sends to signals (normally electronic in nature) that are sent over this medium. The receiving NIC mirrors this process by receiving a set of electronic signals and then translating them into packets for the computer to receive.

MAC Address

Each machine connected to the network is identified by an address built in to its NIC. This address, called the *Medium Access Control* (MAC) address, is a physical address used to uniquely identify every computer on the network.

IP Address

Internet Protocol (IP) addresses are logical (not physical) addresses that are (with one exception—IPv6[1]) always 32 bits in length. These bits are represented in terms of four octets, a format with which nearly everyone who uses the Internet is familiar. Each host address is typically represented as a four-octet IP address; the hypothetical host `sunshine.global.net` might, for example, have IP address `120.10.20.11`. This address in turn corresponds to the particular set of bits shown in Figure 3.1.

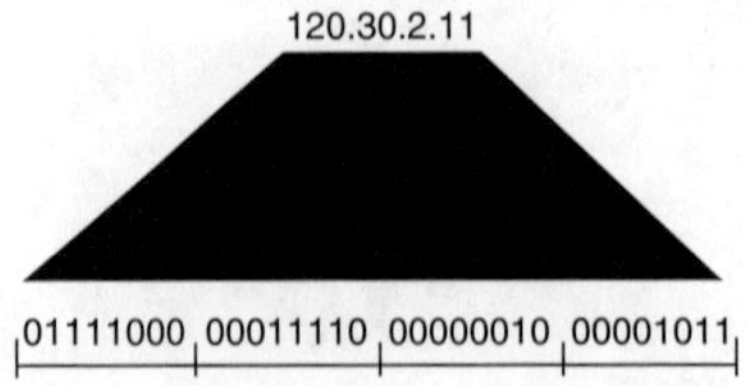

Figure 3.1 *Composition of an IP address in terms of octets (above) and bits (below).*

An Alternative Addressing Convention

Windows NT networking is largely based on the IP protocol. In contrast, Novell Internetwork Packet Exchange (IPX) addressing is a variant of the Xerox Network Service (XNS) addressing scheme originally developed for Ethernets. In the latter scheme, the host address is always 48 bits in length; a node address is always 32 bits. These bits are represented as four-digit hexadecimal numbers. An example of an IPX node address is `41.0000.od00.12bb`. *The Novell addressing scheme is not used in the Internet; and given that Novell NetWare 5.0 runs TCP/IP natively, this addressing scheme is rapidly becoming a thing of the past. It is, nevertheless, still used in reaching NetWare 4.x (and earlier versions) hosts over the network and is therefore relevant to Windows NT networking because of interoperability considerations.*◆

Packet

Data sent over the network consists of blocks of characters (properly known as datagrams, but most people call them packets). Packets consist of a header, a small set of data about the type of packet, sending and destination host, and so forth, followed by the contents (data).

[1] *IPv6, the newest rendition of the IP protocol, is based on 128-bit addressing. There is no IPv6 stack in Windows 2000.*

Networking Protocol

When networked computers communicate with each other, they must share common methods and meanings to successfully do so. When one computer transmits data, for example, the receiving computer must not only prepare to receive it, but also must determine the context and meaning of this data. Protocols provide the solution by establishing methods of communication between computers: how communications are started, parameters that must be passed between machines, the order in which they are to be sent, and many other considerations.

Ethernet

Ethernet is a very widely used protocol that network adaptors connected to cabling media use. It determines the numeric values given to series of electrical signals to form valid Ethernet packets. Its method of networking is based on *carrier sense multiple access collision detect* (CSMA/CD) control in which hosts on the network wait for the right time to send network transmissions to each other. If no traffic is going over the part of the network to which these hosts interface, they start to send their transmissions. If more than one host sends a transmission at once, however, the packets collide with each other, necessitating another transmission attempt. Collisions are not so much of a problem in smaller Ethernets, but the opposite is true in larger ones. Both switching, a mechanism that makes a direct path between ports, and routing are frequently used to deal with these types of problems.

Source Host

The source host initiates a network transmission (for example, packets).

Destination Host

The destination host is the host designated to receive a network transmission.

Broadcast

Networked computers often need to obtain data about the status and availability of other computers or to provide information to other computers. In other cases, computers need something (an IP address, an executable, for example) to locate a particular type of server or something else from a server. This is where broadcasts fit in. Broadcast packets are designed to be sent to every machine within a local network. With a destination address of `255.255.255.255`, these packets can reach every host on the local network, but by default cannot be sent outside of the local network unless they are encapsulated within another routable protocol.

Multicast

Multicast is an optimized multipoint transmission protocol. It is used in networking contexts, such as multimedia transmission and high volume data transfers.

Sniffer

Sniffer is a trademarked name owned by Network Associates. The Sniffer product that Network Associates makes captures packets transmitted over network cabling, dumps the data contents to storage media, and provides a user interface to view the data. The term *sniffer*, however, is a widely used term within the computing community to refer to any physical device or program that captures packet data. Because of trademark considerations, *packet capture device* or *packet capture program* is the appropriate term.

Protocol Analyzer

Having a device or program that captures data is useful; but having a device or program that dumps and sorts the data in different formats and views is even more useful, given the volume of data normally collected. A protocol analyzer does exactly this—it dumps captured network data in different formats and views to make analysis easier.

Socket

A socket is a convention that enables a user or program to reach a particular program on a destination host.

Firewall

A firewall is a host used as a security barrier between networks. Firewalls selectively screen traffic and sometimes also manage connections between one network and another.

Major Network Components

This section provides a brief discussion of the basic components of most networks—repeaters, bridges, hubs, and routers.

Repeaters

In the most basic sense, networks work by sending electrical signals across cables. These signals, however, attenuate as they traverse each cable; at some point along a cable, the signal may fail to carry any further. Devices called *repeaters* are used in digital networks to regenerate signals as they go down cables so that they can reach destination hosts. Repeaters are often used to increase the physical size of LANs, allowing additional systems and peripherals to connect to a preexisting LAN. Note, however, that Ethernet does not need repeaters, because of the limited distances over which traffic to segments travels.

Contrasted with other types of network components, repeaters are in many respects more passive in their functionality. In the most elementary sense, they simply take signals, magnify them, and then send them along a network cable without the capacity to selectively filter, in any way, what is sent. A potential problem in connection with repeaters, therefore, is that a repeater can potentially overwhelm a network with volumes of traffic. Hosts in any part of a network in which repeaters are present can produce an enormous amount of traffic volume even though some, much, or all of this traffic may be superfluous to the systems along the way.

You might think, therefore, that repeaters would be frequent targets of network attacks in the Windows NT or any other networking environment. Gaining unauthorized access to a repeater or sending network traffic to a repeater in a manner that causes the repeater to fail or other possible attack scenarios could conceivably lead to widespread denial-of-service. Attacks against other components of networks (for example, routers and firewalls) are, however, generally not only easier to remotely perpetrate, but they are also more likely to subvert higher-level network functionality, such as routing.

Bridges

A *bridge* is very similar in functionality to a repeater, but operates at Layer 2 of the OSI model. Therefore, a bridge actually *filters* traffic transmitted over the network based on the Layer 2, or MAC, address. Bridges dynamically update their routing tables with source addresses as they receive packet traffic. They determine the MAC address for each machine on the basis of the contents of packets (the MAC addresses of both the source and destination hosts) sent over the network. The destination MAC address of each packet is then used to selectively filter traffic packets in the following manner:

- Packets with unidentified destinations are sent on to every network segment to which the bridge is connected.
- Packets with identified destinations on other network segments to which the bridge is connected are sent on to the segment on which the destination machine resides.
- Packets in which the source and destination address are both within the same network segment are not sent to any other network segment.

Bridges are both good and bad in terms of their contribution to the problem of managing networks. An advantage of bridges (at least compared to repeaters) is that the former are not as passive; they can at least send traffic to other network segments or, if appropriate, keep traffic within a particular local segment. They can also selectively filter traffic on the basis of each packet's destination MAC address. A disadvantage is that bridges cannot filter broadcasts (transmissions from hosts that are intended to reach other computers independently of the computers' addresses).

Hubs

Some types of networks have network cables that go from the connected computers to one single point. *Hubs* (sometimes called concentrators) connect the cables at this point. Hubs vary in sophistication. Some of them just rebroadcast any signals they receive from a particular cable on to every other cable. Others are higher end, in that they function as network switches. They determine packets' destinations and then resend the signal exclusively to the appropriate cable over which the packets must be transmitted to reach this destination.

Routers

Routers are the final network component to be considered in this chapter. Routers, like bridges, route and screen traffic; but whereas bridges operate at Layer 2 and therefore use the MAC address to determine whether to forward traffic, routers operate at Layer 3, and therefore forward traffic based on the network layer address. In addition, routers have knowledge of networks outside the networks to which they are directly connected, and consequently can interconnect one LAN to many others. By contrast, bridges have no intelligence other than to determine which network a certain MAC address exists on. They can be used only to interconnect the networks to which they are directly connected. Whereas bridges can interconnect only networks that use the same data link layer protocol, routers can connect networks with different data link layer protocols, as long as they use the same network layer protocol. The important result is that routers can handle packets on a higher, more abstract level rather than information supplied by any NIC. Consider, for example, the effect of dynamic IP addressing. One machine is assigned one particular IP address for a while, and then a different address sometime afterward. Routers have no particular difficulty dealing with dynamic addressing provided the assigned IP addresses are legitimate and routing tables have been set up and maintained suitably.

The basis for routing, therefore, is routing tables. When a router boots, it has few addresses in its table. Routing protocols, such as the *Address*

Resolution Protocol (ARP), add entries to the tables as packets pass through. Network administrators can also add or delete entries in routine tables as desired. Routers may also support Access Control Lists (ACLs), rule lists specifying whether to allow or deny inbound (and also often outbound) traffic according to certain variables. These variables include source and/or destination IP address, type of protocol (for example, Simple Mail Transfer Protocol [SMTP] and File Transfer Protocol (FTP), and type of packet (SYN, ACK, FIN, and so forth). A router's ACL may block all incoming packets destined for a particular IP address, for example. A bridge, on the other hand, sends and filters packets on the basis of the network segment to which a machine with a certain MAC address is connected.

Domain Name Server

When you send a mail message to an Internet address or hit a Web site, a mechanism needs to translate this address (for example, `http:// security.globalintegrity.com`*) into a numeric IP address. The service that performs this task (called address resolution) is domain name service (DNS). Using its database of addresses and IP addresses, the Address Resolution Protocol (ARP) is used to resolve layer three (IP) addresses to layer 2 (MAC) addresses. Similarly, the Reverse Address Resolution Protocol (RARP) is used to get an IP address from a MAC address. Windows NT supports ARP, but not RARP. DNS does not use ARP at all. DNS resolves a Fully Qualified Domain Name (FQDN) to an IP address, using a forward lookup query. To get an FQDN from an IP address, a reverse lookup is performed. Because so many Internet applications and services depend on DNS, internetworking as we know it would be virtually impossible without this service.*

The Internet consists of a large number of computing domains; each Internet-connected host is part of one domain. The host `security.globalintegrity.com`*, for example, is part of a domain called* `globalintegrity.com`*. A given DNS server can resolve addresses only within its own domain, but it also knows how to forward resolution requests to other DNS servers if it cannot resolve the name. If unable to resolve* `globalintegrity.com`*, the DNS servers within a tree forward the request all the way to the top (the root domain) to find the one that knows about the type of organization (for example,* `.com, .org, .gov, .edu`*). From there the request is forwarded to a DNS server that knows* `.com` *addresses, and then to still another that knows* `globalintegrity`*.*

DNS serves as a convenient target for perpetrators for numerous reasons. At a minimum, its mechanisms are automatic and are not selective concerning the particular host allowed to make queries. One of the most common attacks on DNS servers is "cache poisoning," in which the perpetrator replaces part or all of the name cache it builds with bogus entries.◆

Many vendors' routers also support additional functionality, such as encrypting network traffic sent from one router to another. From a security standpoint, routers are potentially very useful network components. On the other hand, if an intruder gains unauthorized access to or causes disruption of a router, the consequences can be extremely unpalatable for security. An intruder could, for example, change a router's ACLs or set the routing configuration to cause traffic to be sent over a fixed route over the network. Ensuring that this fixed route is used is important in a number of different types of network attacks, including attacks in which an attacker has installed a network traffic capture device on one of the machines along this route.

Because the Internet switches packets instead of using circuits to move packets from one point to another, we often refer to it as a packet-switching network. At this point, you might assume networking consists of an orderly flow of packets from one point through one more routers and finally to the destination point. However, this is not true. Packets may, for example, be too large for a router to handle. In this case, IP routers typically simply discard the packets. In other cases they are broken into fragments. When these fragments reach their destination, they are usually reassembled into a continuous data stream. The process of fragmentation and reassembly is normally transparent to users. In TCP/IP, a transmission's packets do not go over fixed routes, but instead look for the best, most efficient route available. Different packets from the same transmission might therefore go over somewhat different routes from the sending to the receiving host. Packets may arrive out of sequence; the receiving host normally can reconstruct the original order.

Network Layouts

The term *network layout* refers to the way that network computers, network components, and other physical parts of a network, such as cabling, are deployed. Three fundamental types exist: linear, star, and ring. The branching tree is also addressed, although this layout is actually two stars that have been connected.

Linear

In a *linear* layout, all computers are connected to the network on one network cable or segment. The linear layout was extremely common in the past but is rapidly being replaced by the star layout. It is now mostly used in networks to which relatively fewer machines (30) are connected. Figure 3.2 illustrates a linear layout.

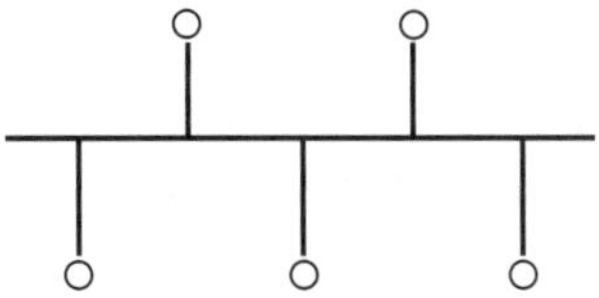

Figure 3.2 *A bus layout.*

Star

In a *star* layout, all computers are directly connected to a hub or a switch, which is a device that allows multiple cables to connect all at one point. Note here that if the interconnecting device in a star network is a hub, the network functions logically, just like a bus network, such that all clients receive all communications. Therefore, a star with a hub is also vulnerable to packet-sniffing attacks. Figure 3.3 shows an example of a star layout.

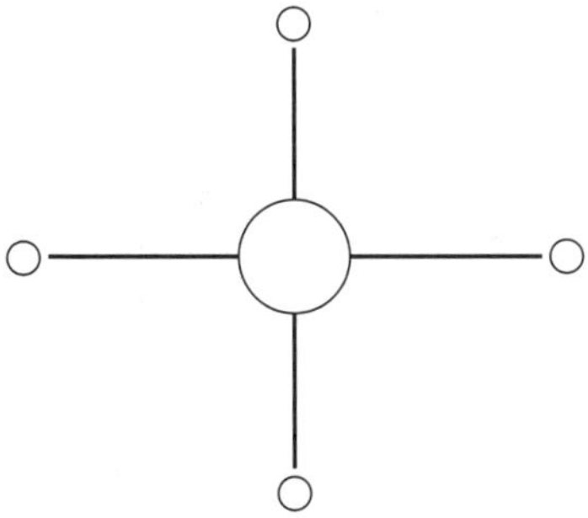

Figure 3.3 *A star layout.*

Branching Tree

In this layout, two or more star layouts are connected to each other (see Figure 3.4).

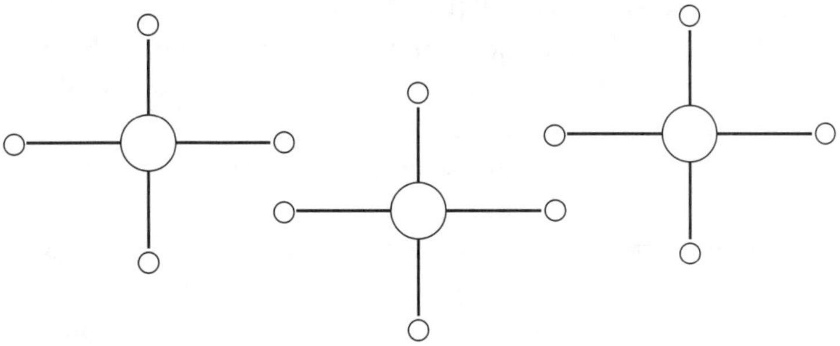

Figure 3.4 *A branching tree layout.*

Ring

A cable can connect to itself, thus forming what amounts to a self-enclosed circuit. In a *ring* layout, all hosts are connected to this circuit (see Figure 3.5).

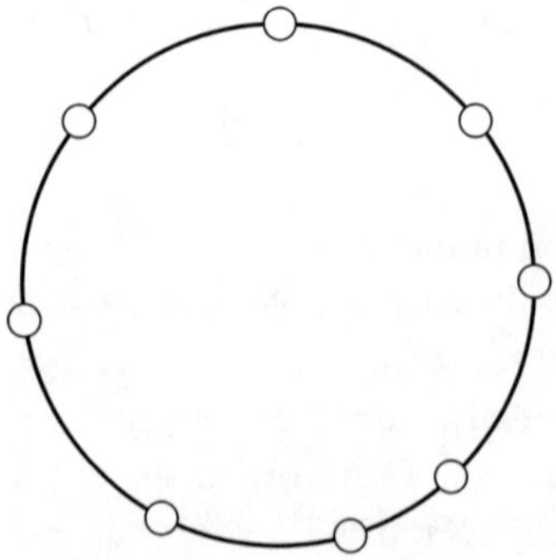

Figure 3.5 *A ring layout.*

Significance

Although other, more sophisticated manifestations of these layouts exist, all can in one form or another be characterized as one of these fundamental types. Modern Ethernets usually use the star and bus layouts together; the star connects systems to a bus together. Layout is also an important consideration in network security because some types of layouts are more vulnerable to certain kinds of attacks than are others. In the bus layout, for example, all computers listen to all packets sent over the network segment to which they are attached. This makes these networks particularly vulnerable to eavesdropping attacks in which one host has a program installed to copy every packet that reaches that host's NIC.

Local Versus Wide Area Networking

Windows NT networking is most fundamentally based on the Internet Protocol. IP addressing is based on the previously discussed *logical* addresses rather than physical addresses (for example, MAC addresses). Packets can therefore reach their destinations regardless of whether they stay within a local network or are sent across network boundaries to an entirely different network. The distinction between a LAN and WAN is, in fact, more arbitrary than anything else. Traditionally, the distinction between a LAN and WAN is based on physical proximity. A network with components entirely within a single building is therefore likely to be considered a LAN. Similarly, a network that connects LANs dispersed over a wide geographical area is likely to be considered a WAN. More importantly, however, than distance over which a network spans is the protocol used. If a network runs Ethernet, it is a LAN. If it runs *Asynchronous Transfer Mode* (ATM) over leased lines, it is a WAN. If ATM switches are installed in a small area, the network should probably be called a LAN; in these cases, Ethernet runs on top of ATM. What is probably more important from a security perspective is the number and type of boundaries between networks. Consider the following examples:

1. Because an IP limited broadcast packet always has the destination address of `255.255.255.255`, it stays within router boundaries. Attacks such as broadcast flooding attacks (attacks in which one or more machines on the network send a high volume of broadcast packets, bringing the network to a virtual standstill), are very likely to be confined within a portion of the network served by a particular router.
2. The preceding example also applies to Network Basic End User Inteface (NetBEUI), a nonroutable protocol used in Microsoft network environments. Attacks that exploit some implementation of NetBEUI are likely to be initiated from *within* a network for the same reason.
3. NetBIOS is a naming convention and an API. NetBIOS traffic is routable if NetBIOS runs over a routable protocol, such as IP. NetBIOS typically runs over both TCP and IP. Because TCP and IP are robust protocols, attacks that expolit this protocol are therefore feasible from locations quite far away from a target Windows NT host.

The term *enterprise networking* is another interesting one. Although often applied to networking within large corporations with computing facilities in different geographical locations, this term is more of a marketing term than anything else. It has virtually no value from a technical viewpoint. Its usefulness in terms of understanding and dealing with security-related issues is therefore also minimal.

The OSI Model

Let's now move on to the next topic—the OSI model and its relationship to Windows NT networking.

The OSI model is a widely used model of viewing and implementing network functionality. This model specifies seven distinct, but interrelated layers of networking, starting with the physical layer and going up to progressively higher layers. Different network functionality occurs at different levels (see Figure 3.6). The layers are as follows:

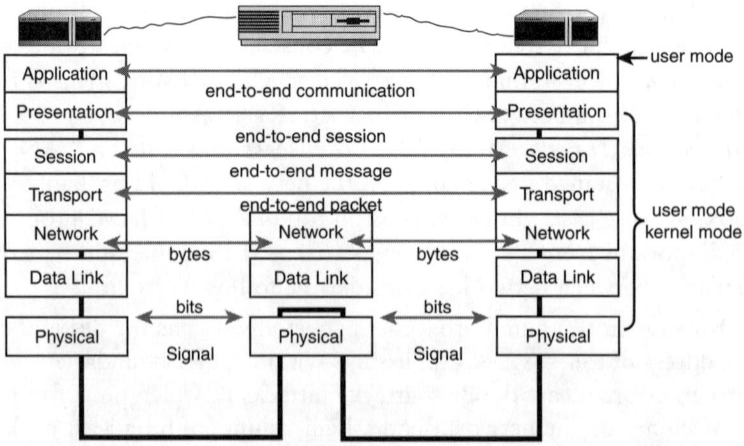

Figure 3.6 *The seven layers of the OSI and their interrelationships.*

- **Physical layer.** The layer at which electrical signals are transmitted over network wires; repeaters work at this layer.
- **Data link layer.** At this layer, data streams identified on the basis of their MAC address are transmitted to computers.
- **Network layer.** This layer supports logical addressability (independent of MAC and Logical Link Control [LLC] addresses) of packets that contain data, such as, source and destination address; routers work at this layer.
- **Transport layer.** Provides reliable end-to-end delivery between hosts, error detection and recovery, and flow control.
- **Session layer.** Whereas the network and transport layers provide connections between hosts, the session layer provides connections between applications on those hosts. The session layer provides a control structure for interprocess communication.
- **Presentation layer.** This layer is responsible for data transformation, such as character set translation, encryption/decryption, and compression.
- **Application layer.** The application layer, the "highest" in the OSI model, provides an interface to applications that run over the network. Note that the application layer does *not* consist of applications per se, only the interface to them.

How to Apply the Model

The OSI Model is, to a large degree, nothing more than an abstraction. Current implementations do not always decompose into neatly defined layers. Nevertheless, the OSI Model provides us with a very useful abstraction mechanism to discuss network funtionality. As two computers communicate across a network, the dialog begins with a top-down set of data transformations within the machine that initiates the communication. The application layer within this computer passes data to the next layer down, the presentation layer, which reformats the data and passes it to the session layer. The session layer again transforms the data for the next layer down, the transport layer, then the network layer, then the data link layer, and finally the physical layer. At this point electrical signals are transmitted along the network medium. The receiving machine receives these signals, which become progressively transformed as the data passes from one layer to the next higher one, starting with the physical layer. In this manner, every layer of one host thus effectively establishes a type of peer-to-peer communication with the same layer on the other host.

Although seven layers exist within this model, the model can be summarized in terms of four basic layers of functionality:

- Below the network layer, each layer focuses on providing an error-free signal from one host to another.
- At the network layer, traffic sent in the form of packets is routed to its intended destination within a network.
- At the transport layer, end-to-end communication between the sending and receiving host occurs.
- Above the transport layer, transmissions depend on the nature of each application involved in these transmissions.

Importance of Understanding the OSI Model

Not every networking expert embraces the OSI model. Critics argue that it adds undue complexity, and that looking only at application, transport, network, and lower layers is all that is necessary to depict that data transformations which occur within the source and destination hosts. In some networking contexts, this view is appropriate. Understanding the OSI model is, nevertheless, extremely helpful in understanding how to secure Windows NT and its many network protocols and services.

Although each layer presents its own set of special challenges from a security perspective, protocols and services at certain layers potentially pose more security-related risk than do others. Attacks, such as IP spoofing, a type of attack in which the attacking host masquerades as another one, capitalize on weaknesses in implementations of programs that utilize the IP protocol, a Layer 3 protocol. The *User Datagram Protocol* (UDP), an efficient, sessionless, and connectionless protocol, poses a different set of security risks. UDP transmissions are sent from one host to another; if the destination host does not receive the transmission, no effort to notify the sending host that the transmission has failed occurs. UDP transmissions are therefore fundamentally less secure than TCP, which attempts to form a virtual connection between a sending and receiving host.

Services and Protocols

Now that you have had a look at the OSI model, the following section examines the Windows NT network environment's specific services and protocols and how they relate to this model.

Relationship to OSI Model

The Windows NT network environment is extremely complex with respect to the types and ranges of services and protocols supported. Figure 3.7 illustrates just how complicated this environment is. The intent here is not to present an exhaustive set of services and protocols in the Windows NT environment, but rather to provide a basic understanding concerning where within the OSI model some of the most fundamental and widely used protocols typically fit. Note also that the level at which a given protocol is utilized depends on the particular implementation based on that protocol, as explained shortly. In other words, one developer may implement a specific layer in a certain protocol, while another may implement the same funtionality in a different protocol.

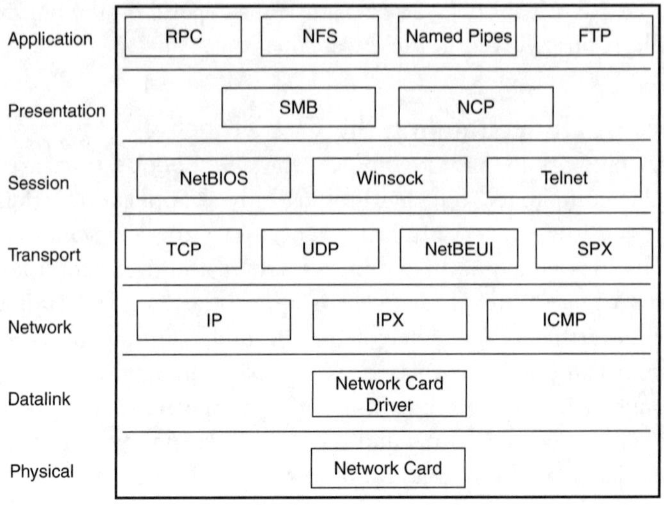

Figure 3.7 *Some major services and protocols in Windows NT networking.*

Layer 3 includes protocols such as IP and Internetwork Packet Exchange (IPX)—a mainstay protocol for Novell NetWare until release 5.0, but also the same protocol that runs in the Windows NT networking environment for interoperability with legacy NetWare hosts. Layer 4 includes the *Transmission Control Protocol* (TCP), the UDP, the NetBEUI, and *Sequenced Packet Exchange* (SPX) protocol (another protocol that in the Windows NT networking environment allows interoperability with NetWare hosts).

Relevance to Security

Although each layer presents its own set of challenges so far as security is concerned, certain layers potentially pose more security-related risk than do others. The physical layer, for example, is the layer vulnerable to packet-capture attacks in which network traffic is captured by a physical or logical (that is, a program) device. Attacks, such as IP spoofing, capitalize on weaknesses in implementations of programs that utilize the IP protocol, a Layer 3 protocol. The UDP, a Layer 4 protocol, is transmitted without provision for notification of the sending host in case the transmission fails or contains one or more errors. In contrast, another Layer 4 protocol, TCP, is a considerably more reliable protocol in that it provides a mechanism for notifying a sending host when something goes wrong with a TCP-based transmission. Therefore the UDP is, in general, more vulnerable to certain types of network attacks than is TCP.

IP Spoofing

IP spoofing is a type of network attack that can be directed against virtually any machine that processes IP traffic. The goal of an IP spoofing attack is to establish a connection between a client unknown to a server by making that client appear to be a legitimate client, and then to exploit a relationship between the server and the bogus client to gain unauthorized access. Here is a well-known way to perpetrate an IP spoofing attack:

1. Make the legitimate client unable to respond to the target server. This can be done by using a utility that "wedges" the legitimate client's ports—making the service or daemon that receives input from each port wait for input that will never come, thereby making the machine unresponsive to other inputs, such as connection request acknowledgements from other servers. This step is necessary because if the legitimate client were able to respond to the target server, the bogus client would not be able to "break in" to their communication.
2. Send a SYN packet from the bogus client to the target server to request that a connection be opened. This packet must indicate that the connection request is from the legitimate client (for example, must bear

the IP address of the legitimate client), even though in reality the packet must originate from the bogus client. The bogus client's request packet includes the *initial sequence number* (ISN) for that client.

3. The target server sends a SYN packet to the legitimate client containing data such as the server's ISN in addition to the client's ISN incremented by one. The legitimate client's ports are wedged, however, so the legitimate client will never respond to this packet.
4. The connection request is dropped if the client does not increment both ISNs (that is, for both the client and the server) and increment them in a manner that the server expects. The software running on the bogus client must then send a reply SYN packet containing the source address of the legitimate client with appropriate ISNs (one for the client and one for the server) incremented by one. Deriving the client's ISN is easy; this ISN is in fact an arbitrary number of which the server is not initially aware. The challenge is guessing the target server's ISN. The best clue concerning the value of the ISN the server has sent to the legitimate client in the first place is within the contents of already captured network traffic; packet dumps can reveal the previous ISNs for the server's connections to other systems. If the target server's ISN for a connection request from an entirely different client began with 24080 a few seconds previously and the ISN is always incremented by one for any new connection request, for example, the next ISN for a new connection is likely to be 24081 if the initial ISN is not random. IP spoofing software that returns a ISN of 24082 from the bogus client to the server would therefore be very likely to correctly anticipate the appropriate ISN.
5. If the bogus client sends the correctly incremented value of both ISNs to the server, the attacker will have established a connection between the two. The attacker can then attempt to exploit a relationship between the two machines to gain unauthorized access to the target server. Windows NT 4.0, for example, supports the (remote shell) **rsh** command that can allow trusted access from one machine to another without requiring that a password be entered.

Although predicted by Steve Bellovin in "Security Problems in the TCP/IP Protocol Suite," (*ACM Computer Communications Review*, Vol. 19, Issue 2, 1989, pp 32–48), the first reported IP spoofing attack was not observed until late 1994. For several years afterward, IP spoofing was one of the most frequently observed types of attack on the Internet. IP spoofing is not now as commonly reported as a few years ago, although it still poses a potentially major threat to organizations, in that so many automated IP spoofing tools are so widely available. The best (albeit not infallible) countermeasure is deploying a firewall or screening router that blocks all incoming packets that indicate they originated from a host within the network protected by the firewall or screening router. This measure prevents spoofing attacks originating from outside one's network, but does not prevent such attacks if they are initiated from within the same network.[2]

Although most observed IP spoofing attacks have targeted UNIX systems (in particular, implementations based on *Berkeley Standard Distribution* [BSD] UNIX), Windows NT is also vulnerable to these attacks. Unless Service Pack 6[3] for Windows NT 4.0 is installed on a given Windows NT host, that host will (under many connection contexts) linearly increment the server's ISN from one connection to the next in a predictable manner, making the machine extremely vulnerable to IP spoofing attacks. Service Pack 4 for Windows NT 4.0 causes a server that receives an IP connection request to generate a reasonably random ISN in the SYN packet it returns to the requesting client, virtually precluding the possibility of IP spoofing. Several ways exist to verify that this service pack has been installed in 4.0 systems. One way to do this is to bring up the Command Prompt and enter **winver**.

If your Windows NT installation includes Service Pack 4 or up, you will obtain the following type of output from an About Windows NT dialog box (see Figure 3.8).

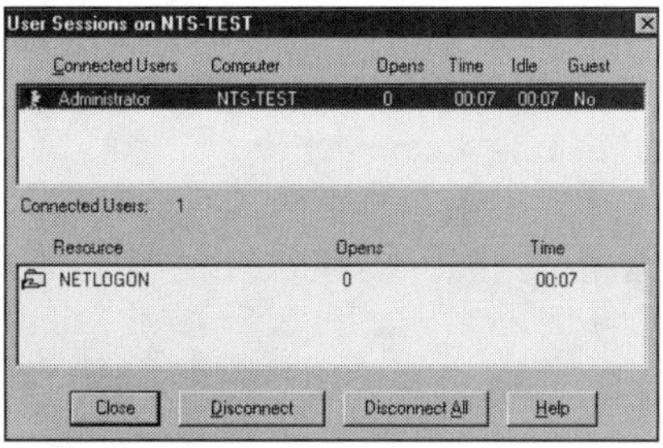

Figure 3.8 *User Panel.*

[2] *IP spoofing is most often initiated by external clients to deceive internal servers that these clients are internal.*

[3] *Actually, this was changed in SP4, not SP6. However, after SP6 it was discovered that there was a bug in the ISN generation. Therefore a new hotfix was issued. It is described in Q243835, and is available for SP4-6.*

Another way you can determine that latest service pack installed is to invoke a Registry Editor, and then check the value of the following key:

Hive: `HKEY_LOCAL_MACHINE`

Key: `Software\Microsoft\WindowsNT\CurrentVersion\`

Value: `CSDVersion`

Another way to determine the service pack level on the local host, as well as hosts across the networks, is to run the SPQuery utility from MTE Software (`http://www.mtesoft.com`). It lists the numbers of installed service packs as standard screen output.

Finally, another way to prevent IP spoofing attacks is to use a firewall or router with ACLs to reject traffic coming into a network that bears the source IP address of any internal host. Any incoming traffic with an internal source address is almost certainly bogus (and could indeed indicate an IP spoofing attack); legitimate incoming traffic should bear the source IP address of some *external* host.

About the Protocols Themselves

The Windows NT networking environment includes a wide variety of protocols, virtually all of which affect security one way or another. What are some of these protocols? Where do they fit into the OSI Model? This section explores these important issues. Figure 3.7, which shows some (but certainly not all) of these protocols, provides an initial overview. Consider the following protocols.

- **Remote Procedure Call (RPC).** RPC is a UDP-based protocol used in setting up communications, such as negotiating the particular ports to be used in establishing a connection.
- **Network File System (NFS).** NFS is a protocol (generally based on UDP) for file sharing that enables a user to connect to remote disks as if connecting to the local machine. Several Windows NT–based NFS implementations (typically based on the SMB protocol) are currently available.
- **Named pipes.** Named pipes are mechanisms that provide a direct channel to services that support applications. They are advantageous because they allow programs to reach them by referring to a name instead of requiring that a full path be specified.
- **File Transfer Protocol (FTP).** FTP is a TCP-based protocol for establishing sessions in which files are transferred between computers.
- **Trivial File Transfer Protocol (TFTP).** TFTP is similar to FTP, although it is not a connection-oriented protocol. Based on UDP, it is used to

download fonts and configuration files to hosts that broadcast their needs. Because it does not confirm whether data are actually being sent to their destination, it involves less overhead to create and maintain connections than does FTP.

- **Simple Mail Transport Protocol (SMTP).** SMTP is the protocol that establishes the structure of Internet mail through a special syntax. It also defines the conventions for setting up SMTP connections, transmitting both the sender and receiver's addresses, and sending the subject and main body of mail messages.[4]
- **Server Message Block (SMB).** SMB is an implementation of redirectors. Redirectors handle client requests for access to remote resources on a drive with a shared directory or another type device (for example, a printer) by taking these requests and reformatting them according to the needs of the protocols that will process these requests. Finally, SMB forwards the requests to either a lower- or higher-level protocol.
- **NetWare Core Protocol (NCP).** NCP is a protocol implemented in Novell NetWare. NCP is used in the Windows NT networking environment for access to remote resources on NetWare machines.
- **Network Basic Input Output System (NetBIOS).** NetBIOS is an *Application Programming Interface* (API) used in the Windows environment to provide session-layer connectivity between machines.
- **Winsock.** Winsock is not a protocol; it is instead a socket (a combination of a service and port) used by APIs for client applications regardless of the underlying protocol. It is commonly used to provide network-based access to Windows applications.
- **Telnet.** Telnet is a protocol that furnishes a command-line interface for emulating a virtual terminal on a remote computer. This in turn enables users to interact with a remote computer.
- **Network Basic End User Interface (NetBEUI).** NetBEUI implements the transport layer and is only used in smaller, local networks because of the fact that it is unroutable. All things considered, NetBEUI is a relatively fast protocol with low overhead.
- **Transmission Control Protocol (TCP).** TCP is the most common transport protocol used today. It is a connection-oriented transport layer protocol that verifies packets sent by one machine (the source machine) arrive at the destination machine. TCP thus establishes a virtual connection between two machines.

[4] *While there are SMTP implementations for NT, it is not a standard protocol.*

- **User Datagram Protocol (UDP).** UDP is a connectionless protocol that does not have built-in guaranteed delivery. One of its main advantages is that it involves less overhead than connection-oriented protocols such as TCP.
- **Sequenced Packet Exchange (SPX).** SPX is a transport layer protocol used primarily in contexts in which Windows NT hosts access Novell NetWare computers.
- **Internet Protocol (IP).** In many respects, IP is described as the protocol that provides the underlying functionality of nearly all higher-layer Internet protocols. Its functionality includes addressing (which includes checking packet headers to determine whether the information therein is correct), fragmentation (in case a router received packets that are too large to handle), and determining each packet's time-to-live (which, if expired, causes the packet to be discarded). IP handles each packet completely independently of any other packets sent over the network.
- **Internetwork Packet Exchange (IPX).** IPX, a routable protocol, is a very fast and highly established protocol, but it cannot be used on the Internet because it supports a different addressing convention from the one used by the IP (see the following section). Novell developed IPX/SPX for use in NetWare, but Microsoft has developed its own implementation of this protocol, the NWLink protocol. This protocol is completely compatible with Novell's IPX/SPX implementation.

The default protocol in most Windows NT network applications is a protocol suite called NetBIOS over TCP/IP (NBT). Numerous problems with NBT have emerged over the years due to dependencies between the NetBIOS and TCP layers of networking, in addition to other reasons. Performance and denial-of-service problems have resulted. As you will see shortly in the section titled "NetBIOS and SMB-Based Vulnerabilities," the NetBIOS layer is also filled with perils and pitfalls, among the more notable of which are dependence on primitive lookup mechanisms to retrieve NetBIOS name data and the capability to crash remote hosts by sending malformed NetBIOS packets or packets with illegal parameters. These and many similar vulnerabilities are discussed in more detail throughout this chapter.

Note again that the protocols described in this section by no means constitute the full range of protocols in the Windows NT networking environment. These protocols are some of the most commonly found ones that also often pose the most serious security-related threats. They are collectivel, only a portion of the possible protocols found within the Windows NT networking environment.

NetBIOS and SMB-Based Networking[5] in Windows NT

The chief focus of this section is the SMB protocol implemented in Windows NT (and the vulnerabilities it presents), although the NetBIOS protocol deservedly gets some of the attention. The *Common Internet File System* (CIFS), which implements the application and presentation layers of the OSI model, is Microsoft's implementation of SMB (a draft standard proposed by Microsoft and several other companies).

Introduction to SMB

SMB packets can be up to 65536 bytes in length, not counting an optional field in the header that indicates how long the packet is. SMB communicates directly with the NetBIOS layer, but it also works in conjunction with lower-layer protocols. At the transport layer, for example, it adds 4 bytes of data concerning transport handling initially transmitted with the TCP stream. SMB itself cannot determine which particular TCP packets are part of each individual session that has been established, so it turns over to TCP the responsibility of actually segregating the sessions. SMB can also, however, work in connection with UDP. In this case SMB sends 12 bytes of filler data to help the receiving system put the packets back in their intended sequence.

SMB also has a built-in mechanism that allows a system to transmit multiple requests within the same session. This allows sending requests in parallel rather than serially. The name of this mechanism is AndX; it is a legacy mechanism from earlier days of networking resulting in part from the need to increase the efficiency of connections.

Structure of SMB Packets

Let's look at the structure of the SMB packet. Associated with each offset is a field that carries designated types of data. Table 3.1 lists each offset, field name, and field length in bytes.

- Note that the first offset contains the optional 4-byte length integer field mentioned previously.
- The header start, a mandatory field, starts at offset 4 and is also 4 bytes in length.

[5] *Many of the facts and ideas in this chapter were developed by Hobbit, an independent vulnerabilities researcher (see* `http://www.avian.org`*). His white paper, "CIFS: Common Insecurities Fail Scrutiny," was the basis for most of the content of this particular section of the book.*

- The SMB command field, 1 byte long, is used to communicate to the receiving system that the packet contains a particular SMB command used in a es the "Key" communication.
- The smb_rcls and smb_err fields, both 2 bytes in length, begin at offsets 9 and 11, respectively. These fields, used to transmit, indicate when something goes wrong in these communications and what the nature of the error condition is.
- The 1-byte smb_flg and 2-byte smb_flg2 fields, beginning at offsets 13 and 14, respectively, are fields used to set flags that indicate the status of the communication between SMB-capable hosts.
- The next field beginning at offset 16 is reserved for data in TCP and UDP information that indicates the sequence of packets.
- The TID ("Tree ID") field (starting at offset 28) is for the 2-byte tree ID, a value used for the "tree connect" mechanism that indicates exactly where in the file system on a host to connect when a session that allows such a connection has been established.
- The PID ("Process ID") field (2 bytes long, starting at offset 30) indicates the process ID of the process associated with the network application on the machine sending the packet.
- The UID is an arbitrary user ID (unrelated to the NT logon ID); this field begins at offset 32 and is also 2 bytes long.
- The MID (2 bytes long, beginning at offset 34) is for the machine ID.
- Offset 36 is the beginning point for the 1-byte parameter word count, a field that tells the receiving system how many of the subsequent smb_vwv fields will follow. These smb_vwv fields contain data used in parsing the data that follow in the variable-length buffers.

Table 3.1 The Structure of the SMB Packet

Offset	Name	Number of Bytes
0	Length integer (optional)	4
4	Header start	4
8	SMB command	1
9	smb_rcls	2
11	smb_err	2
13	smb_flg	1
14	smb_flg2	2
16	(filler)	12
28	TID	2
30	PID	2

Offset	Name	Number of Bytes
32	UID	2
34	MID	2
36	Parameter word count	1
37	smb_vwv0	2
39	smb_vwv1	2
41	smb_vwv2	2
Variable	Buffers	Variable

Relationship with the NetBIOS Layer

Networked clients and servers need to how to communicate with each other. They frequently need, for example, to know each other's IP address and computer name. In conventional TCP/IP-based networking, DNS readily provides this kind of information. In the SMB networking arena, however, clients and servers not only require this type of information, but also need information used by the NetBIOS layer of networking. This layer, immediately below SMB in the OSI stack, has it own conventions for communications among other hosts on the network (that is, the NetBIOS names of other hosts). Capability to determine the NetBIOS name depends on a service called the NetBIOS Name Service (nbname). This service, for which the default port binding is UDP port 137, capitalizes on several different sources, including DNS, the *Windows Internet Name Service* (WINS), direct queries, and broadcasts, to build "name caches" that hold the information about other machines that NetBIOS mechanisms need. Using its own naming conventions, NetBIOS subjects the name that the system administrator assigns to a host to a series of transformations to produce a NetBIOS name.[6] Table 3.2 shows these steps.

Table 3.2 *How NetBIOS Names are Derived*

Step	Result
Convert characters of computer name to ASCII	"GLE" becomes ASCII 71 76 69
Convert ASCII characters to hexadecimal	71 76 69 becomes 47 4C 45
Add 20 until there are 16 byte pairs	47 4C 45 20 20 20 20 20 20 20 20 20 20 20 20 20 20

continues ▶

[6] *For more information on how to encode/decode NetBIOS names, refer to Knowledge Base article Q194203.*

Table 3.2 Continued

Step	Result
Split into two 168-byte hex strings	47 4C 45 20 20 20 20 20, *and* 20 20 20 20 20 20 20 20
Split each byte pair into nibbles (4-bit chunks) of individual bytes	4 7 4 C 4 5 2 0 2 0 2 0 2 0 2 0 2 0 20 2 0 2 0 2 0 2 0 2 0 2 0
Add hex value of "A" (41) to each byte pair	45 48 45 4D 45 46 43 41 43 41 43 41 43 41 43 41 43 41 43 41 43 41 43 41 43 41 43 41 43 41 43 41[7]

If the name is longer than 15 bytes, the additional bytes are truncated. Then a final byte is appended at the end to indicate the status or meaning of the NetBIOS name. Therefore, the NetBIOS name consists of a 15-byte unicast[8] hexadecimal value plus a 1-byte trailing hexadecimal value. This last byte pair can assume any of the hexadecimal values indicated in Table 3.3.

Table 3.3 Meaning of the Trailing Hexadecimal Values of a NetBIOS Name[9]

Value	Meaning or Status
00	Computer names and workgroup names*
01	Master browser
03	Messaging/alerter service; username of user with logon session
20	Names of available resources on server
1B	Name of domain master browser
1C	Name of domain controller
1E	Response to election announcement

You will see NetBIOS names when you use a packet-capture device to examine network traffic. If your protocol analyzer does not convert NetBIOS names back to computer names, you may have to perform this conversion to identify specific machines referenced in packets. Also, because NetBIOS includes mechanisms for identifying computers with NetBIOS and

[7] *The result if the NetBIOS name were to be converted back to ASCII would be EHEMEFCACACACACACACACACACACACACA.*

[8] *Unicast is a format in which each byte pair is separated from the next by a space.*

[9] *This list is not exhaustive.*

other sessions to a given host, you can enter the **nbtstat** command into a Windows command line with the following options to remotely or locally identify these sessions in addition to other information:

```
nbtstat (-a targethost] [-A IPaddress][-c][-n][-r][-R][-s][-S][interval]
```

To get a dump of a host's sessions table with the destination IP addresses, for example, enter the following:

```
nbtstat -S
```

Similarly, given its host name you can get a host to dump its name table (its *name cache*) that it creates by entering the following:

```
nbtstat -a <hostname>
```

You can get a host to dump its name cache given its IP address by entering the following:

```
nbtstat -A <IPaddr>
```

Requests for name cache dump are often called wildcard node status queries. The value of the **nbtstat** command (the execution of which is not limited to priveleged users) to remote attackers goes without saying.

Client/Server Communications

How are SMB-based client/server communications established? A series of conventions are used in which both client and server pass data to each other until, if everything has gone right, the server establishes the SMB connection to a specific point in its hard drive or other device. This negotiation process occurs in four distinct stages: establishing a TCP session, negotiating a dialect, establishing a SMB connection, and accessing resources.

Stage One: Establishing a TCP session

The first stage of the negotiation process begins when a client sends a Session Request Block to the server. The names of both the server and client (in NetBIOS format) are included in the request. The server *does not* check the IP address of client, and immediately creates a TCP connection with the client on port 139 of the server (normally TCP 139) on the server.

Stage Two: Negotiating a Dialect

In this stage, the main purpose is to discover the "highest" version of SMB supported by both client and server. What this in essence means is discovering which implementation of MS Networks (the basic LAN implementation used in Microsoft networking) has been used in both the client and server. The particular implementation is known as the "dialect." The various types of dialects, starting with the earliest and ending with the most recent are as follows:

PC Network Program 1.0
XENIX Core
Microsoft Networks 1.03
LanMan 1.0
Windows for Workgroups 3.1a
LM1.2X002
LanMan 2.1
NT LM 0.12

The client sends the names of all dialects that it supports. Therefore if the client is a Windows NT Workstation 4.0, it will understand the most sophisticated dialect, NT LM 0.12. It will, however, forward to the server all the dialects in the preceding list. When the server receives the dialect name(s) from the client, it responds with a dialect list index showing which to use.[10] It also sets security flags (using the smb_flg and smb_flg2 fields in SMB packets) based on how sophisticated a version of SMB has been negotiated. It may additionally send 8 bytes of ciphertext for authentication; whether this is done depends on the particular authentication program. If any part of the dialect-negotiation process fails, the TCP session is terminated.

Stage Three: Establishing an SMB connection

The third stage of establishing SMB communications between a client and server once again starts with the client. The client forwards a session setup request containing a header that includes data, such as the user ID, domain name, operating system, and other (variable) information. The header is usually only 16 bytes long. The server responds by sending a token incorporating the same types of information included in the session startup request, but this time applicable to the server. Unfortunately as discussed earlier in this chapter, each user ID is not necessarily unique across sessions! If the client has sent a username that the server cannot recognize (that is, the user ID is unknown to the server), one of two results occur: denial of access (and, therefore, failure to create an SMB connection); or creation of a "null session," in which the SMB connection is nevertheless established but without a defined user ID. The big problem here is that the strength of authentication depends on the client, not the server. Incidentally, more negotiation must take place to establish an SMB connection if "share-level" security (an option in Win9x, but not in Windows NT) is in place.

[10] *The server also volunteers its file system type to the client during negotiation.*

Stage Four: Accessing Resources

In the fourth and final stage of the negotiation process between client and server, the server locates the specific point (for example, in the hard drive) to which the SMB connection will be made. The \PIPE\Srvsvc service is used to locate the device, and then a "tree connect" mechanism (based on the *Inter Process Communication* (IPC) mechanism in MS Networks) is used to access the resources (for example, files, directories, named pipes) within this device. The connection request includes the name of the requestor, TID, password (but only in the case in which share-level security is in place), and the name of the type of service being used to access the resource. The client then returns a 2-byte SMB header with the TID to the server after the tree connection is in place to acknowledge to the server that the connection request succeeded. At this point, a share connection is established, allowing the client to access resources with the restrictions imposed by both share permissions and the file system. (Chapters 5, "Configuring Windows NT Server for Security," and 6, "Maintaining Windows NT Security," provide details concerning how these restrictions work.) Because share connections time out if they are not active, a primitive type of SMB echo mechanism keeps the share active.

Null Sessions

Chapter 5 describes Windows NT accounts, groups, and privileges in detail. At this point, you need to be aware that an ID named SYSTEM exists on every Windows NT computer. This ID, which has almost unlimited privileges on the local computer, has no password—you cannot log on to this account. Privileged processes in Windows NT run, almost without exception, as SYSTEM.

Some complications arise when a service that runs as SYSTEM needs to access a remote resource. The destination machine does not recognize, nor give deference to, some other machine's SYSTEM ID. Because the service runs as SYSTEM, it does not have a password to present. The service therefore tries to set up an SMB connection with an undefined (null) username, empty password string, and undefined domain name during stage three of the client/server negotiation process described in the preceding section. The connection that results if the negotiation is successful is on behalf of the anonymous user and is therefore called an anonymous session or null session.

Security-Related Considerations with Null Sessions

Null sessions pose a dilemma. Certain null sessions are created on behalf of processes used in establishing trust between domains and also in other contexts. You can use the Server Manager tool to see the sessions established on any given machine. Open Start, Programs, Administrative Tools, Server Manager. A list of servers in the current domain displays. Double-click any of them to see the sessions established to that server[11]. (Note, however, that null sessions are not limited to share and named-pipe access mechanisms to reach remote resources.) If you click on the Users button, you can determine exactly to whom each session belongs (see Figure 3.8). If you see Anonymous, you can be sure that it indicates that a null session to that computer exists. You can also determine whether null sessions have connected to resources by looking through a system's Audit log for data concerning the user named Anonymous. Although the system and domain do not have a user account for Anonymous, this entry is the one that results from connections opened by null sessions.

The real danger of null sessions is that they are designed to be used by the SYSTEM ID. Yet at the same time, they are unprivileged sessions that can be initiated by the ever dangerous Everyone group on the remote machine. The network result is a default absence of protection for the remote resources that can be accessed via null sessions. The potential for misuse should by now be readily apparent.

Solutions for Null Sessions

The dilemma in dealing with null sessions is that Windows NT, to some degree, depends on them. You could disable them, but at the cost of possible disruption of certain network services (for example, Windows NT's passthrough authentication used in establishing trusted access between domains).

By default, Windows NT systems at least restrict the way null sessions can be opened. They do not allow null sessions to be opened on any system through any existing share or named-pipe access mechanism. *Not* changing the default Registry setting that controls null sessions is in general a good move for the sake of security. It may, however, be necessary for the sake of some applications to override this default. In this case, use a Registry editor to reach the following path:

```
\System\CurrentControlSet\Services\LanmanServer\Parameters
```

If you want to allow null session access through shares and named pipes, you need only to create a subkey named RestrictNullSessAccess under

[11] *The Server Manager tool is installed by default only on Windows NT Server. You can install it on Windows NT Workstation, and even Windows 9x. It is part of the client tools, which are located in the* `\CLIENTS\SRVTOOLS\WINNT_` *or* `WIN95` *directories on the Windows NT Server CD.*

Parameters and set its value to 0. (Note that the key type must be `REG_DWORD`.) Once again, making this modification is not advisable for security's sake in most settings, but it may be necessary to allow a select set of applications to work. To that end, you can specify shares that can be accessed by null users, regardless of the value of `RestrictNullSessAccess`. You can view and edit the names of the individual shares and named pipes through which null sessions can access system resources by examining and editing `NullSessionShares` and `NullSessionPipes` under Parameters. Each item that appears indicates a share or named pipe that can be accessed through null (anonymous) sessions. In this manner, you could selectively limit access via null sessions without disabling null sessions completely, thus reducing the potential for disruption. Finally, if you are running Windows NT 4.0 with Service Pack 3 or higher, you can make another Registry change to restrict access by the anonymous user (as described in Chapter 5).

NetBIOS and SMB-Based Vulnerabilities

NBT is the default network protocol in most built-in Windows NT network functions. This protocol consists of both the NetBIOS (the upper half) and the TCP/IP protocols (the lower half). NetBIOS serves as an abstraction layer in this arrangement. The NetBIOS protocol is used to communicate a considerable amount of information about the status of machines within the network, in particular the nature of processes and sessions running at this layer. Accordingly, this protocol can allow users and processes to query NetBIOS for information helpful in attacking Windows NT hosts and domains. Users with access to a Windows command line can, for example, initiate a node status query to discover information about other machines on the network. The data in the following example shows a data dump from a packet analyzer on a network in which an external user initiated a "wildcard query" (using the **nbtstat -a** command). Note that this query contains a string of 30 zeros followed by 2 zeros, the format used in NetBIOS names. The external user (possibly an attacker) is requesting that the target host dump its NetBIOS name table, a very dangerous request indeed.

```
"Flags""Frame", "Delta
Time", "Destination", "Source", "Protocol", "Summary"
"M",      1,            0, " [90.128.192.131]       ","[141.192.128.233]
","DNS","C ID=15 OP=QUERY
NAME=*<000000000000000000000000000000><00>"
"  ",        2,       1., 5121, "[90.128.192.131]   ","[141.192.128.233]
","DNS","C ID=16 OP=QUERY
NAME=*<000000000000000000000000000000><00>"
"  ",        3,       1., 5108, "[90.128.192.131] ","[141.192.128.233]
","DNS","C ID=17 OP=QUERY
NAME=*<000000000000000000000000000000><00>"
```

In addition, certain commands can allow unauthorized persons to attempt access to administrative shares (default shares set up for the convenience of administrators who must remotely access the systems they administer). Attackers must, however, guess the password of one administrator to successfully do so.

Protocol Analysis in Windows NT Networking

Monitoring network traffic in the Windows NT network environment is extremely important, both in troubleshooting and in discovering possible network-based attacks. You can, for example, use a packet-capture device to determine whether users have initiated NetBIOS status queries (as previously shown in Figure 3.9). Windows NT has a built-in packet-capture program, the Network Monitor *(NM), that comes in two varieties. The simpler version comes with NT Server; it captures only the packets bound for the particular machine on which NM is installed. To install this version, open the Network Control Panel. Click on the Services tab at the top. Click Add. Scroll through the names of services that appear until you reach Network Monitor Tools and Agent, RefSeOK. There is also a Network Monitor Agent service. It is used by the* Systems Management Server *(SMS) version of Network Monitor to remotely capture data. Because of risks due to the potential for unauthorized access, it should not be installed unless there is a particular reason. Now reboot the server. Once NM is running, you need to go from Start to Programs to Administrative Tools to Network Monitor to see this output.*

Another, more powerful version of NM comes with Microsoft's (SMS), a system administration tool that you can purchase. The SMS version can connect to remote computers running the Network Monitor Agent and capture data from there. This latter version is more useful for system administration purposes because it allows packet capture for a potentially wide range of hosts. It also unfortunately poses even greater possible security-related hazards because it allows anyone who obtains unauthorized access to it to view network traffic for potentially many machines on the network. Installing this version is more or less parallel to installing the simpler version except for several steps. You must, for example, find the right path in the SMS Distribution Kit. First locate the top-level SMS directory within this kit, then go down one level to the `NMEXT` *subdirectory, then to your platform (Alpha or i386). Now invoke SETUP.EXE (path:* `SMS_TOP_DIRECTORY\NMEXT\I386\SETUP.EXE`. *Next start the Network Monitor Agent by clicking on Network, Services, Network Monitor Agent, Start, OK. Now reboot the SMS server. After installation, you can find Network Monitor Tools in Network Analysis Tools and the Network Monitor Agent in your system's Control Panel. You must also install the Network Monitor Agent on all computers for which you want to obtain packet dumps. You must then start the capture capability for each of these computers from Network Monitor's Capture menu. Finding the specific capture file for each computer may not be trivial. Choose the Find All Names option from the Capture menu to set the computer name that goes with each particular IP and MAC address. To read the logs for the first time, you may also have to experiment a bit by selecting a variety of different names from the Capture menu until you discover the particular log for each system that runs the Network Monitor Agent.*

Regardless of which version of NM you choose to run, several critical security considerations apply. Having NM packet dumps fall into the wrong hands enables a perpetrator to potentially obtain passwords (some or all of which may be clear text) and data transmitted across the network. Clear text passwords traversing any network pose a high level of security risk because anyone who captures them can use them to illegally log on to systems. You should, therefore, ensure that permissions on your SMS console allow access of any kind only to SMS administrators.

Note that you need to do more than just run a program or suite of programs to capture network traffic. Remember, too, that NM is only one of many available options for dumping packets. Other alternatives include NetXRay by Network General, Surveyer by Shomiti, LANDecoder by Triticom, Observer by Network Instruments, EtherPeek by AG Group, and many others.◆

NetBIOS Solutions

Although piecemeal solutions that control against certain types of unauthorized access exist, no effective, comprehensive solutions for controlling NetBIOS vulnerabilities currently exist. Consider one solution—disabling the bindings between the TCP/IP and NetBIOS layers of networking. To disable these bindings, bring up the Control Panel, double-click on Network, and then click on the Bindings tab. The screen shown in Figure 3.9 displays. To disable NetBIOS over TCP/IP, click the plus sign next to NetBIOS Interface, select WINS Client (TCP/IP), and then click the Disable button. This effectively eliminates the possibility of a long-range attack that exploits weaknesses in NetBIOS, but again at a cost. Disabling these bindings interferes with services such as share access in wide area networking because the NetBIOS protocol (which is not a particularly good wide area protocol) depends on the underlying TCP and IP layers (both of which are well suited for wide area transmissions) in wide area networking.

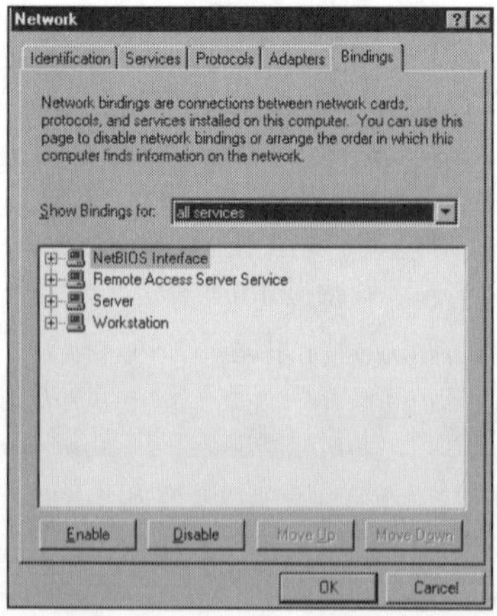

Figure 3.9 *Network panel.*

Consider a second solution, the Policy Editor, a tool in the Windows NT 4.0 Resource Kit that disables all Administrative Shares.
Consider yet another solution: disabling the administrative shares.[12] To disable these shares on a server, set the following Registry value:

Hive: `HKEY_LOCAL_MACHINE`

Key: `System\CurrentControlSet\Services\LanmanServer\Parameters`

Value: `AutoShareServer`

Type: `REG_DWORD`

Data: 1 (default) to create these shares, 0 to disable them.

On workstations, the procedure is the same, but the eegistry value is named `AutoShareWks` instead.

Disabling these shares, however, is in general not advisable because doing so is likely to cause severe disruption or at least inconvenience in system administration activities. Several commercial backup utilities, for example, require remote access to systems via Administrative Shares as they back-up systems. In short, no genuinely suitable solutions for most environments currently exist. Until Microsoft discontinues basing its implementation of Windows NT networking on the NetBIOS API (something that Windows

[12] *When Windows NT boots, it automatically creates certain "administrative" shares. These are so named because they are only available to administrators and are used for administrative purposes. Administrative shares are created for the %systemroot% directory, as well as for all hard drives.*

2000 does), security-related concerns with NetBIOS-related vulnerabilities will continue to be a source of worry.

Problems with SMB/CIFS

Microsoft calls its implementation of SMB the Common Internet File System. The following are some of the most serious types of SMB/CIFS related vulnerabilities and the ways these vulnerabilities could be exploited:

- A perpetrator may repeatedly attempt to gain access to a share even though denied access—the perpetrator may get share access anyway! Flooding a server with share requests can cause it to become so overloaded that it fails to process some of them normally.
- An attacker may break out of the share constraints that exist to gain access to the whole volume, even though the share attaches to a lower point than the root of the volume. This attack, commonly called a "dotdot" attack, requires that the perpetrator repeatedly use the command line (to enter **cd..**, then **cd..**, and so forth, repeatedly) after a TID connect is in place to gain access to a higher point in the file system than the TID specifies. SMB/CIFS-based connection mechanisms may ignore the TID if users repeatedly attempt to gain access to another point in the file system.
- Someone may exploit differences in naming conventions among compatible operating systems to attempt to gain access to files for which access is not allowed.[13] The trick here is initiating an SMB degradation attack in which the client is an older release of Windows or runs a malicious routine that convinces the server that the client understands only a very primitive SMB dialect. The server assumes that the client understands only the 8.3 file naming convention. An attacker must now own one or more file(s) within the same directory or subdirectory that holds a file to which the attacker desires unauthorized access. The attacker may be able to use a command line to access a file that begins with the same 8 characters and has the last 3 character extension as the file to which the attacker has access, even though the file to which the attacker has access and the target file do not have the same name when the extended (256-character5 character) naming convention is used. For example, the target file's name could be MARKETING.XCL and the file owned by the attacker could be MARKETINXXX.XCL. The particular file that the attacker tor access is now a matter of chance; the attacker may now be considered

13 *A Solution for this problem is to disable 8.3 naming by making a Registry change described in Chapter 6.*

the owner of the target file because of confusion over the naming convention used!

- A perpetrator can replay the SMB/CIFS connection creation sequence from a bogus client. If the attacker can do this soon after this sequence is captured through use of a packet-capture device or program, the target server may not be able to detect whether this sequence is from a legitimate client.[14]
- Someone may forge SMB/CIFS request packets. The server will create a TCP session because it does not check the identity of the client.
- An attacker may gain access to shares that currently exist or that have existed recently (even though the share is to another user ID). The relatively primitive conventions involved in CIFS-based networking allow someone to break in to an existing connection and take it over.
- Someone can access resources as an anonymous user through a null session, as exemplified by the mechanisms used by a program called Red Button. Red Button sets up a null session to a designated host, and then exploits the fact that the anonymous user is by default a member of the Everyone group on the target host to read certain key values from the Registry on that machine.
- Someone can send an incorrect IP address but correct computer name to allow rogue hosts to access resources on CIFS servers. Remember, these servers do not check the IP address of clients before creating a session for the client.
- A malicious user may attempt to abuse weaknesses in the CIFS implementation of the SMB protocol to cause denial-of-service. A fairly recent vulnerability of this type results from the way Windows NT Server 4.0 processes SMB logon requests. A perpetrator who does not even have an account on a target system can send an authentication request with SMB packets that contain illegal values. The victim host that receives these packets processes the authentication request anyway, but the illegal data corrupt memory in the kernel. One of two errors typically results:

  ```
  STOP 0x0000000A
  ```

  or

  ```
  STOP 0x00000050
  ```

The server now will either reboot or hang displaying the notorious Blue Screen of Death. Microsoft has developed and distributed a patch for this

[14]*Fixed in Service Pack 3, with the SMB signing feature*

bug; the patch is incorporated into Service Pack 4 (but not 3). This vulnerability illustrates only one of a wide range of vulnerabilities of this nature.

How Serious Are SMB Vulnerabilities?

At the time this chapter is being written, the exposures resulting from Windows NT's implementation of SMB in many respects constitute the most serious type of Windows NT security-related vulnerability. *The basic problem is that many Windows NT network mechanisms and protocols incorporate too many legacy negotiation and connection methods.* The fact that the client for the most part drives the level of security in SMB connectivity is also a serious concern. The resulting exposures potentially allow unauthorized users to remotely obtain copies of critical objects, including the SAM database, proprietary applications, business-critical data, and the like, stored on any Windows NT Server. The sheer potential for denial-of-service is, however, probably the most serious concern in many operational environments.

Chapters 6 and 7 discuss solutions for SMB- and NetBIOS-based vulnerabilities. Many of these solutions involve adopting fundamental network security measures.

Future Solutions

The next release of Windows NT (Windows 2000) incorporates Kerberos, a powerful tool that controls against unauthorized access through use of encryption. Kerberos in and of itself may, however, not solve the entire threat of unauthorized file access using SMB-based exploitation methods because Kerberos does not provide protection at the level of underlying protocols. Chapter 10, "Workstation Security," explores this and related topics in greater detail.

Conclusion

The main purpose of this chapter has been to set the stage for subsequent chapters that describe solutions for Windows NT networking vulnerabilities. This chapter has covered the basics of Windows NT networking itself, describing what networking is, and the functions it serves. This chapter has gone over the types of networks, the major components within networks, and the topologies that characterize them. The OSI model presented us with a systematic view of how data is transformed as it is sent from one computer to the other across a network. The discussion then turned to the services and protocols in the Windows NT networking environment. Windows NT networking is, in fact, no simple matter; it encompasses a large range of protocols and services, most if not all of which translate to challenges when it comes to attempting to implement security. This chapter covered the SMB and NetBIOS layers of networking that Windows NT shares and other network applications utilize. SMB/CIFS's method of establishing connections leaves quite a bit to be desired from the perspective of security. We delved into null sessions and discovered still another cause for concern. Finally, this chapter analyzed the major types of vulnerabilities in, and a few solutions with respect to, the SMB and NetBIOS layers of networking.

Chapter 4, "Basic Windows NT Security Exposures," examines other types of vulnerabilities. In the remaining chapters of this book, we once again look at Windows NT networking mechanisms, but from a different perspective. We will increasingly consider options for dealing with the many vulnerabilities inherent in the way Windows NT networking transpires.

Checklist for System Administrators

1. If you need high levels of security, change the Registry of critical servers to restrict null session access, or at least to limit access via shares and named pipes. Test these changes in a nonproduction environment first to ensure that they do not disrupt your operational environment.
2. Observing the same constraints as in step 1, consider disabling the NetBIOS bindings if security needs so warrant.
3. Ensuring first in a nonproduction environment that no application breaks, consider disabling Administrative shares if security needs so warrant.
4. Install the most recent SP in all your Windows NT hosts, minimally SP5.
5. Ensure that access to devices and programs that capture network traffic is properly limited—only a few of the most trusted system and network administrators should be given such access.

4

Basic Windows NT Security Exposures

"Vulnerabilities and tools that exploit vulnerabilities in operating systems are anything but new. The impact of these vulnerabilities and methods of exploiting them is, however, greater in the Windows NT arena."
*–Eugene Shultz in "Windows NT Security: Kudos, Concerns, and Prescriptions" (*Computers and Security, *Volume 18, 1999, p. 205.)*

Windows NT was first released over six years ago. Windows NT is not yet a mature product; new security-related vulnerabilities have been surfacing at a rapid rate. Some readers may experience some level of discomfort with this chapter because of their confidence in Windows NT's many settings and features that appear to control most, if not all, security-related exposures. But appearances can be deceiving. Just because the Windows NT user interface enables someone to move a pointer to a radio button and then click on an icon that depicts some particular security control feature, it doesn't necessarily mean that this feature works as advertised or can't be circumvented in some way.

This chapter describes the major types of vulnerabilities in Windows NT and assesses their severity. Some of these vulnerabilities (for example, exposure to password guessing) are not unique to Windows NT, but are instead common to virtually all operating systems. Many of these more generic vulnerabilities are relatively easy to control; basic security controls (such as creating and enforcing an organization-wide security policy) are (at least to some degree) likely to counteract the overwhelming majority. Other vulnerabilities, however, are more or less unique to Windows NT and may be considerably more difficult to adequately control. As discussed in Chapter 3, "The Windows NT Network Environment," for example, Windows NT's implementation of the Server Message Block (SMB) protocol may allow unauthorized clients to obtain access to objects stored on servers by bypassing Windows NT's share mechanisms (altogether).

Documenting every single Windows NT vulnerability is not the major focus of this chapter. If it were, this chapter would not only be voluminous, but also would quickly become obsolete; vulnerabilities and their solutions are anything but static. This chapter instead presents sufficient detail about Windows NT security vulnerabilities to enable you to appreciate some of the most deep-seeded problems. At the same time, this chapter takes a reasonably detailed look at some of the most interesting and potentially impacting vulnerabilities. The goal is to better assess security-related risks and select appropriate security control measures, as discussed in all remaining chapters of this book.

Let's begin with some definitions and coverage of the basic types of security exposures that affect systems in general. This will set the background for describing Windows NT–specific vulnerabilities.

Types of Generic Security Exposures

Certain kinds of security exposures are found in *all* systems, Windows NT systems and others such as UNIX, Linux, NetWare, MVS, and so forth. This section covers these exposures.

Doorknob Rattling

Perpetrators initiate "doorknob rattling attacks" to gain information needed to attack systems and networks. Discovering the specific type (for example, Firewall-1, Raptor, CyberGuard, Gauntlet) and version of firewall that guards the entrance to a network is a valuable piece of information for someone intent on attacking systems within that network. Similarly, learning modem dial-in numbers can be very useful to attackers.

Password-Based Attacks

Over the past decades, password guessing has almost certainly been the single most successful type of attack. In these attacks, a perpetrator enters one password after another until either succeeding or getting locked out. Although brute-force attacks have a certain likelihood of success, they are currently less preferred by perpetrators than other types of password-based attacks because they are inefficient. Breaking into an account may literally take thousands (or more) of tries, unless, of course passwords are extremely easy to guess.

Denial of Service

Denial-of-service (DOS) attacks are in many respects a type of "electronic vandalism" in which the goal is to disrupt or crash applications, systems, and network services. You may find it more difficult to understand the motivation for initiating DOS attacks than attacks in which someone gains unauthorized access to one or more systems. Perpetrator motives vary from "joy riding," curiosity, hostility, revenge, gaining respect within the cracker community, and so forth. Still, denial-of-service attacks are now (according to the Computer Emergency Response Team Coordination Center (CERT/CC) at the Software Engineering Institute at Carnegie Mellon University) one of the most commonly reported types of attacks (`www.cert.org`).

Unauthorized Use of Accounts

Gaining unauthorized access to user and system accounts is commonly called a "break-in." Normal user accounts can also be accessed without authorization because (as discussed in the preceding section) users may use easy-to-guess passwords or because social engineers are able to "con" users into giving up their passwords (see the following sidebar). Similarly, unattended logon sessions are a problem if someone can gain access to the session before a screen saver goes into effect to prevent unauthorized access to the live session.

Social Engineering: A Nontechnical Threat Worse Than Most Technical Threats

One of the easiest ways for perpetrators to gain unauthorized access to a user's Windows NT and other systems is through social engineering. Social engineering is a technique in which a perpetrator calls, sends a message, appears in person at a help desk, and so forth to trick someone into giving out information that will enable the perpetrator to obtain unauthorized access. Case studies indicate that help desks are the most frequent targets of social engineering attempts, although system and network administrators and even everyday users may be targets. The stated reason for the target of the social engineering attempt—to reveal a password, encryption key, modem dial-in number, firewall product version, or other piece of information—can be very logical and compelling. On the other hand, some social engineering attacks are so obvious that they are laughable. Consider the following message sent to many AOL customers:

"hello,i am from the AOL assistens department. due to the unexpected shutdown of our computares we have lost all of your accounts info.to keep your account active respond with your password and Screen Name. chat areas are disabeld

continues ▶

▶ *continued*

because of that too. thank you for your time,have a good night. AOL security/assistens TEAM."

The best way to deal with social engineering attempts is to put requirements for training concerning social engineering in your organization's InfoSec policy. You may also want to include requiring any user or technical staff member who is the target of a social engineering attempt to notify your InfoSec manager right away. If one social engineering attempt occurs, it is usually the "tip of the iceberg." Assume that previous attempts have already occurred and expect many more attempts to follow. Knowing that a social engineering effort is in progress as early as possible can help your organization quickly circulate a warning that may reduce the likelihood of success, or, if an incident is already in progress, to reduce the probability of it spreading.◆

Abuse of Trust

Many operating systems provide mechanisms that enable users and system administrators to gain access to systems without fully authenticating to those systems. These mechanisms provide "trusted access." UNIX, for example, allows whomever is listed in a .rhosts file in the root directory to use the **rlogin** command to gain root access to that system and all files within it without having to ever enter a password. Trusted access is convenient, but it is dangerous because it bypasses normal security mechanisms.

Unauthorized Access to Services

It is not necessary to actually break in to a remote system to gain unauthorized access. An attacker needs only to misuse a service that provides remote access. An example is File Transfer Protocol (FTP). If an attacker cannot log on to a domain server using MSV1_0 authentication, the attacker may be able to gain FTP access to that server.

Unauthorized Access to Resources

Unauthorized persons may also gain unauthorized access to resources. One of the easiest ways to do this is to break into an account and then use the access permissions and rights assigned to that account to gain access to resources. Faulty file permissions and bugs in file systems themselves are also sources of concern.

Privilege Escalation

A favorite trick of attackers is to escalate their privilege level after they gain unauthorized access to an account or service. Escalating privileges enables them to not only take full control of the system they have attacked but also to expand the attack against other machines on the network more easily. Privilege escalation results from problems such as break-ins to privileged accounts, exploiting vulnerabilities in poorly written programs, social engineering, and many other causes.

Covering Up Unauthorized Activity

No operating system or application offers ideal auditing capabilities. In most cases, auditing is incomplete, sometimes to the point of allowing perpetrators to engage in certain actions without resulting in appropriate audit entries. Vulnerabilities in auditing programs may allow someone to write a program that masks one's presence from Audit logs. Another technique for covering up unauthorized activity is running a program that generates so much audit data that there is no more space to write more data to the hard drive.

Viruses and Other Malicious Code

Viruses are a universal problem. Systems (such as Windows NT) that run on Intel platforms are particularly vulnerable to viruses. Viruses are not, however, the only type of malicious code that affects Windows NT systems. Malicious executables (for example, Java applets and ActiveX controls) downloaded by browsers can also cause considerable loss and disruption. Chapter 10, "Workstation Security," explains these and other problems with regard to Windows NT systems in detail.

Unauthorized Physical Access

Physical access to computers by unauthorized users typically results in a worst-case scenario. Physical access generally bypasses many of the security-related controls built in to a system and increases the likelihood that someone can gain unauthorized Administrator privileges.

Specific Windows NT Vulnerabilities

Let's now go through some of the most significant Windows NT–specific vulnerabilities, matching them to each of the categories previously discussed.

Doorknob Rattling

The vulnerabilities described in this section are potentially related to security problems in the "doorknob rattling" category. These include NetBIOS status queries, identifying network routers, and probing the Registry.

NetBIOS Status Queries

As covered in Chapter 3, a perpetrator can use the many variations of the **nbtstat** command from a Windows command line to obtain information about NetBIOS names, sessions, host functionality, and even the NetBIOS name cache.

Identifying Network Routes

Using a Windows command line to enter the **tracert** command with an IP address as the argument enables someone to determine the intermediate hops between the querying host and another one. This can enable a perpetrator to discover other hosts to attack. In particular, planting promiscuous network data-capture programs on one or more of the intermediate hosts would be valuable to the attacker; the intermediate hosts could be used to capture critical data such as passwords sent across the network.

Probing the Registry

The Windows NT Registry is a hierarchical database containing data concerning a Windows NT system's hardware, software, and applications environment. This database also serves as a mid-level interface between each machine's kernel, device drivers, hardware recognizer, User Manager for Domains, Server Manager, and other components and programs. To allow system processes to read and sometimes to update Registry values, Windows NT by default permits Everyone to have widespread access to the Registry. Attackers can therefore run executables, such as Red Button, that read critical Registry values such as the build number of the Windows NT release, the service pack that has been installed, the share names (which in and of themselves also reveal whether a Windows NT system is a server or a workstation because workstations do not have the built-in NetLogon share), and other critical data such as the name of the default Administrator account. Additionally, Windows NT 3.51 Server has a flaw in its interface to clients that allows Windows 95 clients remote access to critical server resources (including the Registry).

Many methods exist for obtaining names of accounts and groups from remote Windows NT systems. A perpetrator with Administrator-level privileges in one domain can use the User Manager for Domains on any domain controller within that domain to initiate the process of setting up a trust relationship with another domain. After initiating trust, the perpetrator can use the Windows NT Explorer on any server within the domain to view the account names and groups in the other domain. The perpetrator needs to just highlight any file or folder, then go to File,

Properties, Security, and then click the Permissions button. The account names and groups in the other domain will appear when the perpetrator selects List Accounts From. Note that trust does not have to be in place; it must merely be unilaterally initiated.

Still another way to gather critical information about systems and domains is to create a program that utilizes certain Application Programming Interface (API) calls as follows:

- **NetUserEnum().** This call can be made by the anonymous user. Data returned as the result of making this call includes the names of accounts, full usernames, descriptions for each account (which often contain wording such as "Built-in Account for Administering the System," thereby revealing the privilege level associated with the account), and other values.
- **NetGroupEnum().** This call can be used in a parallel manner to reveal the names of groups as well as the names of users within each group.
- **LookupAccountSid().** This call enables the anonymous user to obtain the names of accounts (including the name of the default Administrator account, even if it has been renamed).
- **NetUserModelsGet().** This call enables the anonymous user to retrieve Account Policy settings (see Chapter 5, "Configuring Windows NT Server for Security," for more information about these) as well as the domain role (for example, Primary Doman Controller (PDC), Backup Domain Controller (BDC), computer name, and machine Security Identifier (SID).
- **NetServerTransportEnum().** This call gives the anonymous user data about the number of adaptors and transports on the probed machine.

The best solutions for security-related vulnerabilities are to do the following:

- Install Microsoft's Local Security Authority 2 hot fix, which substantially limits the anonymous user's access to critical system calls and other sensitive functions.
- Assuming the *Service Pack* (SP) 3 is installed, make a change in the Registry to limit the anonymous user's access to critical resources such as Registry objects. Invoke a Registry editor, such as REGEDT32.EXE, go to `HKEY_LOCAL_MACHINE\System\CurrentControlSet\ Control\Lsa` and add a subkey, RestrictAnonymous. The value should be 1, and the key type should be `REG_DWORD`.[1]

[1] *In Win2K you can restrict all anonymous access by setting the value to 2.*

Password-Based Attacks

The vulnerabilities described in this section potentially enable password-based attacks. These vulnerabilities can allow attackers to readily obtain and crack Windows NT passwords.

Accessing Administrative Shares

Windows NT provides a reasonable barrier to brute-force attacks through its bad logon limit that results in an attacked account becoming locked. One attack technique in Windows NT that is inefficient, but at least not subject to bad logon lockouts, is trying to map to an Administrative share on an NT system. All an attacker needs is a Windows command line, as follows:

```
> net use * \\128.5.83.222\C$  <password> /user:Administrator
```

If the attacker enters the username and password of a user entitled to access an Administrative share (whether it be C$,[2] D$, ADMIN$, the attacker gains access to the share with Administrator-level privileges, affording the ability to change or replace virtually any file accessible through this share. Particularly worrisome is that bad logon limits (that is, values for the number of bad logons for a particular account in a designated time period that, if reached, cause the account to be locked) are not enforced on any administrative share except for IPC$. If the bad logon limit for a Windows NT host or domain is three within 20 minutes, an attacker will be locked out after three unsuccessful logon attempts in 5 minutes against say, the Administrator account. The attacker can, however, attempt to access the C$, D$, WINNT$, or NetLogon shares an infinite number of times without being locked out! Note also that cracking tools that initiate multiple password-guessing attempts against accounts (not just administrative shares) without triggering the bad logon lockout are now available on the Internet.

Password Cracking

The worst problem with Windows NT passwords, however, is that they are much more crackable than you might imagine. Chapter 2, "The Structure of Windows NT Security," has already explained how Windows NT password representations and hashes are derived using both symmetric encryption (based on Data Encryption Standard (DES) and hashing (based on MD-4). A common type of attack against operating systems other than Windows

[2] *Any share name that is followed by a dollar sign ($) is a "hidden share." When you look in the server you will see the names of all shares except for hidden shares.*

NT involves obtaining a copy of the password file and then running a cracking tool against the encrypted password entries. To guard against obtaining a copy of the password file in this manner, Windows NT by default prevents any user (regardless of privilege level) who has a logon shell from accessing the Security Accounts Manager (SAM) database.

Unfortunately, this control measure does not go far enough; the Security Accounts Manager (SAM) database is more accessible than was originally intended. Users with access to the Windows NT backup program can, for example, easily obtain a copy of the SAM database. When someone with Administrator-level privileges makes a copy of the *Emergency Repair Disk* (ERD) using the **RDISK** command, a copy of the SAM database that by default is readable by Everyone, when an ERD is being created, is copied to `%systemroot%\repair\sam._`. In addition, a perpetrator can use one of a number of widely available cracking tools (for example, SAMDump, PWDump2, and l0phtcrack) to obtain a copy of this database.

The greater concern, however, is that Windows NT's algorithm for deriving password representations and hashes is flawed. Each password's representation and hash are both completely predictable, because no step in which, say, a random variation of the encryption and hashing algorithm exists. In other words, a one-to-one relationship between the cleartext password and its encrypted and based representation exists. Consequently, a password-cracking program can readily apply the Windows NT encryption and hashing algorithm to determine the resulting outcomes for a given password, compare them to the entries for corresponding account in the SAM database, and then move on to the next. If a random variation in the encryption and hashing algorithm were used, the cracking program would have to determine the outcomes from every variation—a much slower and more computationally intensive process. The problem is even worse with LM representations because when DES encryption is applied, alphabetic characters are first converted to all uppercase. This procedure further limits the possible LM representations that a password-cracking program must match against entries in the SAM database.

Windows NT Web clients, such as *Microsoft Internet Explorer* (MSIE), furthermore, may send a user's encrypted password to an SMB-capable Web server, potentially making the password available to unauthorized persons in a number of ways. A network data-capture program such as Netcat, a tool that listens for traffic bound for particular ports, is therefore even more useful to an attacker. In addition, password hashes used in logging on to a domain from a Windows NT or Win9x Workstation may be stored on the workstation and thus are potentially available to anyone who can access the workstation. A tool named l0phtcrack can even capture and then crack LM hash-encrypted nonces sent over the network.

Screen Saver Bug Can Allow Unauthorized Password Changes

A perpetrator can exploit a bug in the Windows NT screen saver to change passwords without authorization. The perpetrator must first rename `\winnt\system32\logon.scr` and then copy MUSRMGR.EXE (the executable for the User Manager) to LOGON.SCR. Then the perpetrator must wait for the screen saver to start. At this point, the perpetrator can use the User Manager to change passwords. This bug, which can be exploited only by locally logged on users, is fixed by SP4 or a higher SP.

Passwords Resident in Memory Can Be Read

User IDs and passwords remain in memory even after a user logs on. The purpose is to authenticate users to remote systems where the user's access token(s) are not recognized (because each access token is valid in one and only one system and/or domain). A perpetrator with unauthorized Administrator-level privileges may be able to glean both out of memory by writing a program with System privileges that accesses the memory space assigned to WINLOGON.EXE. Specifically, the program must do the following:

- Use the Task Manager to find WinLogon's Process ID (PID).
- Open WINLOGON.EXE for access to the following processes: `PROCESS_QUERY_INFORMATION and PROCESS_VM_READ.`
- Call ReadProcessMemory for the address `0x00010000` within the page in memory that corresponds to the WinLogon memory space.
- Search the copied area in memory for the values of lMprNotifyUserName and lMprNotifyPassword. The returned values will be the username and password, respectively.

This problem is more pertinent to workstations than servers because it is more common to closely control privileges on servers than on workstations. Normally only a subset of all domain users will be assigned Administrator-level privileges. A higher percentage of workstation users are likely, however, to have Administrator-level privileges. (Remember, many people think that there is no harm in freely handing out Administrator-level privileges on workstations—the adage, "It's just a workstation," is unfortunately, more reality than myth in real-life environments.) A rogue user with Administrator-level privileges on a workstation may therefore be able to discover passwords used for access to domain servers.

Denial-of-Service Vulnerabilities

Windows NT is vulnerable to a wide range of denial-of-service attacks. Denial-of-service attacks often result in a system crash that produces the infamous Blue Screen of Death. The following text shows a real-life Blue Screen of Death message that is all too familiar to those who work in Windows NT environments:

```
STOP; c000021a (Fatal System Error)
The Windows Logon Process system process terminated unexpectedly
With a status of 0xc000000000).
The system has been shut down.
Restart and set the recovery option in the system control panel
Or the /CRASHDEBUG system start option.  If this message reappears,
Contact your system administrator or technical support group.
```

A few notable types of denial-of-service attacks in Windows NT include SYN flooding, the ping of death, packet fragmentation, port binding, sending out-of-range input to the process manager, the `DOMAIN_CREATE_ALIAS` bug, Local Security Authority SubSystem (LSASS) crashes, Remote Access Service (RAS) client buffer overflow, and SMB-based denial-of-service attacks.

SYN Flooding

As explained in the sidebar, "IP Spoofing," in Chapter 3, TCP-based communications involve a sequence of conventions. SYN packets are used to establish communications between an origin and destination system on the network. In Windows NT, the destination machine, by default, accommodates incoming connection requests by allocating memory space for the anticipated connection. If the destination machine receives connection requests from one or more unknown IP addresses, this machine cannot open a connection; it allocates memory space for the connection instead. If connection requests from unknown hosts keep flooding in, memory space can be exceeded, causing the destination machine to crash. SP3 and up for Windows NT 4.0 corrects this problem.

Ping of Death

The **ping** command enables users to determine whether a particular system is alive on the network. Ping packets have a maximum size; exceeding this default could cause problems for the destination machine. Sending an oversized ping packet (which is likely to arrive at the destination host in fragments that have to be recombined) can cause a destination Windows NT system to crash. SP3 and up for Windows NT 4.0 also corrects this problem.

Packet-Fragmentation Attacks

The Windows NT implementations of some widely used network protocols have several deeply seated vulnerabilities that enable a wide range of denial-of-service attacks. For example, a malicious program can send a pair of malformed Internet Protocol (IP) fragments to the target system. The system will then reassemble the fragments into an illegal datagram causing the receiving system to regress into an unstable state and then freeze or crash (often displaying the Blue Screen of Death). An illegal datagram is one that contains unrecognizable values because of offsets in packet fragments that are combined with valid values in the initial fragment. This particular attack, known as the "teardrop" attack, caused tens of thousands of Windows NT systems to crash in March 1998. Microsoft had released a hot fix for this problem, but many system administrators had not installed the fix. SP3 and up contains the proper fix.

Port-Binding Attacks

Windows NT permits any logged on user, regardless of privilege level, to bind to any port. Ports to which users can bind include the ports used by services such as NetBIOS and Remote Procedure Call (RPC). Port-binding programs initiated by users have priority over native NT services that listen on any particular port; this property is the critical weakness that leaves Windows NT hosts vulnerable to port-binding attacks. Only users with Administrator-level privileges should be able to stop shares and other services in a secure environment. Windows NT attempts to establish such an environment through measures (by default) such as restricting access to utilities, such as the Server Manager and to commands such as **net start.**[3] A malicious program can, however, continuously bind to the port through which services, such as share services running on a system, are delivered, disrupting those services. There is currently no adequate control mechanism for this problem except possibly the *packet-screening*[4] solutions discussed in Chapter 7, "Basic Network Security Measures."

In "snork" attacks, a local or remote malicious program binds to one of several high-numbered ports. The service listening for input detects the connection and allocates a disproportionate amount of CPU on its behalf, causing the system to become so bogged down that it slows to a crawl. There is also currently no adequate fix for this problem, except possibly the packet-filtering solutions presented in Chapter 7.

---

[3] *The* net start *command allows administrators to turn services on and off on a particular host. The command net start alerter, for example, starts the Alerter service. In many cases, however, the system administrator must reboot the host before the service actually starts.*

[4] *Packet screening means that a program intercepts incoming traffic and allows or rejects it based on characteristics such as source IP address, destination port, and others.*

Any user can also use the **telnet** command to connect to ports such as 135, 139, and 1028 and then enter unexpected input (**asdfasdfasdfasdfasdf,** for example). If the service that receives this input does not have an adequate way of handling out-of-bounds input, the service may stop ungracefully, causing the system to halt or crash. SP3 and up fixes many of the vulnerabilities of this nature.

A perpetrator can also use the **telnet** command to pipe input from the character generator (Chargen) service to domain name system (DNS), causing the system drive to fill up with garbage input until the system crashes. The syntax for this attack is as follows:

```
telnet [IP address] 19 | telnet [same IP address] 53
```

A good solution for this problem is packet screening (blocking all incoming traffic destined for port 19), as described in Chapter 7. Another solution is not to install the Simple TCP/IP Services when you are installing Windows NT.

Sending Out-of-Range Input to the Process Manager

The Windows NT Process Manager scheduling algorithm has a bug that enables an unprivileged user with local (physical) access to a Windows NT machine to compile and then run a program ("CPU hog") that passes an out-of-range job priority value to the Process Manager. The spawned threads are fed at the expense of other unprivileged threads, causing many system-critical threads to starve. The result is a system crash. SP3 also fixes this bug by having the Process Manager perform more careful bounds checks before it runs programs.

The *DOMAIN_CREATE_ALIAS* Bug

The DOMAIN_CREATE_ALIAS vulnerability enables any logged-on user (regardless of privilege-level) who has an account in a domain to create local groups within that domain, to include other users in that group, and to grant access to objects to that group. The user needs only to enter the following:

```
net localgroup [groupname] /add /[domain
```

The user can reach Windows NT's quota for number of local groups by creating so many groups, making it impossible to create additional groups. Think of the time and resources necessary to delete all the superfluous groups created on hundreds of systems, should someone commit an attack that involves this many hosts. Microsoft has released a hot fix for this vulnerability.

LSASS Crashes

Still another vulnerability enables any user to crash the LSASS on a Windows NT host (both NT Workstation and Server) with either SP4 or SP5. With LSASS crashed, no one can log on, either locally or remotely, to the victim host. Exploiting this bug requires a second machine that runs SP5 or SP6. The perpetrator must set the following Registry value to 3:

```
HKEY_LOCAL_MACHINE\SYSTEM\CurrentControlSet\Control\LSA\LMCompatibilityLevel
```

This change requires that the first machine use NTLMv2, an authentication method in which a dual challenge-response process (from server to client, and then also from client to server) is used. If no one has logged on to the victim host since the last time it was rebooted, it will crash when a client using NTLMv2 authentication connects to it. This bug was fixed in SP6. A hot fix is available for SPs 4 and 5 (note that Microsoft does not provide fixes for new issues with service packs prior to SP4.) Note here also that this bug can be exploited accidentally by legitimate clients as well as perpetrators.

A second and equally serious vulnerability causes LSASS to stop processing security information by using an API, `LsaLookupSids()`, to send faulty arguments that cause it to reach the wrong area in memory. LSASS does not adequately check these arguments. Processing of User-mode authentication stops, disrupting subsequent authentication and necessitating a reboot to correct this condition. This attack can be launched either locally or remotely. All Windows NT 4.0 hosts, regardless of level of SP installed, are vulnerable, and to date no suitable fix has been released.

RAS Client Buffer Overflow Condition

Vulnerability in components of RAS clients can cause these clients to crash. The RAS phonebook contains entries about users, dial-in access, and so forth. The path to this file is `c:\winnt\system32\ras\rasphone.pbk`. If ACLs to this phonebook allow unprivileged users (for example, Everyone) to write, a malicious local user can modify one or more entries to include data of sufficient length to cause the buffer that the RAS client uses to overflow, crashing the client. This is an exploitable buffer overflow, meaning that by carefully constructing these entries, a malicious user could also cause commands to be executed. Microsoft has released a patch for this vulnerability.

SMB-Based Denial-of-Service Attacks

As discussed in Chapter 3, many well-known SMB-based denial-of-service attacks exist. The SMBtorture program, for example, can be used to flood a victim host with random requests (**IPC$ smbtrans requests**) via an anonymous connection to the IPC$ share. The victim host will accept these requests to the point that it becomes flooded, causing it to crash. SP5 and up provides a solution to this problem.

Additionally, sending SMB packets with illegal values can cause the receiving machine to freeze or crash. SP3 and up addresses this problem, at least partially, by enabling system administrators to deny access to certain hosts by disabling LM authentication and requiring SMB signatures. Additional measures described in Chapter 7 provide a more effective solution.

Unauthorized Use of Accounts Vulnerabilities

The vulnerabilities in this section potentially enable the unauthorized use of accounts. This includes access to built-in accounts, user access to other accounts, and using RAS to access accounts.

Built-in Accounts

The accounts most frequently the targets of unauthorized access attempts in Windows NT are the default Administrator and Guest accounts. These are well-known accounts and they too often have no password. Even if someone has assigned a password to these accounts, the password in many instances is easy to guess.

Access to Other Accounts

Other accounts may also be targets. Of course, any user account is a potential target. If a server runs the *Internet Information Server* (IIS), an account named IUSR_[*server name*] is created. Someone can attack this account using normal logon[5] procedures or the telnet program to obtain unauthorized access.

RAS

If the RAS service is not set up properly, it can lead to unauthorized use of accounts. A user not approved for dial-in access can, for example, be granted dial-in access in the RAS phonebook through a system administrator's error in configuring RAS access. Some organizations even make the mistake of allowing all RAS access through a Guest account that has no password! RAS, covered thoroughly in Chapter 8, "Securing Network Services and Protocols," potentially allows one of the quickest and easiest conduits of unauthorized access.

---

[5] *Normally, it is not a domain account. If it is, then the account name may very well not correspond to the server on which IIS is installed. This is especially likely with machines that have been upgraded and renamed.*

Abuse of Trust Vulnerabilities

The vulnerabilities described in this section have the potential to enable an abuse of trust, especially those between domains.

Abuse of Trust Between Domains

Trust between domains is subject to abuse. As discussed earlier in the chapter, simply initiating a trust relationship with another domain allows users to use NT Explorer to see the names and groups of the other domain. Additionally, someone who obtains unauthorized access to a domain controller in one domain and to a domain controller in another domain could set up trust between the two domains without authorization. The purpose of doing so would most likely be to set up a backdoor access mechanism. Note, however, that someone would have to first obtain Administrator level privileges before engaging in these actions.

Revoked Trust Between Domains May Persist

Another vulnerability is that even if one or more system administrators revoke trust between domains, trust continues to work until the PDC updates the BDCs in each domain. This could possibly allow unauthorized access to resources. Currently, the best solution for this problem appears to be to revoke trust, and then to immediately use the Server Manager's Synchronize option under the Server menu in one domain controller in the trusted domain and another in the trusting domain.

PDC Failures Break Trust Links

If the PDCs of both the trusted and trusting domains both go down, the trust link between the domains is broken. The system Administrator(s) of each domain must use the User Manager for Domains to re-create trust. The best solution for this problem is to adopt measures, such as clustering, that help ensure operational continuity.

Remote Shell Access

Although *remote shell* (rsh) and equivalent programs do not use passthrough authentication (in contrast to trusted access between domains), rsh access is in every sense of the word another type of trusted access in Windows NT. Any attacker may be able to use the rsh program to gain unauthorized access to other Windows NT machines, under some circumstances without even having to enter a password. The best solution is to delete this executable altogether and then to regularly verify that unauthorized copies are not installed. If business and operational needs dictate that this executable be present on Windows NT hosts, setting ACLs to allow execution to no one but the minimum number of system administrators who genuinely need to it is the next-best solution.

Unauthorized Access to Services Vulnerabilities

The vulnerabilities described in this section potentially enable unauthorized access to services. Services covered in this section include File Transfer Protocol (FTP), Hypertext Transfer Protocol (HTTP), telnet, and Messenger service.

FTP

FTP programs (especially in FTP *server* programs) that run on Windows NT servers typically have many vulnerabilities. Of course, if FTP is misconfigured it can allow access to resources for which access by FTP users is not intended. Several other problems exist as well, including the following:

- FTP programs used in the Windows NT arena abound with buffer overflow conditions that result problems including illegal code execution and crashes.
- In the Microsoft IIS version of FTP, any user who logs on to an FTP server that is on the same physical machine as a Windows NT domain controller is logged on to the domain. The FTP user is thus a member of the Domain Users group, with all the rights and access afforded to this group. Furthermore, all users who connect via FTP must have local logon privilege. Therefore, if the FTP service is located on a domain controller, all FTP users must have the right to log on to the console of the domain controller. If the FTP server is on a member server or standalone server, the user will be locally logged on to that server (even though the user has remotely accessed the server). The user becomes a member of the Interactive group on that server for the life of the logon session. Consider the security-related risk this entails, especially with the previously discussed default permissions for the `\winnt` and `\system32` directories that Everyone has.
- Even if NT File System (NTFS) permissions are set correctly to guard against access to the root directory, in many FTP servers it is sometimes possible to keep entering **cd..** to gain access to the root of a volume. Mechanisms that define a virtual root directory and limit file system access accordingly sometimes are not coded carefully enough to work reliably under all conditions.
- A recent bug in the WAR FTP server that runs on Windows NT can allow unauthorized access to the SAM database and other critical files.

HTTP

Successful attacks against Web servers (Windows NT Web servers included) are currently one of the greatest security-related threats. The biggest security-related problem in the HTTP arena is Web applications that are not written properly from a security perspective. Problems such as buffer overflows continue to abound. Because the IIS Web server runs as SYSTEM, these overflow commands can run with SYSTEM privileges.

Another problem in many Web servers is that the server may support *server-side includes* that provide the capability to start a program by entering input in a field in the interface to the Web server. The potential for mischief is great if any user can start a rogue program or even enter simple commands such as **net start, net stop, net use,** and **net share/delete.**

Still another problem is the ability to gain access to critical system and business-related files and executables that are not part of the Web server itself because many Web servers use virtual addressing to reach directories and files. An attacker who understands this addressing system's conventions may be able to locate and then subsequently access directories and files that are not part of the Web server. This kind of attack is possible when the web root is not pointed to a separate partition.

Many vulnerabilities, too many to cover here, exist in the IIS Web server, in *Active Server Pages* (ASPs), in *Front Server Pages* (FSPs), and in other Web-related programs that run in the Windows NT arena. Microsoft has fixed many, if not most, of these bugs. Chapter 8 provides direction for countering these many security-related exposures.

telnet

As discussed previously, the telnet client can be misused to cause DOS by binding to a particular port, then sending unexpected input, for example. If the telnet service is installed on a Windows NT host, telnet can also allow someone to gain unauthorized access through attack methods such as brute-force password guessing. By default all telnet traffic also goes over the network in clear text. In general, it is best to avoid installing the telnet service when security needs are high; *secure shell* (ssh) (`www.F-secure.com`) provides a more secure alternative, in that it at least encrypts network traffic.

Messenger Service

The Windows NT Messenger service can be misused to write messages to other Windows NT systems. These messages can prompt users to enter passwords or otherwise engage in reckless actions. Therefore, it is best to delete this service if it is not needed.

Unauthorized Access to Resources Vulnerabilities

The vulnerabilities described in this section potentially enable unauthorized access to resources. The types of vulnerabilities discussed here include inappropriate default permissions, unauthorized access to dynamically linked libraries (DLLs,) NTFS vulnerabilities, and others.

Inappropriate Default Permissions

One of the biggest vulnerabilities in Windows NT regarding unauthorized access to resources is inappropriate default permissions that may allow Everyone the ability to modify read, or sometimes even take ownership of critical files. The following chapter discusses ways to deal with inappropriate default permissions.

Access to DLLs

Much of Windows NT's system functionality depends on DLLs. Because these libraries are dynamically linked, it is much easier to replace them with bogus DLLs than it would if these libraries were statically linked (compiled). One of the potential targets in Windows NT is GINA.DLL, which provides the graphical interface for authentication. A perpetrator could replace this DLL with a bogus one that accomplishes results such as harvesting passwords that users have entered.

Setting permissions on system DLLs that allow only Administrators to write to or delete them and checking these libraries to ensure that they have not been changed are both good countermeasures. Unfortunately, default permissions do not always conform to security needs. In general, permissions that allow Everyone no more than read access are conducive to security; several DLLs, however, by default allow write or even greater access to Everyone.

Vulnerabilities in NTFS

NTFS itself has several vulnerabilities that under certain conditions can allow unauthorized access to resources. Functionally speaking, using NTFS is your only real hope if you want file system security. Why? In a File Allocation Table (FAT) partition, you might as well forget about file system security because FAT does not have functionality to restrict access. Nevertheless, NTFS is less than perfect from a security perspective. The previously discussed vulnerability, in which an NTFS server allows a low-ended client access to files because it assumes that the client understands only the 8.3 naming convention, is a good example. Because Microsoft considers this a feature rather than a problem, it is not likely to ever be fixed.

SMB-Based Vulnerabilities

Finally, remember from Chapter 3 that many vulnerabilities in Windows NT's SMB implementation have surfaced. Exploiting these vulnerabilities can also lead to unauthorized access to resources.

Backdoor Programs

Backdoor programs allow unauthorized access to systems and thus comprise a major security threat. Numerous Windows NT backdoor programs are readily available over the public network.

NetBus

The first backdoor program that gained notoriety in the Windows NT arena was NetBus. This program modifies the Registry in each victim so that the NetBus server starts every time the system boots. How? By adding an entry to `HKEY_LOCAL_MACHINE\Software\Microsoft\Windows\CurrentVersion\Run`, *a Registry key that stores the names of programs that run on logon. It also makes a copy of itself, such that if it is deleted, it will still be present in the victim system, but in a different path* (`C:\windows\ime.exe`).

NetBus enables a perpetrator to perform a number of actions on the victim machine, including mouse control, modifying mouse buttons, starting and stopping the CD-ROM, closing windows, opening URLs in Web browsers, starting programs, taking a snapshot of the desktop, and shutting down the computer, in addition to others. The perpetrator can connect to a victim by using the NetBus client to connect to port 12345.

Although widely considered a malicious backdoor program, NetBus does not necessarily have to be used for malicious purposes. Its author, in fact, is promoting the use of the most recent version as a remote system administration tool.

Several measures help to defend against unauthorized installations of NetBus and a similar tool, BackOrifice2000 (BO2K). One is Jammer (`http://www.start.at`) *The problem with blocking the ports is that setting the backdoor services up to listen to other ports is trivial.*◆

Over the past few years, a new type of Windows NT–based Trojan horse program has emerged on the Internet. This type of program enables someone who has planted a service on a victim machine to remotely control that system. A server program, NetBus (see preceding sidebar), is one such example; another is BackOrifice2000. The main security risk associated with these programs is unauthorized, remote backdoor access to systems.

Note that an attacker must first install and start the service before gaining remote access in this manner. You can use the Find function in the Windows NT Explorer to find the Trojan executables.[6] You can use the **netstat** command (**netstat -a** [*IPaddress*] would be suitable in that it displays ports on which processes are listening) to view all current connections, looking for connections to TCP ports such as port 12345. However, the best detection method is using commercial tools. Many antivirus packages now detect these programs in much the same way that they deal with viruses.

Session Hijacking

Another way to gain unauthorized access to resources is via session hijacking. *Session hijacking* is very similar to IP spoofing (as discussed in Chapter 3), except that it involves commandeering a session already in place by sending forged ACK packets instead of initiating a connection.[7]

Privilege Escalation Vulnerabilities

Inappropriate assignment of users to privileged groups (Local Administrators, for example) results in privilege escalation that can present a formidable threat to the security of Windows NT systems. Inclusion in the Local or Global Administrators groups, in particular, allows a user an enormous amount of control over Windows NT machines. Remember that users with Administrator-level privileges can create new accounts with the same level of privileges, can insert bogus logon scripts that result in the same level of privileges after a logon, and can make many other potentially catastrophic changes to a Windows NT system. Assigning normal users to nonprivileged groups is only the beginning of the control of this problem. Other measures, such as assigning help desk personnel Account Operator rather than full Administrator-level privileges, are good additional steps. These are discussed in more detail in Chapter 5.

The vulnerabilities described in this section have the potential to enable privilege escalation.

RASMAN.EXE Bug Can Allow Privilege Escalation

A vulnerability in Remote Access Connection Manager, RASMAN.EXE, can allow an unprivileged user who is logged on (locally or remotely) and who has access to the *Service Control Manager* (SCM) to run arbitrary code. The

[6] *The services can be renamed and still work.*

[7] *SMB Message Signing (SP4) guards against this.*

result is escalated privileges on a Windows NT host. The cause is a faulty (ACE) Full Control access to Everyone in the Registry path

Hive: `HKEY_LOCAL_MACHINE`

Key: `\SYSTEM\CurrentControlSet\Services\RasMan\Security`

Value: `Security`

This path sets an access control list (ACL) on the service itself. By default, it grants Everyone Full Control access, enabling an unprivileged user to repoint the RASMAN service to a trojan executable. The SCM could thus be misused to start a Trojan horse program than runs with SYSTEM-level privileges. Microsoft has released a patch for this bug.

Exploitation of Bugs in Programs

Any application that runs with elevated privileges presents a potential problem for Windows NT security. If someone can exploit a bug in the application, the user can obtain elevated privileges. The BackOffice applications present a particular challenge because they often execute with SYSTEM-level privileges on the systems on which they run. Attackers who can bypass any of these applications' security mechanisms or can exploit bugs within these applications can gain SYSTEM privileges without authorization.

Buffer Overflow Conditions

As explained earlier in this chapter, exploitation of buffer overflow conditions in applications is one of the most frequently used methods of unauthorized privilege escalation in Windows NT. Microsoft SPs and vendor fixes provide the best solutions.

SecHole

SecHole, a Trojan horse program, is one of a group of programs that can allow locally logged-on users to obtain Administrator-level privileges without authorization. This type of program first finds the memory address of an API call named OpenProcess. The DebugActiveProcess function uses this API. The program then modifies the instructions at this memory address to indicate a success even if a failure in opening a process occurs. It then attempts to open a process (DebugActiveProcess) that it is not allowed to open, producing a bogus success condition that results in Debug-level access to the system (SE_DEBUG privileges). With this level of privilege, it can now spawn a thread that runs instructions contained in a rogue DLL that adds the currently logged-on user to the Administrators group in the local SAM database.

SP4 contains a fix to counter most versions of this program. Installing this SP (or higher) is the best solution at the present time.

Modifying the KnownDLLs List

Yet another vulnerability can allow unauthorized local users to gain Administrator-level access. Windows NT caches operating system libraries (DLLs) in virtual memory and then makes the contents of these libraries available to applications. A data structure, the KnownDLLs list, records the location of each of these libraries. As previously mentioned, not all DLLs are assigned adequate protection by default. In this case, however, the problem is not inappropriate default permissions for DLLs, but rather that a user process can read and write to the KnownDLLs List. A malicious local user can, therefore, call a rogue DLL with the same name as a system DLL, and can then change the KnownDLLs list to point to the rogue DLL code. If a privileged program calls the DLL, it will execute the commands supported by the rogue DLL with SYSTEM privileges. Note, however, that remote users cannot exploit this security-related bug.

This bug is one of the most serious in, terms of potential for damage and disruption, that has surfaced in recent years. Two solutions—one older and inferior, one newer and better—have emerged. The older solution, described in Microsoft advisories, is to add a new Registry value, ProtectionMode, to guard against privilege escalation attempts. This solution is flawed in that adding this new key can adversely affect other services, such as, the Server Service, that run on Windows NT hosts. The newer and better solution is to install a Microsoft hot fix that prevents users' ability to arbitrarily change the KnownDLLs list. If you have already changed the Registry in accordance with the older solution, therefore, you should now delete the new key and apply the hot fix instead.

If you need to change this Registry key back to its previous state, run REGEDT32.EXE; then follow these steps:

1. Find the Registry key named:
   `HKEY_LOCAL_MACHINE\System\CurrentControlSet\Control\Session Manager.`
2. Delete the ProtectionMode key.
3. Click OK. Exit the Registry editor, and then restart.

Covering Up Unauthorized Activity

Windows NT provides a reasonable set of control measures to protect the Security log. If you assign Administrator-level privileges very sparingly, you substantially reduce the threat of an intruder gaining illegal access to the Security log and deleting entries to hide unauthorized activity.

Unfortunately, a few vulnerabilities in logging exist:

- If someone who is not an Administrator has the Manage Audit and Security Log right, that user can clear the Security log, but this action will not be recorded in the Security log (even if Security Logging is correctly configured). Installing SP4 or a higher SP solves this problem.
- If insufficient space has been allocated to the Security log, log entries can be overwritten. A perpetrator could write a program that fills up the log with entries, thereby overwriting entries relevant to the perpetrator.
- Someone could install a program such as RootKit for NT to selectively delete Security log entries.
- If you choose the Clear Log Manually option but the log fills up, the system will stop logging. Chapter 6, "Maintaining Windows NT Security," discusses security logging in more detail.

Viruses and Other Malicious Code

Most small systems are very susceptible to viruses; Windows NT is no exception. Chapter 9, "Virtual Private Networks," explains this problem in detail.◆

Unauthorized Physical Access

Unauthorized physical access to a Windows NT system spells catastrophe. For example, someone with direct physical access to a Windows NT system might be able to reinstall the Windows NT operating system to gain Administrator-level access. Inserting a NTFS DOS disk in the floppy disk drive and then rebooting physical access to a system in which a user is logged on can lead to system access with the same privileges as the legitimate user; a local logon is necessary to exploit hacking tools such as the SecHole program mentioned earlier in this section. Any object on a partition with anything but the NTFS is an easy target, also for reasons elaborated earlier. Rebooting Windows NT can additionally allow unauthorized Administrator-level privileges if the value of the AutoAdminLogon key in the Registry is set to 1. (See Chapter 6 for an explanation of this problem.) Pre-Windows NT 4.0 releases had a bug that allowed any user to bypass the screen saver to gain physical access to a system.

Unauthorized physical access merits strong security-related measures. Locked server rooms are the single most effective measure. Correctly configured screen savers that activate very quickly after inactivity on a machine are also valuable in helping prevent an unauthorized person from using computers with live logon sessions. Other measures, such as removing hard drives when a machine is not in use, locking computer encasements, utilizing boot keys, and so forth, are appropriate in settings that require additional physical security.

Miscellaneous Vulnerabilities

Other Windows NT vulnerabilities do not fit into any of the categories covered in this chapter. When you add the number of these vulnerabilities to the known vulnerabilities in MSIE, Exchange Server, SQL Server, Terminal Server, and the many other products that run in the Windows NT environment, the number of vulnerabilities with which you potentially have to deal to secure your Windows NT environment can be staggering.

CASE STUDY

Assessing the Severity of Windows NT Security-Related Vulnerabilities

An event that occurred in 1998 can teach a valuable lesson about the need to correctly assess the severity of vulnerabilities before reacting strongly to them.

Many mail programs use Multipurpose Internet Mail Extensions (MIME) when sending messages or attachments over the Internet. MIME can also handle news transfers. MIME works by using headers (tags) to inform mail or news clients how the message is formatted in terms of the type of data in each section, how encoding has been performed, the names of attached files, and so on. The header is deleted before the client can read the message. A MIME mail client may load a MIME header into memory and then process it without analyzing critical variables, parameter ranges, and normal conditions of operations. If the header length is greater than the amount of memory allocated, part of the header can overwrite other memory-resident instructions—a classic case of buffer overflow. This exact problem in certain versions of Outlook 98 for Windows, Outlook Express, and Netscape Messenger surfaced on the Internet in mid-1998.

As stated earlier in this chapter, buffer overflows are dangerous. They can allow rogue commands to be executed with the privileges of the account out of which they are run. In the current example, they need to be included in an attachment's tags. An attacker could determine exactly where (in terms of MIME header byte length in the memory a

continues ▸

▸ *continued*

buffer overflow will occur and could then structure this header such that rogue commands will be embedded in the right part.

When this vulnerability surfaced in 1998, it evoked a massive reaction among both security people and reporters. The primary cause for alarm was the sheer number of mail and news clients with this vulnerability. Hysteria proliferated as one newsgroup even publicly called on the vendors to recall their products!

The issue was actually resolved reasonably quickly, however, by the vendors of the mail and news clients making patches available. Over time, people began to realize that the reactions to this vulnerability were, for the most part, badly overblown. The MIME-based programs under discussion run on client, not server, platforms. Vulnerabilities that affect servers are often potentially more dangerous because servers generally have greater functionality and hold the most valuable applications and data. Additionally, many of the client platforms affected were low-end platforms (that is, they were Windows 95 and 98 boxes). The hysteria soon died down; no real-life attacks that exploited this vulnerability were observed.

Conclusion

This chapter has described many of the vulnerabilities in Windows NT that could undermine the security of your Windows NT systems. I hope it has made you realize that, despite having a good basic design and offering many effective security mechanisms, Windows NT is beset with quite a few security-related vulnerabilities. I hope you will be motivated to learn more about these vulnerabilities and to develop a systematic strategy for dealing with them.

The following Web sites will be helpful in providing the type of information you need to find:

`http://www.aelita.com`

`http://www.ataman.com/freebies.html`

`http://www.avian.org`

`http://www.bugnet.com`

`http://come.to/nttools`

`http://www.eeye.com`

`http://www.icsa.com`

`http://www.infowar.co.uk/mnemonix/`

http://www.iss.net

http://www.loa.espri.fr/winnt/

http://www.l0pht.com

http://www.microsoft.com

http://www.nmrc.org

http://www.ntbugtraq.com

http://www.ntresearch.com

http://www.ntsecurity.net

http://www.omna.com

http://www.oliver.efri.hr

http://www.osp.nl

http://www.packetstorm.com

http://rcswww.urz.tu-dresden.de

http://www.rootshell.com

http://www.rtis.com

http://www.securityfocus.com

http://www.somarsoft.com

http://www.sysinternals.com

http://www.win2Ksecadvice.com

This list is by no means exhaustive, but it should give you a good start in your effort to research Windows NT vulnerabilities further.

The main point I want you to take away from this chapter is that you need to take Windows NT's security-related vulnerabilities very seriously. What we have here is a product in which vulnerabilities seem to surface frequently, due in large part to code immaturity, and one in which we are dependent on the vendor for fixes whenever vulnerabilities emerge. Remember that few organizations outside of Microsoft have source code. Whatever you do, remember that Windows NT out-of-the-box is not at all secure and that you will have to invest a lot of time and resources if you want your Windows NT boxes to run more securely.

At the same time, you need to assess the severity of these vulnerabilities in your own environment before you panic! The following case study describes an incident that may provide some perspective.

Checklist for System Administrators

1. (Repeated from Chapter 3) Install the most recent SP in all your Windows NT hosts, minimally, SP5.
2. Install hot fixes as needed. The LSA 2 hot fix that is incorporated in the SPs is a particularly important one to install in most environments.
3. Ensure that every default account (Administrator, Guest, IUSR_[*servername*], and so forth) has a difficult-to-guess password.
4. In cooperation with other system administrators, create procedures to obtain information about new vulnerabilities, evaluate their potential impact, and address them in a manner that considers both costs and benefits.
5. Evaluate the physical security of the Windows NT systems you administer and, if warranted, start working with your management to obtain the resources necessary to make critical servers more physically secure.

5

Configuring Windows NT Server for Security

"A journey of a thousand miles must begin with a single step."
–Lao-tzu (circa 604–531 B.C.)

If a journey of a thousand miles begins with a single step, a reasonable parallel principle exists in the network security arena. Regardless of the nature and complexity of the network environment, security begins at the level of each host. Networks with an abundance of network security defenses, but with unsecured hosts, can make easy targets for attackers.

One of the greatest challenges in working with any computing system is configuring the system correctly right from the start. Finding the time and resources needed is not easy. The alternative, however, is to ignore security and then add measures in a reactive fashion after security-related incidents occur. This alternative generally proves costly and frustrating and leaves valuable data and system resources at unnecessary risk. Remember that Windows NT "out-of-the-box" is not very secure.

This chapter provides recommendations for security-related measures you should adopt and pitfalls you should avoid to achieve an initial configuration that meets your security needs. Remember, retrofitting security is usually considerably more time-consuming and complicated than building it in from the start, so achieving an initial configuration that meets security requirements is a worthy goal. This chapter describes security considerations related to installing Windows NT, namely, the installation process itself as well as how to set up default accounts and partitions appropriately. This chapter also discusses how to secure critical system directories and files, control privileges, secure the Registry, set auditing according to specific needs, and implement other measures that will increase the security of Windows NT systems.

Security Considerations During Windows NT Installation

Three ways to install Windows NT exist:

- Booting from the setup CD.
- **WINNT.EXE.** This executable is for installing Windows NT to replace an already installed 16-bit operating system, such as LAN Manager or OS/2 or for installing when there is no preinstalled operating system on the platform on which Windows NT is to be installed.
- **WINNT32.EXE.** This executable is designed for replacing 32-bit operating systems such as Windows 95 or previous releases of Windows NT (such as Windows NT 3.51).

Windows NT's relative ease of installation is a two-edged sword. On one hand, it allows you the luxury of paying more attention to security (in addition to other) issues. On the other hand, installation is generally so routine that it can be tempting to forget about security-related issues right from the start!

Protecting the Installation Program

One of the first security-related installation issues is protecting the installation program against alteration. In a worst-case scenario, someone could alter this program to contain one or more Trojan horse programs, viruses, or other malicious codes. Ensure that you install Windows NT from a CD-ROM that you consider to be a trusted copy—keep it in a locked cabinet or other safe place. To set up a Windows NT domain, you must start by installing Windows NT Server on one platform using the host's CD-ROM. Most system administrators then use distribution shares or a remote administration tool, such as the *System Management Server* (SMS), to move the software you install (including configuration files) to other machines that are to be part of the same domain. Protecting the CD-ROM you use through good physical security is especially important in the remote installation process because it contains software to be replicated on every additional server throughout the domain.

Partitioning Disk Space

Partitioning disk space in the Windows NT environment is another installation issue that has several important security implications. First and foremost, you need (for the sake of security) at least two partitions, C: and D:. Dedicate C: for your system files and directories; all other files and directories should reside on D: or any other non-system partition you create. Keeping the system directory separate from the rest of your system helps protect system integrity; share access to system directories should be for administrators only. This helps protect against unauthorized access by everyday users. If you were to mix together system and non-system files and directories on the same partition, shares that are set up to allow remote access to users would potentially enable users to reach, and subsequently change or delete, critical systems files (such as dynamic link library (DLL) and other files). Figure 5.1 shows the screen used for partitioning.

Dedicating a physical platform to Windows NT is best for security. Sharing disk space between Windows NT and one or more other operating system(s) creates opportunities to gain access to Windows NT disk space—even if NT File System (NTFS) access permissions are set very stringently. Virus infection is less of a threat when you have a single- rather than a dual-boot configuration because viruses that infect other co-resident operating systems can spread to Windows NT (see Chapter 10, "Workstation Security," for a detailed explanation). On the other hand, you may want to have a dual-boot configuration if you, like so many other users, have trouble running particular DOS applications on the Windows *NT Virtual DOS Machine* (VDM). The VDM does not include all the system calls and other features in MS-DOS and other DOS releases; a shared DOS partition will enable these applications to run correctly. As you will soon see, however, other alternatives, such as using VMWare to run DOS applications within NT are more conducive to security.

The installation panel enables you to choose the file system for each partition. Dedicating every disk partition to NTFS is also extremely important. NTFS permissions are the only ones that Windows NT itself can recognize and thus enforce. If you format any partition with another file system, there is no potential for access control at the file system level. That partition is, for all practical purposes, a File Allocation Table (FAT) partition as far as access restrictions go. Some system administrators prefer to use FAT for each partition, believing that in case of system failure due to causes such as corruption of system files, they can more easily restore a FAT partition. However, this assumption no longer has any basis. Tools, such as NTFS DOS and Emergency Repair Disk (ERD) Commander, enable efficient restoration of an NTFS partition. From a security perspective, NTFS alone is the best choice, and you should, of course, decide whether to dual-partition your hard drive and whether to use NTFS or some other file system based on a careful appraisal of the security-related benefits versus cost.

Security-Related Considerations for Domain Controllers

The first security-related decision you need to make during an installation of Windows NT Server is the domain role of the server you are installing. When you build a domain, the first server you install is the *primary domain controller* (PDC). You then need to determine whether each subsequent system you install will be a *backup domain controller* (BDC). You need only to click on the appropriate option within the Add Computer to Domain panel (see Figure 5.1). You have the option of creating one or more BDCs. BDCs are important not only from an operational but also from a security standpoint because they help provide continuity of operations in case of a denial-of-service attack or other unexpected PDC failure.

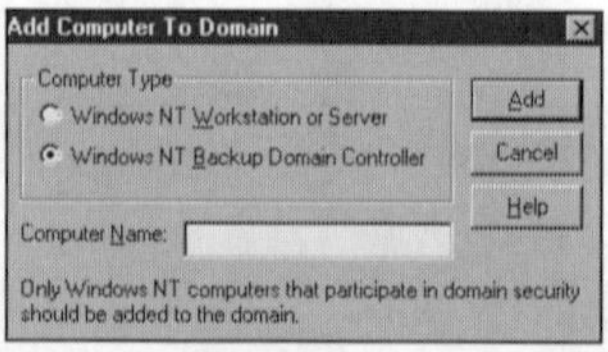

Figure 5.1 *Add Computer to Domain panel.*

Additionally, consider these security-related issues:

- If you have many clients within the same domain but at different, widely separated physical locations, you may want to place a BDC at each remote location to localize authentication. You may recall from Chapter 2, "The Structure of Windows NT Security," that BDCs also act as authentication servers. Placing BDCs in remote portions of networks reduces the amount of authentication-related traffic that goes over the network and, concurrently, the response time for authentication.
- Real-time applications, applications with high memory, or other requirements may not run well on a host that is a PDC or BDC, both of which normally entail significant processing overhead in connection with their role as domain controllers. Additionally, denial-of-service attacks against these applications may cause Windows NT itself to crash. If these applications are on the same physical platform as a domain controller, the threat to continuity of operations increases even more. In many cases, therefore, it is best to run both critical applications and domain controllers on dedicated physical platforms.

- Additionally, if you run an application that is difficult to secure on the same physical platform as a domain controller, an attacker could gain an easy foothold into your domain by exploiting a security-related flaw in the application to gain access to the system. Running applications on member servers (that is, domain servers that are not domain controllers) often makes more sense.

Deciding Between Workgroup and Domain

Another critical consideration at installation time is whether each machine that you install is part of a workgroup or a domain. You can choose the option you prefer through the panel shown in Figure 5.2, accessible through the Control Panel (first choose Network, and then choose Change). The better choice for security is Domain. If you choose Workgroup, you allow users with access to the system to initiate dangerous actions such as discovering resources on the system via workgroup-browsing mechanisms.

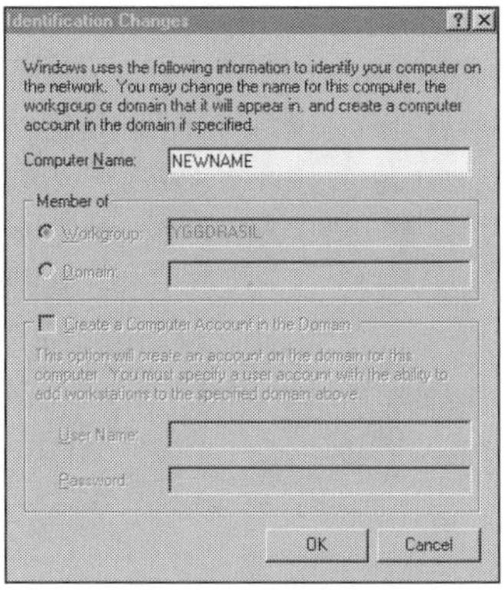

Figure 5.2 *Identification Changes panel.*

If you are installing an independent server, choosing Workgroup or Domain membership is a somewhat more complicated issue. If you click on Domain in the Identification Changes panel (refer to figure 5.2), you receive a prompt for the domain name. Because independent servers have no PDC, you cannot enter this information. The only apparent alternative, therefore, is to choose Workgroup, an unsatisfactory alternative from a security perspective. Fortunately, you still have several other choices:

- You can install the server as the PDC in a one-host domain.
- You can choose Workgroup in the Identification Changes panel but then hide the system so that workgroup-browsing mechanisms cannot

find this system's resources. To do so, invoke the Command Prompt and enter:

```
net config server /hidden:yes
```

- The potential downside to this change is that applications which depend on these browsing mechanisms may break.[1] It is best, therefore, to test this change in a nonproduction environment before making it in production hosts.

Securing Default Accounts

When you install Windows NT, the installation program creates several default accounts. Default accounts in both Windows NT Server and Workstation include the Administrator and Guest accounts.[2] The default Administrator account is a special concern because many attackers are aware that this account exists and that it is privileged. The Password field in the panel for the Administrator account is initially blank. If you leave this field blank, you have an Administrator account without a password immediately after installation. Having an account with no password creates an easy opportunity for unauthorized access, and unless passwords expire (because you have chosen this option in the User Account Policy, as explained later in this chapter), this vulnerability continues to exist indefinitely. Therefore, be sure to enter a password for the Administrator account as soon as you have the opportunity during installation.

Ensure also that the initial password you enter is difficult to guess. A good choice would be two unrelated words connected by a control character, such as "lamp&flag", or the first letters of every word in a well-known phrase such as "Take me out to the ballgame, take me out to the crowd."

In all releases of Windows NT Server and the 4.0 release of Windows NT Workstation, the Guest account is disabled after installation. Is entering a password for this account therefore not important? No: You should take the precaution of entering a password just in case someone who is performing system administration duties later enables the Guest account for some reason. As mentioned previously, an enabled Guest account provides a way intruders know they are likely able to break into a workstation or domain. In every operational setting, you should leave the Guest account disabled. Remember that a better alternative than having a shared Guest

[1] *You could also disable the browsing service altogether. Certain applications will fail, such as remote network backups using at least Veritas BackupExec, but it is nevertheless good practice to disable the browser service in most networks.*

[2] *Of course, when you are creating a domain of Windows NT Server platforms, these accounts are created only once because all accounts are domain accounts.*

account is to create a user account for each person who needs temporary access to the system, for instance when you have someone from another of your corporation's offices staying at your office for several weeks to work on a special project. You can then disable this account when the user no longer needs temporary access. Taking this precaution not only circumvents having shared accounts, which entails high security risk, especially on domains in which many servers reside, but also ensures that users are accountable for their own actions—because every user has a separate account for which activity is recorded in the Security log. Therefore, entering a difficult-to-guess password for the Guest account during system installation is a wise precaution that hardly takes any time at all.

CASE STUDY

A Real-Life Incident Caused by Faulty Installation Procedures

Several years ago, a large corporation started a massive migration from NetWare to Windows NT. They installed several Windows NT domains within their central network and, in anticipation of users' need to obtain dial-in access, enabled the Remote Access Service (RAS) in several of these domains. They did not, however, assign passwords to the default Administrator account. Shortly after the installations were complete, logs in other systems within this network indicated unauthorized activity. The investigation revealed that someone had found one of the RAS servers and had dialed in, obtaining access to the default Administrator account. The attacker then used the Telnet client on the compromised RAS server to access other hosts (including UNIX hosts) within the internal network. Immediately assigning a password to the Administrator account during installation could easily have prevented this incident.

Creating an Emergency Repair Disk

Finally, toward the end of the Windows NT installation procedure, you have the option of creating an ERD (see Figure 5.3). The purpose of the ERD is to enable you to quickly restore corrupted system files without having to perform an entire restore operation. In most cases, it is best to create the ERD during installation; you may need it shortly afterwards. The inconvenience of waiting momentarily for your system to build an ERD during installation is almost certainly outweighed by the prospect of having to reinstall your system if a catastrophic system error occurs before you have had time to back up your system. Be sure to label each ERD you make appropriately, and keep it in a secure location.

System installation should not, however, be the last time you make an ERD; regularly updating the ERD is one of the best things you can do to ensure recoverability of parts of each system (such as the Security Accounts Manager [SAM] database) in case catastrophe strikes.

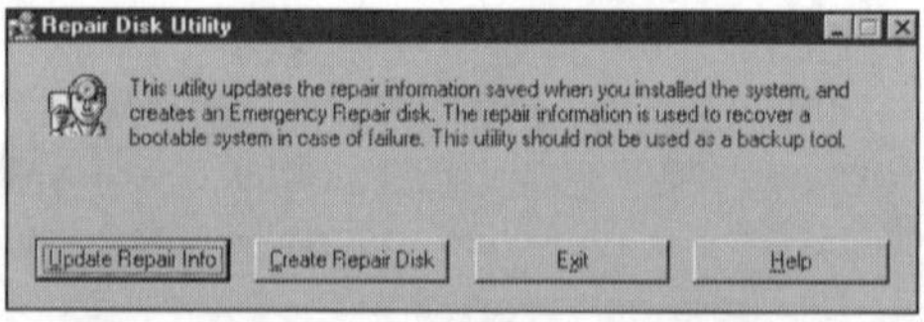

Figure 5.3 *Repair Disk Utility panel.*

Securing Critical Directories

After you have installed a system, your next impulse will almost certainly be to create additional accounts so users can begin using the system. However, you should turn your attention elsewhere—ensure that the most critical components of the system, system directories and files, are secure before you start allowing users to access the system. Failure to secure system files adequately leaves the system wide open to subversion and misuse. Securing directories and files in other partitions is also usually a very important task in most operational environments.

Securing System Directories

The system you have just installed is in big trouble if everyday users are able to delete, add files to, or take ownership of system directories. Following these steps increases security substantially:

- Ensure that Administrators are Creator Owner of the root directory in each volume you have created during installation. In general, do not allow users any more than Read access to each root directory.
- On the C: drive, make sure that critical directories, such as `WINNT` and `SYSTEM32`, are owned by administrators and that they have Full Control Access. The level of access by users should ideally be no more than Read, but applications such as Microsoft Office may not work properly on workstations unless you allow greater access to each. Try Add and Read first, but if this does not work, try Change (even though Change allows users to delete files, subdirectories, and even the directory in question—not exactly optimal from a security standpoint).

- SYSTEM should also get Full Control access to all system directories (that is, directories in the C: partition). In general, nobody else should be given this level of access to system directories. (Administrators and the Creator Owner already have Full Control because they own them.)

Assigning the appropriate permissions during installation is extremely important, but it is only the start of a competent effort to secure files and directories. Any new system directories should normally also have the same permissions as `%systemroot%` and `system32`. Although the Object Manager normally assigns the same permissions for any parent directory to new directories within that directory[2], it is important to check to ensure that new directories have the permissions that you expect. You can use the CACLS program (see Table 5.1 for a short description, including some of the optional switches) or the similar XCACLS program in the Resource Kit.[3] Check also to see that the print spool directory allows Full Control to Administrators, SYSTEM, and Creator Owner. Ensure that only Administrators and SYSTEM (who should have Full Control) have any more than Read access to `\%systemroot%\profiles` to prevent unauthorized users from tampering with settings that control areas such as the user environment or home directory.

***Table 5.1** The Syntax of the CACLS Command*

Command	Operation
/T	Changes ACLs of specified files in current directory and all subdirectories
/E	Edit ACL instead of replacing it
/C	Continue on access denied errors
/G user:perm	Give specific user rights. The value of Perm can be: R Read C Change (write) F Full control
/R user	Revoke specified user's access rights (only valid with /E)

[2] *Whenever files or folders are moved (for example, through using the* **move** *command from the Command Prompt or dragging the icon for a file or folder to another location) within the same physical (not logical) partition, the permissions and ownerships are preserved. When an object is moved to a different physical partition, permissions and ownerships are inherited. When an object is copied, it is always inherited regardless of its destination.*

[3] *Third-party tools, such as Pedestal's NTSEC toolkit and the SuperCACLS tools, are even more powerful than CALCS and XCALCS.*

Another challenge is the `Temp` directory within the C: volume. In general, giving List access to Everyone and Full Control to Administrators, System, and Creator Owner is a good idea.

Set the permissions on all the executables (including DLL files) in the high-level system directories to Full Control for Administrators and Read (Read-Execute) for Everyone. Once again, the owner should in every case be in the Administrators group. This helps protect against unprivileged users installing or modifying executables, such as DLLs. Protecting DLLs is particularly important because DLLs are dynamically linked, not compiled, thus making them especially susceptible to unauthorized replacement. One of the few exceptions to this guideline in setting permissions for DLLs is the case in which processes that run on behalf of users must update certain DLLs. In this case, you would also have to allow Everyone to be able to Write to these files. The reason I make this point is that as you examine permissions for DLLs, you will find some that are not very satisfactory from a security viewpoint. If you tighten these permissions, however, you may cause system failures for previously discussed reasons; so being conservative is a wise idea.

System Drive Directories Caution

The default permissions on the system drive's directories, such as `SYSTEM32`, *are unquestionably dangerous from a security viewpoint. You should seriously consider tightening these permissions but should be careful to ensure that you do not cause disruption and breakage by tightening them too much.*◆

Securing Non-system Directories

Securing directories in partitions other than the system partition is also extremely important. Unauthorized access can lead to unauthorized execution of applications, copying of business-critical and/or sensitive data, and a variety of other negative outcomes. The following recommendations will help in achieving needed levels of file and directory security:

- On partitions other than the system partition, the appropriate permissions for everyday users depend largely on your application environment. If you want to lock down access tightly, try setting the root of your D: and E: drives to Read for normal user access.
    1. Propagate these settings all the way down the entire volume using the Replace Permissions on Subdirectories option in the Directory Permissions panel for the root directory.

2. Highlight the folder for the root directory and then drag down options in the pull-down File menu to Properties.
3. Click on Security.
4. Click on Permissions to be able to view the Permissions panel.
5. If one or more applications break, try assigning user Add and Read permissions for these directories. The best overall compromise between security and keeping everything working, in fact, is to allow Add and Read to users. Allowing Full Control of these directories to users is, of course, the most unsatisfactory solution from a security perspective.

- If users need to store files in certain directories, they will individually (at a minimum) need an Add and Read or perhaps even a Change permission. Assigning permissions such as Change to Everyone is, however, extremely risky in that it enables anyone to delete files from directories.
- The appropriate course of action concerning user home directories varies according to security needs. The strategy that creates the least path of resistance is to allow users to own their own home directories. The main limitation with this course of action, however, is that ownership allows any user to reset permissions for this directory. A user could, for example, reset these permissions to allow Full Control to Everyone. Alternatively, assigning Administrators ownership of all user home directories, and then allowing each user no more than Change access to his or her home directory is more conducive to security. It keeps the ability to change home directory permissions as well as ownership itself in the sole possession of the Administrators. If the required level of security is not high, you may want to allow each user to own his or her home directories. Otherwise, Administrators should have Full Control to every user home directory. Everyone should not normally have any defined access to user home directories; if a need for universal access to home directories emerges, it is best to assign a Read (but not Write) permission to Authenticated Users or Domain Users.
- If your systems have drop-in directories, you should normally ensure that they are in a non-system partition. An Add and Read permission for users and Full Control permission for Administrators are normally appropriate permissions for this type of directory. A number of additional directories, such as the cache directory for browsers, may require the ability to add and/or modify files for Everyone, but not more access for unprivileged users.

Writing to INI files

Unprivileged programs must sometimes write to INI files in the system tree as well as files within the `\winnt\system32\config` path; they obtain access through the Everyone group. If Everyone cannot write to (or create) these files, these programs crash, usually with catastrophic consequences for your system. Users who are not Administrators may not even be able to log on or, if they are able to, they many not be able to see anything but a blank desktop.◆

Is Everyone a Suitable Group for Universal Access in Windows NT?

Windows NT's default universal (world) group is Everyone. If you work with Windows NT for even a short time, you will encounter some permission or privilege that involves the Everyone group. By default, for example, Everyone has Full Control access to every share created. Although virtually every operating system has some kind of universal group, the Everyone group in Windows NT poses several serious security risks not found in others. In Windows NT, the Everyone group consists not only of every user *security identifier* (SID) but also the anonymous user who may have a connection to a particular server or workstation. In fact, anyone who can establish a null session to a remote host is, by default, in the Everyone group. Tools such as Red Button exploit this property; they set up a null session to a remote (or local) machine, and then as a member of the Everyone group read values of critical Registry keys to which Everyone has Read access.

Microsoft has created a fix for the problem of the anonymous user being part of the Everyone group. If a Windows NT 4.0 machine has Service Packs (SPs) 3 or 4 installed, you can use a Registry Editor to change the value of the key `\HKLM\System\CurrentControlSet\Control\LSA\RestrictAnonymous` to 1.

This excludes anonymous from all the access that Everyone receives, thus preventing tools such as Red Button from working. Note also that Pedestal Software makes a tool called NTSEC, which replaces Everyone's access with access by Authenticated Users.

A more fundamental issue is at stake, however. Even if the anonymous user is excluded from certain types of accesses that Everyone receives, the Everyone group continues to pose some degree of security-related risk, as does any universal group. Should you then remove all access granted to it? By no means! The Everyone group is critical to system functionality. The access that this group receives necessarily entails some degree of risk, but depriving this group of all access (especially Write access) causes system processes that expect, but cannot obtain, a certain level of access to particular files and programs to break (possibly even massively). The trick to managing this group from a security standpoint is making sure that both its permissions are appropriate and that it is used in the correct access contexts.

The second issue regarding universal access revolves around the nature of Everyone's access needs. Only system-related programs and processes actually need access through this group. When you are setting up access (for example, through shares and NTFS permissions) to non-system directories, you do not need this group at all. You should use a different (and safer) universal group, Domain Users, in this context. If at a minimum, you have installed SP 3 for Windows NT 4.0, you also have a group named Authenticated Users, a group whose composition is accurately reflected by its name. Use Domain Users or Authenticated Users.

The actions you take to assign permissions and ownerships to system and other directories and files immediately after you have installed Windows NT software is especially important because of Windows NT inheritance mechanisms. In most cases, lower-level folders and files inherit permissions and ownerships from the parent directory (see footnote earlier in this chapter). If you wait to tighten up file permissions and ownerships, it may require considerably more work or, worse yet, your system may be open to simple kinds of attacks in which weak file and directory permissions can easily be exploited to allow unauthorized copying, modification, or deletion of files. Whatever you choose to do, be sure to test settings in a nonoperational environment before moving these changes into production environments. Remember, too, that different organizations have different security needs; no one group of settings is right for all environments.

Achieving Privilege Control

Immediately after installation is the right time to worry about privilege control. You need to create a guiding scheme for determining the users who need a particular subset of privileges and the particular group(s) to which they should be included to obtain the privileges they need. If you don't create this scheme right after installation, it is unlikely that you will ever do it. The result is likely to be privilege escalation—too many users will have superuser privileges. Now a perpetrator needs only to break into one of these many superuser accounts to gain full superuser privileges. Alternatively, only one superuser needs to be dishonest and/or vindictive to cause a catastrophe for every machine within a domain.

The major principle to be followed here is the least-privilege principle; assign users to the least amount of privileges needed for them to get their job done. If you are setting up a domain with 200 servers and 8,000 users, for example, you may need up to five or six system administrators, all of whom should receive full Administrator privileges. Some of the technical staff may do nothing more than make backups; if so, they should be placed in the Backup Operator rather than Local or Domain Administrators group.

Default Privilege levels

Recall from Chapter 2 Windows NT Server's tiers of privileges for interactive users:

- **Administrator.** The privilege level for the "superuser."
- **Operator.** The Operator level of privileges involves a subset of full Administrator privileges. Windows NT Server has four operator groups: Account Operator (for administering unprivileged accounts and groups), Server Operator (for tuning servers, making backups, and so forth), Print Operator (for administering printers), and Backup Operator (for making backups).
- **Users.** This level of privileges allows user-level access, such as being able to access a computer remotely from the network.
- **Guest.** Guest-level privileges are the lowest level of privileges for interactive logon sessions.

After you install Windows NT, you will find that certain groups are afforded certain default rights or privileges from the start (see Table 5.1). Abilities are similar to rights in that they are privileges; the difference is that you can add and remove rights, but you cannot do so with abilities. Abilities are built in and they stay that way. Tables 5.2 and 5.3 show the default abilities in Windows NT Server.

***Table 5.2** Default Rights in Windows NT Server*

Right	Administrator	Account Oper.	Service Oper.	Print Oper.	Backup Oper.	Everyone
Access this computer from network	X					X
Add workstations to domain	X					
Back up files and	X		X		X	

Right	Admin-strator	Account Oper.	Service Oper.	Print Oper.	Back-up Oper.	Every-one
directories						
Change the system time	X		X			
Force shut-down from remote system	X		X			
Load and unload de-vice drivers	X					
Logon locally	X	X	X	X	X	
Manage auditing and security log	X					
Restore files and directories	X		X		X	
Shutdown the system	X	X	X	X	X	
Take owner-ship of files and other ob-jects	X					

Table 5.3. Default Abilities in Windows NT Server

Ability	Admin-strator	Account Oper.	Service Oper.	Print Oper.	Back-up Oper.	Every-one
Create and manage user accounts-	X	X				
Create and manage global groups	X	X				
Create and manage local groups	X	X				

continues ▸

Table 5.3 Continued.

Ability	Administrator	Account Oper.	Service Oper.	Print Oper.	Backup Oper.	Everyone
Assign user rights	X					
Lock Server	X		X			X
Override lock on server	X	X	X	X	X	
Format server's disk drive	X		X			
Create common groups	X					
Create local profile	X					
Share and stop sharing directories	X		X			
Share and stop sharing printers	X			X		

Customizing Rights

You can add or remove rights by bringing up the User Rights panel shown in Figure 5.4. To access this panel, follow these steps:

1. Click on Start.
2. Click on Programs.
3. Click on Administrative Tools.
4. Then either click User Manager for Domains (available when you have access to a domain controller) or User Manager (available when you have local access to a server or access—local or remote—to a workstation).
5. Finally, click User Rights.

Alternatively, to reach the User Manager for Domains, you can bring up the Run menu (by going from Start to Run) and enter the following:

```
C:\>usrmgr
```

To bring up the User Manager (on workstations, member servers, and standalone servers) from the Run menu, enter the following:

```
C:\>musrmgr
```

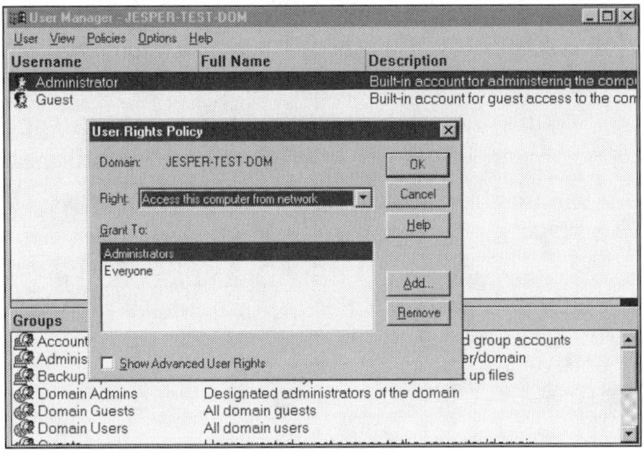

Figure 5.4 *User Rights panel.*

Customizing Windows NT Group Assignments

Windows NT system administrators often complain that the default privileged groups in Windows NT do not give the particular set of permissions needed in an organization's computing environments. Consider, for example, an organization that requires that the system administrator role be separate from the role of system auditor. These requirements dictate that the system administrator be able to do anything to the system except read, change, or delete the Security log. Auditors, according to these requirements, should be able to read, change, or delete the Security log but not to control other functions, such as creating user accounts and changing membership of local and global groups. Windows NT does not support such a separation of duties; the Administrators group's rights include managing the Auditing and Security logs.

One possible solution to this dilemma is to create custom groups with an appropriate set of privileges. For example, you could create your own custom administrator-like group (named something like "Superusers") that could be assigned all the rights of the Administrators group except for the

Manage Auditing and Security Log right. It would also be appropriate to avoid assigning anyone to the Administrators group; anyone who needed to perform system administration duties should be assigned to the Superusers group. This part of the solution would prevent system administrators from reading, changing, or deleting the Audit log. You could then also create another group (perhaps named "Auditors") for people who need to review the Audit logs on systems. This second group would need the following three rights to be able to review the Audit logs: Access this Computer from the Network, Manage Auditing and Security Logs, and Logon Locally.

Although creating custom groups can be an effective solution when problems such as this one arise, creating such groups is usually no small task. Another problem is that many of the rights are still not sufficiently granular for some business needs. Still another alternative solution is to buy a third-party tool that permits more granular assignment of rights. Examples include tools, such as seOS by Security Dynamics and Enterprise Administrator by Mission Critical Software.

Advanced Rights

Certain rights—"advanced" or "special" rights—go well beyond the scope of normal rights in that they allow the person who has them to accomplish actions that affect the internal functionality of Windows NT. Some of these rights are as follows:

- **Act as part of the operating system.** This right allows you access to the operating system as a trusted part of it without interference by the Security Reference Monitor.
- **Create a pagefile.** This right allows you to create one or more files to be used for virtual memory page swapping.
- **Create a token object.** This right enables you to create an access token or some other type of token.
- **Create permanent shared objects.** This right allows you to create a special, permanent object to be shared, such as a permanent device.
- **Increase scheduling priority.** This right permits you to increase the priority of one or more processes.
- **Log on as a service.** This right allows you to log on as a service, such as the Server or NetLogon service.
- **Modify firmware environment.** This right allows you to change the hardware environment.[4]

[4] *This allows a user to modify system-environment variables stored in nonvolatile random access memory (RAM) on systems that support this type of configuration.*

Advanced rights are potentially even more dangerous than "normal" rights, in that they can be used to subvert the internal functionality of a system if they get into the wrong hands. The best course of action to take with respect to these rights, is to be especially stingy with them—assign one or more of them only if a compelling need to have these rights exists. Note that in Windows NT 4.0 Server and Workstation, no group, not even Administrators, is by default assigned these rights. Any person with Administrator-level privileges can, however, assign these rights to Administrators by just scrolling down the list of rights in the User Rights panel, and then highlighting Advanced Rights. Now by clicking at the point where the name of the right meets the particular group or user to which these rights will be assigned, any person with Administrator-level rights can "claim" these rights for Administrators (see Figure 5.5).

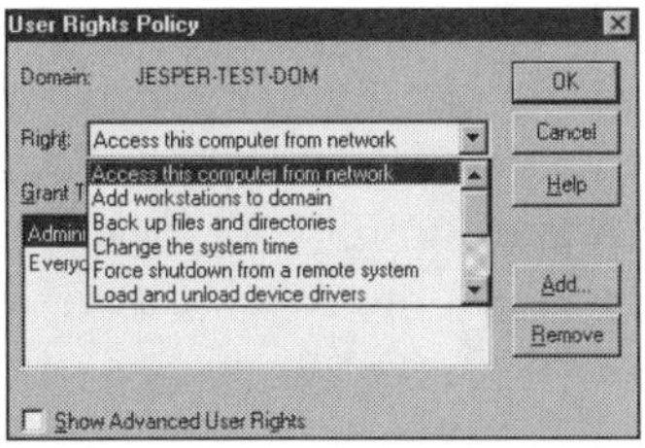

Figure 5.5 *User Rights Policy panel.*

Note also that several "special" groups exist. These are local groups, an integral part of system functionality, created by the system. Each of these groups has at least some particular set of default rights. These groups include the following:

- **Everyone.** The universal group that includes every user, including the anonymous user. The SID for this group always has the value of S-1-1-0.
- **Interactive.** A group of users who are currently logged on locally to a system. It also can include users coming in across the Internet Information Server (IIS) File Transfer Protocol, (FTP) service or over basic authentication to the IIS web service.
- **Network.** This group includes users who are logged on to the system over the network, such as to a server message block (SMB) share or through Microsoft-authenticated Web access
- **SYSTEM.** A user who can bypass most Kernel-mode restrictions to be able to start or stop almost any process within the local machine. This ID is in most respects the most powerful ID in Windows NT; for example, it can create and then assign primary tokens to users.

SYSTEM, paradoxically, has almost no privileges when it comes to remote access. For example, this ID cannot perform a remote shut down.

- **Creator Owner.** This group really represents two different things: the current owner of a particular object (regardless of whether the owner has actually created the object in question) and the person who created the object. These need not necessarily be the same entry.

As implied by their names, these groups are not typical groups. For one thing, all these groups are volatile. As programs run, the composition of each group can change. For example, anyone who logs on locally to a server becomes a member of Everyone, but inclusion in this group ceases when the user logs off. Furthermore, users who have interactively logged on cannot move particular SIDs in and out of any group. On the other hand, you can allow access to each group by changing *access control lists* (ACLs) to build in or remove access for any of these groups. The higher the level of privilege someone has, the more of these groups he or she can view through the NT Explorer. The Administrator can, for example, see all of these groups when scrolling through the panel shown in Figure 5.5. The best thing you can do with respect to securing against unauthorized access via membership in any special group is to leave these groups alone. One exception is the Everyone group; you may want to make modifications to these permissions to reduce the level of access to critical system files and the previously explained `RestrictAnonymous` Registry change. Another exception is SYSTEM, which is often used in impersonation tokens created as the result of running applications that run with elevated privileges.

As a final caution, consider that Windows NT differs from most other operating systems in a number of ways, one of the most important is the way rights are assigned on domain controllers. When you add or remove a right for a particular user or group on a domain controller, that right has been added or deleted for that user or group on all the domain controllers within the same domain. When you add someone to the Domain Administrators group, anyone in that group automatically gets Administrator-level access to all machines, servers, and workstations within the domain. Therefore, it is important to be aware just how widespread rights can be distributed in a Windows NT domain. In most operational settings, it is best to assign the most powerful rights, such as Administrator rights, as conservatively as business and operational needs allow.

What's New? Rights Assignment in Windows 2000

Windows 2000 still has rights in the Windows NT 4.0 sense; however, assigning rights in Windows 2000 can be done in a fundamentally different manner in that maintaining the problematic distinction between "Administrators" and non-administrators is not necessary. Windows 2000 allows rights to be delegated to organizational units (OUs) that consist of groups, individual accounts, and so forth. Part of the task of setting up rights and access in Windows 2000 involves creating OUs and assigning rights and access permissions to OUs. Each lower-tier OU must necessarily have the same or fewer rights as the parent OU. No OU will necessarily have the full set of rights that exists in this new operating system. To use Windows 2000 terminology, rights can be "delegated" to OUs in accordance with an organization's needs. This scheme will, to a large degree, address the problem that Windows NT 4.0 imposes because currently certain privileged groups are given rights and abilities that cannot be revoked. ◆

Securing Accounts and Groups

Securing accounts and groups after you have installed Windows NT is no easy task. The best starting point is to ensure that the default Administrator account and any other accounts with Administrator-level privileges are as secure as possible. The default Administrator account is more likely to be attacked than virtually any other account. In fact, surveys indicate that there is a reasonably high chance that in many domains and workstations it will not even have a password. Additionally, if this account is the only account with Administrator-level privileges, it cannot be locked as the result of too many bad logon attempts unless a tool such as PASSPROP.EXE is installed. An attacker could, therefore, initiate as many password-guessing attempts as desired in a brute-force attack against this account. In light of this, you should strongly consider the following measures:

- Change the name of the default Administrator account.
- Create other accounts for administration purposes.
- Establish a central accounts database.
- Set up a notification process.
- Avoid using the Copy function in the User Manager for Domains (or User Manager).
- Set up user login scripts and policies.
- Create a *separate* account for every Windows NT domain user.

The following sections address these topics in more detail.

Change the Name of the Default Administrator Account

Using the User Manager for Domains or the User Manager, assign it a more neutral, innocuous name (for example, "routine"). If you do this, be sure to change the description of the account in the User Manager from its default wording, "Built-in account for administering the computer."

Create Other Accounts for Administration Purposes

Create one for each administrator and include each in the Domain Administrators group.[5] Also create an unprivileged account for each administrator. Require that each administrator use the privileged account only when performing system administration functions (to avoid hogging system resources unnecessarily and to minimize the potential for catastrophic error resulting from mistakes by the superuser). Install the SU.EXE utility from the Resource Kit to ensure that system administrators can easily switch between their privileged and nonprivileged accounts.

Are Windows NT Systems Defenseless Against Brute-Force Attacks That Target the Default Administrator Account?

We have already examined special security concerns in connection with the default Administrator account. These concerns, however, do not constitute the total set of security-related risks that apply to this account. An attacker can also by default continue to attack the default Administrator account indefinitely without worrying about any bad logon limit lockout. One of the restrictions in Windows NT is that the last remaining account (that is, one not already disabled or deleted and that has Administrator priviledges) cannot be locked out or disabled. If the default Administrator account is the only one with Administrator privileges that exists, security-related risk in domains (as well as workstations) increases substantially due to the threat of brute-force password attacks against this account. Note that the default Administrator can be locked out or disabled if the PASSPROP.EXE tool from the Resource Kit is installed, the bad logons are network (remote) logon attempts, and at least an additional nondisabled, nondeleted account with Administrator-level privileges exists. Under no circumstances can the default Administrator account be deleted, however. ◆

[5] *Note that this way of assigning superuser privileges differs from the best way to do this in UNIX, in which having one root (superuser account) is the most desirable from a security perspective. In UNIX the first account in the* `/etc/passwd` *file with a user ID (UID) of 0 is the account identified in UNIX logs whenever any root user does something. Therefore, UNIX cannot log the actions of each individual root user. In contrast, in Windows NT each superuser's actions can be individually logged. The best alternative in Windows NT, therefore, is to create a separate superuser account for each system administrator.*

Establish a Central Accounts Database

Require every user who needs access to complete a form that includes provisions such as agreeing to keep from revealing passwords to users and refraining from actions, such as attempting to escalate privilege levels without authorization. Every time you create an account for a user, first make the proper entries in the central accounts database.

Set Up a Notification Process

If users leave your organization or are transferred somewhere else, the system administrators need to be immediately informed in order to delete or disable accounts appropriately. The optimal course of action is generally to disable accounts of users who leave for between 30 and 90 days to allow time to find new owners of files in an orderly manner. Then, after 30 or 90 days, it is generally best to delete each disabled account.

Avoid Using the Copy Function in the User Manager for Domains (or User Manager)

This function is an invitation to error: When you copy another account to create a new one, you also copy all the group memberships, logon scripts, profiles, and so forth. You may be giving new accounts considerably too much access and privileges without even knowing it! If you use the Copy function, create a nonfunctional, generic account with minimal group memberships and privileges from which to create new accounts.

Set Up User Logon Scripts and Policies[6]

In certain situations, you may want to set up special logon scripts and policies for individual users. Logon scripts can be useful from a security perspective in that they can limit the user environment. The default path to logon scripts is `\winnt\system32\repl\import\scripts`. You can create a logon script that locks a user in a particular environment, if that user needs access to a system or domain solely for the purpose of running a particular application. In this case, you would need only to create a logon script that causes execution of this application. You need to specify the name of the custom logon script in the User Properties panel that is accessed by bringing up the User Manager for Domains, and then double-clicking on a highlighted username (see Figure 5.6). Next, click on Profile. When the Profile panel for that user appears, enter the name of the path for the custom logon script (see Figure 5.7).

[6] *You can, alternatively, use the System Policy instead, because it directly edits the Registry to affect variables such as program startup.*

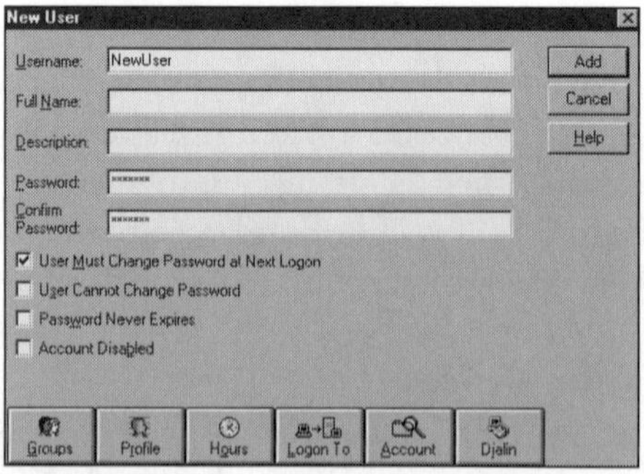

Figure 5.6 *User Properties panel.*

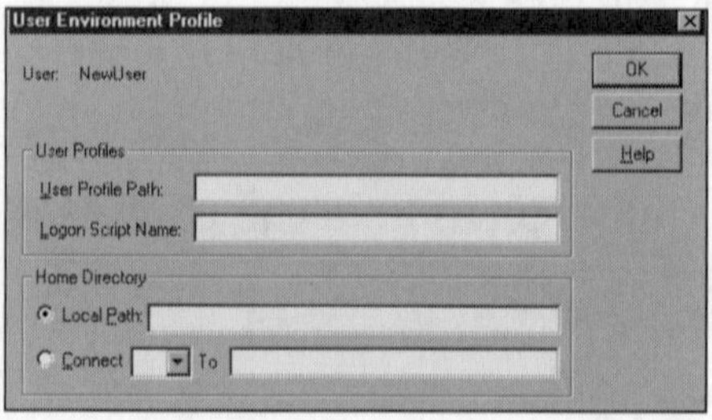

Figure 5.7 *User Environment Profile screen.*

Create a Separate Account for Every Windows NT Domain User

If security is a concern, do not allow any account to be shared. Shared accounts invite catastrophe. If even one user reveals the password to the account, the account can be easily compromised. In short, shared accounts create too many "weak links." These are users who all know the same password and who will not have to face up to the consequences of their actions, if they engage in unauthorized activity because any one of a number of users may have been the person who misused the system.

Installing Appropriate Service Packs and Hot Fixes

Chapter 4, "Basic Windows NT Security Exposures," discussed in detail the types of security-related vulnerabilities that exist in Windows NT and the types of solutions that address them. Your installation may not include the SPs that counter vulnerabilities that cause significant security-related risk in your operational environment. Shortly after installation of Windows NT systems, therefore, you should check the version of SP installed and upgrade it, if necessary. Installing hot fixes for security-related bugs for which no SP exist is also a good idea. ◆

Securing the Registry

The Windows NT Registry is a hierarchical database used for storing parameter values that define software, system, and security configurations. It not only replaces what used to be many INI files in previous Microsoft operating system and networking products, but also provides an interface capability with components, such as device drivers, the Hardware Abstraction Layer in Kernel mode, administrative tools (such as the User Manager for Domains and Server Manager) and many others. The Windows NT Registry contains two types of values, volatile and nonvolatile. Each value is viewable through a Registry editor (such as the Windows NT Registry Editor, REGEDT32.EXE, or the Win 9x. Registry editors, REGEDIT.EXE). As part of the Windows NT file system, the Registry is referred to as a hive. By default, Registry files (that is, the hive) are stored in `%systemroot%\system32\config` and `%systemroot%\profiles`.

Keys

Registry objects are called *keys*[7]. Failure to set appropriate values in the Registry for certain keys could result in malfunction, subversion, or denial of service. Windows NT Server 4.0 has the following six root (top-level) keys in the Registry:

- **HKEY_LOCAL_MACHINE** This keeps volatile and non-volatile data concerning system configuration.
- **HKEY_CLASSES_ROOT** This key holds file association data and data needed for *Object Linking and Embedding* (OLE).
- **HKEY_USERS** This key holds subkeys containing values pertinent to local user accounts.
- **HKEY_CURRENT_USER – HKEY_CURRENT_USER** This key stores data about any users who are currently logged on to a Windows NT machine.
- **HKEY_DYN-DATA** This key contains counters related to system performance.
- **HKEY_CURRENT_CONFIG** This key holds data about a system's hardware configuration.

7 *A subkey is a key that is beneath another key in the Registry key structure. A value is also below another key but is not part of the tree itself. A value could thus more appropriately be called a lateral key. When you use REGEDIT32 to view the Registry, you can choose Tree and Date by pulling down the View menu bar. Registry keys and subkeys are displayed to the left; and values are displayed to the right.*

Each value consists of three pieces of data: the name of the value, the type of value, and data. The types of Registry values include the following:

- **REG_BINARY** To hold binary data greater than 32 bits in length or raw data.
- **REG_DWORD** A double word that may be represented in different formats, such as binary, decimal, and hexadecimal formats. It is always 32 bits in length.
- **REG_DWORD_BIG_ENDIAN** Like `REG_DWORD`, but with the high byte first.
- **REG_EXPAND_SZ** For Unicode string variables.
- **REG_FULL_RESOURCE_DESCRIPTOR** To hold data concerning hardware configuration.
- **REG_LINK** For obtaining the value of one key from another key.
- **REG_MULTI_SZ** To hold several string variables all in one key.
- **REG_NONE** For variables for which the type is not specified.
- **REG_SZ** To hold a standard string variable that represents names, filenames, paths, and so on.

So, for example, a hypothetical value such as `SERVICES:REG_DWORD:0x00` has the name "SERVICES," displayed in a double word value format and has a hexadecimal data of zero. Although data can be displayed as alphabetic characters, binary numbers, decimal numbers, or hexadecimal numbers, the default representation for numeric data is hexadecimal.

A large part of the Registry is (and must, to some extent be) open to access by any user or process. This problem was worse in earlier releases of Windows NT—they came with many weak and sometimes dangerous default Registry permissions from a security standpoint. They allowed unprivileged users (for example, Everyone) to, in many cases, have Full Control over critical keys. Subsequent releases have come with somewhat tighter permissions, but there are still some areas of the Registry in which you can and, in most cases, should tighten permissions if you need a greater level of security. In particular, you need to pay attention to the permissions for the `Winlogon` and `Lsa` keys and all values below them. These keys control critical security-related properties such as authentication, how commands are parsed, the composition of special groups, how auditing works, and so forth.

Registry Permissions

Registry permissions differ somewhat from NTFS permissions. Basic Registry permissions include the following:

- **Read.** Allows you to determine what the value of a key or subkey is, but not to modify it.
- **Full Control.** Enables you to read, modify, delete, and take ownership of a key or subkey.
- **Special Access.** See the following list.

Special Access permissions include the following (which do not have to be assigned on an all-or-none basis—you can assign any combination of the following permissions to a user who has Special Access):

- **Query Value.** Allows you to read the value of a Registry key.
- **Set Value.** Allows you to create or redefine the value of a key.
- **Create Subkey.** Enables you to create a new key somewhere in the Registry tree.
- **Enumerate Subkeys.** Allows you to view subkeys below a particular key.
- **Notify.** Required to register a change notification on a Registry key. A change notifiation allows an application to be notified of changes to a specific Registry key or its subkeys. Regedt32 uses this mechanism—you can verify this by opening the key in Regedit and Regedt32 then deleting the key from Regedit. Regedt32 will automatically update its display to reflect the change. This is parallel to the way NT Explorer makes updates to reflect changes to the folder it is viewing.
- **Create Link.** Enables you to link the values of Registry keys so that one has the value of the other.
- **Delete.** This option allows you to delete a Registry key.
- **Write DAC.** This permission allows you to change the permissions associated with a Registry key.
- **Write Owner.** Write Owner allows you to take ownership of a key.
- **Read Owner.** Enables you to read who the owner of a key is.

You can assign these permissions by invoking REGEDT32, highlighting a particular key, and dragging down the Security menu bar at the top to Permissions (see Figure 5.8).

Figure 5.8 *View of REGEDT32 menu bars (including Security menu bar).*

What are appropriate permissions for Registry keys? To a large degree, the answer depends on the particular group that needs access to the Registry. In the case of Administrators and System, it is necessary to allow Full Control access to most keys. In the case of Everyone, however, allowing the least-possible access without causing system failure or disruption is the best strategy. In many cases the following permissions are appropriate for Everyone: Query Value, Enumerate Subkeys, Notify, and Read Owner. These permissions minimize the possibility of an unauthorized user modifying or deleting one or more Registry keys, something that could result in major disruption or subversion of your Windows NT systems. Registry permissions may be selected through the Registry Key Permissions panel that appears when you choose the Permissions option from the Security menu bar (see Figure 5.9).

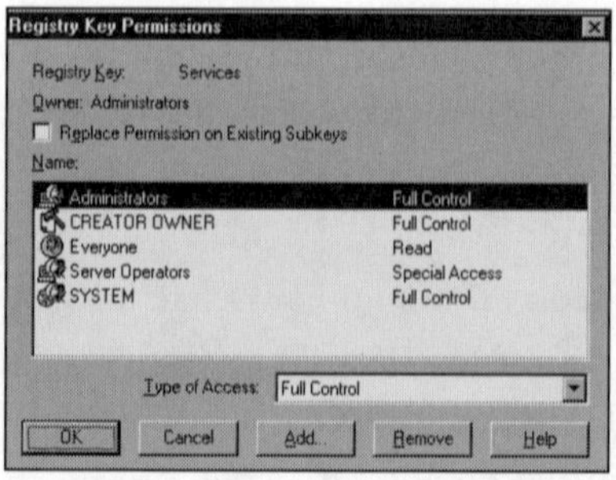

Figure 5.9 *The Registry Key Permissions panel.*

Ownership

Another major consideration is ownership. The best security solution here is to have Administrators be the owner of every Registry key, starting with each HKEY root key all the way down the Registry tree. Having any others (especially unprivileged users) be the owner of *any* key is a potential invitation to disaster because of the close relationship between Registry values and security. If an everyday user needs to install an application, that user should not be the owner of any keys installed. Administrators still should be the owner; you can still assign the level of access that the user needs without having to give ownership to that user. You can examine and reassign ownership by starting REGEDT32, highlighting a particular key, and dragging down the Security menu bar at the top to Owner. The ownership panel is shown in Figure 5.10.

Figure 5.10 *Ownership panel.*

To take ownership, click on the Take Ownership option, and then click on OK.

The Registry is a strange entity. It is not entirely stable; playing with it unnecessarily can result in extremely negative consequences. You need to carefully plan potential changes to the Registry, thoughtfully considering their potential impact. You should always test the changes you intend to make in a nonproduction environment first before implementing them in production machines. Chapter 6, "Maintaining Windows NT Security," discusses additional changes to the Registry that you should consider after you are through with the installation cycle.

What's New? The Windows 2000 Active Directory

Windows 2000 hosts still have a Registry, but the Active Directory (AD) will become the more important focus for the security community. The AD, like the Registry, is protected by ACLs that limit access by OUs. OUs with the appropriate permissions can edit entries in the AD. An important, but currently unresolved issue is the degree to which fixes for the bugs in the Windows 2000 operating system will require AD modifications. ◆

Setting Account Policy and User Properties Parameters

Windows NT has some additional settings that can improve the security of accounts and passwords. These settings are available through the Account Policy and User Properties settings. The Account Policy settings differ from the User Properties settings in that the former apply to *all* accounts, whereas the latter apply only to *one account at a time.*

Account Policy

You can reach the Account Policy panel on a domain controller by bringing up the User Manager for Domains and then dragging down the Policies menu bar until you reach Account. The account panel is shown in Figure 5.11.

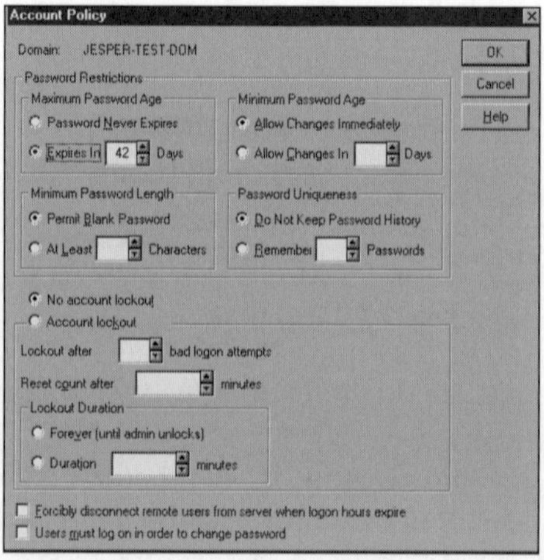

Figure 5.11 *Account Policy panel.*

Note that in Windows NT 4.0 the only default setting is related to password expiration—by default, passwords expire in 42 days. The best alternative for security is to assign reasonable values to the other fields in the Account Policy panel. These fields include the following:

- **Maximum Password Age.** The maximum number of days that a password for an account is valid for a logon.
- **Minimum Password Age.** The minimum number of days that a password is valid for a logon.
- **Minimum Password Length.** The minimum number of characters that must be in a password for a password to be usable.
- **Uniqueness Value.** The number of new passwords that must be chosen before a user can choose a previously chosen one. The actual uniqueness value is the displayed uniqueness value plus one; if the displayed value is 2, the actual value is 3.
- **Lockout After.** The number of failed logons that are allowed with the period of time (in minutes) specified in the next field, Reset Count After. If the Lockout After value is 3 and the Reset Count After value is 20 minutes, the third bad logon within a 20-minute time span would cause the account to be locked. After either a successful logon to the

account in question, or the expiration of 20 minutes after the first bad logon, the Lockout After value goes back to 0.

- **Reset Count After.** Defines the time period in which bad logons are counted, as explained under Lockout After.
- **Lockout Duration.** The time in minutes that an account is locked after the number of bad logons within the Reset Count period has been reached. Note that accounts with Administrator-level privileges are locked for only 30 minutes regardless of the value of this setting.
- **Users Must Logon to Change Password.** Determines whether users must log on to change passwords or if they may change them even if they are not logged on.

Note that when you set or modify Account Policy settings on a domain controller, you cause whatever setting you choose to be propagated to all other domain controllers. These settings then apply to all domain logons, choices of domain passwords, and so forth. If you have Windows NT Workstations that are domain clients, however, you need to set the Account Policy settings individually for each workstation, if you want to control security parameters related to local logons and passwords for each workstation. The domain parameters do not apply to local workstation logons. (Note, however, that in most environments, no accounts should be specified on the workstations beyond the normal Administrator and Guest accounts.)

I recommend the following values for the Account Policy settings:

- **Maximum Password Age.** Values between 30 to 90 days are generally appropriate. The more critical the environment in which Windows NT runs, the more appropriate a lower value is. Remember, however, that if you require users to change passwords too frequently, they will resort to desperate measures that will defeat your good intentions. For example, users who must change passwords every 30 days will choose a password such as "janpassword" during January, "febpassword" during February, "marpassword" during March, and so on.
- **Minimum Password Age.** The purpose of setting a minimum password age is to prevent users who have just changed their passwords from changing them right back again. This value should be low—perhaps 1 day—not so much for reasons related to security, but because requiring that users wait very long to change their passwords prevents users who learn that their password is weak from changing their passwords themselves. The only way they can change passwords quickly is to call a system administrator or help desk, thus potentially resulting in a backlog of help requests.

- **Minimum Password Length.** A good value for this field is 8; certain Windows NT–based cracking tools try every combination of every permissible character to crack a password up to 8 characters in length (although it takes a very long time to crack an 8-character password in this manner). Choosing a password of 8 or more characters, therefore, is very advisable.
- **Uniqueness Value.** The uniqueness value represents how many new passwords a user must choose befre being able to select one that was previously used. (Remember the formula for the uniquenes value is n+1.) A value of 3 or 4 is generally more than sufficient.
- **Lockout After.** A value of 3 for this field is a typical setting in business-critical processing environments. In other environments, a value of 5 is good. Remember that in Windows NT, the major concern is not the susceptibility to brute-force password-guessing attacks as much as the ability to perform an unauthorized logon because someone has obtained the password file and then cracked passwords.
- **Reset Count After.** A value of 480 minutes (8 hours) for this field is generally sufficient. A lower value could allow a patient attacker to wait for a while and then reinitiate attacks after the reset count has been reset. Note that choosing the Forever alternative here means that there will never be a reset period—the number of bad logons for an account will increment with each bad logon, ultimately until the bad logon limit is reached or until there is a successful logon to the account.
- **Lockout Duration.** A value of 8 hours (a reasonably long period of time) is generally sufficient to discourage hackers from continuing efforts to guess passwords for accounts. Note that the Forever option is also available here—Forever means that if an account is locked, an Administrator must reset the account before it can be used again.
- **Users Must Logon to Change Password.** This setting works exactly as advertised. Choosing it is useful for security in that it helps prevent the possibility that an unauthenticated user can change a password.

Although these settings would appear to solve a great proportion of the practical problems organizations experience with user accounts and passwords, Windows NT servers do not reliably enforce all these settings under all conditions. The interface between Windows NT Server and non-Windows NT clients is the problem. If the client is a Windows NT Workstation, these settings appear to be reliably enforced. Otherwise, only the first four (Maximum Password Age, Minimum Password Age, Minimum Password Length, and Password Uniqueness) of the Account Policy settings are reliably enforced. The most important of all these settings in most operational environments are the Maximum Password Age, Minimum Password Length, Lockout After, and Reset Count After. You can count on the first two of these settings being reliably enforced no matter what type of client platform is used to initiate logon requests and change passwords, but you cannot rely on the last two unless the logon or password change attempts are initiated from a Windows NT Workstation.

Account Policy Parameters: A Caveat

Too many Windows NT system administrators get a comfortable feeling about their system's security just because they set the Account Policy parameters tightly (for example, by requiring a minimum password length of 10 characters). All things considered, it is better for security to choose values such as these, but consider also the security benefits versus the costs. Longer passwords are better, true, but having to choose longer passwords will motivate many users to write their passwords down on a slip of paper that they may post in the open (something that your organization's InfoSec policy should prohibit). Consider, too, how easy cracking Windows NT passwords are—longer passwords just take somewhat longer to crack than shorter ones. Finally, remember that not all of the Account Policy settings work reliably when clients are not Windows NT Workstations. ◆

User Properties

User Properties settings for each user can be viewed by double-clicking on the username in the User Manager for Domains. Figure 5.12 shows the User Properties panel.

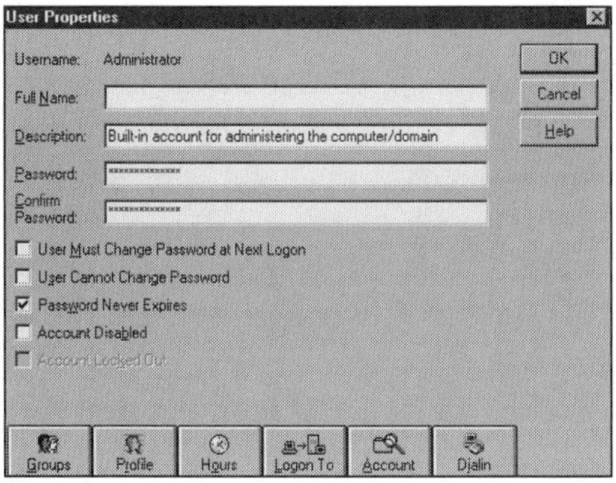

Figure 5.12 *User Properties panel.*

You can change several settings, as follows:

- **User Cannot Change Password.** This option could be useful in operational environments requiring very high levels of security, but there is a high cost associated with choosing this option: System administrators and/or help desk personnel have to change passwords because users cannot. The drain on the time of these people may not be worth the benefits in many situations.
- **Password Never Expires.** This setting is appropriate for accounts such as software installation accounts in which a password change could disrupt installation routines that are expecting a certain password. For normal user and Administrator accounts, however, this is *not* a good alternative. If an attacker obtains password hashes, having the password never expire gives the attacker too much time to crack the passwords.
- **Restrict Logon Hours.** Restricting logon hours can be useful in preventing scenarios such as widespread attacks on user and Administrator accounts during nonworking hours (especially weekends). The main problem with this setting, however, is that in today's work environment it is difficult to predict exactly when each user needs access to a computer. If the access is remote because the user is traveling, limiting logon hours may keep the user from obtaining access when he's in a different time zone. All things considered, you should restrict logon hours only if a very strong business justification for doing so exists.
- **Force Logoff.**[8] This function is intended to log a person off a system or domain if the user exceeds the allocated logon hours (as defined earlier). Although well intentioned, it can frustrate and alienate users and can even be career limiting for whomever has set the Force Logoff setting for other accounts. On the other hand, it can help protect systems from attacks during times few users access these system (for example, Saturday night at midnight).

Note that at the bottom of the User Properties panel three selections appear: one for Groups, one for Profiles, and one for Dial-in. You can click on Groups and adjust each user's group memberships. Double-clicking on the Profiles box displays the panel depicted in Figure 5.13.

[8] *This only works for users who are coming in remotely, and it is in the wrong context.*

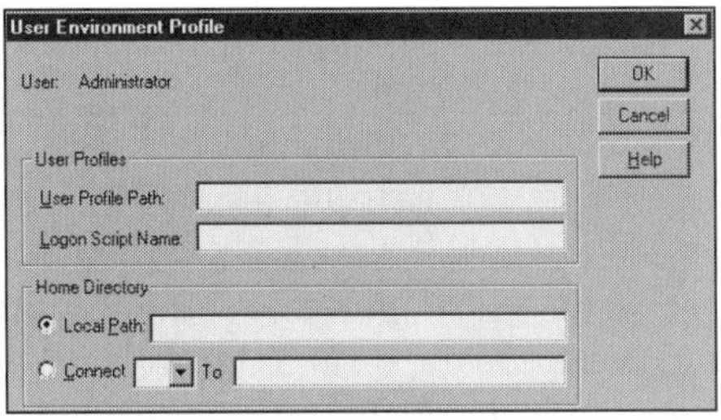

Figure 5.13 *User Environment Profile panel.*

The Profile panel is used primarily to set each user's environment. It can be useful for security in that you can specify the path to the logon script that will be executed on behalf of the user when the user logs on. You can limit the user's environment in this manner by including in the logon script the path to an executable that will constitute a captive (restricted) environment for the user. This is normally practical only in special cases, such as production applications that require multiple users to share the same account. Finally, you can set dial-in access characteristics through the Dial-in box. (Chapter 8, "Securing Network Services and Protocols," discusses RAS security.)

Enabling Auditing

Windows NT can produce three kinds of logs: the System log, the Security log (also called the Audit log), and the Application log. Table 5.4 shows the similarities and differences among these logs. Note that the System log is *not* configurable; it runs continuously, capturing events such as the starting or stopping of system and network services, failure of drivers to execute properly, and when share limits are exceeded. The critical logging capability for the purposes of this book is security logging/auditing, which (if turned on and correctly configured) records security events, such as successful and failed logons and logoffs, access to files and printers, exercise of user rights, and so on. Note that any Application log data captured is the result of logging capabilities built in to the application itself. Many applications that run on Windows NT do not incorporate any capability of sending log data to the Application log; others do.

Table 5.4 Windows NT Logging Capabilities

Type of Log	Function	Configurable?
System	Logs wide variety of system related events including errors, warnings, and other data.	No

continues ▶

Table 5.4 Continued

Type of Log	Function	Configurable?
Security (Audit)	Logs security-related data including logons/logoffs, accesses to objects, use of rights, when users start and stop program, and other data.	Yes
Application	Logs application status during run time.	Yes

Windows NT auditing capabilities are based on the functionality of the Event Log Service. The Event Log Service continuously writes to three log files: SYSTEM.LOG, SECURITY.LOG, and APPLICATION.LOG—each of which temporarily holds data until they can be written out to SYSEVENT.EVT, SECEVENT.EVT, and APPEVENT.EVT, respectively (see Figure 5.14). Only the .EVT version of each file (but not any .LOG version) is viewable using the Event Viewer within the Administrative Tools.

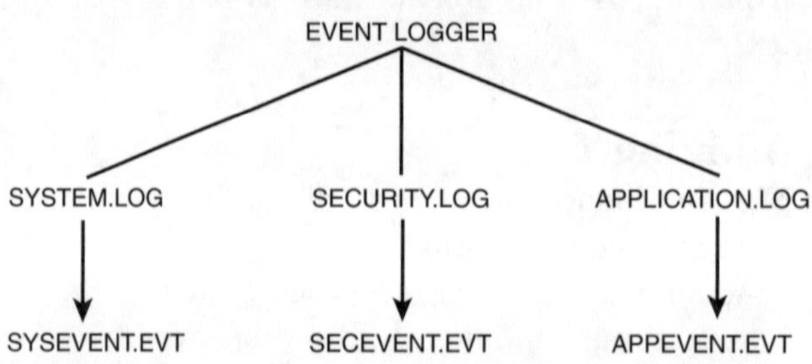

Figure 5.14 *How the Event Viewer writes to files.*

The most basic practical consideration in using Windows NT's auditing capabilities is determining whether to turn on auditing in the first place and, if so, how much audit data you need to capture. In all but very low-risk systems (for example, in an open computing environment), your best bet is to turn auditing on. To turn on auditing, you need only to navigate your way from Start to Programs to Administrative Tools to User Manager for Domains and then pull down the Policies menu bar to Auditing. The Audit panel is shown in Figure 5.15. First click on Audit These Events to enable auditing. Now you need to decide which of the following seven event categories you want to enable:

- **Logon and Logoff.** Both local and remote logons and logoffs.
- **File and Object Access.** Results in log entries for access to particular files, directories, printers, and/or Registry objects (*if* such logging has been turned on for individual files).
- **Use of User Rights.** Produces log entries for use of user rights, such as Manage Auditing and Security Log, Change System Time, Take Ownership of Files and Objects, and so on, but excludes logons/logoffs, restarts, and shutdowns—all of which are included in other event categories.
- **User and Group Management.** Results in log entries for events, such as password selection or change, creation, change or deletion of accounts and/or groups, lockout of accounts, and so on.
- **Security Policy Changes.** Leads to data reflecting any change in any User Manager or User Manager for Domains policy (user rights, account, audit, or trust).
- **Restart, Shutdown and System.** Produces data about object accesses by processes, system operations, and aborted processes for users.
- **Process Tracking.** User attempts to start and stop programs.

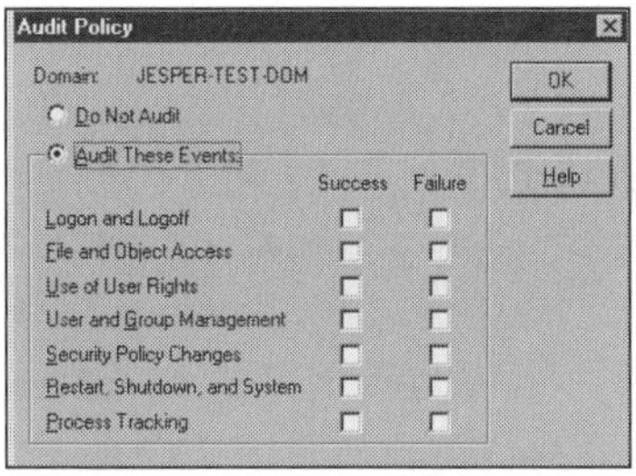

Figure 5.15 *Audit Policy panel.*

Which of these event categories are most important?[9] The answer depends on the needs of your particular environment. Normally, the most essential events to record are logons and logoffs. At a minimum, you will want to at least know who is getting access to a system and who is trying unsuccessfully to get access. The next most important event category in many operational environments is File and Object Access. It is frequently important to capture accesses to critical files and directories as well as to critical Registry keys and printers. The File and Object Access category does exactly this (although you have to determine exactly which objects are the

[9] *Note that just as in the case of User Manager for Domain settings, the audit settings you choose for one domain controller are propagated to all domain controllers.*

ones for which you want to capture access and also the level of access about which you want to log information, as explained a bit later in this chapter). The next most important event category in many environments is User of User Rights because of the risks associated with unauthorized use of user rights. Obtaining data related to other event categories, such as User and Group Management and Process Tracking, may also be valuable. You, other system administrators, InfoSec staff, and business unit managers will have to determine your own logging priorities.

One thing is certain: Enabling *all* event categories results in a flood of data that no one is likely to inspect and use. Choosing some subset of all the event categories is, therefore, generally the wisest decision.

In the case of File and Object Access, you must also choose the particular group or individuals for whom you want to capture data relevant to each event category. All things considered, the best choice is to select the Everyone group in each case because of the all-inclusiveness of this group; you will obtain a more thorough picture of what is happening on each system.

For each event category, you also need to record successes, failures, or both. The best choice is to select both. So, for example, if you choose to record logon/logoff successes but not failures, no Audit log entry is recorded if someone has attempted a bad logon.

In the case of File and Object Access, you need also to set the particular actions you want to record. For each file for which you want to record accesses, you need to choose some or all of the options in Table 5.5 (also see Table 5.6).

Table 5.5 Audit Options for Files

Event	Meaning
Read	Captures reading file contents, attributes, ownership, and/or permissions
Write	Records adding to or modifying file contents, changing attributes, or displaying any ownerships or permissions
Execute	Logs displaying file attributes, file ownerships, or permissions; running an executable
Delete	Self-explanatory
Change Permissions	Self-explanatory
Take Ownership	Self-explanatory

If you choose to audit access to directories (or folders, as they appear on your desktop), you must choose from among the following directory access-related events.

Table 5.6 Audit Options for Directories

Event	Meaning
Read	Logs reading names, attributes, ownerships, or permissions of a directory
Write	Records changing attributes, creating subdirectories and files within subdirectories, or displaying ownerships or permissions
Execute	Records displaying attributes, changing ownerships or permissions, or changing subdirectories
Add	Captures when somebody adds one or more directories
Delete	Records deleting directories
Change Permissions	Self-explanatory
Take Ownership	Self-explanatory

At this point, if you have the impression that setting auditing for a good portion of the files and directories on each server is an overwhelming task, you are right on track! Fortunately, the Directory Audit panel has a setting that can take a lot of the work out of the process. The Replace Auditing on Existing Files option, shown in Figure 5.16, enables you to click on a radio button to have the same audit settings for the directory for which the panel applies recursively propagated to all files beneath that directory.

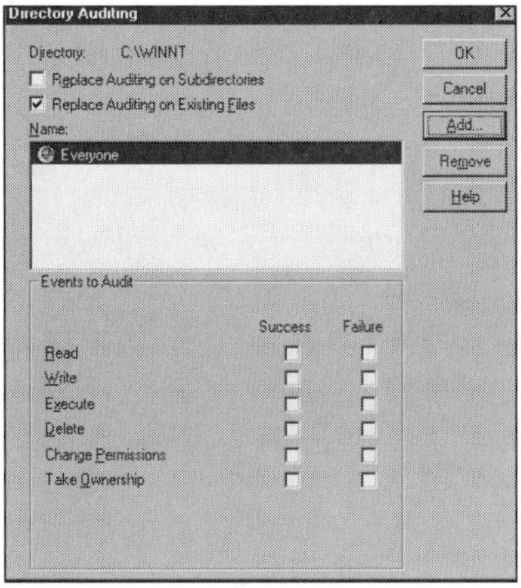

Figure 5.16 *Directory Auditing panel.*

So, for example, if you have chosen to audit Delete and Take Ownership access for Everyone to the directory, all files within that directory and all files within all lower-level directories will also have auditing set so that

Delete and Take Ownership access is recorded for Everyone. A similar option is the Replace Auditing on Subdirectories setting. If you choose this alternative, the same level of auditing selected for the directory for which the panel applies is recursively propagated to all lower-level directories.

There is yet another consideration when you set auditing; you have to set parameters that determine both the maximum size of each of the three logs the Event Logger produces as well as what happens when the logs fill up. You need to access the Event Log Settings panel, shown in Figure 5.17, by going from Start to Programs to Administrative Tools to Event Viewer. Pull down the Log menu bar to the Log Settings option. After the Event Log Settings panel appears, you can pull down other options from the Change Settings
For field to view settings for other (Security and Application) logs.

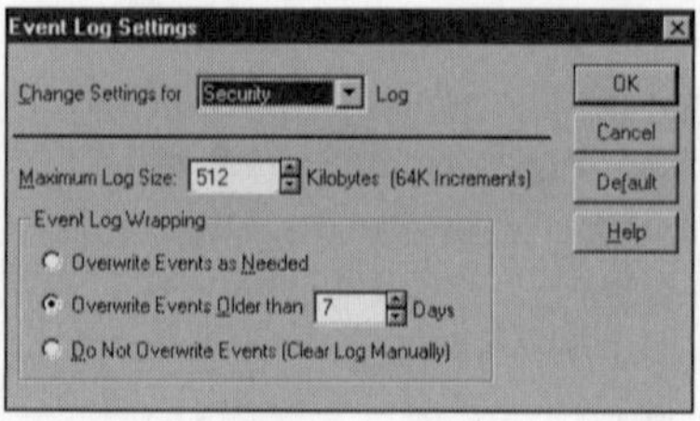

Figure 5.17 *Event Log Settings panel.*

The first consideration is log size; the default is only 512K. You can use the up arrow to increase the log size. The default of only 512K for each of the three logs is much too small for most deployments of Windows NT Servers (and even a few deployments of Windows NT Workstation, in which auditing is generally less critical than in servers). The exact setting you need for log size depends on how much logging you capture and how often you purge the logs. At a minimum, however, you should increase the size of the Security log by a factor of 5 to 10 (and perhaps by a factor of 10 to 20 on domain controllers). Remember, too, that you can set this value for the System and Application Log as well.

The second consideration is choosing a setting that determines what happens when each of the three logs fills up. As shown in Figure 5.17, you have the choice of three settings:

- **Overwrite Events as Needed.** This setting causes the Event Logger to overwrite log data only if the log fills up; it then overwrites the oldest events first if an overwrite is necessary
- **Overwrite Events Older than __ Days.** You choose the value of the number of days by using the up or down arrows in the Event Log

Settings panel. If you set the value to 7, after 7 days have expired, all entries that are 7 days old are deleted if you have chosen the value of 7 days.

- **Do Not Overwrite Events / Clear Log Manually.** This means "Don't automatically overwrite or clear any entry; I'd rather do it myself."

The worst setting of the three alternative Event Log Settings is generally Do Not Overwrite Events. If you choose this event and forget to clear the logs manually, they will fill up. If they fill up, one of two outcomes occurs: Log data are randomly overwritten or the system crashes. Neither alternative is normally very acceptable. The best overall alternative is Overwrite Events as Needed, because it results in log data overwrites only if the logs fill; otherwise a system does not delete log data. The second-best alternative is generally Overwrite Events After __ Days. This alternative can result in loss of audit and other data. If you have a good backup strategy (for example, you make full backups once a week and incremental backups daily), you will back up the logs enough that you should not lose very much data, if the logs are purged after the specified number of days have expired.

Dealing with auditing is not a simple matter. The major issues to be resolved are performance and disk capacity issues versus security. If you capture too much log data, system performance suffers, and your disk space fills up (sometimes unnecessarily). Enabling two particular event categories, File and Object Access and Process Tracking, is particularly detrimental to system performance. On the other hand, if you do not audit sufficiently, you may not be able to tell whether someone has been tampering with your system. The resolution of this issue, therefore, depends on your own cost versus benefit analysis.

How Do You Determine a User's Last Logon in Windows NT?

Windows NT can log a moderate amount of information about logons, logoffs, access to objects, and so forth. This information is, however, not always available in a format that a system administrator can really use. Determining a particular user's last logon can be a particularly arduous task. You can use the Command Prompt to enter ***net user [username}/[domain]*** *to see the last logon time for a user; but this information is only part of a large amount of displayed information—not efficient enough for a busy system administrator. Fortunately, a public domain tool called NTLAST is available. This tool lists the last logon for any particular user. To determine the last logon for user CBROWN, use the command prompt to enter the following:*

```
ntlast cbrown
```

This tool is currently available from
`http://www.ntobjectives.com/ntlastv2.htm.` ◆

Installing Antivirus Software

Another wise move is to install antivirus software on your servers and workstations. Chapter 10, "Workstation Security," covers viruses and other types of malicious code in detail. Suffice it to say at this point, despite the fact that virus attacks have become rather commonplace compared to some of the kinds of attack techniques that have emerged in the last few years, few problems can disable Windows NT systems so rapidly and widely as virus infections. Installing antivirus software right away is, therefore, an extremely important step in increasing the security of your Windows NT systems.

Conclusion

Reading this chapter should have reinforced a point made earlier in this book: Windows NT is not all that secure out-of-the-box. You need to do a lot of work during installation, and immediately afterward, if you want your Windows NT systems to run more securely than the default configuration allows. Some of the work involves adopting simple measures, such as ensuring that default accounts have difficult-to-guess passwords; other security-related tasks may go well beyond the scope of these measures. Having a set of standard procedures that specify the specific measures to be implemented is the most important step. Unless you create sound installation procedures from a security perspective and put them in place, it is likely that some of your Windows NT systems will differ considerably from others in terms of security level; the weaker systems will create weak links that will make your network considerably easier to attack.

A final caveat: Securing your Windows NT systems right away is one of the major steps you can employ to ensure that your Windows NT environment is sufficiently secure. Remember the case study in this chapter about the newly installed Windows NT domain. No one gave a password to the default Administrator account; a "lucky" perpetrator found the RAS dial-in number and logged on remotely to the domain as Administrator without even having to enter a password. Then the "fun" began. The newly installed domain contained virtually no data or applications of any value to anyone, but the perpetrator used to connect to other systems within the network. If the installer had followed the recommendations in this chapter, this very serious incident would in all likelihood never have happened.

Checklist for System Administrators

1. Physically secure your installation media.
2. Set up at least two partitions, one of which is a dedicated system partition. Ensure that every partition is an NTFS partition. Deploy multiple BDCs and place them in parts of the network where they can authenticate clients with a minimum amount of traffic having to be sent across the network. Set permissions (especially permissions for universal access) in a manner that minimizes the likelihood of unauthorized deletions and modifications, and in certain cases, unauthorized reads. Avoid giving Full Control to Everyone.
3. Whenever possible, choose domain rather than workgroup membership for every host, except for a public Web server.
4. Password the default Administrator and Guest accounts. Rename the default Administrator account if possible, and then create multiple accounts with Administrator privileges for system administrators.
5. Check the SP level of each installed system and upgrade to the desired SP whenever possible. Install hot fixes as needed.
6. Make an ERD for each system during installation. Ensure that each ERD is physically secure.
7. Ensure that administrators own every directory in the system partition and the root directory of every other volume.
8. Secure the Registry by ensuring that Administrators own every key and that, in general, Everyone has only Special Access (Read, Enumerate Subkeys, Notify, and so forth).
9. Set the Account Policy settings in accordance with your organization's security policy and business needs. Be sure, at the very least, to assign appropriate values to the minimum password length, maximum password age, bad logon count, and reset period.
10. Enable auditing on all business-critical hosts, capturing successful and failed logons and logoffs. Increase the size of the Security log in proportion to the amount of data it holds and avoid choosing the Clear This Log Manually option.
11. Install and update antivirus software.

6

Maintaining Windows NT Security

"If you stop getting better, you stop getting good."
–Anonymous

This chapter continues the theme that Chapter 5, "Configuring Windows NT Server for Security," introduced: Network security begins with an adequate level of system security. At this point, I will assume that you have implemented many, if not most, of the techniques presented in the preceding chapter, using a cost-benefit analysis as appropriate for your own organization. Not everything you need to do to elevate Windows NT security needs to get done immediately after installation, or later for that matter. However, other measures may be very important. Certain critical steps in securing systems actually need to be done more or less continuously throughout the life cycles of systems—consider shares, for example. You may create numerous shares when installing domain servers, but chances are that you will set up (and possibly delete) additional shares in time. Failure to secure shares may lead to unauthorized access to objects on the machine, on which these shares have been created. Topics such as share security are among the main topics of this chapter.

This chapter addresses security maintenance, implementing additional security-related measures after installation, and inspecting systems' configurations and settings. It also includes adopting measures to minimize the likelihood of authorized changes in the future. Despite the fact that greater levels of hype surround other areas of Windows NT security, initial configuration and setup, security maintenance is just as important. Your Windows NT (or any other type of system) will not be secure if you do not regularly implement appropriate security-related measures that include, at a minimum, inspecting those systems to ensure that unauthorized changes have not occurred. Remember, that most security-related events involve some degree of unauthorized changes to systems and networks. Topics covered in this chapter include

- Share security
- Securing trust
- Making backups
- Checking integrity
- Installing service packs and hot fixes
- Making Registry modifications
- Setting alerts
- Using fault-tolerance solutions
- Employing other methods that increase security

Securing Administrative Shares

This section explores Securing Administrative Shares, an extremely important step in making Windows NT more secure.

What are Administrative Shares?

One of the continuous tasks of system administration involves setting up shares. Certain shares (known as default shares, or administrative shares) are created every time a Windows NT system boots. On Windows NT Server, for example, the built-in shares[1] are ADMIN$, IPC$, NETLOGON[2], and a share for every local partition. If a system has only a C: partition (something that is not good for security, as explained in the pre-ceding chapter), the only additional share is C$. If a system has two partitions, C: and D:, the additional default partition access shares are C$ and D$. The shares that are created are essentially the same regardless of whether the host is a server or workstation, except that the NETLOGON share is created on domain controllers, but not other systems when the system boots.

Whenever you want to connect to an administrative share, you must use the Command Prompt to enter the following:

```
C:\>net use * \\<IPaddress>\<sharename>
```

[1] *The "$" indicates that each share is hidden, that is, if you enter* **net view** *from the Command Prompt, these shares are not listed. The Server Manager also does not display these shares. All three shares that are not named after a partition are to the* `%systemdrive%`*. The ADMIN$ share, for example, allows access to the* `%systemroot%` *directory within this drive. The IPC$ share is for interprocess communication, and is used to support remote access to named pipes and other objects associated with IPC.*

[2] *Only on domain controllers, not on member servers. Also, a print server will have a PRINT$ share that holds printer drivers for clients to download.*

For example, you could do the following from virtually any Windows command line on any host that supports such a command line:

```
C:\>net use * \\72.45.68.199\C$
```

To attempt to connect to the C$ share for the machine with an Internet Protocol (IP) address of `72.45.68.199`, you need access to a Windows command line (for example, on Windows NT, Win9x, Windows for Workgroups, Microsoft Local Area Network [LAN] Manager, SAMBA client, DEC Pathworks, and a Disk Operating System [DOS] network client). You must enter the password of anyone who can access this and other administrative shares on this command line by default, that is, any person with Administrator-level privileges on that machine. Alternatively, you can enter the preceding command shown, and then wait for the system to prompt for entry of a password.

Security-Related Vulnerabilities

As discussed in previous chapters, the major security-related risk with administrative shares is that (except for the IPC$ share) access to shares is not restricted by bad logon limits. An attacker can enter one username-password combination after another or (more advantageously for the attacker) can use an automated program to accomplish the same purpose. In fact, tools that present password after password to gain access to administrative shares are available on the Internet. A secondary risk is that someone can run a tool, such as Red Button, to learn whether a Windows NT system is a domain controller or another type of host. Remember, a server has more administrative shares than a workstation. This type of information can be very useful to someone interested in attacking systems.

Solutions for Shares Risks

One possible solution for the security risks presented by administrative shares is to disable them manually every time any Windows NT system boots. The ADMIN$ share, for example, can be manually disabled by invoking the Windows NT Explorer, highlighting the icon for the `WINNT` directory, and then dragging down from File to Properties. Next you need to click on Sharing. Note that you have the choice of sharing or not sharing the *`WINNT`* directory (see Figure 6.1). If you click on Not Shared, no one can access the ADMIN$ share. Alternatively, you can use the Command Prompt to enter the following:

```
net share <sharename> /delete
```

The major problem with either of these solutions is that the next time the machine boots, the default administrative shares are re-created.

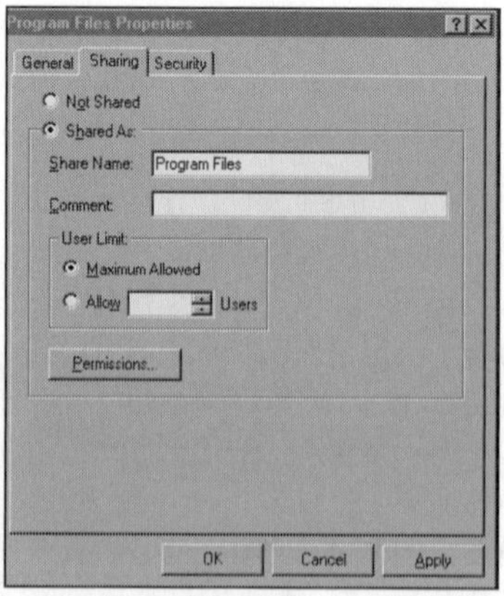

Figure 6.1 *Sharing panel.*

Policy Editor

A second solution for securing administrative shares is to use the Windows NT Policy Editor within the Resource Kit. You can use this tool to enter a setting that disables all administrative shares—the shares will not be created when a machine boots. To do this, follow these steps:

1. Install the Policy Editor program from the Resource Kit CD-ROM.[3]
2. Use the Command Prompt to enter **poledit**.[4]
3. The Policy Editor dialog box displays.
4. Pull down the File menu to Open Registry.
5. Double-click on Default Computer.
6. Open `WindowsNetwork\Sharing\CreateHiddenDriveShares`.
7. Uncheck the box next to this option.
8. Click on OK.
9. Pull down the File menu and select Save.

Although this solution sounds good superficially, it presents several substantial complications; the worst is that it disables all administrative shares on a server except for IPC$. Disabling these shares is likely to have catastrophic consequences for programs such as remote backup programs.

---

[3] *Policy Editor Program is installed by default on Servers. It is also available in the Support\SRVTools directory on the Server CD.*

[4] *If you install the policy editor from the Server Tools it shows up on the Administrative Tools menu.*

Command Line

Another potentially good solution for securing administrative shares is to execute a command that disables administrative shares every time a system boots. The `net share` command is most suitable for this purpose. Using AUTOEXNT from Resource Kit, include one `net share <share>/delete` command in the associated batch file to delete each administrative share you do not need.

Note that only certain administrative shares are safe to disable (with the previous exceptions noted)—namely C$, D$ (if the D: partition exists), E$ (if the E: partition exists), ADMIN$, and NETLOGON (sometimes, but be careful here, too). If the NETLOGON is disabled you will break both domain synchronization and domain logons, which ostensibly is the reason they are domain controllers. The best way to execute the `net share` commands, so that these shares are disabled from one boot to another, is to use *AUTOEXNT*, a Resource Kit tool that enables the system administrator to include the names of commands and programs to be run during boot time.

Securing Other Shares

Administering a Windows NT system invariably requires creating numerous shares to allow users and programs remote access to volumes. The chief problem from a security perspective is that these shares, by default, allow Full Control to Everyone. This permission potentially allows an everyday user to engage in disruptive actions, such as using a hacking utility to change ownership of the share, locking out all other users from accessing it, or deleting it altogether.

Resetting Permissions

Table 6.1 shows Windows NT share permissions.

Table 6.1 *Windows NT Share Permissions*

Share	Description
No Access	No share connection can be made to directory.
Read	Display subdirectory names and filenames.
	Display file data and attributes.
	Execute files.
	Change subdirectories.
Change	All permissions associated with Read, as well as the following:
	Add files

continues ▶

Table 6.1 Continued

Share	Description
	Create subdirectories Change or append file data Change file attributes Delete files and subdirectories.
Full Control	All permissions associated with Change, as well as the following: Change permissions Take ownership.

You can set these permissions by using the Server Manager on domain controllers. Go from Start to Programs to Administrative Tools to Server Manager. Alternatively, enter **svrmgr** in the Run menu. When you reach the Server Manager, pull down the Share menu until you reach the Create Shares option as the panel shown in Figure 6.2 displays. Pull down the options in the Security file menu until you reach Permissions. You can set permissions as desired. In the case of Windows NT Workstation, go from Start to Settings to Control Panel to Server, and then go to Shares.

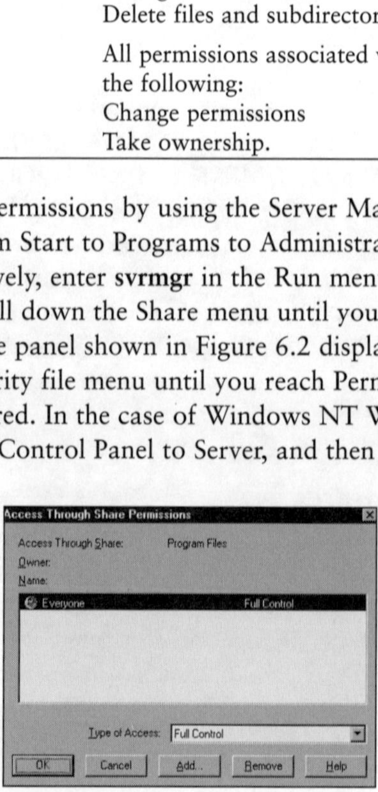

Figure 6.2 *Access Through Share Permissions panel.*

Choosing Share Permissions

What share permissions are appropriate in Windows NT? The answer to this question first requires an understanding of how share permissions and NT File Systems (NTFS) permissions work with each other. With respect to any one object (for example, a directory), NTFS permissions for a given user are cumulative, with the exception that if that user is assigned one No Access permission with respect to that object, all other access permissions are void. The user literally has no access. The more groups a user is assigned to, the more NTFS permissions that a user is likely to accumulate. Remember that permissions can also be assigned directly to a user account or to a group to which that account belongs. The same applies to share permissions that allow a user to remotely reach the object in question. Relevant share permissions that affect access to that object also accumulate with the exception that one No Access share permission wipes out all other positive share accesses. The overall access given to a user who accesses the object remotely, that is, by logging on to the domain from a workstation is the result of applying the least-access rule between the applicable NTFS permissions and share permissions. If a user's cumulative NTFS permissions for a directory are Change and the cumulative share permissions are Read, that user's level of remote access to that directory is Read—Read is the least access between a Change and a Read.

Share and NTFS Permissions

The interplay between share and NTFS permissions is a potentially very strong security feature in Windows NT. This interplay is like a "two-lock" security system; for a user to get to an object remotely, that user must have both the right NTFS permissions and the right share permissions. Unfortunately, the fact that the default share allows Full Control to Everyone to some degree defeats this two-lock system. Therefore, the best practical measure to take is to change the default permissions for every nondefault share to the following:

- **Change.** For Domain Users or Authenticated Users (assuming that you have installed at least Service Pack 3 for Windows NT 4.0).
- **Full Control.** For Administrators and the Creator Owners of objects accessible through the share. Note that anything less causes disruption of remote Creator Owner actions such as changing permissions. Administrators, however, can easily circumvent such problems because of the default rights afforded to them.

The method of setting share permissions recommended in this chapter prevents everyday users from engaging in potentially disruptive actions, such as using tools that change share permissions. This advice applies to nonboot partitions (for example, the D: and E: drives). It does not apply to shares to the C: system drive. You should *not* normally allow users to remotely access the C: drive in the first place. Only Administrators typically need to reach the system drive remotely. Built-in administrative shares will by default already exist. See the previous section for recommendations for securing this drive. Remember too, that if you are *not* dealing with some system-related aspect of Windows NT and need to build in universal access, the universal access groups, Domain Users and Authenticated Users, are better from a security perspective than is the Everyone group.

Share Ownership

Note that the interplay between NTFS permissions and share permissions is difficult (or potentially difficult) to determine, especially for users who are in multiple groups and is difficult to check. Tools, such as SomarSoft DumpSec (`http://www.somarsoft.com`) display file and directory permissions and ownerships, but do not take into account the permissions and ownerships of the shares that are created to reach the files and directories. Pedestal Software's ListACL (`http://www.pedestalsoftware.com`) lists permissions on files and directories, and the ShareListACL tool lists permissions on shares. *Appropriately setting the permissions of shares immediately after you create them is extremely important.* If you don't set the share permissions correctly when you create each share, it is unlikely that those permissions will ever be changed later.

Securing Trust Relationships

Trust in Windows NT is always between domains, not between individual servers and/or workstations. It means that a link between domains has been established such that users in one domain can view and/or potentially access some or all of the resources in another domain. Consider the two hypothetical domains in Figure 6.3. If Domain A is trusted by Domain B, this means that some or all users in Domain A can see—and perhaps read, execute, or delete resources—within Domain B.

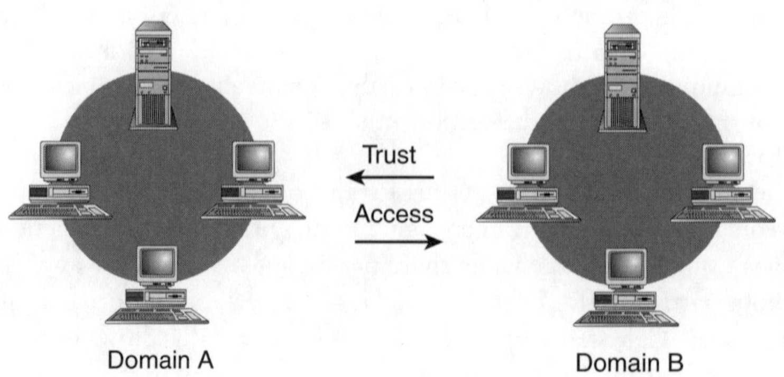

Figure 6.3 *Trust and access in interdomain trust between two hypothetical domains.*

Preparing to Establish Trust Relationships

Setting up trust requires implementing several measures. First, you have to make the appropriate entries in a trust panel in one domain controller in both the trusting and trusted domains (see Figure 6.4). Then you have to enter a password in the next panel that appears (see Figure 6.5). This password must be identical in both the trusting and trusted domains. Finally, you need to include one or more global groups from the trust*ed* domain in one or more local groups in the trust*ing* domain to set up the actual access.

Note that one domain may trust another domain, yet users from the trusted domain may not be able to obtain access to resources in the trust*ing* domain if no group in the trust*ed* domain is included in any group in the trust*ing* domain. No access is also the result if the local group in the trust*ing* domain, in which one or more groups from the trust*ed* domain, is included does not have any access to resources within its own domain.

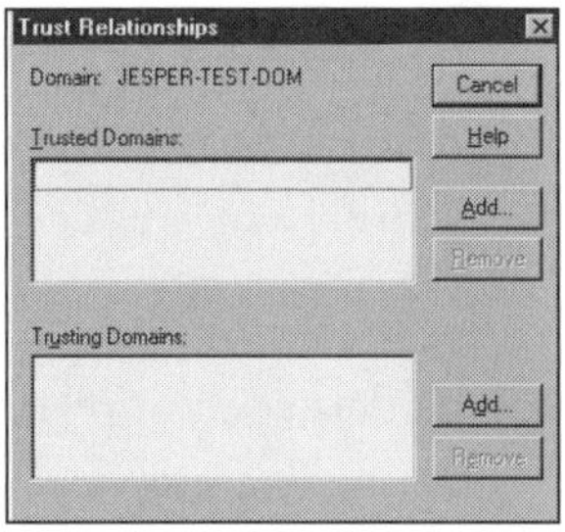

Figure 6.4 *Trust Relationships panel.*

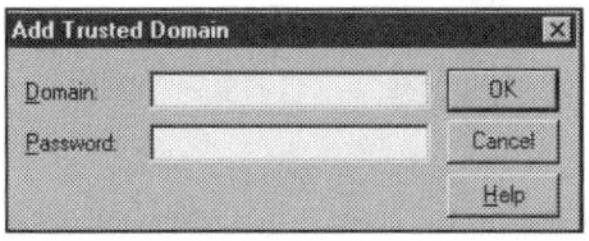

Figure 6.5 *Trust Password Entry panel.*

The level and extent of trusted access depends on the level and extent of access of the local group in which one or more global groups from the trusted domain are included. If the system administrator has built in very little access for the local group within the trusting domain, users from the trusted domain(s) can obtain only very little access to resources within the trusting domain. On the other hand, if the local group has a very great degree of access, users from the trusted domain(s) also receive this same degree of access when they access resources in the trusting domain. Figure 6.6 shows an example. Suppose that Domain C trusts both Domains A and B. Suppose further that Domain A has a global group named Personnel and that Domain B has a global group named Administration. Suppose too, that these groups are included in Domain C's local Operations group after trust between the domains is established. When users in DomainA\Personnel and DomainB\Administration access resources in Domain C, they access them with the same level of access (in terms of permissions and user rights/abilities) as users in DomainC\Operations. Note that users in DomainA\Personnel and DomainB\Administration may access resources in their own home (trusted) domain with a greater or lesser level of access than they do for resources in the trusting domain.

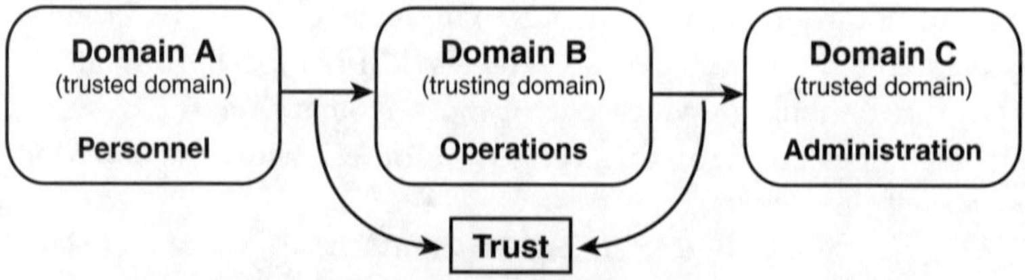

Figure 6.6 *How global groups obtain access to resources within trusting domains.*

Trust Models

Windows NT offers several models of trust relationships between domains including the following:

- **No trust.** In this alternative, no trust between domains exists. Note that although this variation of the trust theme is in some respects easier to secure, it also presents the most barriers to users who need access to resources in remote domains.
- **Complete trust.** The complete trust model is in effect a peer-to-peer trust model—every domain trusts every other domain. Sometimes nicknamed the "helter-skelter" model of trust by critics, this variation is the potentially least secure of all alternatives because it offers no central control over trust relationships. Figure 6.7 illustrates complete trust between four domains.

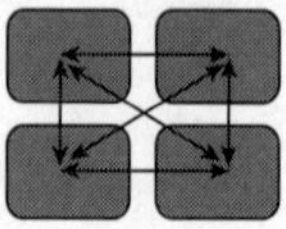

Figure 6.7 *The complete trust model.*

- **Master domain model.** As the name implies, the master domain model requires implementation of a master domain in which accounts and global groups exist. Resources do not normally exist within the master domain, but rather within each of a number of resource domains. Each resource domain trusts the master (accounts) domain. The resource domains contain only local accounts into which global groups from the master domain are included to set up trusted access. This type of domain model is conducive to security because trust can be managed centrally from the master domain. Figure 6.8 shows an example of this model. A variant on the master domain model is where you have a domain to contain untrusted users' accounts. For example, a university may have a domain to contain students' accounts and another to contain faculty accounts. The faculty domain is trusted by the student domain so that faculty can gain access to resources in the student domain. However, there is no trust of the student domain in the faculty domain. Hence, students are barred from being allowed any access in the faculty domain. This arrangement, which allows fundamentally untrusted users to be isolated, can also be seen in organizations that have separate domains for temporaries and consultants.

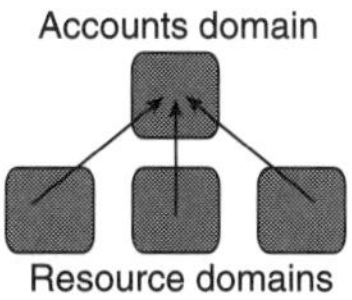

Figure 6.8 *The master domain model of trust.*

- **Multiple master domain model.** The multiple master domain model (see Figure 6.9) is very similar to the master domain model except that accounts and global groups are divided between more than one master (accounts) domain. It is used when the number of accounts exceeds the practical limit[5] for the number of accounts in Windows NT 4.0, namely approximately 30,000 accounts. Both master domains trust each other. This model, like the master domain model, is conducive to security in that it provides a large degree of central control over trust relationships.

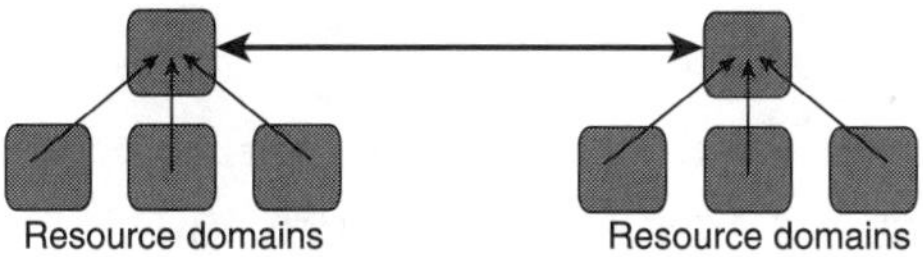

Figure 6.9 *The multiple master domain model of trust.*

[5] *The Windows NT 4.0 SAM database can hold 40,000 authentication objects (for example, accounts, groups, computers) per domain. When the number of accounts exceeds approximately 30,000, domain controllers can exhibit strange and unpredictable behaviors (for example, error messages indicating that a newly created accounts already exists) when a system administrator creates, disables, or deletes a new account.*

Passthrough Authentication: What Makes Trust Work?

Passthrough authentication means that a user in a trusted domain is allowed access to resources within a trusting domain. Before passthrough authentication can occur, however, trust must initially be established between two domains. A Local Security Authority (LSA) object, the trusted domain object, must be passed to and from both the trusting and trusted domains. This object is in effect a trust password shared between the two domains. On the PDC in the trusting domain, the trusted object is stored in a hidden file, `G$$<TrustedDomainName>`. This PDC propagates the trusted domain object(s) to all domain controllers within its own domain. On the primary domain controller (PDC) in the trusted domain, the trusted domain object is stored in an account within an authentication database that is originally created when trust between two domains is initially established. This account is by default named `INTERDOMAIN_TRUST_ACCOUNT` when the master domain or multiple master domain model is used. Otherwise, the account's name is RESOURCE$. In either case, the account exists in `\WINNT\SYSTEM32\CONFIG\SAM\SAM\Domains\Account\User\Names`. This account is also propagated to all domain controllers.

During the process of establishing trust between domains that trust each other through a master domain or multiple master domain model, the PDC of the trust*ed* domain passes this object to a domain controller in the trust*ing* domain. This domain controller then tries to create a session with the PDC in the trusted domain using the trusted domain object in its RESOURCE$ account. The PDC in the trusted domain will not be able to connect to this session because the normal logon session does not recognize the account used for trust when the master domain or multiple master domain model is used. The PDC in the trust*ed* domain therefore now records the error[6], determining that trust can exist between the two domains. This PDC then uses RPC transactions involving remote API calls to create a null session to the trusting domain. The NetLogon service in the trust*ing* domain subsequently creates a session on the basis of trust-related information stored in its User Manager for Domains to create the trusted link between the two domains. The User Manager for Domains in the trust*ing* domain also creates what is called a secret object (a transparent password) for each user who is allowed trusted access to that domain. One secret object exists for each user whom the trusting domain trusts.

After trust between domains has been established, any user in a trusted domain who is in the appropriate (trusted) global group can initiate access to

[6] *The error code is the hexadecimal value* `0xc000198`. *The name of the error is* `Status_Nologon_Interdomain_Trust_Account`.

a resource within a trusting domain. The user's action (for example, clicking *on* a share name *for* a share *to* a drive *within* a trusting domain) initiates passthrough authentication. The user, of course, is unaware of all the transparent events that occur and does not have to enter an additional password or anything else to be able to connect to a share in the trusting domain. When the trusting domain receives the passthrough authentication request, it sends a challenge to a domain controller within the trusted domain. If the user is allowed trusted access, the trusted domain responds by sending the secret object for the user, and an access token that it creates, back to a domain controller within the trusted domain. The user is now allowed to access the resources available (based on the local group to which the user's global group or account has been included). Note also that if the user needs access to a *different* domain resource (or the same, previously accessed resource but at a different level of access), passthrough authentication for the new level of access must once again occur. If the user logs off, then logs on to the home (trusted) domain once again, each passthrough authentication must once again be performed to allow access to the trusting domain(s).

Trust objects are volatile. Both the trust*ed* and trust*ing* domains', trusted domain objects, and secret objects are changed every seven days. The PDC of the trusting domain initiates these changes. It sets the OldPassword field of each LSA object to the former NewPassword value and assigns the new value to the NewPassword field for each object. The PDC of each domain then replicates the updated LSA objects to backup domain controllers (BDCs) within their own domains using the NetLogon service. This update process, which is initiated by the `I_NetServerPasswordSet` Romote Procedure Call (RPC) to the PDC of the trusted domain, helps guarantee that both PDCs (that is, the PDCs for *both* the trust*ed* and trust*ing* domain) have a viable password if one of the PDCs does not update the objects properly, if the LSA replication process goes awry, or if a PDC crashes during the update process. The final result is that any domain controller in the trusting domain can potentially connect to any domain controller in a trusted domain provided that a trust link between both domains is established.

If trust is revoked, the process of updating the trusted domain and secret objects within each domain ceases to occur. Similarly, if one or both of the PDCs in the trusting and trusted domain becomes nonfunctional and no one promotes the a BDC, the update process for these LSA objects is halted. In both cases, disruption of passthrough authentication results. The disruption does not occur immediately—one vulnerability in Windows NT is that trust relationships persist after trust has been revoked.

So what does all of this mean to security? The answer is that passthrough authentication is both complex and almost completely transparent to users, as well as system administrators. Even the LSA's trusted domain object is unknown to Administrators. The very minute that the Administrators from a trusted and trusting domain enter the trust password, the string that they enter is used by a cryptographic algorithm to produce the trusted domain object. The major point here is that compared to other security-related weaknesses in Windows NT, passthrough authentication is not a particular problem. Denial of service because of simultaneous crashes of PDCs in the trusted and trusting domains is the greatest threat. As of the time this book went to press, I am not aware of any Windows NT cracking tool that exploits trust relationships.

Transitive Trusts

In Windows NT, transitive trust (in which Domain A trusts Domain B, Domain B trusts Domain C, so Domain A effectively trusts Domain C) is *impossible*. The reason is that to set up a trust relationship in which A trusts B, you have to include a global group from A in a local group in B. Now A's trust stops because it is embedded in the local group in B. Windows NT's group inclusion rules do not allow a local group to be included in any other group, so the local group in B cannot be included in a local group (or any other group, for that matter) in C. The bottom line is that trust is so complex, transparent, and so limited in its pervasiveness (see the "Passthrough Authentication" sidebar) that subverting it is extremely difficult. Trust is not something that you have to lie awake at night worrying about if you have set it up properly in the first place and do not make changes that defeat security over time.

Securing Trusts

To ensure that trust between domains is secure as possible, consider implementing the following practical trust management measures:

- Avoid trust relationships completely when a domain contains extremely critical information or runs very critical services. Although trust is not the most dangerous function in Windows NT, it should not be implemented in some deployment contexts. Having a domain in which servers compute statements that go to stockholders trust any other domain, for example, is probably unwise from a security standpoint.
- In general, avoid bidirectional trust (in which Domain A trusts Domain B and vice versa). This trust arrangement is one of peer-to-peer trust, the most risky way to set up trust. Setting up a master domain or a

multiple master domain model is much better for security because it allows better central control over critical variables related to trust.

- Determine the identity of users before including global groups from trusted domains in local groups from trusting domains. You can do this by invoking the Windows NT Explorer on any domain controller after you complete the Trust Relationships panel in the User Manager for Domains. The groups and users from a domain that is to be trusted will now be visible if you highlight any file or folder in the Explorer, then go from File to Properties to Security, and click on Add. Keep scrolling down to view these new names and groups.
- Control trust by limiting privileges and access permissions for the local groups that include global groups from other domains. *The local groups are, for all practical purposes, the containment point for trust.* As mentioned previously, if you want users from a trusted domain to have little access to resources in the trusting domain, you can easily accomplish this goal by drastically limiting the privileges and access permissions for the local group(s) that include the users from the trusted domain.
- Regularly check the identity of users in the groups from trusted domains. Also review the trust relationships that exist and their directionality. Resource Kit tools such as NetDom and NlMon can greatly assist in this latter activity. Commercial tools such as the Enterprise Security Manager by Axent (`http://www.axent.com`), Kane Security Analyst by Intrusion.com (`http://www.intrusion.com`), and NOS Admin Manager by BindView (`http://www.bindview.com`) can also be very helpful.

What's New? Trust in Windows 2000

Windows 2000 supports trusted access between domains, but the nature of this trust differs substantially from Windows NT 4.0 trust. In Windows 2000, trust is based on Kerberos; trusting domains exchange Kerberos keys. Trust in Windows 2000 is established by default for all domains that have the same Active Directory. Trust is by default both bidirectional and transitive (such that if Domain A trusts B, and B trusts C, then A trusts C). It is still possible to establish trust between a Windows NT 4.0 domain and a Windows 2000 domain. In this case, trust is based on the Windows NT 4.0 mechanisms. Some security experts are concerned that trust in Windows 2000 is potentially more dangerous than in Windows NT 4.0, in part because of the default trust in the former. ◆

Making Backups

Backups are another important part of security maintenance in Windows NT. Making regular backups (particularly of critical systems) serves several extremely important functions:

- Making regular backups minimizes the possibility of losing online data. If worse comes to worse, you can always restore data from backups.
- It provides a good way of checking the integrity of critical system, data and application files. All you have to do is compare a current object on a system to the object stored on a backup—any change may indicate some kind of integrity problem.
- Restoring from backups is the best solution for bringing severely compromised or damaged systems back to their normal status.
- If a security-related incident occurs, making a backup right away is one of the wisest moves. It not only enables you to determine what is wrong by working on a "clone" system based on the original compromised system without having to work directly on the compromised system, but it preserves evidence—evidence that may be used in an investigation or even in a court of law. Backups copy programs such as cracking utilities that attackers may try to delete after they realize that someone has been monitoring them. Backups preserve such programs in addition to other evidence (for example, in the form of personal files) of unauthorized activity.

Backup Options

Windows NT offers the following three types of backup:

- **Full.** Every file and directory object is backed up, and the A (archive) bit is reset to indicate that the file has been backed up.
- **Differential.** Only files that have changed since the last full or differential backup are backed up. The backed up files do not contain information contained in an incrementally backed up file. A differential backup resets the A bit to indicate the file is a backed up version.
- **Incremental.** Only files that changed since the last full backup are included in the backup—each backed up file contains information that indicates the file has been incrementally backed up. An incremental backup does not reset the A bit on backed up files.

The types of backups your organization decides to make depend on your particular needs. An often-used backup strategy in commercial organizations is to make a full backup once a week and to make incremental backups daily.[7]

The native backup program in Windows NT is *BACKUP.EXE*. Many commercial backup programs deliver considerably more sophisticated functionality and are easier to use. These programs include their own executables installed during backup software setup. Some of the most popular commercial backup programs include

- Veritas' BackupExec, `http://www.veritas.com/us/`
- IBM's ADSM, `http://www.storage.ibm.com/storage/software/adsm/adsmhome.htm`
- Computer Associates' ArcServe, `http://support.cai.com/arcservesupp.html`
- Legato Systems' Celestra, `http://www.legato.com/`

Some backup tools such as Legato and Veritas can back up not only Windows NT systems, but also systems such as UNIX systems—a real advantage. Each particular tool has its own specific strong points and weaknesses.

Backup and Security

The following procedures enable you to get the maximum security-related advantages from the backup process:

- Make both full and incremental (or differential) backups according to a schedule. Adhere to the schedule vigorously. Unless you systematically schedule backups, backups are not likely to be made regularly.
- Use NTFS to maximize security of backups. Like any other program in Windows NT, backup programs cannot read (and thus store with the backup) any permissions except NTFS permissions. The same is true of ownerships. If you want to preserve permissions and ownerships in a backup, you have to back up from NTFS, not from other partitions.
- Realize that the backup operation is only the beginning of the whole backup cycle. Unless you put other sound backup measures into effect, the value of backups is likely to be limited. These measures include recording data about each backup (noting anomalies and so on), manually ensuring the goodness of each backup by attempting to restore a few randomly selected files, correctly labeling backups, storing backups in a place where unauthorized access is unlikely, rotating them offsite, and so forth.

---

[7] *Most commercial backup programs do not support differential backups, because recovering from one of those is extremely cumbersome. It is much easier to recover from incremental backups.*

- Periodically test to ensure that you can operationally restore (data, software, documentation, and so on) critical systems, especially network servers (for example, Domain Name Servers [DNS] and Dynamic Host Configuration Protocol [DHCP] servers) and application servers.
- Your backup package should have a backup scheduler that enables you to run the backup program as a batch job. Limit any access to this scheduler to personnel authorized to make backups. Don't allow others to have access; they may insert Trojan horse programs or schedule unauthorized backup jobs that may disrupt ongoing operations.
- Ensure that the system date and time on each system to be backed up are correct. If not, incremental (differential backups) may not be valid because they are so dependent on elapsed time. In addition, if you ever have to use a backup as evidence in a court of law, the correctness of the system data and time has much to do with the admissibility of the backup as evidence.
- Include workstations in your backup strategy. Even though the best security policy is to prohibit storing sensitive and valuable files on workstations, users will almost certainly store such files on their own workstations. If you don't include workstations in the backup strategy for your organization, valuable information assets that are accidentally deleted or become corrupted may be lost.
- Remember that restoring data to another partition on the same system or to another system affects how ownerships and permissions are restored. If you back up the C: drive on a system and restore the backup to the same drive, ownerships and permissions are preserved. If you restore to the D: drive, however, inheritance mechanisms are likely to (depending on the particular backup program used) determine the ownerships and permissions that apply to every file and folder.
- Be suspicious of logs captured by software packages that perform backups. Open files are likely to be missed during a backup, yet logs may indicate that all files have been backed up.
- Backed up information on tape is subject to unauthorized reading. It doesn't make much sense to set appropriate permissions and ownerships on files and directories, but then leave backup tapes that include the same files and directories in a publicly accessible area.
- Use the least-privilege principle with respect to Backup Operator rights, as discussed in Chapter 5.

Even if you make backups regularly, you will probably also want to regularly create *Emergency Repair Disks* (ERDs) for your critical servers. ERDs provide a convenient means of restoring certain parts of a system, particularly the system partition and the Registry.

Procedures for Making Emergency Repair Disks

Having an updated ERD is a critical part of any strategy for securing Windows NT systems; it provides assurance of the integrity of the Security Accounts Manager (SAM) database as well as one of the easiest recovery methods in case the this database becomes corrupted. After you have finished installing each system, you must initiate the creation of the ERD from that point on. You have several options when creating an ERD, the most basic of which is to invoke the Command Prompt and enter the following:

```
C:\>RDISK
```

This produces a backup written to the path `\%systemroot%\repair\` (Note that whatever data is in the *SAM.___* file is overwritten.) After the write is finished, a prompt gives you the option of backing up to floppy disk. If you choose this option, the data in `\%systemroot%\repair\` is written to a floppy disk immediately after the write to the hard drive. The problem with this option, however, is that it does not back up the SAM database. In most cases, a better alternative is to enter the following:

```
C:\>RDISK/S
```

The **/S** option ensures that all information in the SAM database is backed up. Now there are additional considerations. If you create an ERD for a domain controller, that domain controller's SAM database is likely to be very large—too large to store in entirety on a floppy. A better alternative is to suppress the write to floppy disk by entering the following:

```
C:\>RDISK/S-
```

After the write to the hard drive has been complete, you can use a Zip utility to zip the ERD, and then either use your NT Explorer to drag the icon for the zipped file to your A: drive or use the Command Prompt to enter the following:

```
C:\move C:\%systemroot%\repair\sam.___.zip a:\
```

This technique also offers the advantage of writing the *SAM.___* data to an independent (separate) medium from the one on which the SAM database is stored. If partitions within your hard drive become corrupted, you can rebuild from completely separate media—the floppy disk. If you ever need to rebuild critical system files from your ERD, you need only unzip the

SAM.___ data, expand it, and then copy it back to the original path. Good system administrators recognize the value of up-to-date ERDs. Many organizations require that ERDs be made once a week for each critical Windows NT Server.

Integrity Checking

Another critical step to ensure Windows NT systems are secure is to check the integrity of your systems. Integrity checking verifies that system configuration (including critical security-related settings), permissions, ownerships, accounts, group memberships, and executables have not been changed accidentally or maliciously. Although potentially tedious and time-consuming, integrity checking is one of the most critical parts of securing Windows NT (or for that matter, any type of system). Depending on the criticality of each system, you should check the system every one to six months. Critical systems such as a bank's financial transactions systems should be checked very frequently; other less-critical systems can generally be checked less often without undue negative consequences.[8]

The bad news is that, by default, inspecting Windows NT systems for integrity involves accessing utilities such as the User Manager for Domains, Server Manager, Event Viewer, Windows NT Explorer, and others—for each system. The task is indeed unmanageable if you choose to use normal access methods to check integrity. Fortunately, there are alternative methods of integrity checking. One is to use a third-party security administration tool such as:

- Axent Technologies' Enterprise Security Manager (ESM), `http://www.axent.com/Axent/Public/`
- Security Dynamic Technologies' Kane Security Analyst, (licensed to ODS Networks, Inc), `http://www.ods.com/security/products/ksa.shtml`
- BindView's NOSadmin, `http://www.anti-hacker.net/`
- Centrax Corporation's Centrax tool, http://solutions.sun.com/catalogs/all/Systems_Administration/Network_Administration/32731.html

Many of these tools enable you to define a policy that includes desired settings, and to evaluate the actual system settings compared to those

[8] *The major concern associated with inspecting less-critical systems infrequently is that these systems may in effect become "orphan systems" that are functionally excluded from system administration. Orphan systems become weak links in network security.*

defined by the policy. Another alternative (a potentially good one, because it is free) is to use the *Security Configuration Manager* (SCM) included in Service Pack 4 for Windows NT 4.0.

Using the Security Configuration Manager

The SCM provides a number of useful security-related capabilities. It performs a security evaluation on multiple Windows NT systems in addition to enabling system administrators to set the security configuration on these systems. One of the major potential advantages is that it allows centralization of system management from the *Microsoft Management Console* (MMC).

The basis for SCM's functionality is security configuration templates. These are *INF* files stored in the path `%systemroot%\security`. These templates provide two types of functionality: evaluation and modification of configuration. SCM also accommodates extensions to expand the functionality of this tool. You can use SCM to create different types of templates, including templates for policy settings, auditing, Registry values, user rights, group definitions, and the system services that run. Policy settings include (among other things) those that affect passwords, Kerberos-based authentication parameters, trust, account lockout parameters, system and network access parameters, and inheritance of access permissions.

SCM works in two modes: Configured System Analysis (which stores data about the host configurations and settings and checks this data against the template used to configure the host) and Unconfigured System Analysis. In Unconfigured System Analysis mode, you can use a command-line utility, SECEDIT, to build and modify templates.

The main downside with SCM is that many bugs in this tool have been reported. Among the problems that have surfaced is that systems that run SCM may crash; templates also may not propagate to other hosts correctly.[8] The SCM shipped with the CD-ROM for Service Pack 4 of Windows NT 4.0 is not the same version that is shipped with Windows 2000. The Windows 2000 version of SCM includes additional features such as the capability to assign security descriptors that apply to the objects in the Windows 2000 Active Directory and the ability to remotely analyze systems and apply security settings.

---

8 *SCM tool has serious memory leaks and hence does not scale. It also changes the ACL editor. I've tried applying a set of permissions to a directory hierarchy using both the new ACL editor and the SCM proper. The hierarchy had about 60,000 files. Both tools crunched for about 3 hours and then came back and said that they had essentially run out of memory (except the actual error message was not that useful). I would be really wary of using this tool in a production environment.*

Checking Ownerships, Permissions and Privileges

Items of particular interest during system administration activity are permissions and ownerships of high-level directories such as the root of each non-system volume and `%systemroot%`, `system32` in the C: partition, as well as shares (especially shares to critical resources). Examining permissions and ownerships of dynamic link library *(DLL)* and *EXE* files within the C: partition is also very critical. All the policy settings—Account, Trust, User Rights, and Trust Relationship—in the User Manager for Domains are so critical to domain security that they need to be regularly examined, as do the log settings in the Event Viewer. You should also regularly inspect memberships in privileged groups (for example, Local Administrators, Server Operators, and so forth) as well as in groups that get access to critical resources.

Tools for Integrity Checking

Another approach to integrity checking is not as broad (and therefore not as suitable in many operational environments), but from a technical perspective it is very simple and powerful. Tools are now available in the Windows NT arena that check the integrity of files. These tools, called "tripwire" tools, use cryptographic algorithms to compute a crypto checksum for each file defined in a configuration file. If anything is even slightly changed in a tripwired file, the crypto checksum also changes. Two of the leading tripwire tools for Windows NT are Tripwire for NT by Tripwire (`http://www.tripwiresecurity.com`)[10] and Enterprise Security Manager by Axent (`http://www.axent.com`). Pedestal Software (`http://www.pedestalsoftware.com`) also makes a tool called Intact, which has similar functionality. You can deploy one of these tools and just periodically check whether checksums for any number of critical files have changed. Note that a tripwire tool can even detect changes in file permissions, because access control list(s) (ACL)s in NTFS are contained in file headers. The same principle applies to ownerships.

You should also regularly check the Task Scheduler in systems to ensure that bogus (and possibly malicious) batch jobs have not been added. You can inspect this scheduler if you have IE4 by opening explore and checking the Scheduled Tasks entry. If you have IE3 or earlier, you can check the tasks at the command line by entering the `at` command.

Alternatively, you can tripwire this file to discover any unauthorized modifications.

---

[10] *Interestingly, the original version of Tripwire, developed by the COAST (now called CERIAS) Laboratory at Purdue University, has turned out to be one of the most valuable security tools in the UNIX arena.*

Be sure also to inspect the integrity of logon scripts (path: `\winnt\system32\repl\import\scripts`). In the Novell NetWare arena, numerous bogus logon scripts that produce results such as unauthorized privilege escalation have now circulated widely. It is only a matter of time before the same is true in the Windows NT arena. The best way to check the integrity of logon scripts is to tripwire them.

Installing Service Packs (SPs) and Hot Fixes

As previously mentioned, Service Packs (SP)s and hot fixes are potentially very useful in countering the security-related vulnerabilities that continually emerge in Windows NT. The downside is that many service packs that have been released have not functioned correctly after their initial release. Even corrected versions of some service pack releases (for example, Service Pack 4 for Windows NT 4.0) have continued to present significant difficulties, including failing to actually fix the vulnerabilities and inflicting system instability (including a significant elevation in the tendency to crash). Appendix C, "Significant Security-Related Features of Service Packs 3 through 6a for Windows NT 4.0," lists the many security-related SP features in Service Packs 3–6.

In most cases, the best strategy with respect to SPs and hot fixes is to wait for a while after they are initially released before you install them on a large-scale basis. You might install them on a few, noncritical machines shortly after they are released for the purpose of discovering how well they work and what their limitations are. You should also closely monitor newsgroup postings (such as WIN2KSECADVICE postings) to watch for reports of problems with the new SPs and hot fixes. *The major mistake people make with SPs and hot fixes is to prematurely install them on production servers.*[11] Another mistake is not installing them at all. Installing them in the wrong order can also sometimes prove catastrophic. Some fixes, such as SP6a's features that substantially reduce Windows NT vulnerability to IP-spoofing attacks, are very valuable from a security perspective.

It is safe to assume that sooner or later you will and *must* (for the sake of security) install each SP and hot fix after the major bugs in them have been eliminated.

---

[11] *If you can, make a duplicate of your production servers, using a ghosting program (big disadvantage: you have to take the machine off line to create the image) or just using a backup program. Then apply this image to a test machine and install the SP on that.*

Useful Registry Changes

Chapter 5 covered how to secure the Registry in terms of permissions, ownerships, user access to Registry edit tools, and so forth. After you have secured the Registry, the next step is to consider whether any additional changes to the Registry are useful from the standpoint of your organization's security needs. These changes focus on modifying Registry values and adding additional keys. Numerous changes go hand in hand with SPs; many features in SPs do not go into effect until appropriate Registry modifications are made. The same is true with some hot fixes.

Cautions and Preparations

The Registry is truly a strange beast. One ill-advised modification can cause serious system or network disruption or even subversion of security. Additionally, one of the main problems in effectively dealing with the Registry is the mindset that UNIX system administrators bring with them when they transition to Windows NT administration. To a large degree, UNIX system administration involves making changes to critical configuration files, especially in the */dev*, */etc*, */usr*, and */var* directories. Many UNIX system administrators assume that the same basic principle applies to Windows NT security; the greatest public manifestation of this mindset is in many of the so-called Windows NT security checklists that describe one Registry hack after another as a prescription for good Windows NT security. As well-intentioned as many of these checklists are, they frequently miss the mark, prescribing largely superfluous or sometimes costly changes (from the standpoint of system performance or functionality limitation). Although there are some similarities in dealing with the Windows NT Registry and UNIX configuration files, hacking away at the Registry is no panacea for Windows NT security.

Before you modify the Registry of any Windows NT machine, you should first back up the Registry. Creating an ERD may turn out to be the easiest method in many cases. Other techniques for backing up and restoring the Registry are also available. The Resource Kit for Windows NT 4.0 offers two Registry backup utilities: *REGBACK.EXE* and *REGREST.EXE*. You can use REGBACK to back up the Registry to virtually any directory; after using this tool, be sure that permissions for this directory do not allow universal Read and/or Write access. REGBACK also compresses the Registry by removing wasted space within the hives. Domain controllers tend to have large Registries; having compressed backup versions makes options such as writing to a floppy disk possible. You can use REGREST to restore the Registry from a REGBACK backup. If you use REGREST, however, it is best that you first boot to a neutral installation.

REGEDT32

To modify the Registry, you need a Registry Editor. REGEDT32, the Windows NT Registry Editor, is one of the best choices because not only does it enable you to change permissions and ownerships (unlike REGEDIT, the Win9x Registry Editor[12]), but it also saves files in a compressed format that is still viewable using this tool. You can, therefore, use REGEDT32 to view and change either the Registry or any hive—a major advantage. REGEDT32 offers several modes in the Editor dialog box:

- Binary (for editing binary or hexadecimal values)
- DWORD (for editing binary, hexadecimal, or decimal values)
- Multistring
- String

You should be careful of DWORD mode because it allows the display of decimal values. The default display value is hexadecimal. It is very easy to see a decimal value and assume that it is a hex value, or vice versa. Worse yet, you might make the same error when you edit values. It is best to use DWORD mode only to read, not change, values.

Other choices are available such as REDEDIT and third-party tools.

REGEDIT

REGEDIT (the Win9x Registry Editor) is preferred by many Windows NT system administrators because of its superior Find feature and ease of use. REGEDIT has several significant limitations, however:

- It does not support changing Registry permissions and ownerships.
- When you use it to save part or all of the Registry as a hive, it writes the data in a format that is viewable only through a text editor (for example, the NotePad Editor).
- You cannot set permissions, ownerships, and auditing for Registry keys.
- You cannot view or edit the value data types `REG_EXPAND_SZ` and `REG_MULTI_SZ`. It actually does so, but with sometimes disastrous results (as per the following).

[12] *Note that the Windows NT Registry differs completely from the Win9x Registry. REGEDIT, the Win9x Registry Editor, however, can be used to edit either Registry. The same is not true for REGEDT32.*

- If you try to view a `REG_EXPAND_SZ` value, REGEDIT incorrectly shows it as a binary data type. If you try to change either of these data types, REGEDIT saves it as the `REG_SZ` type; the key now no longer works as expected. This can have disastrous effects and can actually keep the system from booting in severe cases.

Third-Party Tools

Still another option is to use a third-party tool such as Axent's Enterprise Security Manager to view and edit the Registry. You can also use NT Diagnostics to view the Registry, although, unfortunately, this utility does not enable you to make any changes. Finally, Policy Editor allows the system administrator to view and edit the Registry.

Hacking the Registry

All the following procedures describe how you can use REGEDT32 to hack the Registry. To invoke this editor, just go from Start to Run, and then enter the following:

```
REGEDT32
```

Whenever you need to add a key or value, first click on the folder for the key under which you want to add the new one. This highlights the folder for the "parent" key. Next go to the Edit menu bar and drag down until you reach Add Value (see Figure 6.10). Add Value also enables you to add a value. The main practical significance is that you can view this type of value only in the right portion of the screen when you have opted for the Tree and Data display option under the View menu.

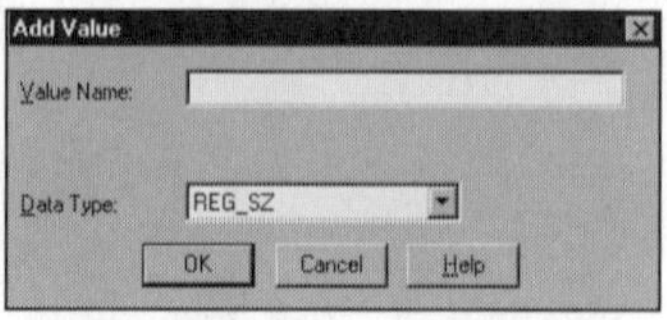

Figure 6.10 *Add Value panel.*

You now need to enter the name of the value you want to add as well as the type of value in the Add Value panel. Note that the value type you specify is critical. If the value type should be `REG_MULTI_SZ` but you choose `REG_DWORD`, it is extremely unlikely that the changes you are making will actually work. In some cases, the changes may be disruptive to your system. After you finish specifying the name and type of the value you are creating, click on OK. Another panel displays (see Figure 6.11). The particular name of this second panel will be <_______> Editor. The first word of the name depends on the type of value (string, double word, and so on). Therefore, if you choose to create a value that is in a double-word format (after you select DWORD in the Add Value panel) another panel titled DWORD Editor) displays. Note also that Registry entries are not case sensitive!

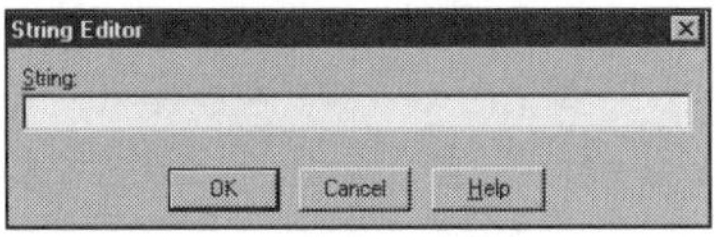

Figure 6.11 *String Editor panel.*

Enter the data the value should have, and then click on OK. Finally, bring up a Tree and Data view to inspect the Registry tree to ensure that the value is where it is supposed to be and confirm that the data and type you have intended to assign are indeed as you expect (see Figure 6.12). It is so easy to make a mistake when you have a GUI interface.

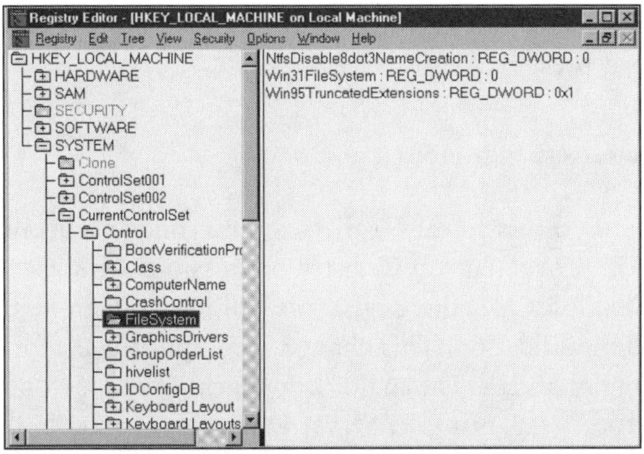

Figure 6.12 *Tree and Data view.*

In many cases a Registry value already exists; some Registry changes therefore involve only a change in the data in a value. In these cases, you need to ensure that you have selected the Tree and Data view of your Registry. On the right side of the screen, move the pointer to, and then double-click on, the line that contains the name of the value you want to edit (refer to Figure 6.12). The same editor shown in the Figure 6.11 appears, enabling you to change the value.

Which particular Registry changes are likely to be useful in your operational environment? Although the focus is on useful changes, a few changes are covered here because, although they are highly touted in some circles, they may involve more cost than benefit. A few are in fact outright dangerous to the health of your system or to your sanity! These hacks are organized into three groupings: recommended, recommended in some but not other environments ("partially recommended"), and not recommended at all. In all cases, I assume that you have at least installed SP 3 (and sometimes also SP 4) for Windows NT 4.0 first, although running the most recent SP available is generally best for security. Many of these changes will not work at all if your systems are not at least running SP4.

Recommended Changes

Restrict the anonymous user from certain types of access that Everyone gets. The advantages of this hack were discussed in several previous chapters. In brief, this hack prevents the anonymous user from obtaining access to many of the resources that Everyone can access.

Hive: `HKEY_LOCAL_MACHINE`

Key: `\System\CurrentControlSet\Control\LSA`

Value: `RestrictAnonymous`

Type: `REG_DWORD`

Data: 1

Targets: Servers and workstations

Restrict *remote* access to the Registry to everyone except Administrators. Despite the improvements in Registry permissions with each subsequent release of Windows NT, the Registry is still too vulnerable to unauthorized reading and modification. This change accomplishes exactly what the name implies—remote access. The major drawback is that it stops "near-Administrators" (for example, Server Operators) from obtaining access to the Registry, thus in some cases escalating the number of people who have to be given full Administrator rights to be able to perform their jobs.

```
HKLM\System\CurrentControlSet\Control\
SecurePipeServers\WinReg
```

Type: It doesn't matter—you don't change this.

Value: This also doesn't matter—you don't change this, either. What you have to do here is only to ensure that the `WinReg` key has the proper permissions: Full Control to Administrators and System, Read to Everyone.

Targets: Servers and workstations.

Restrict access to service settings to only Administrators. This setting determines whether users can change entries below Services in:

`HKLM\System\CurrentControlSet\Services`

Type: It doesn't matter once again—you don't change this.

Value: This also doesn't matter—you don't change this, either. Ensure only that the `Services` key has the proper permissions: Full Control to Administrators and System, Read to Everyone.

Targets: Servers and workstations

Restrict Scheduler access to only Administrators. The Scheduler poses a high degree of security risk in that it runs as SYSTEM. Access by non-Administrators can enable them to schedule commands that run with virtually unlimited privileges, potentially allowing complete subversion of system security. The impetus for making this change, therefore, is reasonably clear-cut; as few people as possible should have access to the Scheduler.[13]

`HKLM\System\CurrentControlSet\Control\LSA\`
`SubmitControl`

Type: `REG_DWORD`

Value: 1

Targets: Servers and workstations

Enable the display of a logon message. Many, if not most, major organizations have some kind of requirement for warning against unauthorized access to their systems. Normally, this warning is included in the logon screen. Windows NT allows you to write both a caption (title) as well as a logon message, and then have this message displayed immediately after each user presses the Ctrl+Alt+Del sequence to initiate a logon. The user has to click on OK before the logon panel itself appears. Changing the Registry is actually only one of several ways you can ensure that a logon message displays. Note also that it is easy to fit in more characters than the LegalNoticeText field appears to allow by using the NotePad Editor to paste in a text message from a file.

`HKLM\Software\Microsoft\Windows NT\`
`CurrentVersion\Winlogon`

Type: `REG_SZ`

Value: Whatever text you want to insert

Target: Primarily workstations, but it is also a good idea to do this on servers

[13] *This has no effect if MSTASK.EXE (IE4) has been installed. You can't restrict access to that scheduler, AFAIK.*

Allow extended filenames on all file systems. Chapter 3, "The Windows NT Network Environment," describes a vulnerability in which an attacker can gain unauthorized access to files by convincing the target platform that the attacker's platform is based on an old implementation of Server Message Block (SMB) that understands only the 8.3 naming convention for file systems. This next hack fixes the problem by requiring the system on which this change is made to always assume that it and any client use the extended filename system (255 characters).

`HKLM\System\CurrentControlSet\Control\FileSystem\NtfsDisable8dot3NameCreation`

Type: `REG_DWORD`

Value: 1

Target: Servers and workstations

Clear system pagefile during shutdown. By default, the system pagefile is *not* cleared during shutdown. Someone could write an Application Programming Interface (API) that could copy critical objects such as crypto keys and password hashes from it. Clearing the system pagefile during shutdown precludes such attacks.

`HKLM\System\CurrentControlSet\Control\`
`Session Manager\MemoryManagement\`
`ClearPageFileAtShutdown`

Type: `REG_DWORD`

Value: 1

Targets: Servers and workstations

Restrict ability to add print drivers. Print drivers often run with SYSTEM privileges. If a user can install one or more print drivers (the default Registry setting), that person could install a malicious program that runs as system instead. If you change the `Server` key value to 1, only Administrators and Server Operators (or, in the case of workstations, Power Users) and Print Operators can add print drivers. The disadvantage is that printers are user-specific, so Administrators can't install them for users. However, if the printers are hosted on NT print servers, users can still connect to them and print, without installing print drivers. But, in a NetWare environment, this is a serious problem.

`HKLM\System\CurrentControlSet\Print\Providers\`
`Lanman Print Services\Servers`

Key: `AddPrintDrivers`

Type: `REG_DWORD`

Value: 1

Targets: Servers and workstations, but making this change on servers is far more important

Put base objects in Protected mode. Access to certain base objects such as threads and semaphores is not by default restricted to Kernel mode processes. Making this Registry change puts them in Protected mode, making unauthorized access to and modification of these objects much less likely.

```
HKLM\System\CurrentControlSet\Control\
Session Manager\ProtectionMode
```

Type: `REG_DWORD`

Value: 1

Targets: Servers and workstations, but making this change on servers is more important

Disable IP source routing (requires that at least SP5 has been installed). As mentioned previously, source routing is dangerous in that it is necessary for certain kinds of network attacks. You can disable source routing at the host level by making the following changes:

```
HKLM\System\CurrentControlSet\Services\TCPIP\
Parameters\DisableIPSourceRouting
```

Type: `REG_DWORD`

Value: 0 – default (enables source routing)

1 – Disables source routing if IP forwarding is also enabled

2 – Disables all IP source routing

Targets: Servers and workstations, but making this change on servers is in many respects more important

Partially Recommended Hacks

Remove the name of the last user to log on. If you make this hack, the username will be blank in the logon panel that comes up on the machine on which this change is made whenever any user attempts to log on (either directly to that machine or using that machine as a client). This may keep a perpetrator from learning the names of user accounts to attack. Although this hack seems to offer a lot of security value, the advantages are offset by the practical problems it causes. Many users do not, for example, remember their username and may consequently burden your help desk or system administrators. This hack therefore makes only the "partially recommended" list.

`KLM\Software\Microsoft\Windows NT\`
`CurrentVersion\Winlogon`

Create new key called `DontDisplayLastUserName` under `Winlogon`

Type: `REG_SZ`

Value: 1

Targets: Primarily workstations

Enable logging that captures system backups. As mentioned previously, one of the exposures in Windows NT event logging is that the Event Logger omits certain, possibly critical events. If you make this change, system backups are recorded in entirety. If you back up all 2,000 files on a server, 2,000 audit entries result. This is exactly the downside of this hack—namely, that you can run out of disk space very quickly. Therefore, I have given only a partial recommendation for this hack, which is most appropriate when extremely valuable files reside on a server, and it is important to know about any accesses, including access by a backup program.

`HKLM\System\CurrentControlSet\Control\Lsa\`
`FullPrivilegeAuditing`

Type: `REG_Binary`

Value: 1

Targets: Servers and workstations

Restrict Guest access to System and Application log. By default, these logs are readable by every user, even the Guest user. Although, I hope you have left the Guest account disabled on all your Windows NT 4.0 systems—someone (perhaps even a perpetrator) who gains access as Guest can read the System and Application logs. No significant disadvantages for this hack appear to exist—on the other hand, it really does nothing more than provide a little extra security to those who have already implemented good security measures such as leaving the Guest account disabled.

`HKLM\System\CurrentControlSet\Services\EventLog\`
`<LogFileName>`

Key: `RestrictGuestAccess`

Type: `REG_DWORD`

Value: 1

Targets: Servers and workstations

Disable cached logons. Cached logons are a mixed blessing. They make client authentication possible in environments where remote MSV1_0 authentication would be impossible. On the other hand, they elevate security risk by not only leaving the workstation in charge of authentication, but also by leaving cache files in workstations (which are usually not secured as well as are servers) that an intruder might access to copy password hashes for domain access. Whether you implement this hack should probably depend more on whether user logons are all within a local network or not. If they are not, you should be more willing to allow cached logons. (Note that by default, 10 cached logons are allowed.)

`HKLM\Software\Microsoft\Windows NT\`
`CurrentVersion\Winlogon`

Create a key named `CachedLogonsCount`

Type: `REG_SZ`

Value: 1 or greater, with a maximum of 10—the higher the number, the greater the number times a user can log on when a domain controller is not available. Set to 0 to disable cached logons.

Targets: Workstations

Disable LAN Manager (LM) authentication (requires that at least an SP4 installation). This setting is designed to eliminate the use of the LM challenge-response mechanism because of its inherent security flaws. In addition, the setting can be used to implement a stronger form of authentication for hosts running SP4 or higher. This effectively limits types of hosts with which a Windows NT computer can communicate. The potential advantage for security is that you can reject authentication requests from low-end clients. The potential downside, depending on the setting chosen, is that if all clients are not Windows NT Workstations (or higher) running SP4 or higher, you can lock out authentication requests that prevent users from remotely accessing hosts within a domain.

`HKLM\System\CurrentControlSet\Control\Lsa\`
`LMCompatibilityLevel`

Type: `REG_DWORD`

Value: 0–5 (0 is default)

- **Level 0.** Send LM response and NTLM response; never use NTLMv2 session security.
- **Level 1.** Use NTLMv2 session security if negotiated.
- **Level 2.** Send NTLM authentication only.
- **Level 3.** Send NTLMv2 authentication only.
- **Level 4.** DC/Server refuses LM authentication.
- **Level 5.** DC/Server refuses LM and NTLM authentication (accepts only NTLMv2).

Levels 0–3 apply to all computers when acting as clients. Levels 4 and 5 apply only to the authenticating server (normally a domain controller). If you have nothing but Windows NT 4.0 Workstations that run SP4 as clients, Level 5 (recommended value in this environment) increases security considerably. If a client cannot use NTLMv2 authentication (a type of double challenge-response between the client and server and also between the server and client), the client's authentication request is rejected. The problem with settings 4 and 5 is that they do not stop the clients from sending down-level hashes, which can be captured and decrypted. A value of 0 (necessary in environments with clients other than Windows NT) causes the host to send both LM and NTLMv1 responses, thus accommodating weaker authentication. A value of 1 causes the host to negotiate NTLMv2, if possible, but allows it to downgrade if necessary. A value of 2 causes the host to send only NTLMv1 requests. A value of 3 causes the host to send only the NTLMv2 response. For this to work, the server connected to (DC if in a domain) needs to understand NTLMV2, for example run SP4 or higher. A value of 4 causes the server to accept only NTLMv1 and NTLMv2 requests and to reject LM authentication altogether (a reasonable alternative in an all-Windows NT environment in which some hosts run SP3, others run SP4 and up).

This hack targets servers and workstations, but making this change on clients is more important.

Require SMB signatures. This fix, which requires the installation of SP3 or up, requires that a host that needs to authenticate to another first present an SMB signature. Without a signature, a remote Windows NT system cannot establish such a connection. The main value, therefore, is to lock out "man-in-the-middle" clients (that is, clients inserted between the legitimate client and server that can obtain the same access to server resources as the legitimate client). The downside is that this fix can lock out low-end clients (pre-Windows 98) from authenticating.

To require message signing on the server, set the following value:

```
HKLM\System\CurrentControlSet\Services\
LanManServer\Parameters\ RequireSecuritySignature
```

Type: `REG_DWORD`

Value: 1

Targets: Servers running the Server Service

To require message signing on the clients, set the following value:

```
HKLM\System\CurrentControlSet\Services\Rdr\
Parameters\ RequireSecuritySignature
```

Type: `REG_DWORD`

Value: 1

Target: Clients running the Workstation Service

Enable SMB signatures. This fix enables a client to present an SMB signature during attempts to connect with a server that requires them. An SMB signature provides some assurance of the integrity of the SMB traffic sent. Note that a different path for enabling this feature on the client is required than from this signature on servers.
To enable this on the clients, set the following value:

`HKLM\System\CurrentControlSet\Services\Rdr\`
`Parameters\ EnableSecuritySignature`

Type: `REG_DWORD`

Value: 1

Targets: Any machine running the Workstation Service

To enable this on machines running the Server Service, set this value:

Hive: `HKEY_LOCAL_MACHINE`

Key: `System\CurrentControlSet\Services\`
`LanManServer\Parameters`

Value: `EnableSecuritySignature`

Type: `REG_DWORD`

Data: 1

`Targets: primarily workstations`

Prevent use of standard Registry Editors. If you don't want anyone to access the Registry using tools such as REGEDT32 and REGEDIT, this change is for you; it definitely makes your Registry more secure. Remember, however, that someone may still be able to access the Registry through a third-party tool or custom API. The downside is potential inconvenience to system administrators[14]—REGEDT32 and REGEDIT are the two most widely used Registry Editors.

`HKEY_CURRENT_USER\Software\Microsoft\Windows\`
`CurrentVersion\Policies\System\`
`DisableRegistryTools`

Type: `REG_DWORD`

Value: 1

Targets: Servers (and possibly workstations in environments requiring high levels of security)

---

[14] *You can set this using System Policy and disable this setting for Administrators.*

Prevent anyone from being able to shut down a system without logging on. Unless you make this change, someone who is not logged on can invoke the shutdown panel by pressing Ctrl+Alt+Del on the desktop. On the other hand, good physical security is probably the best solution for controlling against unauthorized shutdown and other similar threats.

`HKLM\Software\Microsoft\Windows NT\`
`CurrentVersion\Winlogon`

Key: `ShutdownWithoutLogon`

Type: `REG_DWORD`

Value: 1

Targets: Both servers and workstations

AllocateFloppies. This Registry modification disables remote access to the floppy disk drive. This is a reasonable thing to do in some circumstances. However, it also disables remote access to Administrators. A better way to control access to the floppy disk drive is using the FLOPLOCK program from the Resource Kit, which allows ACLs to be assigned for floppy drive access.

`HKLM\Software\Microsoft\WindowsNT\CurrentVersion\Winlogon`

Create new key named `AllocateFloppies`

Type: `REG_SZ`

Value: 1

Targets: Both servers and workstations

AllocateCDROMS. This hack can disable the CD-ROM and is thus similar in logic (with similar advantages and drawbacks) to the AllocateFloppies hack.

`HKLM\Software\Microsoft\WindowsNT\CurrentVersion\Winlogon`

Create new key named `AllocateCDROMS`

Type: `REG_SZ`

Value: 1

Targets: Both servers and workstations

Not Recommended Hacks

CrashOnAuditFail. This Registry entry causes a system to crash whenever the Event Logger has an error condition that disrupts audit logging or the Security (Audit) log fills. In most cases, a crash is a highly undesirable outcome.

`HKLM\System\CurrentControlSet\Control\Lsa`

Create new key named `CrashOnAuditFail`

Type: `REG_DWORD`

Value: 1

Targets: Both servers and workstations

AutoAdminLogon. This hack allows anyone who is physically present when a Windows NT system boots to gain access to an automatically set up logon session with Administrator privileges, even though the user has not entered any username or password. This Registry modification is therefore potentially very dangerous.

`HKEY_LOCAL_MACHINE\SOFTWARE\Microsoft\`
`Windows NT\CurrentVersion\Winlogon`

Type: `REG_SZ`

Value: 0 to disable AutoAdminLogon, 1 to enable it

Targets: Both servers and workstations

When turning off AutoAdminLogon, also make sure you delete the entries DefaultDomainName, DefaultUserName, and DefaultPassword in the same location. These contain the domain name, username, and password of the administrative user who is automatically logged on.

RestrictNullSessAccess. As mentioned previously in Chapter 3, "the Windows NT Security Exposures," changing the default value of this key (path: `HKLM\System\CurrentControlSet\Services\ LanmanServer\Parameters`) to 0 allows null session access through shares and named pipes. Doing so increases the dangers of null sessions substantially.

Windows NT Security Consulting: Caveat Emptor

Windows NT security consulting work performed for organizations is not always "up to par." Consider a consulting recommendation recently made to an organization—that this organization secure its Windows NT–based applications by embedding security control in the Registry (for example, to depend on Registry key settings to control application security). This recommendation was seriously flawed. The Windows NT Registry is one of the most difficult parts of Windows NT to secure because of the potential need for any process (privileged or unprivileged) to access the Registry and because the Registry is accessible through many different access methods. In addition, if application security is controlled at the level of the Registry, application developers or troubleshooters may have to be the owners of certain Registry keys, a highly undesirable practice from a security perspective. The bottom line is that the Registry is by no means conducive to application security in Windows NT; basing application security on Registry settings is risky if not downright dangerous.◆

Alerts

If used correctly, Windows NT's logging capabilities can help you spot activity such as logon attempts by unauthorized people and access to critical resources by users for whom such access is not authorized. One of the problems with logging, however, is that the Event Logger dumps data to files while you, the system administrator, carry on with your other activities. You may or may not read log data shortly after critical events occur. Windows NT fortunately offers a complementary capability to logging—namely, alerting. Alerts, like the Event Logger's logs, are triggered whenever certain events occur, but they display in the form of messages sent only to designated persons. These people invoke the Performance Monitor of the system(s) that receive(s) these messages, and then scroll through a queue of incoming messages. Windows NT's alerting capability is more conducive to real-time intervention by system administrators for two reasons:

- Alert messages will almost certainly be less voluminous than the logs that the Event Logger produces.
- The messages can be sent to a central console to which system administrators have continual access.

The Security (Audit) log is configured through selecting one or more of seven event categories in the User Manager for Domain's Audit Policy panel (please refer to Figure 5.16 if you need a quick reminder concerning these seven categories).

Alerting is similar to the Security log in this respect, except that in alerting the categories of events are called *counters*. The number of counters is also greater than the number of event categories in security logging. Counters include Bytes Transmitted Per Second, Errors Granted Access, Errors Logon, and scores more. Errors Granted Access indicates that a user or program attempted to access a resource but did not have the necessary permissions or rights. The Errors Logon Counter is for failed logon attempts. Note that with the exception of Errors Granted Access and Errors Logon, most of the counters are not very related to security.

In Windows NT Servers, you can enable alerting by going from Start to Programs to Administrative Tools to Server Manager. Pull down the Computer menu to Services. Scroll through the list of services until you come to Alerter. Highlight it, and click on OK (see Figure 6.13). In Windows NT Workstations, you go from Start to Settings to Control Panel, and then double-click on the Services icon. A list of services (just like the Windows NT Server panel in Figure 6.13) displays. Highlight Alerter, click on Start, ensure that it is set to Automatic, and then click on OK. You also must access the same panel and start the Messenger service in any system that is to receive the alerts.

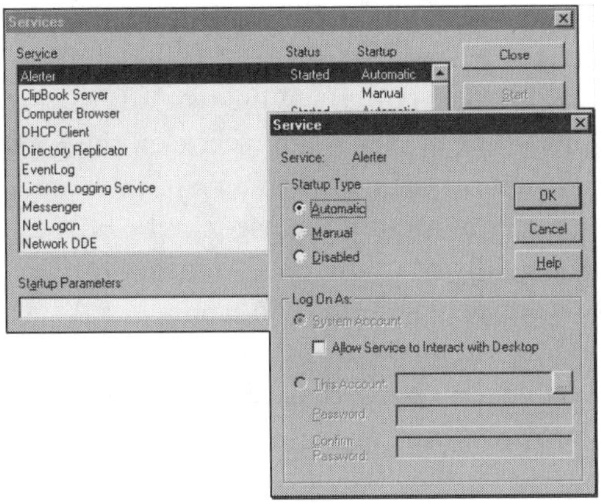

Figure 6.13 *Service panel from which you can enable the Alerter service.*

Just *enabling* the Alerting service is not enough; you next have to set alerting parameters. Do this by going from Start to Programs to Administrative Tools to Performance Monitor. (Alternatively, you can invoke the **Run** command and just enter **perfmon**.) Pull down the View menu bar until you reach Alert; select this option. Then pull down the Edit menu bar until you find Add to Alert. After you select Add to Alert, the panel in Figure 6.14 comes up. You need to ensure that the default computer and server listed in the uppermost field is correct (it should be). Next, scroll through the counters until you find the one you want. Highlight it, and then determine what your alert criteria will be. You can Alert If the event designated by the counter is over or under the numeric value indicated in the Instance field. So, for example, you could select the Errors Logon counter, and then click on the Over option in Alert If, and then enter the value of two in Instance. These settings cause an alert to be generated any time more than two bad logons occur (no matter which particular user or combination of users has (have) caused the failed logons).

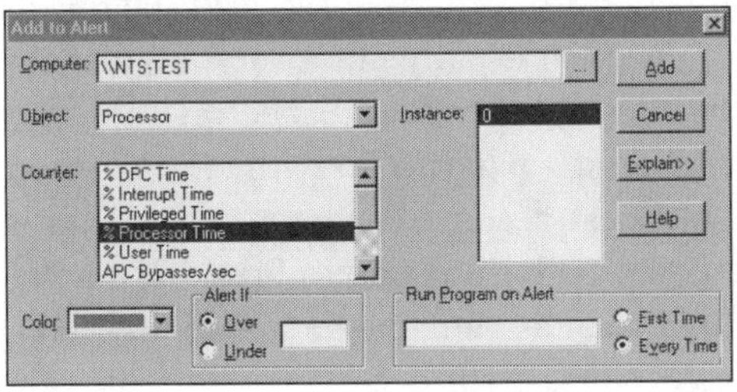

Figure 6.14 *The Add to Alert panel.*

Last, you have to set Alert Notification. Do this by invoking the Server Manager, then selecting Server, and then clicking on Alerts. The panel shown in Figure 6.15 comes up. (In Windows NT Workstation, you can bring up the Control Panel, then double-click on the Server icon, and then click on Alerts.) You need to enter the name of the computer to which alerts will be sent or the username(s) of the user(s) who will receive them. Be sure to use the username(s) listed in the User Manager for Domains or the Alert service will not recognize your entry. To read alerts, bring up the Performance Monitor on the system to which alerts are sent (which in certain cases could be the system that generates the alerts). Pull down the View menu bar to Alerts. Any alert messages display; you can scroll through them. After you have finished reading each, you can delete it (using the Delete Alert option under the Edit menu bar) and move on. You can edit any Alert by using the Edit Alert Entry function, which is also under the Edit menu bar. You can save the alert settings by using the Save Alert Settings As function under the File menu bar.

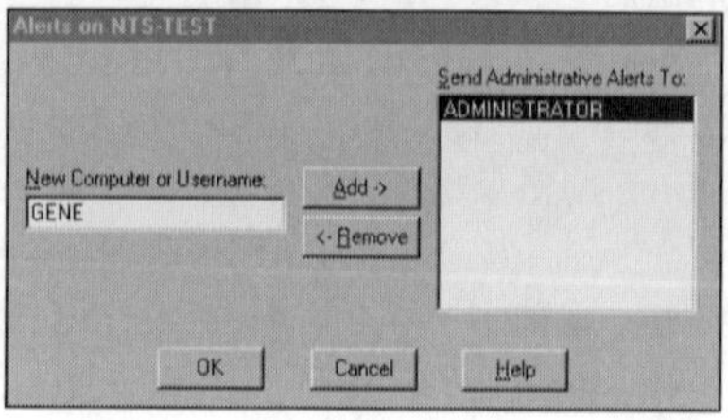

Figure 6.15 *The Add Notification panel.*

Alerting is potentially a very valuable function. It provides a good way to send prompt notification when certain critical events occur, provides a sizeable range of counters, is extremely configurable, and enables you to direct alerts to certain people at designated locations. On the downside, alerts are somewhat tedious to configure, most of the counters are not very related to security, and if the Alerting service is enabled, it causes a performance hit (although usually not a very large one). When you install Windows NT, the Alerting service is turned off.

The choices concerning what to do with alerting should depend on your operational and business needs. Alerting is certainly most useful if you suspect that someone has been trying to break into systems or gain illegal access to something such as valuable data files. Receiving an alert whenever a logon or resource access error occurs may be very valuable. Note that if in a domain you want to be alerted if a user has a failed logon attempt, you need to set alerting on *all* domain controllers. In most environments, the

Alerting service is less critical in workstations than in servers (because more critical data and applications are likely to reside in servers).

Fault Tolerance

Fault tolerance refers to continued availability despite outages and failures. The major types of fault tolerance apply to data and systems. Fault tolerance has shifted from a more-or-less minor concern a decade ago to a truly major concern in today's computing environments. Availability of systems and services has in fact become the *most* important security- and operations-related concern in many organizations.

Windows NT supports several types of fault tolerance by providing interfaces to the hardware used to implement fault-tolerance solutions. Several types of these solutions are commonly used in Windows NT environments: uninterruptable power supplies, symmetric multiprocessing, clustering, redundant array of independent disks, and data replication.

Uninterruptable Power Supplies

Uninterruptable power supplies (UPSs) are in essence very large batteries that can be used to power systems in case of power failure. Windows NT interfaces with UPSs to determine whether power failures have occurred and to produce an alert if the Alerting service is set appropriately. UPSs are extremely important not only to keep computing operations running, but they also can prevent damage to hardware in addition to possible data losses that can result from a sudden loss of power.

Symmetric Multiprocessing

Symmetric multiprocessing (SMP) refers to the workload-balancing capabilities of Windows NT that helps keep systems from crashing by distributing the load on additional processors when one processor begins to experience too great a load.

Clustering

Clustering capabilities can help ensure operational continuity. Clustering creates a pool of processors within a group of machines such that if one or more processors become overloaded or crash, others compensate.

Redundant Array of Independent Disks

Redundant array of independent disks (RAID) works through a disk controller that ensures that data from one drive is written to one or more redundant drives (see Figure 6.16). Windows NT supports several different types of RAID solutions:

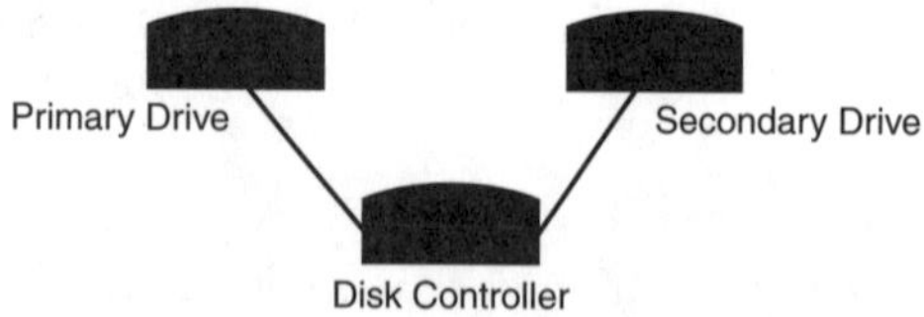

Figure 6.16 *Redundant array of independent disks hardware architecture.*

- **Striping (RAID-0).** With the striping method, data are written as data stripes to two or more disks within the RAID hardware architecture. If two drives are installed, the data stripes are spread evenly across both drives. RAID-0 is used only to speed performance. It does not increase fault tolerance. On the contrary, it actually decreases fault tolerance because if any one of the drives in the stripe set fails, all data on the stripe set are lost.
- **Mirroring (RAID-1).** This is perhaps the most easy-to-understand RAID solution. With mirroring, the same data stored on one drive are mirrored to another. The most sophisticated version of RAID is striped data sets with parity distributed across redundant drives.
- **Striping with parity (RAID-5).** As implied by its name, this last solution also produces data stripes written to several drives. The problem with striping is that if one of the redundant drives fails, part of the redundantly stored data are not available. To counter this potential problem, data are also stored as high-level parity code. Parity in this case is the result of applying a cryptographic algorithm to data, yielding a special, compact output. It is possible to rebuild original data from this output, which (like data stripes) is distributed among the redundant drives. Therefore if one redundant drive fails, it is possible to recover data from the others, even if the desired data have been written to a data stripe on the failed drive.

Data Replication

Data replication also provides data duplication, but uses different mechanisms from RAID's. In data replication, the Windows NT Replicator service continually exports data from an export server to an import server. The goal is to mirror on the import server the contents (data, applications, and so forth) on the export server (see Figure 6.17). Data replication requires that the Windows NT Replicator group have Full Control of all replicated directories. One of the most important security-related considerations regarding data replication, therefore, is to limit membership in the Replicator group to the Replicator account. Everyday users should *not* be members of Replicator—if they are, they can subvert data replication and gain unintended access to files and applications. Although data replication is a reasonably effective fault-tolerance solution, RAID solutions are currently used considerably more in the Windows NT arena because of RAID's superior performance characteristics in addition to other reasons.

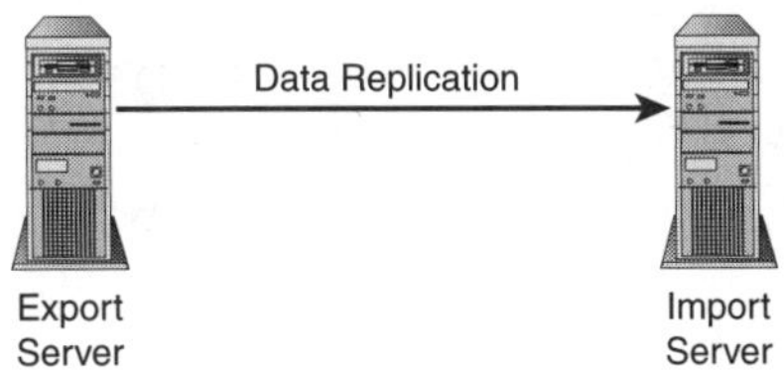

Figure 6.17 *Windows NT data replication.*

Fault-tolerance solutions are especially important in Windows NT, where denial of service is the overall biggest security concern. You should investigate how Windows NT's interface to these solutions can be used in your operational environment.

Conclusion

This chapter has described some important things you can do to elevate security in your Windows NT systems after these systems have been deployed. Security maintenance is truly at the heart of what needs to be done to keep systems running securely—but it is not easy. This chapter is lengthy for a reason: There are many things to be done time and time again if you want your systems to be secure. The key is to develop sound, written procedures and to get buy-in from both other system administrators and managers. Without these elements in place, it is unlikely that effective security maintenance will ever transpire.

Let's turn our attention to networking and network-based services to look closely at security-related vulnerabilities in addition to solutions for countering these vulnerabilities.

Checklist for System Administrators

1. Determine the best course of action in dealing with administrative shares, and then implement the solution. In general, it is best to disable ADMIN$, C$, D$, and shares for other partitions if doing so does not cause network applications to break.
2. Secure other shares as needed. At a minimum, change the default permission that allows Full Control to Everyone. Ensure that no user shares allow access to the system drive.
3. Ensure that no unexpected trust relationships have been set up, that the trust model is appropriate for business needs, and that the appropriate global groups in trusted domains are included in the appropriate local groups in trusting domains.
4. Set up procedures for making backups that meet your organization's business and operational needs. Ensure that backup media are properly labeled and are stored in a secure location.
5. Establish procedures for checking the integrity of systems. Using a tripwire tool to help in this regard is advisable.
6. Continue to evaluate and install SPs and hot fixes as appropriate.
7. Make the essential changes in the Registry that make systems more secure. In particular, restricting anonymous access, restricting remote access to service accounts to only Administrators, displaying a logon message, allowing extended filename creation, clearing the system pagefile at shutdown, putting base objects in Protected mode, and disabling IP source routing are good moves for security. Try to keep the Registry as stable as possible and test changes in a nonproduction environment first.
8. Enable the Alerting service as security needs dictate. Set up a central alerting console to receive the alert messages that hosts send.
9. Implement fault-tolerance solutions as needed. If you use the Replicator function in Windows NT, be sure that users are not members of the Replicator group.

7

Basic Network Security Measures

"Effective Windows NT network security is at best elusive, and quite difficult at worst."
–Professor Gene Spafford

Chapter 5, "Configuring Windows NT Server for Security," and Chapter 6, "Maintaining Windows NT Security," described the most critical measures for securing Windows NT at the system level, starting from system installation and extending into the maintenance phase. I hope by now you agree with the widely accepted notion that trying to secure networks without trying to secure the systems within is for the most part a futile exercise. Now it is time to turn our attention to the most important things you can do to elevate network security itself.

Network security in Windows NT involves more considerations than you might imagine. These include deploying Windows NT properly in the first place, implementing host-based security measures, designing and implementing firewall solutions, using sound net-work architecture solutions, implementing *virtual private networks* (VPNs), implementing monitoring and intrusion-detection measures, ensuring that interoperability programs are secure, and many others. Some of these con-siderations are specific to Windows NT, whereas others are part of what might be described as plain, everyday good network security solutions—solutions that are effective regardless of the specific platforms connected to the network. These solutions are explored in detail in this and following chapters.

Windows NT's Strengths and Weaknesses in Network Security

If security is your main consideration, Windows NT as a *standalone* entity provides no great cause for concern. If you use a tool such as the C2 Configuration Manager, you can make a standalone Windows NT system sufficiently secure.[1] Consider, in contrast, Windows NT in terms of the potential for *network* security. Windows NT presents something of a dilemma. Granted, Windows NT has numerous features that can substantially elevate network security. One of the benefits of MSV1_0 authentication, for example, is that it is designed to avoid sending cleartext passwords across the network (provided, of course, that the client understands MSV1_0 challenge-response mechanisms). You can also easily control the set of network services that run on each Windows NT machine. Windows NT even offers a packet-filtering capability that enables a system administrator to block or reject or accept service requests on the basis of the particular protocol (Transmission Control Protocol [TCP], User Datagram Protocol [UDP], or Internet Protocol [IP]) and destination port.

The major downside of Windows NT network security is that Windows NT networking is based on implementations of older and largely nonmainstream mechanisms, such as Server Message Block (SMB) protocol and the NetBIOS Application Programming Interface (API). Securing SMB and NetBIOS are truly the formidable challenges.

SMB authentication is largely driven by the client. This problem is directly related to the fact that SMB protocols are *inclusive*—any later protocol version must also support all the previous versions' functionalities. Because later protocols tend to be more security conscious, this backward compatibility can allow a malicious client to "dumb down," in effect bypassing many of the built-in security mechanisms. SMB also includes mechanisms such as the AndX mechanism (discussed in Chapter 3, "The Windows NT Network Environment").

NetBIOS is to some degree dependent on query mechanisms available to anyone, regardless of privilege level. These mechanisms provide updates concerning NetBIOS names, network addresses, ongoing sessions, and so forth.

NetBEUI is not much better from a security perspective. Because it is not a routable protocol, however, its dangers are at least limited mostly to local network environments.

Another critical area in Windows NT network security is the *Distributed Component Object Model* (DCOM). DCOM, the main thrust of most of Microsoft's new client/server technology, includes functions such as

[1] *Never overlook the importance of physical security. Even the most rigorously secured machine can be compromised through unsecured physical access.*

Windows Messaging, distributed Internet applications, the *Internet Information Server* (IIS), the *Internet Explorer* (IE), DirectDraw and DirectSound, and others. DCOM is Remote Procedure Call (RPC)-based and therefore utilizes the underlying mechanisms of the RPC protocol. RPC implementations (which invariably depend on the efficient but less-than-reliable UDP protocol at the transport layer) are not noted for their security capabilities. Worse yet, most DCOM applications do not use any of the security functionality that may be built into RPC, thus leaving a Windows NT network even more vulnerable to attacks. To further complicate matters, DCOM programmers are too often focused on application functionality, not security. Although DCOM is not a "showstopper" from a security perspective, you really must nevertheless take it into consideration in your Windows NT network security strategy.

Configuring and Starting DCOM Applications

To set up DCOM, as well as the highly related COM 32-bit applications, Windows NT offers the DCOM Configuration Tool for applications. Before you use this tool, you must go through a few initial steps. You need to invoke DCOM Configuration to determine the properties (for example, security and location) of the application. On the host on which the client application runs, you also need to specify where the server application for this client will be accessed or how it will be started. Similarly, you must designate the name of the user account(s) allowed to access or invoke the application. Default access permissions are defined in a Registry value named `HKLM\Software\Microsoft\Ole\DefaultAccessPermission`.

To start the DCOM Configuration Tool, go to Start, select Run, and then enter ***dcomcnfg***. ◆

Deploying Windows NT Properly

Deploying Windows NT systems properly is one of the most critical considerations in Windows NT network security. The first and foremost consideration is choosing whether to run Windows NT in the first place. In other words, you should deploy Windows NT when business and operational needs dictate that it should be deployed—and avoid using Windows NT when these needs indicate otherwise. Issues to consider when making this decision include degree of required security, existing homogenous environments, and other interoperability issues.

The number of security-related vulnerabilities that have surfaced in this product in relatively few years (especially the number of network-related vulnerabilities) dictate its use in low- to moderate-risk environments. At this point, I don't in general advise that you use Windows NT in business-critical environments (for example, environments in which critical financial applications run) unless you are prepared to devote considerable additional effort and resources (for example, installing an intrusion-detection system and then monitoring and maintaining it properly) to secure your Windows NT systems and networks.

Another important consideration is whether Windows NT will be used in a homogeneous network environment (that is, an environment in which Windows NT Servers and Workstations are used exclusively) or whether it is deployed in a heterogeneous environment. The latter is far more common. Despite some inherent security-related vulnerabilities in the Windows NT network environment, however, deploying Windows NT in a homogenous environment (that is, running only Windows NT Servers and clients) is the best option from the perspective of Windows NT security. Why? Interoperability too often entails the cost of the liabilities of backward compatibility. Additionally, interoperability in software too often includes shortcut mechanisms that provide connectivity and/or functionality at the expense of security. Also consider that Microsoft has designed the highest level of NT security for environments in which one NT box communicates with another.

SAMBA Client provides a good example of the dangers of a mixed-platform environment. SAMBA Client is an application designed to enable UNIX workstations to connect to resources on PC-based platforms. This application is, in fact, a client implementation of the SMB protocol. Although certain SAMBA Client implementations are more secure than others, in general SAMBA Client spells potential trouble in the Windows NT arena; it uses SMB-based connectivity mechanisms independently of built-in NT share mechanisms (as you will read shortly, the SMB protocol is very conducive to security.). Worse yet, tools that disable SAMBA security features to allow SAMBA Client to function as a network attack tool are widely available on the Internet. The real problem with SAMBA Client, therefore, is that someone with access to a UNIX workstation may be able to gain unauthorized access to resources on Windows NT platforms or, minimally, to cause the NT platforms to crash. This problem is so serious that certain Microsoft employees have declared SAMBA an "illegal client." Don't get me wrong, it is a very useful tool; but because it is so easily modified, it can (and has already been many times) used for malicious purposes.

Firewall Solutions

In the most fundamental sense, firewalls are a security barrier between two networks. Firewall hosts insulate one network from security-related threats originating in another network. The most common deployment of firewalls is insulating the gateway to an organization's internal network from the Internet. Firewalls are now so common that failure to deploy them could conceivably constitute failure to exercise "due care" (that is, reasonable precaution) in one's InfoSec practice.

When "push comes to shove," the basic problem with Windows NT from a network security perspective is that its own security mechanisms are insufficient to allow it to fend for itself on the network. If you want Windows NT systems to be secure, therefore, you have to deploy effective security solutions other than setting Windows NT network security-related parameters appropriately. Firewalls provide one of the best mechanisms in this regard. One thing that is reasonably nice about Windows NT from a security perspective is that many of the security-related threats in this product can be controlled by just blocking input destined for dangerous ports. Firewalls are well-suited for this purpose. Although firewalls that do little more than screening traffic bound for certain ports are certainly the least sophisticated, they can serve a very critical function in the Windows NT networking environment.

Finding the Best Firewall

Regardless of the specific types of platforms connected to your networks (see the section titled "Identifying the Best Platform" in this chapter), firewalling them is an extremely important step for the sake of security. Many vendors make firewall products—which is best in the Windows NT network environment? The answer is that vendor firewalls vary in quality, but what generally is more important is the level of functionality that the firewall provides. Firewalls generally provide one or more of the following functions: packet filtering, state-conscious packet filtering, and proxies.

Packet Filtering

Packet filtering is screening input on the basis of characteristics of that input. At the most basic level, for example, a firewall might allow packets from one particular IP address range but reject packets from all other IP addresses. Other bases of filtering include type of protocol (for example, NCP, and SMB), port number, packet direction, packet state (that is, ACK, SYN, established), and other criteria.

State-Conscious ("Stateful") Packet Filtering

Packet filtering may in some settings be sufficient, but in some kinds of reasonably sophisticated attacks a program can send packets that impersonate packets which would normally be sent in a continuing connection to a destination host. The program could, for example, send ACK packets even though SYN packets had never been sent to establish a connection. Sending ACK packets in this manner could fool a simple firewall; it would receive the ACK packets and assume that the packets were legitimate because they were part of a continuing connection. A state-conscious firewall keeps track of the state of all incoming connections; among other things, the firewall blocks all unfamiliar ACK and FIN packets (that is, packets that are not part of a continuing connection).

Proxies

Proxies ("application gateways") are "store-and-forward" connections. In a proxy schema, a proxy server is the intermediate destination of an incoming connection, but the connection stops at this point (see Figure 7.1). The proxy server then initiates a *new* connection to the true destination system. Proxies are advantageous in that they result in a central point of control for incoming connections. If a network administrator sees a malicious connection, it is easy to kill it. Another advantage of proxies is that they enable firewall administrators to embody rules in the proxy mechanisms. At the most elementary level, proxies can require that users enter a password to connect to a remote system. Better yet (given the limitations of password-based security), proxy applications can be used to effectively monitor the security of connections. If incoming input appears to be attack-related (for example, someone from an unknown address tries to execute the **net use** command on a Windows NT Server within an internal network), the proxy program can kill the connection, log it, and possibly also send an alert.

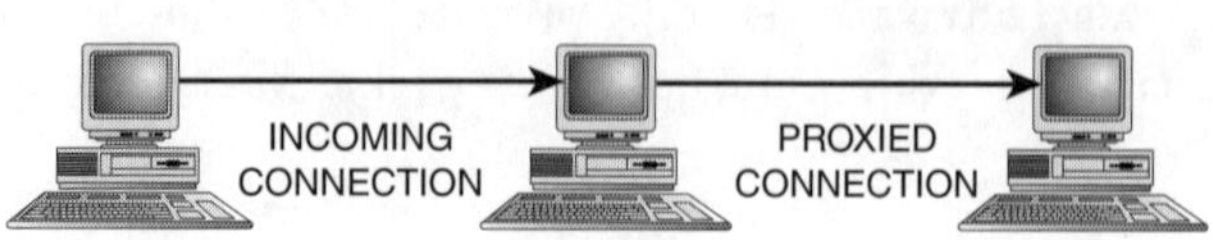

Figure 7.1 *Schematic of proxy connections.*

Identifying the Best Platform

Another firewall issue in the networking arena is whether it is better to use a Windows NT–based firewall or a UNIX-based one. This issue often disintegrates into a "techno-religious debate." A number of individuals from the perpetrator community have made Internet postings in which they claim it is ridiculously easy to defeat Windows NT–based firewalls. Because false bragging runs rampant in this community, however, the validity of these claims is suspect. What is most important is how the firewall is configured after it has been installed and deployed. Not all vendors do as good a job of paying attention to critical considerations, such as the number of network services run by default.

All things considered, a Windows NT firewall with very few services running is more secure as a network entity than a UNIX firewall with a full complement of services running. A Windows NT firewall configured and deployed properly is also likely to be more secure than a UNIX firewall that is not. One of the main disadvantages of Windows NT firewalls is that Windows NT has several flaws in virtual memory management. They impair performance under conditions of high throughput. Windows NT systems are, for example, prone to "page fault" conditions in which a link between a virtual or physical address is not specified in a pagefile. The Virtual Memory Manager (VMM) consequently must go to the paging table to locate the needed information instead of continuing with normal operations.

Implementing a Suitable Packet-Screening Capability

Packet screening is almost certainly the most effective single network security control mechanism in the Windows NT network environment. To implement a suitable packet-screening capability, it is first necessary to be aware of the services that typically run in Windows NT's network environments and the ports used to initially connect to these services. Table 7.1 lists the services and ports, although this list is by no means exhaustive.

Table 7.1 *Familiar Services and Ports Used in Initiating Service Requests in Windows NT Networking*

Service	Port
Echo	UDP 7
Chargen (character generator)	UDP 19
FTP	TCP 20 and 21
Telnet	TCP 23
SMTP (Simple Mail Transfer Protocol)	TCP 25
WINS (Windows Internet Name Service)	UDP 42
DNS (Domain Name Service)	UDP (and sometimes TCP) 53

continues ▶

Table 7.1 Continued

Service	Port
DHCP (Dynamic Host Configuration Protocol)	UDP 67 (request), 68 (reply), and 69
HTTP (Hypertext Transfer Protocol)	TCP 80
POP3 (v3 of Post Office Protocol)	TCP 110
NNTP (Network News Transfer Protocol)	TCP 119
NTP (Network Time Protocol)	TCP 123
RPC (Remote Procedure Call) (primary RPC port)	TCP and UDP 135
Nbname (NetBIOS Name Service)	UDP (and sometimes TCP) 137
Nbdatagram (NetBIOS Datagram)	UDP 138
Nbsession (NetBIOS Session)	TCP (and sometimes UDP) 139
SNMP (Simple Network Management Protocol)	UDP 161 and 162
RPC (Remote Procedure Call) (secondary RPC port)	TCP and UDP 1024 and higher[2]
Microsoft CIFS (SMB in Windows 2000)	TCP and UDP 445

The Risk Factor with Windows NT Services

Any service can, of course, be the target of an attack. Consider, however, the services listed in Table 7.1 and what they contribute to the risk factor in your Windows NT networks. The Echo service can, for example, be used to launch an echo attack. All a perpetrator must do is issue a spoofed echo to a system, and then have that system echo the input back to the spoofed address. The spoofed machine now re-echoes the input it receives back. In not too long a period of time, both machines crash because they are flooded with echo input. The character-generator service, discussed previously in Chapter 4, "Basic Windows NT Security Exposures," can also be used to launch denial-of-service attacks. Note, however, that these vulnerabilities do not apply exclusively to Windows NT systems. You can also launch echo and chargen attacks against UNIX and NetWare systems, for example.

All things considered, the services that a pose the greatest problem for Windows NT network environments are RPC and the NetBIOS-based services (Nbname, Nbdatagram, and Nbsession). Recall from Chapter 3, that RPC is based on the UDP protocol, making this service especially difficult to secure. To date the majority of RPC attacks in the Windows NT

[2] *RPC also uses ports 1024–1028, but this service's port utilization is not limited to this range. Sometimes even higher numbered ports, such as 1032, are utilized.*

arena have been denial-of-service (DOS) attacks. The Nbname service is subject to probe attacks in which perpetrators can gather NetBIOS-related data useful in attacking systems. The Nbdatagram service is used in client/server communications and in broadcasts; it is vulnerable to DOS attacks. Finally, the Nbsession service is used in establishing and maintaining sessions. Tools such as l0phtcrack listen for traffic bound for this port on a victim machine to capture passwords. Session- and share-hijacking tools also target the default Nbsession port.

Knowing about these "trouble ports" is important because a good Windows NT network security strategy entails selectively blocking some or all of these ports. A good firewall, of course, is based on the premise that whatever is not permitted is denied. Your initial strategy should, therefore, be to block all ports unless a business and/or operational reason for leaving these ports open exists. You should implement this strategy in a network security design that blocks packets at two levels: the external gateway and the inner firewall.

The External Gateway

Figure 7.2 depicts two firewalls, one (the uppermost one in the diagram) placed at the external gateway to the internal network. Relative to the other, this firewall is the outer firewall. The basic strategy is to block most incoming services requests. Allowing SMTP-based traffic from the outside to mail servers within the internal network[3] is one possible exception. In an environment with very high security needs, it is appropriate to have a *demilitarized zone* (DMZ) with hosts that spool the incoming traffic if you are just using a filtering router as your primary means of protection. If on the other hand the external server supports proxies, the resulting direct connection into the internal network eliminates a large number of possible security-related problems. In short, avoid allowing an untrusted user to connect directly to an internal machine, regardless of the destination port and other considerations.

A firewall[4] strategy based on high security needs therefore might allow incoming traffic bound for TCP port 25 but deny all other traffic. You may also have a business- and/or operations-related reason to allow certain File

[3] *Another possible strategy is to place mail servers on the DMZ. This leaves them more vulnerable to attack from external sources, but can boost network performance in that less mail-related traffic will in all likelihood need to be passed through the firewall.*

[4] *You do not have to deploy a firewall per se to implement a suitable firewalling strategy. You can also use Microsoft's Routing and Remote Access Service (RRAS) to achieve similar results. Advantages of using commercial firewall products as opposed to RRAS and similar solutions is the superior performance and logging capabilities and the addition of a stateful packet filter in the former.*

Transfer Protocol (FTP), HTTP, and, perhaps even NNTP traffic to certain internal servers. If your need for security is not quite so high, you might allow even more types of incoming service requests from the outside. The main strategy to adopt if you want to fend against externally initiated attacks against internal Windows NT systems is to block service requests bound for the ports through which perpetrators and rogue programs generally attempt to exploit Windows NT networking vulnerabilities. The most important ports to be used in a filtering strategy include the following:

- TCP 42
- TCP and UDP 135
- UDP 137
- UDP 138
- TCP and UDP 139
- TCP and UDP 1024, and higher

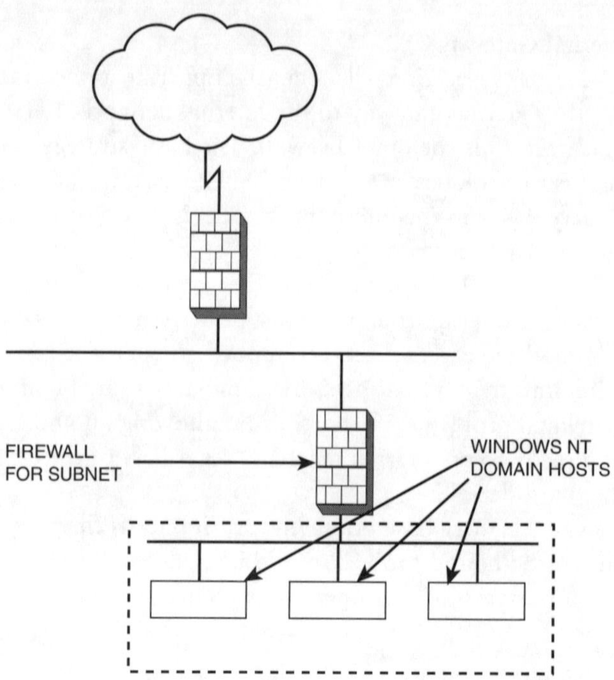

Figure 7.2 *Deployment of firewalls within a network with Windows NT systems.*

The Inner Firewall

Figure 7.2 depicts an inner firewall that selectively screens input to a subnet. A firewall that provides security in this manner creates a "screened subnet." Screened subnets are one of the best measures for network security. Attacks may, after all, originate either from external sources, or they may originate from within one's internal network. Setting up a packet-screening strategy for a firewall that protects a subnet protects that subnet independently whether the origin of attack is from the outside or from another part of the internal network. Note, however, that screened subnets have limitations in that they cannot protect themselves from attacks which originate from within the subnet itself. Subnet-based packet-filtering strategies generally differ from gateway-based ones. If you were to block traffic destined for port TCP port 139 at the entrance to a subnet with a multitude of Windows NT machines, for example, you could seriously disrupt functionality.

Screen Strategies

Establishing suitable rules for screened subnets is often not as easy as doing so at the level of the external gateway. Consider, for example, the scenario in which a Windows NT domain in one subnet extends trust to a domain in another subnet. If you set up a packet-filtering strategy in one subnet that blocks all traffic bound for ports, such as TCP port 139 in hosts within the subnet, for example, the result is disruption of passthrough authentication. You also disrupt MSV1_0 authentication and share access between clients in one subnet and servers in another. The bottom line is that at each inner (subnet) firewall you need to allow traffic to and from other IP addresses of Windows NT (and Win9x) machines in other subnets that need to communicate with Windows NT and Win9x machines within the subnet in question. In general, this requires allowing traffic bound for the following ports of these machines:

- TCP 42 (if you use WINS)
- TCP and UDP 135
- UDP 137
- UDP 138
- TCP and UDP 139
- TCP and UDP 1024, and higher

An effective screening strategy also allows incoming and outgoing service requests based on the other necessary services such as mail, news, file transfers, and others. If you determine that clients in the IP address range `72.33.89.222` through `77.33.89.254` in one internal subnet need access to an FTP server with an IP address of `72.33.90.121` in another subnet, for example, you would include a rule in the second subnet's firewall that allows incoming FTP requests with destination IP address `72.22.90.121` from the source IP address range 72.33.89.222 through 77.33.89.254. Remember, too, that if you allow any SAMBA Client connections, SAMBA is an SMB implementation that utilizes basically the same RPC and NetBIOS ports that a Windows NT or Win9x client would.

Setting up suitable screening rules, especially for inner (subnet) firewalls, is more difficult in real-life than you might imagine. Complicating factors include the sheer number of services that run, the need for dynamic assignment of IP addresses to clients because of the limited availability of address space in today's network environment, and political factors (for example, conflicting operational needs among organizations). Consider, too, that when a Windows NT Server receives a connection request and starts a session to a client, the server typically moves that session to a higher port, making prediction and control of continuing sessions on the basis of port number virtually impossible. (See the "Trusted Ports in Windows NT?" sidebar for a discussion of trusted ports.) One practical implication is that even though you may be able to elevate security substantially, you never can *completely* control Windows NT network security using packet-screening measures.[5] If you carefully design and implement a sound packet-screening strategy, on the other hand, you can *mostly* control against the kinds of security threats described in previous chapters of this book. In most cases (and certainly in business-critical network environments), therefore, expending the resources and living with somewhat reduced network throughput that invariably results is more than justified by the substantial increase in security for your Windows NT systems.

Filtering Outbound Traffic

This section considers only inbound traffic-filtering rules. You may also want to screen outgoing traffic (for example, outbound packets bound for UDP port 138) to control against certain kinds of dangerous service requests that originate from inside a given network or subnet. ◆

Your ability to secure a Windows NT installation is directly proportional to the number and complexity of services that you run on the machine. If you run nothing more than SMB file and print sharing, achieving security is considerably easier than if you run DCOM-based programs with random ports.

[5] *Packets from continuing connections are handled somewhat differently by stateful firewalls and screening routers. Stateful firewalls know about ongoing connections and pass these packets through accordingly. Screening routers generally require that the router administrator modify ACLs to set the "established" rule for each desired continuing connection from source to destination host. When packets bound for a particular host reach the router, the screening program searches its ACLs and allows them to pass through because they are part of an established connection.*

Trusted Ports in Windows NT?

If you are familiar with the UNIX operating system's networking conventions, you know what "trusted ports" are. Trusted ports, port numbers 0 through 1023, allow only root-initiated processes to bind to them. Therefore if a UNIX server needs to listen on port 20 for FTP, for example, by convention that server can connect to port 20 only if root initiates the connection request. This convention provides some small level of security to client programs that connect to a low-numbered port, because they can provide some assurance that a root-level user actually started the server. This assumption was a major design consideration in early firewalls, and is still even used in some firewalls today.

Windows NT does not *have trusted ports. Any process, regardless of privilege level, can potentially bind to any port in Windows NT networking. There are in fact several reasons why having trusted ports would not work in this network environment. Recall from Chapter 3, for example, that because SYSTEM rights apply only locally, SYSTEM processes use null sessions (which do not by any stretch of the imagination have elevated privilege levels) to connect remotely to other computers. The absence of trusted ports in Windows NT is, however, no catastrophe from a security perspective; trusted ports in UNIX have not been all that helpful in providing security control. If a network were to consist of all UNIX machines, trusted ports would elevate security substantially. Today's networks tend to be heterogeneous, however; a UNIX box that receives a connection request initiated by an MS-DOS–based networking client usually considers the request to be from the "root user" on the MS-DOS box. It is easy, therefore, for users of non-UNIX platforms to circumvent the trusted-ports convention anyway.* ◆

Proxies in the Windows NT Networking Environment

As discussed previously in this chapter, proxy servers provide potentially stronger security than packet screening if proxies are configured appropriately. Why then shouldn't you forget about packet screening and just use proxies to protect your Windows NT systems in the network environment? The answer is that perhaps you should, but proxies and Windows NT do not always live well together. Proxy connections, for example, do not always work well in conjunction with MSV1_0 authentication because proxies may disrupt the flow of data between the client and server. Multiple proxy connections for client/server communications magnify the problem considerably. Therefore, if you are thinking about deploying one or more proxy-capable firewall(s) to protect your Windows NT systems in an internal network, you should be a little wary of rushing right ahead. In sum, proxy-based network security solutions can and may work; and if they do, they will provide a higher degree of security if they are designed and implemented correctly. Remember, however, that it is also possible that they will cause disruption of Windows NT networking.

What's New? Packet Filtering in Windows 2000

Appropriate packet-filtering strategies in Windows 2000 vary according to the way Windows 2000 is deployed. If you run Windows NT 4.0 and Windows 2000 systems in the same domain ("mixed mode"), Windows 2000 uses the same networking mechanisms that Windows NT 4.0 currently uses. The same packet-filtering strategy discussed in this chapter is, in this case, appropriate. If a domain consists of all Windows 2000 systems, many of the filtering rules presented in this chapter are no longer necessary. The NetBIOS name and NetBIOS session services are, for the most part, no longer needed[6] *in the latter deployment context, allowing both external and internal firewalls to screen out all traffic destined for ports 137 and 139. Windows 2000 utilizes the* Lightweight Directory Access Protocol *(LDAP) extensively; the default LDAP static port binding is TCP 389. The default static port for SMB sessions is now TCP and UDP 445. If Windows NT and Windows 2000 domains establish trust links, however, trust is based on Windows NT 4.0 mechanisms; the same filtering rules presented in this chapter are once again suitable in this context.* ♦

Architectural Solutions

This section deals with a very important consideration related to network architecture. Where within your network should you place critical servers and even domains themselves? Specifically, this section covers placement of Web servers, FTP servers, Gopher WAIS and Archie servers, mail servers, news servers, and firewalls.

Web Servers

Where should you locate your Web servers? These are a number of alternatives and related security issues.

Because of the immense popularly of Web-based services, this discussion starts with the proper placement of Windows NT Web servers. The first thing you need to consider is whether each Web server is an external or internal Web server. The former is located *outside* your internal network, either on a true DMZ (sometimes more precisely called an "external DMZ"—that is, one without any firewall-based protection, as shown in Figure 7.3) or on an "internal DMZ, (that is, a protected segment behind the firewall).

---

[6] *Assuming that NetBIOS over TCP/IP has been disabled.*

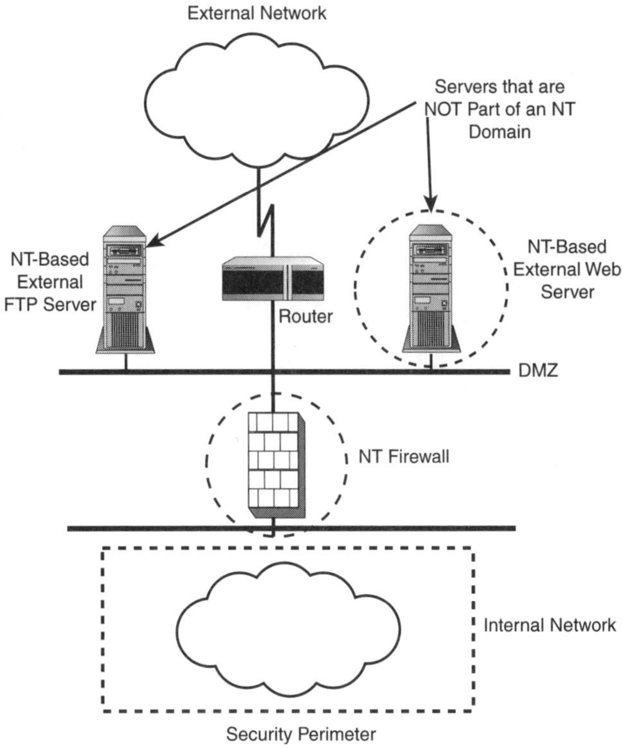

Figure 7.3 *Recommended placement of external Web servers, external FTP servers, and firewalls.*

Protecting External Web Servers

External Web servers are usually intended for public access; the security-related risk is therefore typically extremely high. Someone from virtually anywhere can readily attack almost any external Web server. Providing firewall-based protection for external Web servers is the best thing to do for the sake of security. A downside, however, is the impact on throughput; the Web users will experience slower performance than if the Web server had been placed on the DMZ and the traffic bound for the Web server will slow down the firewall itself. The major tradeoff in this case, therefore, is security versus performance.

If you place your external Web servers on a DMZ, you should be especially cautious with respect to the Web server's relationship to other machines within your network. Any machine on a DMZ should be considered a "throwaway" machine,—that is, if someone breaks into that machine, the intruder will not have an advantage with respect to attacking machines within the internal network. As such, a Windows NT–based Web server on a DMZ should not be part of any Windows NT domain within your internal network (refer to Figure 7.3 once again). If the Web server were part of the domain and if a perpetrator were to gain unauthorized access to the Web server, many bad scenarios could follow. The attacker could at a minimum install a packet-capturing device or program on the compromised Web server to capture data, such as passwords, sent between machines as noninteractive remote logons between these machines occur. You may think: "We don't log in and users don't access those machines." Remember that if you use any of the native Windows NT administration tools that use SMB authentication to the IPC$ share, the path over which the authentication-related traffic travels is a primary target for password-capture programs.

If the external Web server is on a protected segment behind the firewall (that is, an internal DMZ), the Web server *could* have the same level of protection as many hosts within your internal network. Nevertheless, this particular deployment of the Web server *does* open a major connectivity avenue into your internal network.[7] It is therefore in all likelihood better to keep *any* external Windows NT Web server from being part of any Windows NT domain within your internal network for reasons similar to those concerning potential domain membership for Web servers on a DMZ. If the domain hosts within your internal network are in screened subnets, from a networking standpoint they will still be afforded a higher level of protection (that is, through both an outer and an inner firewall) than if they are not. Having different levels of network security for hosts within a domain is not a good idea because the hosts afforded a lower level of network security will create weak links within the domain. The bottom line is that from a security perspective, each Windows NT domain should be treated as a single "zone" within your network; all machines within a zone should have the same level of security.

---

[7] *The Microsoft MDAC/RDS exploit as detailed in security bulletin MS99-025 enables an attacker to execute arbitrary commands on a vulnerable IIS server. This vulnerability provides one of many superb reasons why you should keep public an IIS server outside of your internal networks.*

Protecting Internal Web Servers

Internal Web servers generally have a different set of associated security risks. Their placement within the network makes them potentially more resistant to attacks from the outside if they are properly firewalled. On the other hand, more sensitive information tends to be available through internal Web servers; these servers are intended for access only by internal employees, contractors, and so forth. If someone changed the content of a Web page on an internal Web server used to disseminate sensitive employee salary information, for example, the results could be catastrophic. Remember, too, that although many more attacks now originate from external sources, the deadliest and costliest of attacks continue to originate from within.

From a network architecture perspective, the optimal strategy for securing internal Web servers is to determine who is supposed to access the information they hold, and then ensure that they are placed in the right portion of the network. If many people, some of whom are employees and some of whom are from the population at large, need access to a Web server, it is generally better from a security perspective to place that server on a DMZ. Alternatively, it may be better to split the server function by implementing two virtual servers—one an internal server for employees, the other an external server for public access. It is not generally advisable to deploy the physical platform that houses both servers on an internal network, however. At any rate, deploying Windows NT Web servers as member servers in Windows NT domains is generally acceptable from a security perspective because these servers do not present the same types of dangers that external Web servers (which should not be member servers) do. The growing number of bugs discovered in most types and versions of Web servers available in the Windows NT arena, however, make Web servers poor candidates to share the same hardware platforms with other critical services.

Note that three-tier Web applications (in which the client and Web server are outside the network, but multiple servers such as the database servers are inside the internal network) in theory violate some of the principles in this chapter. These applications can nevertheless be secure if programmers follow basic principles of writing secure applications (for example, ensuring that elevated privileges are rescinded at every exit from every routine) when developing the client and server software.[8]

[8] *The other thing you can do is to multi-host these machines. On the Web server, you disable IP on the internal interface, and disable Internet Packet Exchange (IPX) on the external interface. On the SQL Server (or any data server) you disable IP on the external interface and disable IPX on the internal interface. This breaks the link of IP across the firewall, allowing you to still communicate with the Web server.*

FTP Servers

The logic of placing Windows NT FTP servers within a network parallels the logic for dealing with Windows NT Web servers. In general, external FTP servers should be placed on the DMZ and should neither be member servers nor installed on the same physical platform as a domain controller (see Figure 7.3). Deploying internal FTP servers as member servers or independent servers is in general safer from a security perspective for the same reason that deploying internal Web servers in this manner is. Running FTP servers on the same platforms as domain controllers not only increases the likelihood of a successful attack that causes Windows NT itself to crash, but also introduces potential authentication-related vulnerabilities discussed in the next chapter. Remember, finally, that FTP servers are likely to be run on the same physical machine as WWW servers.[9] Hopefully constraints used in deploying WWW servers are therefore likely to also be used in deploying FTP servers, making decisions about FTP server deployment easier.

Gopher/WAIS/Archie Servers

Securing Gopher, Archie, and other similiar services is becoming a moot point. The usage of these protocols is diminishing with the advent of other Web-based services that perform the same functions. The fact that they are extremely difficult to secure is therefore a secondary worry. Note that they many security-related vulnerabilities in these protocols relate in large part to their very nature—they are designed for easy, public access. Suffice it to say that in the Windows NT network environment, Gopher and Archie servers belong *outside* of any internal network (for example, on the DMZ) and should not be part of any Windows NT domain.

Mail Servers

Several different vendor implementations of mail servers are available in the Windows NT arena. In general, if you need a high amount of security, you should deploy your mail server behind a firewall—either on a protected segment or within your internal network. Then have a mail proxy (mail-relay) machine forward mail from the Internet to the mail host. This proxy would be configured to strip out any improper commands, and perform other checks if needed. Having mail servers behind one or more firewalls provides more protection. This deployment can also reduce traffic, because internal mail will not be traversing the DMZ. In this scenario, only Internet-based mail flows in and out of the firewall, reducing the likelihood of an organization's internal mail leaking out.

9 *IIS has a built-in FTP server that is widely used.*

Whether a mail server is a member server within a domain depends on where the mail server is located. External mail servers should be independent servers; internal mail servers can be member servers.

News Servers

If you use Microsoft Exchange, chances are you use the Exchange Server as both a mail server and a news server. You may, alternatively, have a separate news server. In either case, Network News Transfer Protocol (NNTP) implementations generally have numerous security-related vulnerabilities associated with them. One, for example, enables an attacker to use a news server to obtain copies of critical system configuration files from other machines on the local network. It is best, therefore, to deploy news servers within one's internal network where the level of protection is likely to be highest. Use proxies!

Firewalls

By now, the question concerning firewalls is not if, but *where* and *how* to deploy them. We have already covered the difference between outer and inner firewalls and how both can be used advantageously to increase security in the Windows NT network environment. The next major issue is this: If you deploy Windows NT–based firewalls, should you allow them to be member servers or perhaps even domain controllers? The answer is "no." Many vendors who make Windows NT–based firewalls strip down Windows NT capabilities so much that the firewall is by default likely to not be capable of participating in a domain, anyway. If a Windows NT firewall can be part of a domain, the best thing to do is to deploy that machine as a domain-independent entity (see Figure 7.3 once again). The reason is the zone principle. Firewalls are potentially subject to all kinds of attacks from external sources. They also in reality provide a single point of failure from a security standpoint. Mixing firewalls in the same domain as internal Windows NT hosts does not, therefore, make sense. Furthermore, domain message and other traffic bogs down the firewall.

System-Based Network Security Measures

We have already seen how securing individual systems is such an important part of Windows NT security. Additional host-based measures are also part of Windows NT network security. Windows NT 4.0, for example, offers a packet-filtering capability for each network adaptor installed on a Windows NT Server or Workstation. This feature (not available in previous releases) enables a system administrator to determine what kinds of traffic, such as TCP, UDP, and IP bound for any particular port number can actually be passed up the network stack. This section describes systems-based packet filtering and several other systems-based approaches to increasing Windows NT network security.

System-Based Packet Filtering

To enable and configure system-based packet filtering, follow these steps:

1. Go to the Control Panel.
2. Double-click on the Network icon.
3. Click on the Protocols tab.
4. Double-click on TCP/IP Protocol.
5. Click on Advanced, Enable Security, and then click on Configure.
6. A panel similar to the one in Figure 7.4 displays. First you have to choose the network adaptor card for which the settings you choose will apply.

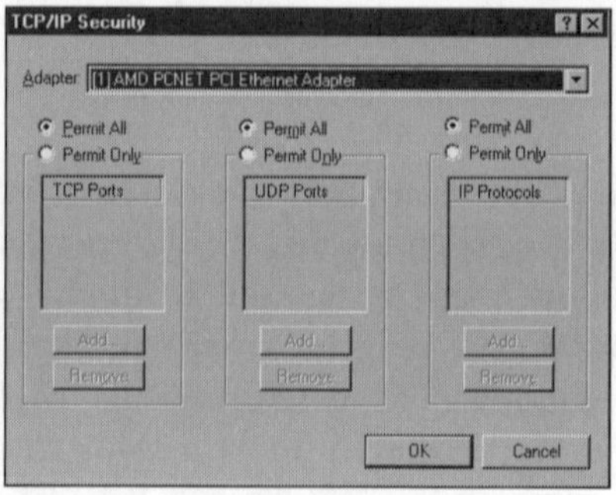

Figure 7.4 *Windows NT packet-filtering panel.*

7. Click on Add or Remove for the particular protocol for which you want to add or remove filtering. For example, you can click on Permit All (the default setting) to permit all inbound UDP traffic to a particular interface card. Alternatively, you can click on Permit Only, and then click on Add. You can then can type in the number of the UDP port for which you want to allow traffic (for example, **135**).
8. Finally, click on OK.

You can, of course, do similar things with TCP and IP packets. Note that you have to restart the system for the picket-filtering rules you have selected to go into effect.

System-based packet filtering in and of itself is a good network security control measure. Used in connection with firewalls, it becomes an extremely strong solution because it provides in effect a "second lock" in your network security strategy. Things are not always as they appear to be, however, and the Windows NT packet-filtering capability is no exception. This capability has the following inherent weaknesses:

- **Lack of flexibility in screening logic.** The Windows NT packet filter is essentially an "all-or-none" capability in that it either allows traffic through a port or blocks it entirely. This packet filter does not, however, allow accepting or denying incoming packets on the basis of IP address. A built-in packet filter that allows, for example, TCP packets from certain IP addresses but rejects all others is much more suited to today's operational needs than one that does not. Unfortunately, the Windows NT packet-filtering capability is one that does not do this. Furthermore, it is severely lacking in that it does not have the capability to selectively deny connections to certain ports and protocol.
- **It can be circumvented (although not easily).** Internet postings indicate that it is possible to write a program which establishes a connection to a target port on a Windows NT system despite the fact that the system has port filtering in place to prevent such a connection. The basic problem is that a rogue program's processes can bind at a lower level of the NBT stack than do the packet filter's. The only way to *totally* disable ports in Windows NT appears to be to halt NETBT.SYS.
- **A configuration mistake can be catastrophic.** If you block incoming UDP traffic bound for port 135 and TCP traffic bound for port 139, for example, you disrupt basic Windows NT functionality, such as network authentication and sharing.
- **Performance liabilities.** Another possible liability of installing a packet filter concerns performance. If you implement Windows NT's packet-filtering capability on a system, that system will suffer a small but noticeable performance hit.

All things considered, the Windows NT packet-filtering capability can be helpful. Its logic, however, is so rudimentary that it is usually difficult to justify the time and effort in configuring it. It may also provide a false sense of security. I suggest that you use it in a pinch, for example, when systems are being attacked and other control alternatives are not immediately available, or when traffic patterns are extremely predictable (that is, Web servers should only expect incoming traffic on port 80 or 443).

Disabling the NetBIOS Bindings to TCP/IP

In Chapter 3, I covered another system-based network solution—disabling the NetBIOS bindings to TCP/IP. This solution prevents a range of attacks that exploit NetBIOS, but at the same time can interfere with wide area communications between systems.

Using Third-Party Vendor Solutions

The number of third-party security solutions in the Windows NT arena is growing at an astounding rate. Some of these solutions are good, but others are not. Again, *caveat emptor* should be the prevailing principle. One of the better vendor solutions is the improved TCP/IP stack for Windows NT systems that Hummingbird Communications (`http://www.hummingbird.com`) makes. This improved TCP/IP stack not only enhances network performance, but also lessens the likelihood of successful TCP/IP-based attacks (for example, denial-of-service attacks).

Another potentially useful third-party network security solution is Nuke Nabber, a packet-filtering tool (`http://www.webzone.net/DDG_Computing/Dalnet/servhelp/detect/detect.html`). This tool works in a manner very similar to Windows NT's packet filter. Nuke Nabber is considerably better, however, in that it allows the use of conditional logic in establishing filtering rules; it enables you to specify the specific IP addresses or ranges of addresses from which packets are or are not allowed.

The commercial version of S/KEY by Bellcore (`http://www.ietf.org/html.characters/otp-charter.html`) is a tool for keeping clear-text passwords off the network. S/KEY, which works in connection with both Windows NT and other platforms, works in connection with both Windows NT's MSV1_0 package and the UNIX `/bin/login` or `/sbin/login` programs. A user enters a number of parameters to set up S/KEY sessions and then enters a password. The client encrypts the password with secret key encryption before it is sent over the network; the server decrypts the password. During the next user session, the user enters the same password, but the client and server change the encryption key they share in a manner that they both understand. Therefore, a different encrypted password goes over the network each time. The same thing also happens during subsequent sessions. Despite some advantages, one of S/KEY's limitations is that programs, such as l0phtcrack, can capture the encrypted password that goes over the network and crack it anyway.

Developing a Strategy for Deploying Third-Party Windows NT Security Tools

An operating system product, such as Windows NT, or any other will never deliver all the functionality that it ideally should. What should you do about the gap between your requirements and what Windows NT delivers?

One solution is to purchase and install third-party tools. These tools can potentially be extremely valuable in improving security, as well as addressing other needs. Microsoft in fact actively promotes many of these tools by posting a list of partners and the products they make on its Knowledge Base site (`http://microsoft.com`).

Dealing with third-party security tools, however, is not as straightforward as one might imagine. Each tool has its own bugs and idiosyncrasies; installing and maintaining tools generally requires significant time and effort. It is very important, therefore, to develop a strategy for choosing and deploying third-party tools above all else. Realistically speaking, it you have a large installation base for Windows NT, using more than one or two tools to enhance security will be all that you can handle. Your best bet, all things considered, is to make a decision concerning the value of each tool based on a set of weighted criteria. You might consider how well the product addresses your needs, the cost, how often upgrades are released, the compatibility with the existing environment, the compatibility with other third-party tools, the reputation and responsiveness of the vendor, the number and seriousness of bugs in the product, and other factors. Note that cost really entails not only the purchase cost, but also the cost of maintenance and upgrades.

What is the bottom line? First and foremost, *third-party tools are no substitute for security built in to an operating system itself.* Security directly built in to an operating system is more seamless and is generally harder to defeat. No matter how good each tool is, tools are add-ons—helpful, perhaps, but they are (from an operational standpoint) an extra piece of baggage to the already complex Windows NT operating system. The responsibility for providing the potential for security rests squarely on the shoulders of operating system vendors; pointing to a third-party product to fix a security-related vulnerability in an operating system is not an acceptable response. Second, *don't get fooled into adopting a tools-based approach ("Tools Myopia") to Windows NT security*. Analysts are constantly comparing one tool to another and talking about the difference in security value resulting from deploying Tool 1 versus Tool 2. It is easy to get lost in this rhetoric; the so-called expert analysts have done the Windows NT and other user communities a great disservice. The most important thing you can do to make Windows NT more secure is to configure systems appropriately and deploy appropriate network security mechanisms. Tools help, but they do not circumvent the need for good basic system and network security measures!

Virtual Private Networks (VPNs)

VPNs encrypt network traffic between two machines, such that if someone has captured this traffic, it is not visible in plain text. VPNs also provide a strong security control solution against threats, such as unauthorized capture of clear-text passwords going over the network. Chapter 9, "Virtual Private Networks," covers VPNs in detail. ◆

Monitoring and Intrusion Detection

The complexity of Windows NT's networking environment and the plethora of security-related vulnerabilities that exist in this environment dictate that you not rely on Windows NT security logging to monitor the security state of your Windows NT systems. Security logging also does not record a number of critical events that occur at the SMB and NetBIOS layers of networking—events that could indicate that an attack has occurred. If your need for security is high, you might want to deploy network monitoring and possibly even intrusion-detection tools.

Packet-Capture Devices and Programs

The simplest type of network monitoring is using a physical device or network interface program that captures and dumps packets. They record all traffic that reaches a network adapter card, providing packet dumps that reveal virtually everything that has occurred either at the level of a single host or within the entire network segment on which the device or program has been installed. What the device or program can capture depends on the topology of your network (for example, the ethernet topology is most conducive to whole segment packet capture), the type of cabling, and the type of network interface card you have installed. Recall from Chapter 3 the packet-dump results depicting a real-life wildcard attack—an illustration of the value of a network-capture capability. Some of the downsides of packet dumping devices or programs are that they may fall into the wrong hands and also that you need a very high-capacity storage device, such as a worm drive, to dump the voluminous output that results. Sifting through this output can, in fact, be a nearly overwhelming task. Some vendors, such as Network Associates, help quite a bit in this regard by providing an easy-to-use user interface in their product Net X-Ray. (Go to `http://www.nai.com` for additional information on this product.)

When you install certain Microsoft BackOffice products, you also by default install a protocol -capture program, *Network Monitor* (NM). You have to go from Start to Programs to Administrative Tools to Netmon to start NM. You also have to ensure that the Network Monitor Agent is started. (Go from Start to Settings to Control Panel to Network to Services, highlight Network Monitor Agent, and then click on Start if NM has not been started, and then reboot.) Figure 7.5 shows a packet-dump screen from the higher-ended version of NM that comes with the *Systems Management Server* (SMS). (In SMS go to `D:\NMEXT\I386\SETUP.EXE` and then reboot.) You can learn useful information, such as the number or type of packet transmissions from one particular computer to another. This type of information is very useful, for example, in determining the machine that has initiated packet-flooding attacks. The packet data dumps can be useful in determining the nature of the communications (client authentication, establishment of a share connection, and so forth). Be sure, at a minimum, to assign stringent permissions for NM access—usually only allow system administrators to obtain any kind of access to this program.

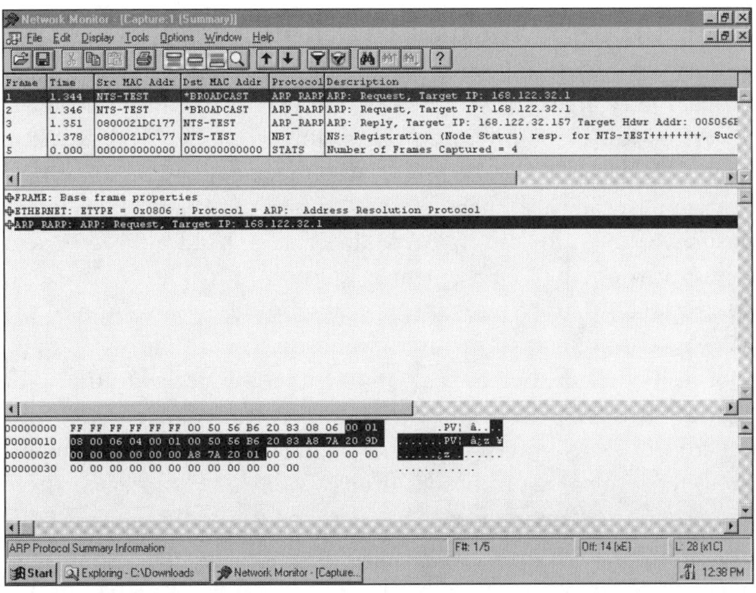

Figure 7.5 *Screen from the Network Monitor Frame Viewer.*

Intrusion-Detection Tools

Intrusion-detection tools go a step further than monitoring tools in that the former generally match data they collect to data pattern "signatures" of known attack patterns stored in databases to determine whether each recorded network event constituted an attack. Some of these tools go even further by using an expert system engine to infer whether an attack has occurred.

Many different vendors now make intrusion-detection tools that find network-based attacks on Windows NT systems. Some vendors include Internet Security Systems (`http://www.iss.net`), Network Associates (`http://www.nai.com`), Cisco (`http://www.cisco.com`), Secure Computing (`http://www.securecomputing.com`), and Network Flight Recorder (`http://www.nfr.net`). Each tool has its advantages and disadvantages. Intrusion detection may seem a bit esoteric to you, but it is rapidly becoming mainstream technology in the business arena. Simply put, no matter what you do to any system or network, many residual vulnerabilities will remain. Furthermore, the worst attacks will in all likelihood continue to be initiated by insiders who are to some degree trusted. Having intrusion-detection capability compensates to a large degree for many of these concerns. With sound intrusion-detection capabilities in place, you can at least discover intrusions and misuse quickly and do something about it.

Securing Interoperability Programs

Windows NT Server 4.0 offers several programs that provide interoperability between Windows NT and other platforms, such as NetWare boxes. These programs (for example, the NetWare Redirector and Gateway Services for NetWare–GSNW) are generally easy to set up and use. Unfortunately, they also may introduce a number of security-related exposures. GSNW, for example, requires that a Windows NT system administrator obtain, and then enter a password for the NetWare platform to be accessed.[10] GSNW uses this password to set up a session to the NetWare platform every time users want to access resources on that platform. By default users actually have superuser access to the NetWare platform. NDS for NT is a good tool, but several vulnerabilities in this product have also surfaced (for example, one of which allows unauthorized users to retrieve password hashes from Windows NT systems).

No program of any type ever has perfect security. In the case of interoperability programs, the main security-related considerations are issues such as the default privilege level for sessions, the strength of the authentication mechanisms, the type and robustness of access control mechanisms, whether the interoperability program in question provides ways to bypass or defeat intrinsic Windows NT security mechanisms, and so on. The main point here is that you should talk to the vendors of interoperability programs and experiment with these programs in a test

[10] *In the overwhelming majority of the GSNW implementations I have seen, the supervisor password is used for access to Novell hosts. The result, intentionally or unintentionally, is superuser access to those hosts.*

environment to learn of their strengths and weakness, and then make your decision concerning their deployment accordingly.

Interoperablility Programs and Security: Beware!

If security is a significant consideration in your environment, you need to be especially wary of programs that allow interoperability between Windows NT and other platforms. Most of these programs build in a few security mechanisms but leave gaping vulnerabilities that are easy to overlook unless you are willing to spend the time and resources necessary to discover how these programs really work. Again, caveat emptor.

Secure System Administration Methods

The last topic in this chapter is secure system administration methods in the Windows NT arena. You will find other books that do a great deal of justice to this topic, so our discussion won't be lengthy. The most used method of system administration in Windows NT since its inception has almost certainly been gaining physical access to Windows NT systems and then logging on locally with Administrator-level rights. To the degree that server platforms are centrally located (hopefully in a locked server room), this method may work reasonably well. To the degree that servers are located in different buildings miles apart, this method is not very practical. Usually workstations are dispersed everywhere, so logging in locally to them on a regular basis is usually out of the question.

Assuming that you need some kind of remote access to systems to administer them, you have a number of options.

Logging On to One or More Domain Controllers, and Then Accessing Administrative Shares

This method is good in some respects because domain controllers work in harmony with each other with respect to areas such as policy settings anyway. To the degree that you have to install software on member servers and workstations, you may need to rely on access to administrative shares. The main limitation is that share access may be a bit cumbersome; it does not let you have access to the range of resources and view of the desktop on each machine you reach that you would have if you were a locally logged-on user.

Remote Control Programs

A remote control program such as pcANYWHERE gives you a much richer view of what is going on in each machine you reach remotely. It also enables you to easily make changes to that system from the workstation on which pcANYWHERE runs. The main limitation so far as security goes is that most remote control programs do not incorporate a sufficient amount of security for programs that provide this level of control over other, remote systems. Ideally, you would logon to the remote control program using a different password than you use for access to the systems themselves (or, better yet, you would also use third-party authentication methods to access the remote control program). The remote program would then provide an encrypted session[11] using strong encryption technology, and would incorporate strong auditing capabilities. Overall, however, remote control programs are one of the least-secure ways to remotely administer other machines. Some of them *do not* require any kind of password at all, and many of them do not encrypt remote sessions!

Remote Access Service

Chapter 8, "Securing Network Services and Protocols," discusses Remote Access Service (RAS) in detail. The problem with RAS as a conduit for system administration access is that unless you set it up properly, RAS can provide an easy avenue of access to attackers. At a minimum, if you use RAS to remotely administer systems, you should dedicate the RAS links to system administrators. If you allow system administrators and users to obtain RAS connectivity from one RAS server, in all likelihood you are making a big mistake. Users may be able to exploit vulnerabilities in the RAS server to gain remote Administrator-level privileges without authorization. If you use RAS, you should also select the settings that produce encrypted passwords and data transmissions.

Commercial System Administration Tools

Some very high-quality system administration tools are on the market today. These tools can provide a very high-ended interface to remote systems and can incorporate powerful "push-pull" capabilities. Many of them encrypt all sessions and provide strong auditing; unfortunately, others do not. The strongest solutions from a security standpoint are generally the comprehensive system administration tools, such as IBM's Tivoli, Computer Associate's Unicenter TNG, and Microsoft's SMS. Unfortunately, some of the most financially costly solutions are also in this category.

---

[11] *Note that the latest release of pcANYWHERE at least provides session encryption.*

Telnet Access

If you install the Telnet server in the Windows NT Resource Kit (or buy a commercial version from companies such as Georgia Softworks `www.georgiasoftworks.com`) on each Windows NT system that you want to remotely access, you can invoke a Telnet client on a central machine to obtain command-line access to remote systems via TCP port 23. Windows NT itself offers a limited set of commands (for example, **net user, net group, net localgroup**, and **net accounts**) for administering remote systems. You can, however, also install tools in the Resource Kit (see Appendix D, "Useful Security-Related Tools from the Windows NT 4.0 Resource Kit") that allow command -line control over certain functions. RASLIST, for example, enables a system or network administrator to obtain a listing of all RAS servers on hosts within a domain. The main limitation with Telnet is that, by default, all session traffic is in clear text.

Secure Shell Access

The final remote system administration access method considered here is *secure shell* (ssh). This tool, which establishes a session on TCP port 22 of each remote host, allows command-line control of remote systems. Similar to Telnet in functionality, you can invoke the same Resource Kit programs listed in Table 7.2 (as well as certain **net** commands) using ssh. It is, however, more secure than Telnet in that it encrypts all session traffic. You can find out more about this program at `http://www.F-secure.com`.

The Importance of Encrypting System Administrator Sessions

Clear-text traffic that traverses a network poses a major threat to security! Ensure at a minimum that the remote administrator method you use encrypts all sessions. ◆

Conclusion

To reiterate, Windows NT (or any other operating system, for that matter) is not easy to secure in a network environment. As a network entity, in fact, Windows NT is in many respects currently more exposure-prone than are other, competing operating systems. Both its relative immaturity and reliance on implementations of older, nonmainstream protocols constitute a large part of the challenge of defending Windows NT in the network environment. The battle is mostly winnable but requires a great deal of planning, effort, and resources. Avoiding using Windows NT in high-risk operational environments, installing properly configured firewalls, designing sound network architectures, and running services only if you need them are several of the potentially most effective network security solutions. Employing other solutions such as VPNs and using secure remote administration methods is also worth your strong consideration. A few solutions, such as the built-in Windows NT packet-filtering capability are not, however, what they appear to be.

The next release of Windows NT is likely to improve the network security potential of Windows NT substantially through the integration of Kerberos into this product. If this next release works as advertised, the time of its release will be the best time to also deploy Windows NT in high-risk environments.

Checklist for System Administrators

1. Windows NT network security requires considering the contribution of clients to overall network security. To the maximum degree possible, work to ensure that many, perhaps (in certain settings, all) clients are Windows NT Workstation clients.
2. Ensure that firewalls are in place to shield Windows NT hosts from network-based attacks and that they filter traffic appropriately. In addition to normal screening that blocks incoming traffic bound for ports such as TCP and UDP 7, TCP 11, TCP and UDP 19, and so forth, at a minimum (for the sake of Windows NT network security) block all externally originated traffic bound for the following ports: TCP 42, TCP and UDP 135, UDP 137, UDP 138, TCP and UDP 139, and TCP and UDP 1024–1029.
3. Ensure that servers that run network services such as WWW, FTP, mail, and news are placed properly within the network architecture. Servers that allow access to the public should be located on a DMZ and should be independent of any internal Windows NT domains.
4. On critical servers, install host-based packet filters that block dangerous incoming service requests.
5. Test the feasibility of disabling NetBIOS bindings to TCP/IP and if you discover that no disruption of networking occurs, disable them.
6. Obtain demo copies of third-party tools that hold the greatest promise of meeting your network security needs. Obtain and install one or two of the most suitable tools.
7. Develop a policy for monitoring and intrusion detection, and then obtain and install the intrusion-detection tool that most closely meets the requirements in this policy.

8. Closely examine interoperability programs to determine whether they introduce significant security-related vulnerabilities. If they do, determine and deploy a suitable course of action (obtaining and installing vendor-provided patches, using a different program, and so forth).
9. Analyze the security-related vulnerabilities associated with current methods of remote system administration. Close these vulnerabilities as time and resources permit. Consider migrating to other, more secure methods if current methods are not conducive to security. At a minimum, try to ensure that all remote administrator sessions are encrypted.

8

Securing Network Services and Protocols

"Security services in the Windows NT network environment pose yet anther level of challenge. Network services are in and of themselves more difficult to secure."
– Gene Schultz

Chapter 7, "Basic Network Security Measures," covered the basic types of network security control mechanisms that you need to put in place to defend your Windows NT systems from a wide range of network-based attacks. And as previously mentioned, running only the services that you really need to run is a basic network security measure which yields high security dividends in the Windows NT arena. Disabling services, such as the Alerter service, may not prove catastrophic as far as your operational needs go, but what about the services that you *really do* need? You will not in all likelihood be inclined to disable these services, but they will in all likelihood introduce vulnerabilities besides those that exist in the Windows NT operating system. What do you do? What are the cost-benefit tradeoffs? This chapter covers these questions, with a focus on the most popular and frequently used services, such as Web and FTP services, mail services, SNMP, DHCP, WINS, DNS, and RAS.

Securing Web Services

One of the main complications in securing Windows NT Web services is that several different Windows NT–based Web servers are available. Among the major options are the *Internet Information Server* (IIS) by Microsoft, the iPlanet Enterprise Server and Netscape Enterprise Server, and the Apache Server by Apache. The particular one(s) you select and implement make(s) a big difference in terms of the security vulnerabilities and methods of achieving security control. This section focuses on securing IIS, however, because of the relative preponderance of this product in the Windows NT Web arena. In addition, IIS is tightly integrated with Windows NT and is required for several other services to run, such as new versions of Exchange Server.

Overview of IIS Security Mechanisms

IIS security to a large degree depends on Windows NT security mechanisms. For instance, three authentication scenarios[1] are possible for users who initiate Web access:

- The MSV1_0 package can use challenge-response authentication in which users are authenticated on the basis of their ability to supply the correct password for a specific account. The Web browser must be capable of participating in challenge-response authentication (that is, only MSIE is supported). In this scenario, passwords of any type (encrypted or clear text) do not go across the network—only encrypted nonces do.
- MSV1_0 can authenticate users to specific accounts, but if the Web browser is not capable of participating in challenge-response authentication, clear-text passwords go over the net. This scenario occurs when users initiate Web access from most browsers other than MSIE browsers.
- Users do not need to have any account; they can just be authenticated as anonymous users. In this case, the Web client is accessing resources without being authenticated. The server impersonates the default "" anonymous account for each client.

After a user has been authenticated, basic Windows NT privilege and object access mechanisms determine the particular resources that IIS Web users can and cannot access, in addition to the level of access they can obtain. When a user authenticates to the Web server on a domain-independent server or member server, the user's access is limited to resources on that platform; the user *is not* a domain user (see Figure 8.1). If a user authenticates to the Web server that has been implemented on a domain controller, however, the authentication is *domain authentication*; the user can *potentially* access any resource on any server and workstation within the domain.

IIS also has some additional security capabilities besides the basic Windows NT mechanisms. For example, IIS enables a Web administrator to limit all user access to an IIS-accessible volume to Read, Write, Execute

[1] *Remember that non-Microsoft Web servers have their own authentication methods, which differ from Windows NT's.*

scripts, or Run executable files. IIS additionally provides the capability to encrypt data sent between the client and server systems using *Secure Sockets Layer* (SSL), as well as other types of encryption. The *Internet Service Manager* (ISM) enables webmasters to manage all aspects of the IIS server.

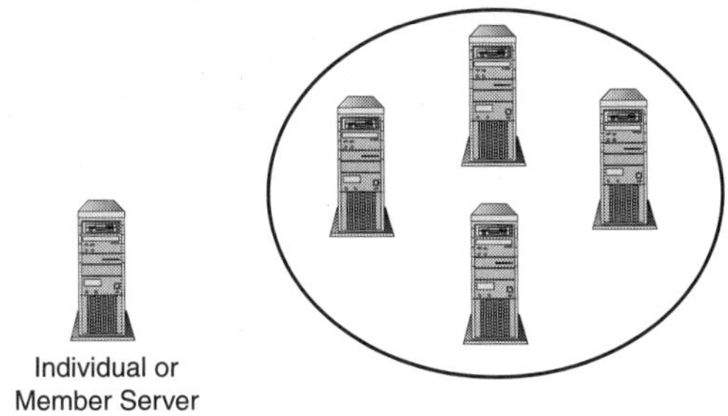

Figure 8.1 *IIS authentication in an independent or member server versus in a domain controller. In the first case (in the left), IIS-authenticated users can obtain access only to resources on the individual or member server. In the second case, IIS-authenticated users can potentially obtain access to any resource on any domain server or workstation.*

Security-Related Vulnerabilities

The downside of IIS security has been the sheer number of security-related vulnerabilities that have emerged in both IIS and the widely used, related browser, MS Internet Explorer (as well as other Web browsers). Some of the vulnerabilities in IIS itself include the following:

- Default sample pages are installed and usually never removed. These sample pages have a significant amount of vulnerabilities, and allow everything from remote retrieval of any file on the IIS server, to execution of remote programs on the IIS server.
- Incompatibility of authentication schemes among browsers (MSIE versus non-MSIE browsers) drives clear-text authentication as the common denominator. An unauthorized packet capture device could capture clear-text passwords that could be used later in gaining unauthorized access.
- Limiting user access to a specific point in the file system and below sometimes is a problem in IIS. Several bugs have allowed a user to whom NT File System (NTFS) permissions allow no access to a higher-level directory to access this directory even though NTFS should contain the highest point in the file system to which access occurs.
- In IIS an account called anonymous per se does not by default exist. Instead, IUSR_<servername> is the default account for anonymous

access. The actual name of this account varies. If the name of the computer that houses the Web server is COMP002, for example, the name of the anonymous account name is IUSR_COMP002. This account is either a domain account if the IIS Web server is on a domain controller. It is a local account if it is on an individual server platform and is created when IIS is installed.[2] The IUSR_servername account has a randomly generated password. It can be the target of password-guessing attacks that result in unauthorized access not only to the Web server but possibly also to domains, depending on whether the IIS Web server runs on a domain controller.

- By default every Web client access request is anonymous. Anonymous authentication is thus the "least common denominator." Although necessary in most operational contexts, anonymous access is not conducive to security because it enables virtually anyone to gain a foothold in the system that allows this type of access.
- IIS runs as SYSTEM. Anyone who capitalizes on security-vulnerabilities, such as buffer overflow conditions in IIS Web applications, can potentially gain SYSTEM-level privileges.
- As previously mentioned, users are either authenticated as domain or local users. While logged on to an IIS Web server, local users are actually included in the Interactive group on the system that runs the Web server. Local access short-circuits a vast number of Windows NT security mechanisms that are part of other types of remote accesses. Protection against the local user's unauthorized access to resources is limited; they include formatting all partitions with NTFS and then properly assigning NTFS permissions in addition to applying the least-privilege principle.
- The fact that IIS can be run on a domain controller can potentially spell catastrophe for a domain. By default, a user who obtains Web access becomes a member of the Authenticated Users group. If the Web server is on a domain controller, this means that the user gains access to the domain resources available to this group, even if the Guest account is disabled. A clever user can authenticate to a Web server, and then use these default memberships to gain unauthorized access to domain resources not intended to be available to web users.
- By default, IIS installs the Web and File Transfer Protocol (FTP) root directories on the C: drive. If IIS is installed on this drive, IIS access can potentially allow any user to obtain access to (and possibly modify, depending on permissions) system files.

[2] *All Windws NT accounts (including the default IUSR_<servername> account instaled with IIS) are either local or domain accounts.*

- IIS versions 3.0 and 4.0 have been vulnerable to a number of different types of denial-of-service attacks, one of the simplest of which is sending a malformed HTTP GET request to an IIS Web server, causing the server to devote all of its resources to processing this request. The server hangs, necessitating either a stop or restart of the Web server or a reboot.
- Another, similar bug causes data corruption if two virtual servers reside on the same physical platform. Sending a malformed GET request to one virtual server causes INETINFO.EXE to crash. When this happens, the file handles created for this virtual server are deleted. When the other virtual server is brought down (for example, as a part of maintenance activity), it needs the appropriate file handles to be able to write to Temp files that save data changes. The file handles are missing, however, because of what happened when the first virtual server's INETINFO.EXE crashed.
- A bug in IIS enables a malicious user to send a malformed GET request that causes the server to devote a disproportionately high amount of CPU to this request, causing the server to crash. Microsoft has released a hot fix for this vulnerability.
- Sending certain, nonstandard characters in a URL can allow unauthorized access to files that are not supposed to be accessed via WWW.

Where Should You Go to Get Patches for Windows NT Vulnerabilities?

Microsoft has released patches and/or configuration recommendations for the vast majority of known IIS vulnerabilities. You can download them from `http://www.microsoft.com/downloads`. ◆

This coverage of vulnerabilities in IIS is by no means exhaustive. New vulnerabilities surface frequently. These also do not include vulnerabilities associated with many of the related programming languages and functions such as ActiveX (see Chapter 10, "Workstation Security"), Active Server Pages, FrontPage, and so forth. Suffice it to say that many associated vulnerabilities exist; your choice concerning whether to use them should be based on a careful analysis of costs versus benefits. It is very important to keep an eye on the Microsoft security site (`http://www.microsoft.com/security`); the fixes[3] are announced there as soon as they are released, as well as other public web sites.

[3] *Not all patches (fixes) are released publicly. If Microsoft does not deem the audience for the patch to be a general audience, they will not release a publicly available patch. To get these "specific" patches, you must have a support contract with Microsoft.*

Securing IIS

Securing IIS is not an easy matter. You have to resolve many issues, including the ones described in this section.

How to Deploy IIS Servers

Almost certainly the most basic consideration in Windows NT security is the particular version of Web server that you implement. Each has its own particular set of vulnerabilities. One of the most serious security-related concerns with IIS is that it runs as SYSTEM. Many other competing Web servers do not. IIS has many advantages; in general, however, security is not one of them. If security is a major consideration, you may want to consider implementing another Web server that does not run as SYSTEM.

If you decide that the IIS Web server best meets your needs, and decide to use it as your external Web server, you should be aware that it takes a substantial amount of effort to get it secure. Many vulnerabilities exist and can result in undesirable consequences, such as having someone change the substance of the Web pages to content that results in embarrassment, dissemination of bogus information, and so forth. You can substantially elevate the security of an external IIS Web server, but it is not a quick and easy task.[4] As an internal Web server, however, IIS is, all things considered, potentially sufficiently secure[5] from a security standpoint if one or more firewalls and other defenses protect it from the potential massive onslaught of externally originated attacks.

Another very important consideration is whether you want to dedicate the Windows NT machine on which IIS runs to Web services. Remember, IIS Web users are either domain users or local users on this machine. Considering the dangers of local logons, in general it is best for the sake of security to dedicate machines on which IIS runs to IIS functionality. If you do this, it at least precludes the possibility that someone who can subvert IIS security can gain unauthorized access to other applications and databases that reside on the same physical machine. Most importantly, it is best to (wherever practicable) *avoid* running IIS on any domain controller; mixing IIS and domain control functions on the same machine exposes the domain to attacks through exploitation of Web vulnerabilities.

---

[4] *This is not to say that securing other Web servers is trivial. Securing IIS in general takes quite a bit of careful analysis and effort; failing to fix even one of the many default vulnerabilities can readily result in compromise of the entire server.*

[5] *The point here is that although IIS has its share of security-related exposures, defense measures, such as firewalls, can compensate to some degree. Although there is nothing sacred about the security of internal networks, a server within an internal network protected by one or more properly configured and maintained firewall(s) is, all things considered, safer than an external server.*

As discussed in Chapter 7, if the IIS server is an *external* Web server, it should not in any case be on a machine that is a member server. Remember, all machines on the demilitarized zone (DMZ) should be "throwaway machines"; unauthorized access to these machines should not increase the likelihood of compromise for machines within the internal network ("security perimeter"). If the IIS server is an *internal* Web server (that is, the server runs on a platform inside your organization's internal network, as discussed in Chapter 7), however, deploying it as member server is not quite as much of a security concern. Nevertheless, the risk of doing so is higher than if the Web server is on a machine that is an independent server.

Authentication Issues

To determine the type(s) of Web authentication you will allow, you must use the ISM. Open the ISM, going from Start to Programs to Option Pack to Internet Information Server to Internet Service Manager, and then select the Web server you are administering. Next go to Properties, then to Directory Security, and then to Anonymous Access and Authentication Control. The screen shown in Figure 8.2 displays. The options for authentication include Allow Anonymous, Basic Authentication (Clear Text), or Windows NT Challenge/Response authentication. In general, challenge-response authentication is the best for security because it requires authentication to a specific account and does not allow clear-text passwords to be sent over the net. You can select challenge-response authentication (the default type of IIS authentication) by clicking on the Security tab of the ISM, and then clicking on Windows NT Challenge/Response. Anonymous authentication, in contrast, potentially allows anyone to gain access to an IIS server; it is therefore the weakest from a security standpoint. In the case of an external Web server, user access is almost always through anonymous authentication, especially if this server is intended for public access. External Web servers generally entail more security risk to the servers themselves, but less risk to the internal network.

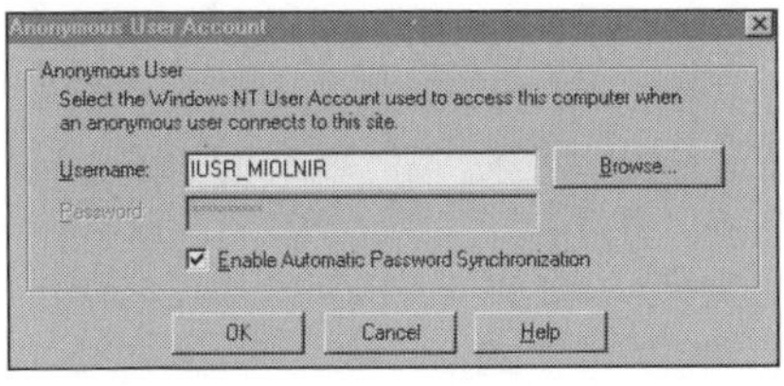

Figure 8.2 *Anonymous User Account panel for IIS 4.0.*

In the case of an *internal* Web server, the potentially best solution from the perspective of security is to require authentication to a specific user account using challenge-response authentication, but this solution is not always practical considering that many browsers are not MSIE browsers.

Enable Secure Sockets Layer (SSL) encryption to prevent clear-text transmission of session traffic. This also helps ensure the integrity of the data transmitted between the Web client and server, and also helps guarantee that client data is transmitted to the right server. IIS supports versions 2.0 and 3.0 of SSL. Enabling this encryption (see following sidebar) is no easy task in IIS Web servers.

How to Enable SSL Encryption on an IIS Web Server

To enable SSL encryption, you must first obtain a digital certificate from a certificate authority (CA), such as Verisign (`http://www.verisign.com`). The ISM assists you in generating a key request. You then contact the CA and apply for the certificate. When the CA approves your application and sends you the key, you will use the ISM to install the new key. You must go from Properties to Directory Security to Secure Communications. After doing this, you have a valid certificate, and can begin using secure communications.

After you have enabled SSL on the server, you must next enable security for specific directories on the Web server. At this point, any SSL client that connects with the directory gets a secure channel connection. The strength of encryption (40 or 128 bits) available depends on the U.S. Export Control Act restrictions applicable to the country in which the copy of Windows NT Server itself was purchased. ◆

To change the anonymous account or password, use the Edit function after you go from Properties to Directory Security to the Anonymous Access and Authentication Control screen for the Web server you are administering (see Figure 8.2). The Anonymous Logon dialog box appears (see Figure 8.3). Check the Enable Automatic Password Synchronization box, and then go to the User Manager or User Manager for Domains (the latter case applies only if IIS is implemented on a domain controller) and reset the password. IIS will be notified. After editing this dialog box, click on OK.

Note that for versions 3.0 and earlier, all the fields from the previously discussed screens and panels are incorporated into a single screen. You must also manually synchronize passwords for all accounts used for anonymous Web access.[6] For each change you enter in the Anonymous Logon panel; you must make the same change in the User Manager or User Manager for Domains, as appropriate.

[6] *For later IIS versions (that is, versions 4.0 and higher), IIS synchronizes passwords automatically.*

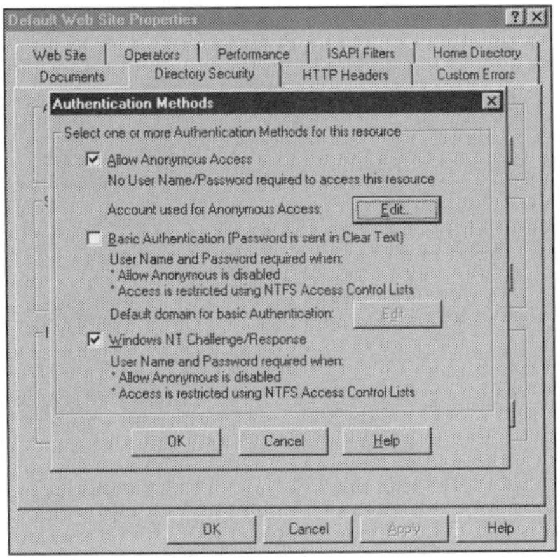

Figure 8.3 *Authentication Methods panel. This panel is used in IIS version 4.0 and higher.*

To secure Web-accessible volumes, dedicate each volume intended for Web access (because of the potential problem of not being able to contain HTTP users' access to the intended point in the file system). Also, always format each Web-accessible partition using NTFS.

To secure your IIS server, you need to employ many measures that you should adopt for *any* Web server (that is, regardless of whether it is an IIS Web server). You should, for example, avoid Web server implementations that execute batch files. Batch files are set up via the Windows NT Scheduler. The problem with batch files is that an attacker could plant a batch file that, when executed, accomplishes catastrophic results, such as extracting a copy of the SAM database.

In general, you should also set up a directory structure in your Web server that looks something like the one shown in Figure 8.4. When you install IIS, a default directory with a path `C:\Inetpub`[7] is created. Subdirectories below `Inetpub` store content, such as Web server files, HTML files, and a directory named `WWWROOT` (the default directory containing the default document displayed to users who are connected to an IIS Web server). The default document in the `WWWROOT` directory is basically the *default* home page for the Web site. DEFAULT.HTM within this directory is the *actual* home page (that is, the document that, if present, comes up on client browsers when users reach a Web site).

[7] *It is best if a Web server is* not *on your C: (system) drive to lessen the likelihood that someone could gain access to system directories and files by accessing the Web server. Therefore, the fact that IIS installs on the C: drive by default has strong negative implications for security.*

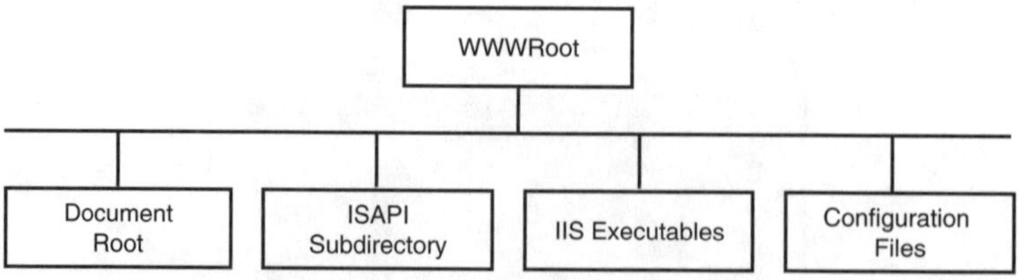

Figure 8.4 *Recommended directory structure for IIS Web servers.*

Set a No Access permission for the IUSR_<servername> account to the entire file system structure, and then remove it from the specific directories that you want the anonymous user to be able to access.

For the sake of security, it is important for `WWWROOT` (not some higher-level directory) to be the root directory for Web access. Below this directory should be subdirectories, such as document root (to store the Web-accessible content for users), and minimally for other subdirectories for APIs and system executables. The rationale for setting up the directory structure depicted in Figure 8.4 is that if someone gains unauthorized access to one part, he still doesn't at that point have access to every file and directory within the directory structure. If, in contrast, you place all content files, executables, and configuration parameters in a single directory, someone who gains unauthorized access to that directory now potentially has access to everything all at once.

You should avoid "server-side includes" in CGI scripts. Server-side includes enable users to invoke executables from fields in Web forms. A malicious user could, for example, enter a dangerous command, such as

```
net start <service>
```

or even invoke a malicious executable by entering its path in a Web form field. Finally, ISAPI scripts should incorporate suitable privilege control; if a routine runs with elevated privileges, the privilege level should be returned to its normal level at the exit from this routine.

Heeding the following recommendations will also elevate IIS Web security considerably:

- Set permissions properly. It is easy to be deluded into thinking that Web-based access to resources is secure if settings, such as authentication parameters, are selected properly. This by no means is the case. In the case of anonymous IIS Web access to a member server, for example, the anonymous user gets the same access as the Everyone group gets on that server. Be careful! The safest overall course is to use the ISM to set Read and/or Execute access for an entire Web-accessible volume.

- To reduce the recently discussed problem of Web users getting potential access to the Web server as Everyone, remove the Log On Locally right from the Everyone account. Only Administrators, IUSR_<servername>, and possibly IWAM_<servername> should (under most circumstances) have this right on the Web server.
- Regularly check the Security log of each system on which the IIS Web server runs to ensure that access to system resources by Web users is appropriate and authorized. If you permit anonymous IIS logons, regularly verify that IUSR_<computer name> in each system's Security Log is not engaging in actions such as attempting to exercise user rights and attempting to modify system files. IIS has its own logging capabilities. To configure them, bring up the Properties sheet for the Web server (as described earlier), and then click on the Web Site tab. After you have verified that logging is enabled, you need to set the Properties (the screen that appears is shown in Figure 8.5), such as deciding whether you want to write the IIS log data to a file or to a SQL or ODBC database. If you want the log data to be written to a file, you have to choose whether you want a new file that holds the log data to be opened daily, weekly, monthly, or when it reaches a size that you specify. You also have to specify the name of the parent directory for these files. Note that the log entries are not part of the Security Log or any of the other two Windows NT logs. If you want log data sent to a SQL/ODBC database, you must enter the ODBC data source name, database table name, and a username and password for access to the database.

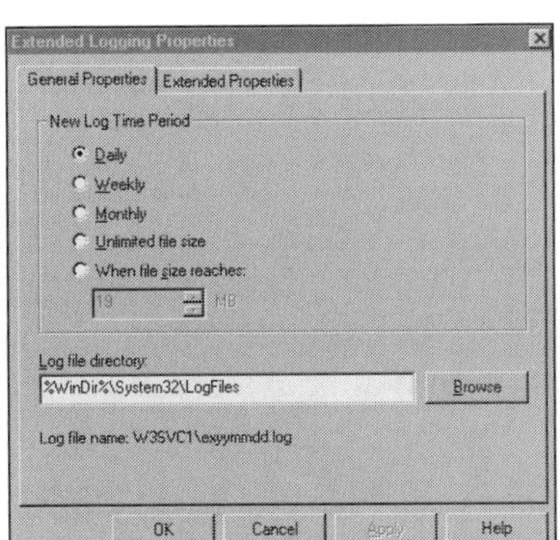

Figure 8.5 *Detailed Logging Properties screen for IIS.*

- Enable IP address–filtering capability, a feature that IIS supports, if you need higher than average levels of Web security. To set this capability's parameters, you must again bring up the ISM, go to Properties on the site you want to restrict (or properties on the server itself if you want to restrict the entire server), then to Directory Security, and then go to IP Address and Domain Name Restrictions. The screen shown in Figure 8.6 displays. The trick here is to determine for each IP address specified (through clicking on the Add option) whether to allow or deny access to the Web server.

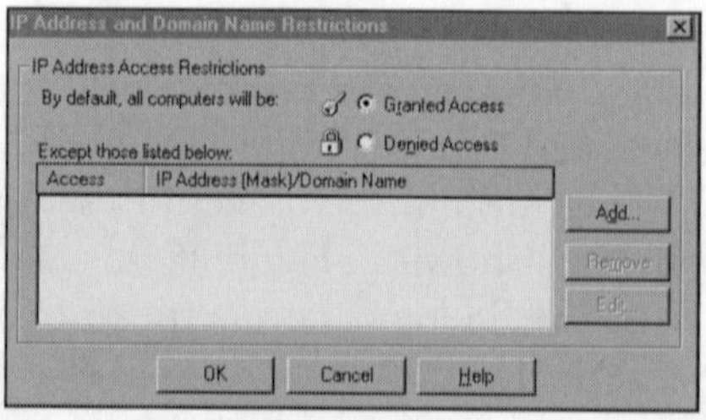

Figure 8.6 *IP Address and Domain Name Restrictions screen for IIS Service Properties.*

The IIS filtering capability is potentially very useful; you can use it to block out undesirable IP addresses, such as IP addresses of business competitors. At the same time, however, it is important to realize that an IP address in a packet header by itself constitutes minimal proof of the true network identity of any computer. Attacks such as IP spoofing and session hijacking, exemplify the weakness of identification based on IP addresses.

You may also want to use the built-in packet filter in Windows NT to filter incoming traffic. This filter, described in Chapter 7, can be particularly useful if all legitimate traffic to your Web server is exclusively through TCP port 80. Blocking all other ports makes sense if the Windows NT platform that houses the Web server is dedicated to Web services.[8]

- Disable the NetBIOS bindings to TCP/IP on the Windows NT machine that houses the IIS server. Although it is possible to obtain NetBIOS-based access to Windows NT Web servers, we have already seen the dangers associated with the NetBIOS layer of networking. Web access

[8] *Another opinion is to install the Routing and Remote Access Service (RRAS), a tool that (among other things) can selectively filter network traffic and use it to selectively limit traffic on the web server.*

entails its own set of security-related threats; it is important to avoid exacerbating these threats by introducing additional NetBIOS-related ones. Disabling the Server and Workstation Services on dedicated IIS servers can also help prevent a number of known attacks on Windows NT systems; in most cases, you will not disrupt Web services, unless you are hosting files served from a different computer.

- Promptly evaluate, and then install (as appropriate) Microsoft fixes for IIS security-related vulnerabilities soon after they become available.

Securing FTP

Microsoft's IIS Server functionality does not stop with Web servers. IIS also enables the system administrator to install an FTP server. The IIS FTP server enables clients to establish remote sessions in character mode, providing rather robust FTP services to a wide variety of clients. To reach an FTP server using a command line, the user must just enter a command with the following syntax:

```
C:\>ftp <name or IP address of FTP site>
```

Security-Related Vulnerabilities

Some of the major security-related vulnerabilities in IIS FTP include the following:

- If the IIS FTP server is not a domain controller, each FTP user is treated as a locally logged on user. You should now be familiar with the dangers of local logons.
- By default, IIS FTP access is anonymous; the FTP client logs on using "anonymous" as the username. We have already seen anonymous access of any type is dangerous (even though in many operational contexts it may be necessary).
- The IIS FTP server has trouble containing the highest point of FTP access within an FTP-accessible volume. In other words, users may be able to access directories and files above the point in the file system that FTP access should allow. All objects in a volume may therefore be accessible independently of NTFS directory (folder) permissions. For example, NTFS permissions may be Read (but nothing else) to Everyone (allowing access to *lower-level* subdirectories), but an anonymous FTP user may be able to reach higher-level directories anyway.
- The IIS FTP server also runs as SYSTEM. Malicious users may be able to circumvent NTFS permissions if they are able to execute commands and programs as SYSTEM.

- FTP users are either local users on the individual Windows NT machine on which the IIS FTP server runs or domain users. Each case has its own particular set of security liabilities, as discussed earlier. In either case, the anonymous user is also by default a member of the Everyone group on the individual system that houses the Web server or a member of Domain Users within the domain if the system is a domain controller.
- The IIS FTP server is vulnerable to a variety of denial-of-service attacks.

Buffer-Overflow Attacks Against the IIS FTP Server

With all the known buffer-overflow attacks against the IIS Web server, it is easy to overlook the possibility that such attacks can also occur with the IIS FTP server. Consider, however, the **NLST** *command in FTP. Any user with either anonymous or account-specific access to an IIS FTP server (IIS 4) can log on, and can then enter* **ls** *from the command line followed by a space, then at least 316 consecutive characters, and then finally* **<ENTER>**. *The result is that the FTP connection is broken; the following message displays on the client:*

```
>ftp: get:Connection reset by peer
```

If an attacker sends 505 "A" characters as an argument to the **ls** *command, however, the FTP connection is not only closed, but an additional error message appears on the client. The contents of this message are as follows:*

```
The instruction at '0x722c9262' referenced memory at "0x41414141'."
```

The hexadecimal values of `41` *indicates a buffer-overflow condition. (Recall that capital "A's" hexadecimal value is* `41`*.) A perpetrator could therefore also carefully structure the characters sent to cause commands in the overflow input to be executed. Because the IIS FTP server runs as SYSTEM, any overflow commands are executed with SYSTEM privileges.* ◆

Control Measures

Fortunately, just as in the case of the IIS Web server, numerous security control measures for the IIS FTP server are available. To configure an IIS FTP server securely, in fact, you need to mirror many of the actions needed to secure an IIS Web server. Some of the most important control measures include the following:

- Choose the type of authentication allowed wisely. Choices include allowing access by anonymous users or only by authenticated users. If you set up an FTP server for a development team, anonymous access is not appropriate; every developer should have a separate account with its own, difficult-to-guess password (although by default this is a clear-text password[9]). To control anonymous access, open ISM, and then select the FTP server you want to administer. The FTP Service Properties panel shown in Figure 8.7 displays. To enable anonymous access, click on Allow Anonymous Connections. (Note that you can assign a username and password to the anonymous user—by default it will be IUSR_servername.)

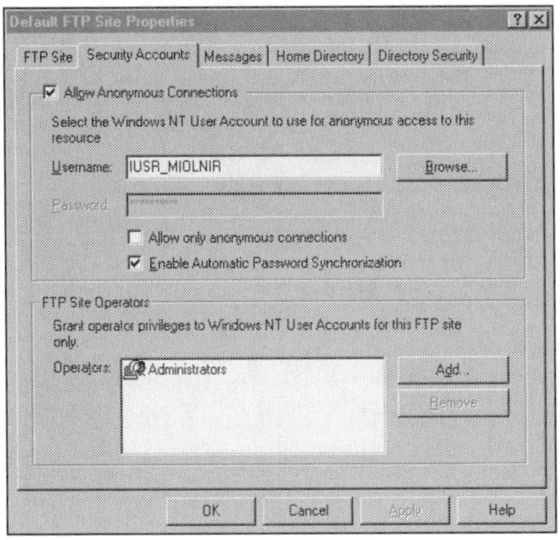

Figure 8.7 *FTP Security Accounts Properties panel.*

- Enable FTP logging. IIS FTP logging is parallel to IIS Web logging, as explained in the preceding section. As in the case of the IIS Web server, the text logs are sent to `\%systemroot%\System32\LogFiles`. Data concerning username, IP address of the client, name of file accessed, type of access (for example, open), date, and time is written as ASCII data to this path. Two cautions are appropriate:
    1. This file will fill in time—although you can choose the Automatically Open New Log option in the FTP Service Properties panel, you may want to archive, and then purge this file on a regular basis as part of your Web-administration activities.
    2. Set access permissions to this file to allow only Administrators the ability to Read, Modify, and/or Delete this file.
- When security is a critically important consideration, ensure that the home directory for FTP access is *not* on the C: partition. This could allow unauthorized access to system files (potentially by every user if you allow anonymous access). Verify this in the Home Directory tab in the Properties of the FTP server in the ISM. The screen shown in Figure 8.8 displays.

[9]*This is an instance where a one-time password such as S/Key or SecureID would be of benefit.*

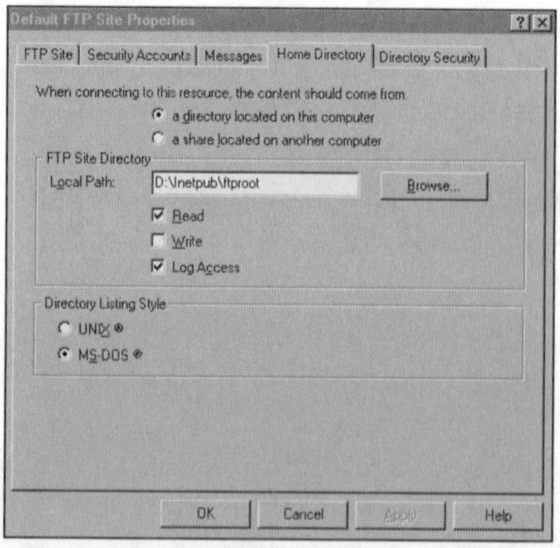

Figure 8.8 *FTP Home Directory Properties panel.*

You can easily change the partition on which the FTP home directory resides by entering another partition name. Additionally, except in environments in which security needs are low, it is best to dedicate FTP-accessible volumes to FTP access alone.

- As in the case of IIS Web servers, deploy each machine that houses an IIS FTP server wisely. In general, you should place FTP servers that allow anonymous access in a DMZ and all other FTP servers within your internal network.
- Set up the FTP server's directory structure properly (see Figure 8.9). `FTPROOT` should be the root directory for your FTP server. Below this directory should be four subdirectories, `PUB` (for public access), `INCOMING` (a "drop-in" subdirectory that allows anyone to contribute postings and/or executables to the FTP site), and `SERVER` (for the IIS FTP server programs).[10]

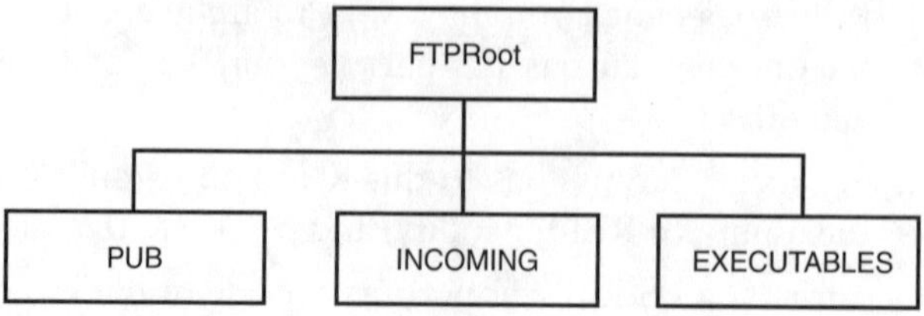

Figure 8.9 *Recommended directory structure for FTP server.*

[10] *You cannot create true drop-in directories on NT IIS FTP. You won't be able to write to a directory unless you have read to it. Also, if you have write, it means you also have delete.*

- Use the ISM to set access permissions. In general, Everyone should be able to Read in FTPROOT (the home directory), Read in PUB, Write in INCOMING, and Read in SERVER. All these directories (except FTPROOT) will be virtual directories, and can have different access permissions set. You need to set these permissions in the Properties section of each directory. This will be the Home Directory tab for FTPROOT, and the Virtual Directory tab for PUB, INCOMING, and SERVER. For FTPROOT (the others are similar), the screen shown in Figure 8.8 displays. You can select the permissions you want for the directory. This thus enables you to create multiple directories (one home directory and the other virtual directories) with their own permissions.
- You may want to filter out incoming FTP connections from certain IP addresses, just as in the previously explained case of your IIS Web server. To do this, double-click on the Internet Service Manager, then double-click on the name of the FTP server, and then click on the Advanced tab when you see the FTP Service Properties panel. You can enter any "exceptions" (that is, exclusions) to FTP access.
- Promptly obtain, test, and install vendor-supplied fixes as appropriate.

Your options concerning FTP servers are by no means limited to the IIS FTP server. The WAR FTP server, for example, is rapidly gaining in popularity within the user community. No matter which particular FTP server you choose, however, you will be faced with the task of dealing with inherent security-related vulnerabilities and vendor fixes. Some of the most critical security-related issues with which you need to deal are:

- Use of clear-text passwords
- Improper settings that allow users to put files on your FTP server[11]
- Buffer-overflow conditions

Mail Services

As in the case of Web and FTP services in the Windows NT arena, the particular security-related challenges you must face with mail services depend on the particular mail server you install. Some of the more popular mail servers include Microsoft Exchange, IBM's Domino Server, the Vintra Mail Server, and Seattle Laboratories' SL-Mail Server.

[11] *This is also known as a "warez" site—a place that makes pirated software available.*

Deployment Considerations Revisited

One of the first major security-related considerations with mail servers in general is placement of the Windows NT mail server within your network. Again, you must decide whether to deploy your mail server outside your network's security perimeter or within it. Placing it outside this perimeter is better from an internal network security standpoint because it limits the ability of a compromised mail server to reach internal machines. At the same time, however, the mail server (which in this case is normally on the DMZ) is more vulnerable to external attacks than if it were placed behind the firewall(s). Alternatively, an internal mail server is protected by the firewall(s), but compromise of the machine leaves the entire internal network open. The decision concerning where you deploy each mail server, therefore, depends on how comfortable you are with the security of the server, and the ramifications of a compromised server. This eventually boils down to risk analysis and cost-benefit tradeoffs.

Packet-Filtering Rules

After you have decided where to place your mail server(s), you should configure your firewall appropriately to provide the level of network security you need. The appropriate packet-filtering strategy for external versus internal mail servers is different. Consider the data in Table 8.1.

Table 8.1 A Look at Some Major Mail-Related Services and Default Port Conventions in Microsoft Exchange Server

PORT	SERVICE	AUTHENTICATION	REFERENCE
TCP 25	SMTP		RFC 821
TCP 110	POP3	Basic or CHAP	RFC 1734
UDP 135	Location service	Used by Exchange clients	
TCP 143	IMAP4	Basic or CHAP	RFC 2060, 2061
TCP 389	LDAP	Basic	RFC 1777
TCP 636	LDAP with SSL		
TCP 993	IMAP4 with SSL		
TCP 995	POP3 with SSL		

Each particular mail server will, of course, utilize a certain set of services and ports, some of which may differ from those in Table 8.1. The major point of Table 8.1 is that quite a number of ports and services are likely to be utilized. Consider, for example, an external Exchange Server. By default it initiates communications with other Exchange mail servers using the *Remote Procedure Call* (RPC), although it is possible to configure Exchange Server to use SMTP-based communications with external Exchange Servers. Internal Microsoft clients (Outlook, Exchange mail client) initiate communications with the Exchange Server using RPC. Other clients (for example, Eudora) use the *Post Office Protocol* (POP), version 3. Still other protocols such as the *Lightweight Directory Access Protocol* (LDAP) and the *Internet Mail Address Protocol* (IMAP) may also be utilized.

Security of the POP Protocol in Windows NT

The POP protocol supports Kerberos and MD5 hashes (known as KPOP and APOP, respectively), for authentication. They prevent the standard clear-text POP username and passwords from traversing the network. Unfortunately, the Exchange Server and Microsoft clients do not support these features. The clear-text nature of POP traffic in these arenas is therefore a security concern. ◆

Packet Filtering for External Mail Servers

One of the main security-related considerations regarding external mail servers is communications between each external mail server and internal clients. External mail server-to-external mail server communications is not affected by the firewall(s) because external mail servers are not behind firewalls. You need, however, at a minimum almost certainly to allow POP3[12] connections outbound from the internal network and through the firewall to external mail servers to allow clients to download mail. This necessitates implementing a firewall rule that permits traffic from IP addresses of internal mail clients bound for TCP port 110 of the external mail server. LDAP, SSL, and other types of connections between clients and mail servers require additional modifications of the firewall's rules for outbound access (see Table 8.1 again).

Packet Filtering for Internal Mail Servers

One of the primary security-related concerns regarding internal mail servers (and also mail servers that are on an internal DMZ—a protected segment immediately behind the firewall but not within the internal network) is communications between each internal mail server and external mail servers (called "site connectors" and "Internet connectors" in the Microsoft Exchange arena). A firewall-filtering strategy in this case must differ from the one described for external mail servers. You need to allow inbound

[12] *You can configure Outlook to use the POP protocol.*

traffic destined for either UDP port 135 or TCP port 25[13] (depending on the type of mail server used and its configuration) of the internal mail server from your ISP's mail server and possibly other sources. A *Virtual Private Network* (VPN) solution is far preferable to allowing incoming traffic destined for port 110 at the external gatewary. You may also have to allow inbound connections for TCP port 110 if users who travel are to access mail over the Internet. (Note that this method of mail access is questionable from a security perspective, as will be explained shortly.)

Choosing and Securing a Mail Server

Numerous vulnerabilities in Windows NT–based mail servers have emerged over the years. Many of these vulnerabilities allow denial-of-service attacks, although others allow unauthorized access to resources on the machine that houses the mail server itself. At the same time, Exchange offers some very effective security control measures including spamming control (through "turf lists") and digital signatures. The best course of action is to read Win2Ksecadvice (`www.win2ksecadvice.com`), Security Focus (`www.securityfocus.com`), and NTbugtraq (`www.ntbugtraq.com`) and obtain as much information you can from the vendors, and then to decide which particular mail server to use based on tradeoffs between security considerations, performance, reliability, and other criteria. After you deploy the server(s), you need to keep up with vulnerability notices and available fixes, just as is necessary in the Windows NT security arena in general.

Additional Issues

One subject beyond the scope of this book is the security issues associated with email content. You can secure connections to mail servers and configure these servers correctly, yet have users send messages with undesirable content. HTML, MIME, VBScript, active content, and encryption all also raise many security issues. These issues are very complex and the answers are usually very specific to each organization. Consider email confidentiality (secure email), for example. There are multiple options (for example, Pretty Good Privacy [PGP]) for this functionality, none of which are universally supported. As far as mail content goes, many organizations deploy *guards*, hosts that screen network traffic for messages containing objectionable words, certain kinds of programs, and so forth. An example is Trend Micro's ScanMail (`http://www.trendmicro.com`). These and other important issues require decisive resolution, regardless of the particular mail system

[13] *If the inbound traffic is from regular SMTP servers, you don't need port 135. However, if you have a gateway Exchange server in the DMZ and an internal server, you can hard code the RPC port to use in the registry.*

and configuration used. The foundation for all decisions and security-related measures should be your organization's InfoSec policy.

Network News Transfer Protocol Services

Securing network news services is also a challenging task. In many ways, the issues that pertain to security in this area are similar to the issues concerning mail (especially with the content of the messages). *Network News Transfer Protocol* (NNTP) servers connect to external news servers during news transfers; clients connect to designated news servers to download news. One of the major differences, however, is that news connections from server-to-server and from client-to-server are all by convention initiated on TCP port 119; there is in this case no long list of default-port conventions.

The NNTP protocol is not as conducive to security as many other network protocols, so special care and precaution in securing news services is in order. A bug in numerous implementations of NNTP, for example, allows an attacker with access to a client to do more than download news; the attacker can actually download system files from the NNTP server. One of the potentially most dangerous targets in this kind of attack is the Security Accounts Manager (SAM) database. NNTP has also historically been vulnerable to denial-of-service attacks.

As in the case of mail servers, it is important to determine whether a news server should be an external server or an internal one. The same kinds of security and performance tradeoffs discussed in the preceding section apply to deploying news servers. In general, it is safer to deploy news servers within one's internal network, but doing so can negatively impact on performance. Internal news servers require that the firewalls allow traffic from an ISP news server and possibly others that is destined for TCP port 119 of the news server to get through, but that all other traffic bound for this port (regardless of destination address) be blocked. External news servers require a somewhat different set of firewall rules. In this latter case, news clients must be able to reach the external news server via TCP port 119, but all other traffic (inbound or outbound) destined for TCP port 119 on any other host should be blocked. Checking for NNTP-related bugs that affect Windows NT–based implementations of this protocol and obtaining, testing, and possibly installing any fixes that become available is also a very important part of a strategy to secure Windows NT news servers.

Simple Network Management Protocol

Its name, *Simple Network Management Protocol* (SNMP), implies that something about this protocol is simple; but this is yet another case of a misnomer. SNMP is actually a complex architecture that has evolved out of the *Simple Gateway Monitoring Protocol* (SGMP) specifications well over a decade ago. SGMP provided a genuinely simple way to monitor gateways (for example, routers). SNMP's functionality, in contrast, is by no means confined to routers. Its goal is in fact to provide facilities for monitoring and controlling networks, although SNMP v.1 and possibly v.2 actually do considerably better in monitoring network *nodes* than *networks* per se. The *control* side of SNMP functionality is not as far along as the monitoring side, either; SNMP v.3 introduces considerably more control-related functionality.

The second version of SNMP, SNMP v.2, is for the most part implemented in Windows NT. This version was originally supposed to incorporate better security mechanisms than in v.1, but the Internet Engineering Task Force (IETF) working group that drafted the Request For Comment (RFC) for this version of the protocol could not agree on a variety of security-related issues. Two working groups emerged, consequently, one that focused on a version called SNMPv2u and another that focused on SNMPv2*. Microsoft's version is ostensibly an independent implementation based on SNMP v.2.

SNMP Functionality in Windows NT

The Windows NT implementation of SNMP serves several functions, including the following:

- System and network management (although the version of SNMP shipped with Windows NT 4.0 is purely an agent and does not accomplish any of this function by itself).
- Status and security updates. The main functionality here relates to SNMP traps, special kinds of data sent from network monitoring stations running monitoring "agents" (such as the SNMP Service included with NT 4.0) to an SNMP console running SNMP Manager software. Traps, which indicate that certain conditions in remote machines exist, include notification concerning bad logon attempts. This type of trap could be very useful if someone is gaining widespread, unauthorized access to your Windows NT machines, but no one knows where the intruder will strike next.

How to Enable and Configure SNMP

First install the SNMP Service on every Windows NT machine that will be an agent. Bring up the Control Panel and double-click on the Network icon. Now click on the Services tab, click on Add, and then highlight the SNMP Service from among the list of services that will appear (see Figure 8.10), and finally click on OK. This starts the SNMP Service.

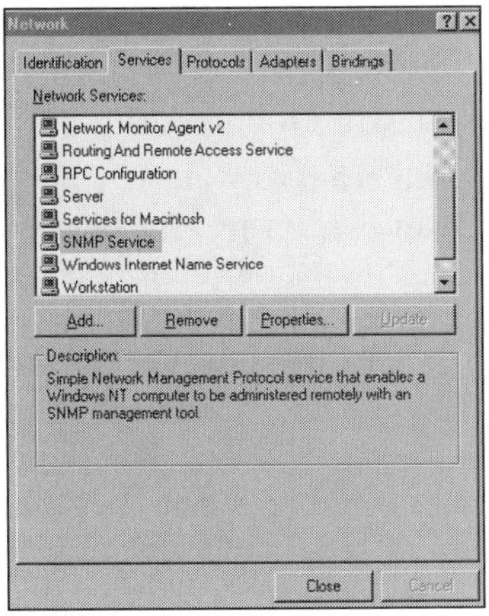

Figure 8.10 *Select Network Service panel.*

The next step is to select appropriate settings on the SNMP console. Go once again to the Control Panel, double-click on the Network icon, click on the Services tab, and then double-click on the SNMP Service. The SNMP Properties panel displays (see Figure 8.11). You have these configuration options:

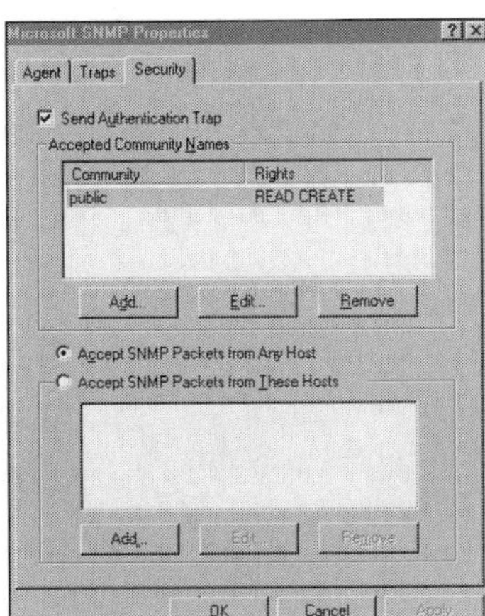

Figure 8.11 *SNMP Properties panel.*

- **Send Authentication Trap.** If you check this box, the SNMP Agent software sends a trap to the Manager (SNMP console) every time a failed logon attempt occurs. Note that you must either enable this capability or leave it disabled. If you enable it, you cannot selectively send traps based on certain users' failed logons but suppress traps when other users have bad logons; it is an all-or-none capability. After you have clicked on this option, you can enter a community name (a type of SNMP password for access) in the box immediately below.

- **Accept SNMP Packets from Any Host.** You can click on this box to receive SNMP management packets from any host running an SNMP management console, or you can check the Only Accept SNMP Packets from These Hosts option instead. If you click on the latter, you must enter the host names from which the SNMP Agent will accept these packets in the box immediately below, and then click OK. The original goal of this option was to limit the number of hosts from which SNMP attacks could be initiated. It can serve the useful purpose of limiting the amount of SNMP traffic if configured properly.

Security-Related Vulnerabilities

SNMP is based on the User Datagram Protocol (UDP). For this and other reasons, the security potential of this protocol is limited. SNMP attacks have historically been one of the most frequent types of attacks on routers, but they can also lead to compromise of any SNMP server and agent platform. The following are among the best known SNMP-related vulnerabilities in the Windows NT arena:

- Community strings (strings that are in effect passwords for access to a set of hosts that compromise an "SNMP community") are vulnerable to brute-force attacks. The easiest way to misuse SNMP to gain illegal access to SNMP-capable hosts, in fact, is to initiate an SNMP connection to the target host, and then to guess the community string. Exacerbating this problem is the fact that the community string has a default value that very few people ever change. The default community string for Read access, for example, is "public."
- In pre-Service Pack 4 Windows NT systems running the SNMP Agent, the default community string is not set to Read Only, but rather allows both a Read and Create (Write). Anyone who knows and enters this string for SNMP access therefore has the ability to modify SNMP configuration parameters. (This vulnerability is fixed by Service Pack 4; Read and Create are now two separate permissions after this Service Pack has been installed. Prior to SP4, there was not an option for Read Only, it was only Read Create.)
- The Windows NT implementation of SNMP is subject to sizeable memory leaks. An attacker can initiate queries to an SNMP Agent to gain access to information held in the target system's memory. Service Pack 6 fixes this vulnerability.
- In Windows NT, SNMP traffic goes across the net in clear text unless a VPN solution is in place.

- Usernames can be remotely retrieved via SNMP, even if regular remote mechanisms are controlled through solutions such as those previously discussed (for example, the Restrict Anonymous Registry change).

Solutions

Making SNMP more secure in the Windows NT environment requires that you address several important issues:

- Do you really need to run SNMP? You may find that other programs and/or protocols serve the same purpose, but without as high a level of security exposure. You might, for example, consider using the Windows NT Alerting service in lieu of SNMP because the former (although by no means perfect) generally introduces fewer security-related vulnerabilities.
- If you need to run SNMP, evaluate whether you need to run Windows NT's implementation of this protocol. Other SNMP implementations such as Hewlett-Packard's Open View (`http://www.hp.com`) are generally considered to be more secure. You may, therefore, want to evaluate and possibly use other SNMP implementations. Note that other implementations are likely to offer more functionality, too.
- If you run SNMP, be sure to change the default community strings to difficult-to-guess values immediately after you install this service.
- Use packet filtering at the entrance to screened subnets to guard against a variety of SNMP attacks. You should definitely use an *external* firewall to filter all incoming traffic bound for UDP ports 161 and 162 (the default SNMP ports). But equally importantly, at the entrance to each subnet you should screen out all incoming SNMP traffic originating from systems that do not run SNMP. This reduces the impact of SNMP vulnerabilities by stopping the kinds of attacks mentioned earlier in this section at the external gateway to your network and subnets.

SNMP: Do You Really Need It?

The most basic consideration in securing Windows NT's SNMP is determining whether you need this protocol. Your systems will in general be safer if you do not enable SNMP in the first place. ◆

Dynamic Host Configuration Protocol

Another important security-related consideration is securing *Dynamic Host*

Configuration Protocol (DHCP). This section explores DHCP security.

How DHCP Works

DHCP automatically assigns IP addresses to machines on the net. Among the major reasons for dynamic addressing is lack of available address space. (For example, the range of addresses from `128.4.69.1` through `128.4.69.200` is available, but there are 30 servers and 200 client workstations.) Normally, you would want to assign a fixed address to every server; dynamic addressing for servers would cause major disruption of network services and applications. You would assign an IP address to each client as the client needs it for a certain period of time. The assignment is in the form of an address "lease." In the Windows NT implementation of DHCP, leases last for three days by default. If the DHCP administrator does not renew the lease, the lease is automatically renewed.

The procedures involved in lease assignment are shown in Figure 8.12. The client first initiates a lease request by broadcasting over the net using the DHCP protocol. The DHCP server responds by offering a lease to the client, using a broadcast message. The client acknowledges the lease offer by sending a DCHP acknowledgement. Finally, the DCHP sends its acknowledgement to indicate to the client that the lease is in place.

Figure 8.12 *How DHCP leases are assigned.*

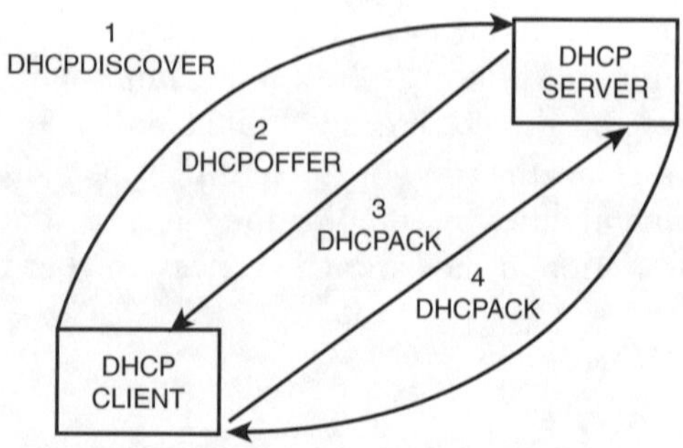

Security-Related Vulnerabilities

Unlike some of the other services in the Windows NT environment, relatively little about DHCP vulnerabilities in the Windows NT environment has surfaced on the net, so far. The main security-related concern is DHCP's susceptibility to denial-of-service attacks. A perpetrator can, for example, bring down a DHCP server very quickly by flooding it with lease requests.

A perpetrator with unauthorized access to a DHCP server could also engage in undesirable actions, such as modifying or erasing the DHCP tables. Another attack scenario is placing an illicit DHCP server within a network and having it respond to a client's DHCP discovery broadcast before the legitimate DHCP server can. If a perpetrator has also broken into the router, it is possible to circumvent normal DHCP services within a network. The bogus DHCP server can assign bogus IP addresses to clients, and then have traffic sent to a bogus network. Remember, too, that in the stack of protocols used by DHCP, the transport protocol is UDP, making security control in network environments very difficult to achieve.

Solutions

The best bet for protecting DHCP servers is deploying packet-screening solutions in a manner very similar to the one described in the preceding section. The difference is the specific ports involved. DHCP clients and servers by default utilize UDP ports 67 through 69. Blocking all incoming traffic destined for these ports at the external gateways provides a very effective first step. Implementing a selective screening strategy that allows DHCP clients and servers to freely communicate via these ports but that blocks traffic bound for these ports that has been sent by other machines is the second step. Ensuring that you keep abreast of vulnerabilities in Windows NT's implementation of DHCP and that you obtain and install fixes in an appropriate manner is also critical in keeping DHCP as secure as possible.

Windows Internet Name Service

The *Windows Internet Name Service* (WINS) is also a cause for concern as far as the security of Windows NT networks goes. This section discusses WINS security issues.

How WINS Works

WINS is the complementary service to DHCP. Its purpose is to map Network Basic Input Output System (NetBIOS) names to IP addresses. It also attempts to prevent DHCP from assigning the same Internet Protocol (IP) address to two different host names by notifying the DHCP server if this occurs.

Security-Related Vulnerabilities

The list of known WINS vulnerabilities is not currently a long one. One of the simpler, yet useful attacks, is gathering information from the WINS server. As discussed earlier, NetBIOS names tell about services running on a machine. A WINS server can be queried for this information from its tables, allowing a perpetrator to obtain information about an entire network from a single host (as opposed to scanning all the hosts, thus possibly setting off an IDS). Additionally, WINS, just like DHCP, is vulnerable to denial-of-service attacks and attacks in which WINS tables are subverted.

Solutions

The best bet for protecting WINS servers is nearly identical to the one previously discussed for DCHP. External firewalls as well as firewalls that screen the entrances to subnets together provide a strong security solution for protecting WINS. WINS data replication occurs between WINS servers on port 42; clients communicate with WINS servers on port 137 (NetBIOS name port). Implementing a packet-filtering strategy that allows for legitimate WINS-based traffic between certain hosts but blocks other hosts from obtaining access via these ports is the most important first step in securing this service. Discovering WINS-related vulnerabilities, evaluating them, and applying patches as appropriate are also critical in protecting WINS. Another very important step is to ensure that the WINS servers are always set to Replicate Only with Partners. Otherwise, anyone can set up a rogue WINS server and download the entire database from a production WINS server. This is the default setting.

Domain Name Service

Domain Name Service (DNS) runs on a variety of platforms, among which are Windows NT Servers. DNS is an extremely complicated service; many books that cover DNS exclusively and extensively are now available. Dealing with the details of DNS is beyond the scope of a book on Windows NT security. Suffice it to say at this point, however, that security vulnerabilities on Windows NT DNS servers are very similar to other platforms. The major decision to be made is what platform to use to run each DNS server,[14] and then determining the specific security features supported by that implementation that need to be enabled.

Suppose, for example, that an attacker could modify the DNS cache to cause a bogus entry to point to your trusted internal Web server. The user could put the DNS name in the browser, which could then do a DNS lookup and get the bad data (that is, an invalid IP address). The client browser would then connect to the target machine, possibly even sending

14 *This is even more difficult in Windows 2000 because DNS is tightly integrated with the Active Directory.*

authentication information at this point.[15] DNS is also very vulnerable to denial-of-service attacks. The security implications should by now be quite apparent.

Although securing DNS is a very complex issue, here are a few especially relevant security considerations in the Windows NT network environment:

- In environments with a need for high levels of security, dedicate each Windows NT–based DNS server to DNS. No other service should run on the same physical platform. It is especially important to avoid running DNS on any domain controller for the same reason that it is unwise to run any other network server with significant security-related vulnerabilities on a domain controller. Vulnerabilities in DNS could lead to subversion of the domain controller if the two are housed within the same physical platform.
- In environments with high-security needs, run DNS servers as *stand-alone servers*. At a minimum, it is unwise to bog down DNS servers with domain-related traffic. Remember, too, that DNS implementations are typically vulnerability-riddled; exploitation of one or more vulnerabilities on a DNS server on a physical platform that is also a member server could give an attacker an advantage in attacking other servers within the domain.
- Run "split DNS." It is generally best to have an external DNS server and an internal DNS server. Only the former responds to externally originated DNS queries, but does not leak any information about the identity of internal hosts to the outside world. The internal DNS server, which is protected by the firewall(s), responds only to queries initiated by internal hosts and resolves only the host names and addresses of these hosts by itself. For external hosts, the internal server could forward the queries to the external server.
- Ensure that you keep up to date on your domain name registrations. Although this is not an NT-specific issue, it is crucially important. Incidents have occurred in which attackers have monitored the expiration date of public registrations and immediately reregistered an expired host name to their own IP address, thereby not only denying the rightful owner the name, but now also redirecting unsuspecting users to a hostile site.

---

[15] *This depends on the browser settings, most of which are insecure.*

DNS Security: A Caveat

If you follow the suggestions for securing DNS on Windows NT platforms in this section, you should not walk away with the feeling that DNS is now secure. I have just presented a few suggestions here to help you control Windows NT–specific security vulnerabilities. ◆

Remote Access Service

The *Remote Access Service* (RAS) also poses a set of critical security-related issues. This section explores these issues and presents solutions.

How RAS Works

Several vendors have their own implementations of RAS that work in the Windows NT environment. This section considers only the Windows NT RAS implementation (including the more "industrial-strength" RRAS). RAS enables users to connect remotely to an individual Windows NT system or domain fairly similarly to how they would do it if they were local users (although the communications rate will almost certainly not be as fast). The most common access route is via conventional modem dial-in, although Windows NT RAS also supports access via X.25, *Integrated Systems Digital Networks* (ISDN), and VPNs.

Security-Related Vulnerabilities

RAS constitutes a potentially huge set of vulnerabilities for Windows NT systems. The major problem is *not* that the Windows NT implementation of RAS is in and of itself vulnerability ridden. The real problem is that "war dialers" that can sweep whole ranges of phone numbers and quickly identify modem dial-in tones, recording the number for future use by attackers. This is a major problem, because most users are not very security conscious. Therefore, they set up their machines to allow the easiest remote access method, which in many cases means installing an unsecured modem on the desktop.

Think of the number of attackers who can potentially reach a system or network by making a RAS connection, and then by guessing a password! Furthermore, RAS access can provide a quick and easy way for someone with a sufficient level of privileges to bypass network security defenses by creating an unauthorized dial-in access route to systems within a security perimeter.

Another major security-related vulnerability in the Windows NT implementation of RAS is that default authentication requires entry of only one password—"one-step (or "one-factor") authentication." Requiring nothing but the entry of a password to authenticate users is, as discussed previously, dangerous. Requiring only the same for *dial-in users* constitutes an even greater vulnerability! Note that if a RAS server is part of a domain, that server assumes the authentication role of a domain controller with respect to RAS access. If a user initiates such access, and then enters the correct username and password for RAS access, the RAS server by default authenticates the user to the domain. The scope of the user's access is not only the resources on the RAS server, but also potentially any resource within the entire domain!

Another significant vulnerability is that by default RAS session traffic goes across the net in clear text. Anyone able to monitor the traffic (which is mostly over public phone lines[16]) could, therefore, capture passwords, encryption keys used by applications, data transmitted over the PSTN, and other critical data.

Solutions

Windows NT RAS has some strong security control features, but they must be configured correctly if they are to be effective. RAS, for example, can use the *Challenge Handshake Authentication Protocol* (CHAP)[17] to negotiate the strongest encryption link possible between a RAS client and a RAS server during authentication. CHAP recognizes sufficiently strong[18] encryption protocols such as DES, MD4 (MS-CHAP), and MD-5, and will by default negotiate a DES-encrypted link between a Windows NT RAS server and a Windows NT or Win9x RAS client during authentication. If the client is a Shiva LAN Rover or other Shiva client, the *Shiva Password Authentication Protocol* (SPAP) is used to negotiate an encrypted link between the client and the Windows NT RAS server. If both the client and server do not support at least one common encryption protocol between them, communication between the client and protocol will be determined by the *Password Authentication Protocol* (PAP), which will just create a clear-text link. Table 8.2 lists authentication methods with the various client and server pairs in Windows NT RAS-based communications.

---

16 *This is also known as the Public Switched Telephone Network (PSTN).*

17 *MS-CHAPv2, even stronger from a security perspective, is available with SP4 and higher.*

18 *"Strong" in this context means strong enough to deter casual cryptoanalytic attacks. It does not, however, refer to the "strong" cryptography used by the U.S. National Security Agency.*

Table 8.2 RAS Authentication Options

Authentication	Client	Server
MS-CHAP (MD4)	NT, Win9x	Windows NT
MD5-CHAP	ANY	Non-Windows
DES	WFW, RAS 1.1a	Any
SPAP	Shiva clients	NT and Shiva
PAP (clear text)	Any	Any
RC4 (data only)	NT, Win9x	Windows NT

Despite the many positive security features available with Windows NT RAS server, you need to resolve a rather extensive set of issues if you want to establish suitable levels of security. These considerations include the following:

- Do users and system administrators really need RAS, or would another service do? If system administrators need to reach remote machines for administration purposes, could they use a less risky method (for example, using a leased-line connection and the secure shell program)?
- If you need some kind of dial-in access, does RAS itself afford the level of control you need? One of the problems with RAS is that it is in and of itself not all that conducive to central control. One system administrator can set up a RAS server within one Windows NT domain; another can set up another such server within another. Suppose that the domains trust each other. It is very possible that one RAS server is much less secure than the other, creating a weak link concerning domain access. In many cases, having a *central modem bank* with an authentication server that authenticates all access to all platforms (Windows NT, NetWare, UNIX, and so forth) is more suitable because it allows for more central control of and more consistent security for the ever-dangerous dial-in access.
- Be sure that if you allow and use RAS, RAS connections go to the appropriate destination. If sales staff need to dial in to obtain updates from a customer contact database, for example, allowing each dial-in user to authenticate to a domain increases the likelihood of disruption and loss considerably.
- Avoid allowing any workstation (Windows NT or Win9x) to run the RAS. Privilege control and security in general are usually much more difficult to control in workstations. Allowing RAS connections to workstations provides an opportunity for rogue users to set up back-door connections that bypass other security controls such as firewalls. You can see whether RAS is running if you have a remote command line on a workstation by just entering the following:

  ```
  C:\> net start
  ```

The listing will contain the name of the Remote Access Service if this service is running. In addition, the previously discussed RASLIST tool in the Resource Kit provides a listing of all hosts within a domain that run RAS servers. This works by doing NetBIOS name queries and listing those hosts that have registered `<computername><06>`. The 16th byte in a NetBIOS name denotes the type of the name. `<06>` denotes the RAS service and is registered by all hosts running the RAS service. Therefore, another way to find rogue RAS servers is to check the name registrations in your WINS database. To find RAS clients, look for `<21>`.

- An important consideration is the type(s) of RAS connection(s) you will allow. Should RAS connections be inbound, outbound, or both? As you can well imagine, the decision you make will drastically impact on RAS security. If you choose only outbound connections, for example, you have precluded the possibility that someone will dial in and gain unauthorized access to your RAS server.
- To choose the type of connections you will allow, go to the Control Panel of the RAS server, double-click on Network, and then click on the Remote Access Service. When the Remote Access Setup panel appears, click on Properties, and then click on Configure. (Alternatively, you can double-click on Remote Access Service, and then click on Configure.) The Configure Port Usage panel shown in Figure 8.13 displays. Note that in this panel, the following options appear: Dial Out Only, Receive Calls, and Dial Out and Receive Calls.

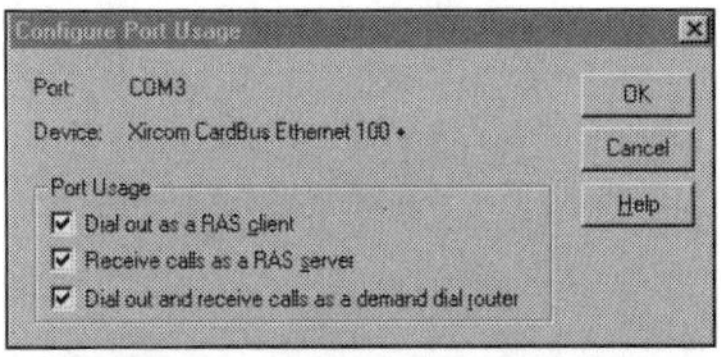

Figure 8.13 *Configure Port Usage panel.*

A good rule for determining the appropriate Configure Port Usage setting is using the "here-and-now rule." Allow only what current business and operational needs dictate; do not choose a setting based on anticipated future needs, or you will create unnecessary, additional routes of unauthorized access. Remember, RAS is in every sense of the word is one of the most potentially dangerous services that runs in the Windows NT environment.

- As you initially set up RAS, you will see a selection named Network within the Remote Access Setup panel. Click on this option. The

Network Configuration panel shown in Figure 8.14 displays. This panel contains some incredibly important choices for security. First, you need to specify dial-out protocols (NetBEUI, TCP/IP and/or IPX) and the types of clients (NetBEUI-, TCP/IP-, and/or IPX-capable clients) that are allowed to connect to the RAS server. On a host running the RRAS service, the panel looks slightly different, because it now has an option for Dial Out and Receive Calls as a Demand Dial Router. You may want to employ a method called "protocol isolation," using a different protocol for inbound connections from the one you use for outbound connections, if you require both kinds of connections on a specific RAS server. Protocol isolation makes RAS-based attacks more difficult to accomplish; the attacker must know how to exploit two different protocols. A common way of achieving protocol isolation is allowing inbound TCP/IP connections and outbound NetBEUI connections. Another advantage of this strategy from a security standpoint is that because outbound connections are NetBEUI connections, they, in and of themselves, cannot get through routers.[19] Remember, NetBEUI is not a routable protocol.

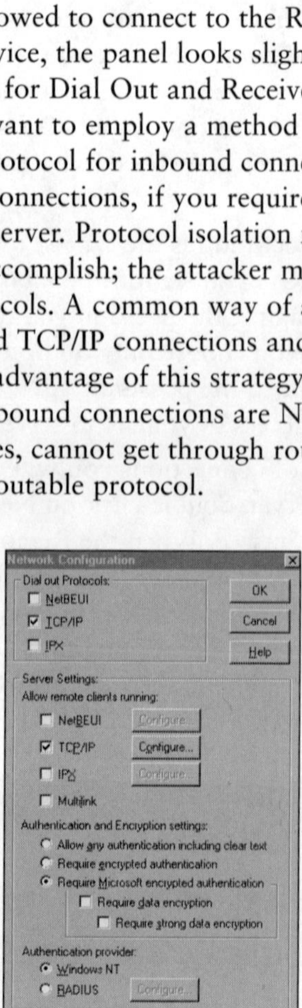

Figure 8.14 *Network Configuration panel.*[20]

The Encryption settings options in the Network Configuration panel are also extremely important. You must choose among authentication selections such as Allow Any Authentication Including Clear Text (a

---

[19] *It is still possible, however, to encapsulate Network Basic End User Interface (NetBEUI) packets in another protocol to tunnel NetBEUI traffic through routers.*

[20] *This dialog looks different in RRAS. There is a "Require strong data encryption" option, and also a RADIUS authentication option.*

bad option as far as security is concerned), Require Encrypted Authentication (which results in the "best" encryption link common to the client and server, but prevents clear-text authentication), or Require Microsoft Encrypted Authentication (the default when the client is a Windows NT or Win9x Workstation). The final option, Require Data Encryption, *does not* affect how passwords are sent over the net. It instead determines whether the session established after authentication has occurred will be encrypted using the "best" encryption link (as explained earlier in this section). The Require Data encryption option is therefore also a very important option; clear-text sessions can allow attackers to capture your organization's data.

- In environments with high-security needs, it is important to log RAS connections and attempted RAS logons. By default, the Audit log on a RAS server *will not* specially record events related to *RAS usage* per se. It does, of course, record logons, logoffs, and access to resources if you configure auditing appropriately. It *does not*, however, record whether a failed logon was an attempt to obtain RAS access unless you enable RAS auditing. RAS auditing dumps RAS-related entries[21] in the RAS servers' System log. You can then correlate the System log entries with Audit log entries to determine the origin of logons, failed logon attempts, and so forth. To enable RAS logging, you can make the following Registry change:

  ```
  HKLM\System\CurrentControlSet\Services\RasMan\Parameters\Logging
  ```

  You need to assign a value of 1 to `Logging`, which is a `REG_DWORD` subkey.

- You may also want to log Point-To-Point (PPP) activity. This may increase your ability to discover variables such as whether a particular RAS connection was a conventional dial-in connection. Logging PPP activity is, however, more important from the standpoint of system and network troubleshooting than from a security perspective. If you want to enable PPP logging, you must modify the Registry one more time, as follows:

  ```
  HKLM\System\CurrentControlSet\Services\RasMan\PPP\Logging
  ```

  The value of the `Logging` subkey must again be 1. The key type is once again `REG_DWORD`.

[21] *RAS logging records almost everything including passwords!*

What's New? RAS Authentication in Windows 2000

Windows 2000 supports RAS connectivity. To combat many of the security-related vulnerabilities, Windows 2000 interfaces with a variety of authentication methods that include smart card– and certificate-based authentication. Although CryptoAPI still provides the cryptographic interface, in Windows 2000 CryptoAPI is part of a larger authentication architecture discussed in Chapter 11, "Security Considerations for Windows 2000." ◆

- It is easy to become distracted by all the things you must potentially do to secure RAS. When all is said and done, the most important single thing you can do to make RAS more secure is to interface RAS authentication with a third-party authentication product! Chapter 5, "Configuring Windows NT Server for Security," has already extensively covered the importance of third-party authentication, so we will not belabor this point. Third-party authentication is even more important in RAS authentication than it is in normal Windows NT authentication because of the special dangers associated with RAS. Windows NT's CryptoAPI provides the necessary authentication capability. In addition, the RRAS free add-on for NT Server enables you to use RADIUS authentication, for additional security.

CASE STUDY A Costly Incident Due to Unsecured Dial-Ins

Several years ago, a large financial institution noticed that unauthorized money transfers from its central facility to banks around the world were occurring. Cooperating with the law enforcement community, investigators discovered that the money transfers were being initiated through dial-in connections originating in Europe. The perpetrators originally broke into machines used by system administrators to learn of modem dial-in routes, and then reached servers that controlled financial transactions. Dial-in access was not secured; all the perpetrators had to do to gain remote access was enter the username and password needed for access to the target hosts. This security-conscious institution had overlooked one important consideration—ensuring that dial-in access had the necessary additional security controls. Fortunately for this institution, it recovered the majority of the money that had been illegally transferred. Learning its lesson well, it subsequently implemented third-party authentication for dial-ins using smart card technology.

Conclusion

This chapter has covered the types of network services in the Windows NT environment that pose special security risks, the nature of the vulnerabilities they introduce, potential solutions, and tradeoffs related to these solutions. Web services, SNMP, DNS, and RAS are the three services that are currently the most frequent targets of attacks in this environment. Elevating the level of security in a Windows NT network environment requires an appreciation of just how much danger certain network environments introduce. You can put firewalls in place, configure systems appropriately, but install and run a certain network service without bothering about security and create a fatally weak security link. After understanding the risks created by network services in the Windows NT network environment, the next step is to just disable (or in many cases just to refrain from installing) services that are too dangerous from a security perspective to justify the benefits of running them.

The focus of this book next turns to security considerations related to clients on the network. As you may suspect, security concerns are not limited to Windows NT servers and the services they support. The next chapter provides a detailed look at vulnerabilities introduced by clients.

Security Checklist for Administrators

1. Ensure to the maximum degree possible that servers in the Windows NT environment run on dedicated platforms. Avoid implementing external servers as member servers or on domain controllers.
2. Determine the particular Web server (IIS, iPlanet, Apache, or another) that best meets your organization's security needs.
3. Deploy Web servers in a manner compatible with these needs. Deploying IIS in particular as an internal rather than external Web server is a wise idea. In general, it is also preferable to dedicate one Web server to one physical platform for the sake of security
4. Adopt the following security measures with the IIS Web server:
    - Choose a suitable authentication method. Challenge-response is most conducive to security, but it does not work with browsers other than the MSIE browser.
    - Secure the anonymous account. Assign a strong password and allow users No Access to files not intended for anonymous Web user access.
    - Enable SSL encryption.

- Dedicate Web-accessible volumes to the purpose of Web access—do not include files not intended for this type of access.
- Ensure that the Web server is installed on a drive other than the C: drive.
- Set up a suitable directory structure with several subdirectories for Web page content, scripts, and so forth under `WWWROOT`.
- Ensure that access permissions are appropriate. Allowing Read Only access is most conducive to security.
- Remove the Log On Locally right from the Everyone account.
- Enable logging and regularly read log entries.

5. Choose the type of FTP server you use wisely—numerous options are available.
6. Deploy FTP servers in a parallel manner to securely deploying Web servers.
7. Adopt the following security measures with the IIS FTP server:
    - Choose the appropriate authentication method. The more secure method is authenticating via individual accounts. This method is not, however, practical for public FTP access.
    - Enable FTP logging and regularly read log entries.
    - Ensure that the FTP home directory is installed on a drive other than the C: drive.
    - Set up a suitable directory structure that consists of multiple subdirectories.
    - Set appropriate permissions. Again, Read Only access is best for security.
    - If security needs dictate, implement traffic filtering on the FTP server.
8. Ensure that mail servers are properly deployed, as discussed in Chapter 7.
9. In Microsoft Exchange, use SMTP rather than RPC for connectivity to Internet connectors.
10. Implement a suitable packet-filtering strategy for internal mail servers that blocks incoming traffic bound for all but a limited set of ports on the mail server.

11. Deploy news servers in accordance with security needs. As in the case of mail servers, it is generally best for security to run news servers as internal servers.
12. Implement a packet-filtering strategy that blocks all incoming traffic to news servers other than traffic via TCP 119.
13. Consider whether you need SNMP; if strong business and/or operational needs do not dictate its use, avoid using it. If you need SNMP, strongly consider using an implementation other than Microsoft's.
14. Set SNMP traps to report bad logons if security needs require this functionality.
15. Change the default community string to a difficult-to-guess string.
16. Filter incoming SNMP traffic according to business and operational needs.
17. Protect DCHP and WINS servers by selectivity filtering incoming traffic bound for UDP ports 67 through 69 and TCP port 42.
18. Install split DNS.
19. Keep up with the latest vulnerabilities and install fixes as needed.

9

Virtual Private Networks

"Anyone who is dumb enough to send stuff in the clear deserves to have it captured and read."
–An anonymous attacker

After you have set up an appropriate level of basic network security and have ensured that the services you run are sufficiently secure, you might be tempted to think that the level of network security you have established is high. Although it is certainly true that many effective network security controls are now in place, justifying some degree of confidence and assurance, yet another potential threat alluded to in Chapter 7, "Basic Network Security Measures," still needs to be addressed. What if someone captures network traffic without authorization? This person could dump data in packets to glean passwords and steal sensitive information.

Unauthorized capture of clear-text traffic going over the network at any point is potentially a worst-case scenario. Most organizations are not very aware of just how much traffic—such as file transfers containing original research data, marketing plans, communication between high-level managers, and other valuable information—goes across networks in clear text. Organizations too often assume that as long as the boundaries to the outside world are protected properly, internal networks are safe. Yet just one saboteur can capture enough information to drive any corporation out of business and to expose secrets of agencies, boards, and research institutions that can give significant advantages to rivals and/or cause extreme embarrassment. We need, therefore, to turn our attention to the problem of securing network communications. This chapter covers Microsoft's *virtual private network* (VPN) capability in Windows NT.

What Are VPNs?

In a small local area network (LAN) with few, very trusted users and good physical security, clear-text data going over network wires is not likely to elevate security-related risk very much. The further this data is transmitted, the greater the risk (because there are more discrete points at which clear-text data can be captured without authorization). Sending clear-text data from one point to another over *a public network*, however, raises security-related concerns to an entirely different level. VPNs are secure "tunnels" over a public network, most notably the Internet. This secure tunnel allows two private, internal networks to communicate over the public network without compromising the communications that flow over them. The two networks may be corporate LANs, a single remote machine from the vast pool of "road warriors" that your company has, or an employee working from home.

From a user perspective, each user is on the internal network. Each has access to all the resources available to someone who is physically connected to the local LAN. The speed (bandwidth) is probably the only noticeable difference in a true VPN configuration.

From a connectivity standpoint (that is, bits going over the wire), however, there is a significant difference regarding virtual private networking. The VPN must package up all the bits, encrypt them (to keep the "private" in VPN), and then send them over the public network to the destination.

Is the Focus on VPNs in General or Windows NT VPNs?

This is not *a chapter on VPNs per se. This chapter covers only the Windows NT implementation of VPNs, namely MS Point-to-Point Tunneling Protocol (although a good deal of the information presented here also applies to other VPNs). Other books and articles cover other implementations of VPNs, such as Merike Kaeo's Designing Network Security (Indianapolis, Cisco Press, 1999).* ♦

Features and Functions

All VPNs have certain functions and features that make them VPNs. These functions deal with encryption, authentication, tunneling, and prevention of internal network access via any other means than the VPN itself.

Encryption and Authentication

The *P* in VPN stands for "private." This means that in some manner the data in the communications is not generally available for others to see. In the context of public networks, and the Internet as a specific example, this means that the data must be encrypted. That is OK, except now you need to ensure that you are encrypting with the person you choose. This is where authentication comes in.

Tunneling

You have to have a way to get packets that should only be on the internal network "transported" over to the other side of the VPN link. This is where tunneling comes in. We take a packet that has only internal information in it, and package it up for transport over the public network. The VPN then uses a "tunnel" as the transport mechanism of this packet.

Limiting Access to Internal Networks

You need to protect your internal network, so by definition a VPN has some firewall capability. It will not allow any external traffic into the internal network unless it goes through the VPN and thus acts as a firewall.

CASE STUDY **Clear-Text Network Traffic**

Recognizing that clear-text traffic sent across a public network results in major security-related risk does not by any means require extensive security-related experience. But does any real-world evidence exist to corroborate that security-related threats concerning the unauthorized capture of clear-text network traffic are real? The answer is definitely "yes." From late 1993 through 1996, a number of perpetrators installed packet-capturing programs on hosts connected to the same Ethernet segments to which Internet Service Providers (ISP) routers were connected. The perpetrators gleaned clear-text passwords and then broke into one account after another. At one point, one investigator reported that some perpetrators had captured so many passwords that they had to "stockpile" them, saving them for use much later.

Security Exposures in VPNs

Security exposures in VPNs are related to the potential to compromise one of the functional areas of the VPN previously described. If someone can compromise any of these functions, the VPN itself is breached, and the internal network's security may be compromised. The following is a basic description of the problems that occur if a specific function is compromised:

- **Authentication.** An authentication-related compromise (guessing the correct username and password combination, for example) would allow someone to access the VPN as an unauthorized user. That person may then have full access to the entire internal network, depending on how the VPN is configured. This scenario is, unfortunately, an all-too-likely one, especially if you are using reusable passwords for authentication. By default Windows NT uses reusable passwords for VPN authentication.

- **Encryption.** An encryption compromise, such as the theft of a cryptographic session key, would allow an attacker to view the data within the VPN. Although not directly compromising the internal network, as the authentication compromise does, this has the potential to leak information, which may be highly damaging to the company. This problem is, in general, not as likely to occur as the previously discussed authentication compromise. An encryption compromise be far more disruptive to a company. Think about the fallout from a leak of private medical information or credit card numbers. By default, the encryption keys used by Windows NT are not particularly strong[1] by today's cryptographic standards and can lead to compromise.
- **Firewall.** Similar to an authentication compromise, a failure of the firewall function of VPNs could potentially allow some level of access to the internal network, in terms of unauthorized incoming sessions.
- **Tunnel.** A compromise of the tunneling function of VPNs results in somewhat different consequences from ones now discussed. If the other previously discussed functions are not compromised, this kind of compromise results only in *denial of service* (DoS), providing the previous three features are sufficiently strong. Compromising the tunnel could allow the attacker to corrupt the data or send it elsewhere. Although this is not a direct threat to the data or the internal network, it would definitely be a DoS and possibly a data-theft scenario.

Microsoft Built-In VPN: Point-to-Point Tunneling Protocol

Now that we have looked at some of the functions and potential weaknesses of VPNs, let's turn our attention to Windows NT's *Point-to-Point Tunneling Protocol* (PPTP).

PPTP is a network protocol that enables you to encapsulate *Point-to-Point Protocol* (PPP) frames into Internet Protocol (IP) datagrams for transmission over IP-based networks such as the Internet. PPTP uses a "control" connection over TCP establish, maintain, and end "tunnel" portions of the VPN. PPTP also uses *generic routing encapsulation* (GRE) to encapsulate the PPP frames in the tunnel.

PPTP supports three network protocols (IP, IPX, and NetBEUI), and is most often used to provide client/server VPN connectivity over public networks. It also assumes that an IP connection already exists between the PPTP client and PPTP server. Whether it is a dial-up connection that has already been established or a dedicated line does not matter. What matters is that the IP connection already exists and is up and running.

[1] *See the PPTP analysis by Bruce Schneier and Peter Mudge at* `http://www.counterpane.com/pptp.html`.

About Windows NT PPTP

Note that the PPTP discussed here is not actually a Microsoft proprietary protocol. This PPTP is instead a protocol specified in an Internet draft developed by the PPTP Forum, which includes Microsoft Corporation, Ascend Communications, 3Com, and ECI Telematics. ◆

PPTP and VPN Functions

We know that machines that provide VPN services should have a certain set of functions: authentication, encryption, tunneling, and firewalls. The following sections explain what Microsoft does to provide these functions.

Authentication

PPTP servers require a username and password. The format of this information is determined by the server configuration. The supported authentication protocols are as follows[2]:

- **MD4.** For Remote Access Service (RAS) *clients* to non-NT RAS servers only
- **MS-CHAP.** For Windows NT, Windows for Workgroups (WfW), and Win9x RAS
- **CHAP.** DataEncryption Standard (DES) down-level RAS and other clients
- **SPAP.** For Shiva LAN Rover or Shiva Client
- **PAP.** Password Authentication Protocol

Windows NT PPTP attempts to negotiate the highest level of authentication possible between the client and server, depending on the particular authentication protocols that both support. The configuration options and the corresponding authentication mechanisms are as follows:

- **Allow any authentication including clear text.** This option supports any of the previously discussed protocols, including PAP (clear text).
- **Require encrypted authentication.** This one supports all the previously discussed protocols *except for* PAP.
- **Require Microsoft-encrypted authentication.** This option limits encryption during authentication to MS-CHAP alone. Choosing this protocol is required if you also want data encryption.

[2] *RRAS also supports RADIUS authentication, enabling virtually any authentication protocol.*

Using Windows NT PPTP: An Important Caveat

It is also important to realize that the MS-CHAP protocol is required for data encryption. Therefore, PPTP is really viable as a VPN solution only if you are running Windows-based clients such as Windows NT and Win9X. ♦

More About PPTP Authentication Options

By default PPTP uses one-step authentication, which it authenticates each user directly to the Windows NT Server without requiring any additional steps. The user needs only to enter a username and password. This process can substantially elevate security-related risk, especially if the PPTP server is a member of a domain within your internal network. If you allow one-step authentication, you should seriously consider deploying the PPTP server as an independent server, that is not part of any domain (see Chapter 8, "Securing Network Services and Protocols," for more explanation).

If you do not use third-party authentication to authenticate RAS users, you should also strongly consider running the PPTP server as an independent server. Clients can authenticate to the PPTP server and then authenticate to the internal domain in which they will access resources. This scheme elevates security somewhat but only if you require the use of *separate* passwords for the initial and the domain authentications—a very wise move indeed.

Encryption

Windows NT PPTP uses Microsoft *Point-to-Point Encryption* (MPPE)[3] to encrypt the data, that is, the PPP payload in the GRE packet. It uses the PPP encryption and compression mechanism as well as the *Compression Control Protocol* (CCP) to negotiate the type of encryption. The encryption key is derived from the user password. RC4 is used to create the key. The key length is 40 bits by default (unless you have the 128-bit upgrade[4], which is available overseas now) and is used to encrypt all data passed over the data connection. Encryption is enabled when you select the Require Data Encryption option in the PPTP server authentication configuration.[5]

It is important to understand that MPPE provides only link-level encryption, that is, data link layer in Open Systems Interconnect (OSI) seven-layer model between the two machines running the VPN endpoints. It is not end-to-end encryption between the client and server.

---

[3] *MS-CHAP must be used in order to use MPPE.*

[4] *Only available in the United States and Canada.*

[5] *Routing RAS also has a checkbox for "Require Strong Encryption" which I believe requires 128-bit encryption for the connection.*

Tunneling

PPTP uses the IP protocol's GRE protocol to tunnel PPP packets.

Firewall

By default, a Windows NT Server running a PPTP VPN does not provide any type of firewall protection at all. You need to enable packet filtering (as discussed later in this chapter) to get any type of protection from external traffic. It is probably better to place this type of server behind a real firewall to protect it.

PPTP Improvements in Service Pack 4

Service Pack (SP) 4 contains several improvements in PPTP.[6] This section describes each improvement.

MS-CHAPv2

Microsoft has improved the strength of its proprietary authentication protocol MS-CHAP in Windows NT SP4 and higher. MS-CHAPv2 does not use the weak LAN Manager password; it now uses client input into the challenge-response mechanism to provide some minimal mutual authentication, as well as to prevent replay attacks. MS-CHAPv2 also improves the password-changing protocol, which makes masquerading as a PPTP server for the purposes of stealing passwords by using the password-changing protocol considerably more difficult.

Unique Session Keys for Data Encryption

PPTP servers running on Windows NT SP4 machines and higher use unique session keys for client-to-server and server-to-client communications. The keys are derived from the password-hash and MS-CHAPv2 challenge. Because the challenge is different for the client-to-server and server-to-client authentication, so are the keys. Note that because the challenges are visible as they traverse the network, the encryption is only as strong as the user password. On the other hand, this method of creating session keys helps prevent replay attacks. The session keys are updates every 265 packets.

Security-Related Vulnerabilities That Still Remain

Despite the fixes and enhancements in SP4, several significant security-related vulnerabilities in Microsoft's PPTP remain. These include problems regarding the control channel and key generation.

[6] *There is also a PPTP hot fix for NT 4.0 SP3.*

Control Channel

As mentioned earlier, the control channel is used to perform "maintenance" on the PPTP channels; this is a very critical operation and should be secure. In the current versions of Microsoft's PPTP, the control operations are done in clear text without authentication.

Key Generation

The generation of keys is still only as strong as the user password, which (as you should recall from Chapter 2, "The Structure of Windows NT Security") is very susceptible to cracking. This result is weak encryption. Additionally, the RC4 algorithm has been cracked under certain circumstances, namely when the same key is used to encrypt multiple data streams, which is exactly what PPTP does!.

Configuring PPTP

You can use two configurations to implement Microsoft's PPTP VPN solutions: Client/server using RAS and a network-to-network configuration using RRAS. This section discusses the RAS implementation in detail, then briefly also covers the *Routing and Remote Access Service* (RRAS) service. This is not to suggest that the network-to-network implementation is not used, but you should be using a more robust VPN solution if you are connecting two networks together. Several commercial VPN solutions are listed later in this chapter.

Client/Server: Configuring PPTP on the Server

A PPTP server requires RAS, even if you are going to use it only over an IP-based network. The RAS service actually implements the PPTP protocol in Windows NT. You use the Install PPTP option in the Protocols tab in the Network Control Panel. After installation, you have to use the same interface to configure or remove PPTP.

The following steps explain how to install and configure a PPTP server on Windows NT. It is assumed that the system has been sufficiently hardened for this purpose.

Three major configuration steps apply when setting up a Windows NT based PPTP server, as follows:

1. Installing PPTP and then selecting the number of VPN devices
2. Adding the VPN devices as RAS ports and devices
3. Configuring encryption and authentication options

Installing PPTP

The installation steps are discussed, along with the appropriate screen shots. This installation is quite simple.

First you open the Network properties in the Control Panel. Then select the Protocols tab, as shown in Figure 9.1.

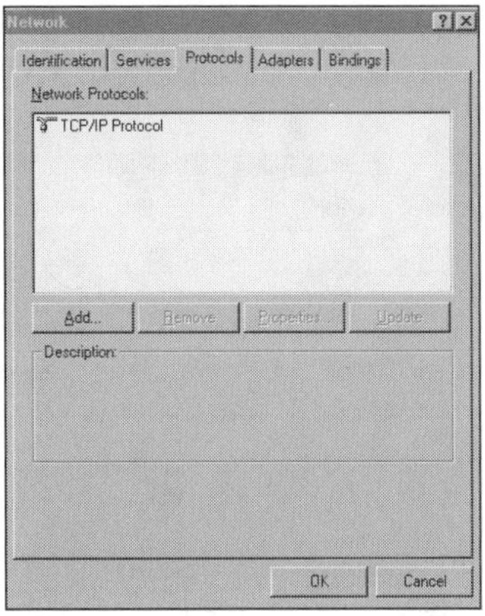

Figure 9.1 *The Network panel with the Protocols tab.*

Using the Add button, you add the Point-to-Point Tunneling Protocol, as seen in Figure 9.2.

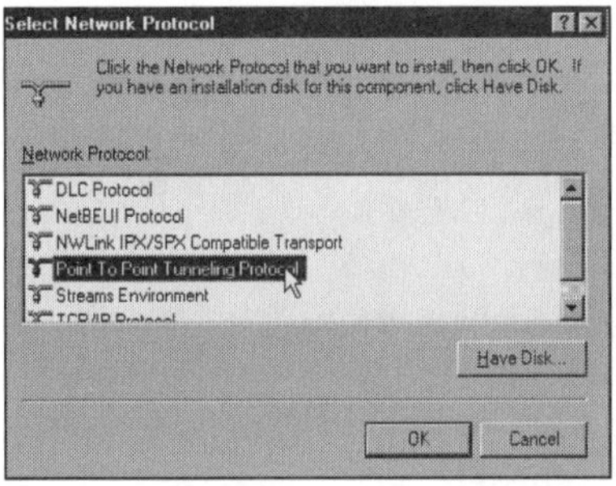

Figure 9.2 *The Select Network Protocol panel.*

You receive a prompt to enter the number of simultaneous VPN connections you want this server to support (see Figure 9.3). This number ranges from 1 to 256. You should normally leave it at the default of 1 for the installation.

Figure 9.3 *The PPTP Configuration panel.*

Next the RAS setup panel is displayed, you must now add the newly configured VPN connection to the list of RAS-capable devices (see Figure 9.4).

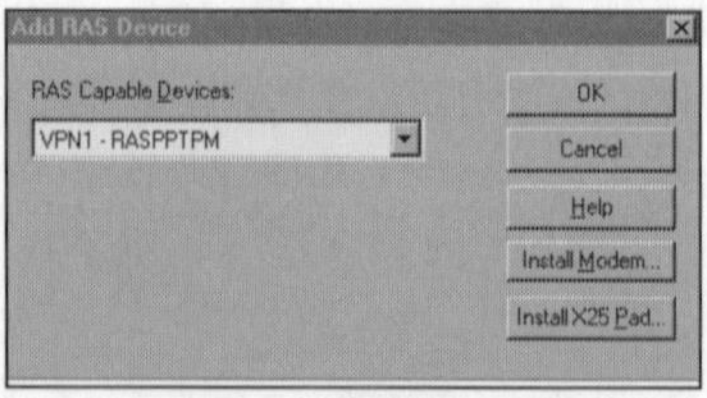

Figure 9.4 *The Add RAS Device panel.*

Next the Remote Access Setup panel displays (see Figure 9.5). In this panel, you configure the device you just added.

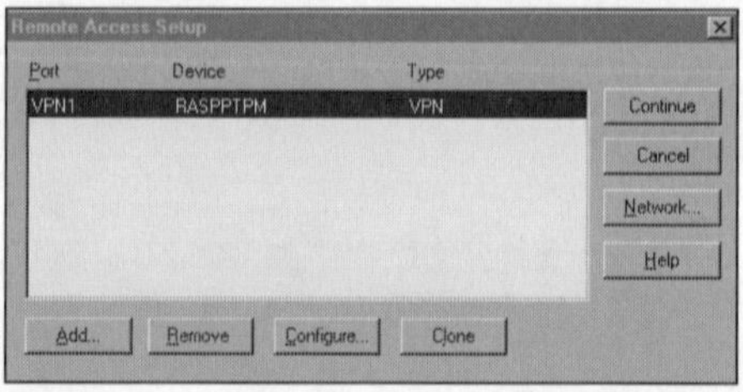

Figure 9.5 *The Remote Access Setup panel.*

There are two sets of configurations that you will want to validate: Configure and Network.

- **Configure.** This option is used to determine in what direction the RAS connections (PPTP in this case) can be made. For a PPTP server, the Receive Calls Only option should be selected (see Figure 9.6).
- **Network.** This option is used to determine which network protocols can be used by the PPTP clients and what encryption and authentication settings are used.

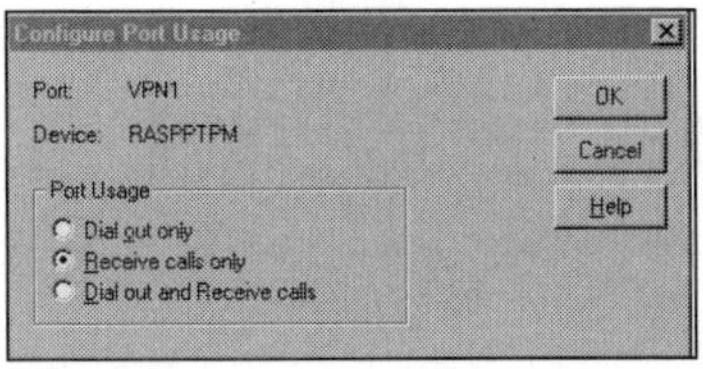

Figure 9.6 *The Configure Port Usage panel showing Port Usage options.*

Configuring Encryption and Authentication Options

The Encryption settings are used to configure both authentication and encryption for the PPTP links (see Figure 9.7). As described previously, to implement a PPTP VPN (with emphasis on *private*), you need to click on Require Microsoft Encrypted Authentication and Require Data Encryption. The configuration option for TCP/IP in the RAS Server TCP/IP Configuration panel enables you to set up the options for client IP address assignment and the internal network access options (the computer only or the entire internal network—see Figure 9.8). This latter option basically determines whether the PPTP server acts as an endpoint or a router. In Figure 9.8, the PPTP server is set up to allow clients to access the entire internal network (that is, unpack and decrypt the packets and then forward them to the internal IP network). It is important to note that IP Forwarding must be enabled for this option to work. See the section titled "Configuring LAN Routing" later in this chapter).

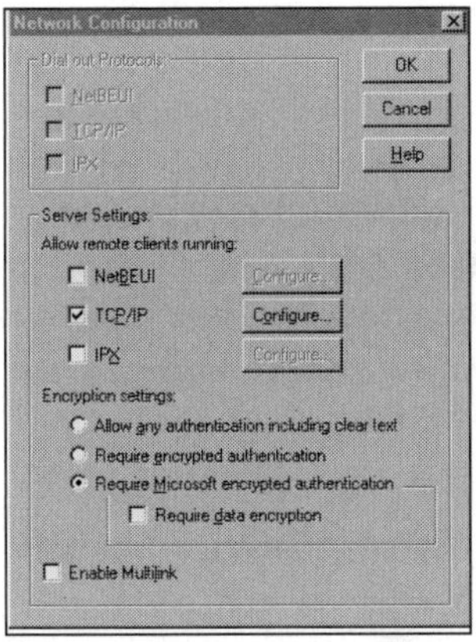

Figure 9.7 *Network Configuration panel showing Encryption settings.*

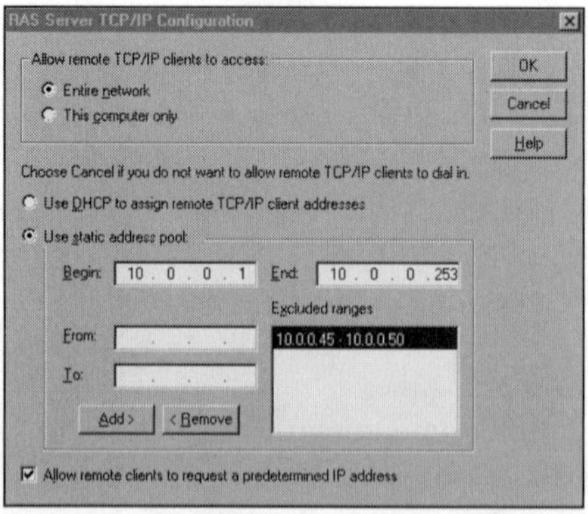

Figure 9.8 *RAS Server TCP/IP Configuration panel showing address assignment options.*

How to Check the Strength of PPTP Encryption

Once you choose the appropriate encryption settings, how can you verify that the encryption you have chosen is as strong as you think it is? One good solution is to use a packet-analysis tool such as the Network Monitor in the Systems Management Server (SMS). If you have enabled Windows NT PPTP with compression, you will see a line called "CCP Value" (for Compression Control Protocol Value) in the dumped-out packet fields. This line contains four octets of values. Ignore the first two octets; only the last two octets are important in verifying encryption strength. If the third octet contains the value 0x01, this means that 40-bit encryption based on the user's NT password hash is being used. (You should by now realize that given how easy NT password hashes are to crack, this constitutes the worst case when encryption is in place.) If the fourth octet contains the value 0x41, this means that 128-bit encryption is being used. If the fourth octet contains the value 0x20, this means that 40-bit encryption (not based on the user's NT password hash) is being used. 40-bit encryption not based on the user's NT password hash is not particularly strong, but it is certainly stronger than 40-bit encryption based on the user's NT password hash, as well as the true worst case...no encryption at all. ◆

The inbound clients are assigned an IP address in the range `10.0.0.1` to `10.0.0.253`, with `10.0.0.45` to `10.0.0.50` being excluded. It also allows the clients to request an IP address from the allowed range; and if it is not already allocated, it gives the client that IP. Assigning IP addresses from a range enables you to control address assignment directly from this panel and is, in general, the better way to perform address assignment. If you select the alternate choice, use DHCP to Assign Remote TCP/IP Addresses; DHCP assigns IP addresses to RAS clients as well as others from the range of addresses available for leasing. This is not necessarily bad for security, but often it is convenient to control and know about the IP address range assigned to RAS as (opposed to other) clients. One security-related advantage that assigning addresses from the address pool offers is that if suspicious activity originates from a known IP address within a network, whoever investigates this activity can usually quickly determine whether the host from which the activity has originated is an RAS client.

Post-Installation Configuration

That's it. Now you have the PPTP server installed. You now need to go back and do a couple of administrative "clean-ups" and take care of certain additional basic Windows NT security measures.

Number of Simultaneous PPTP Connections to Support

I have already recommended that during the setup, you should normally choose the default of one PPTP connection to the RAS server. This undoubtedly will not be large enough, so you will need to add more. If you are unsure of the number of connections you will need, start small (say, 5) then increase it if necessary. Do not allow more than you need; remember, less is almost always better in security. To configure this, open the Properties for the Point-to-Point Protocol in the Protocol tab of the Network Control Panel, as the screen shown in Figure 9.9 displays. You can change the number of PPTP devices to any number between 1 and 256. In Figure 9.9 the value 5 has been chosen.

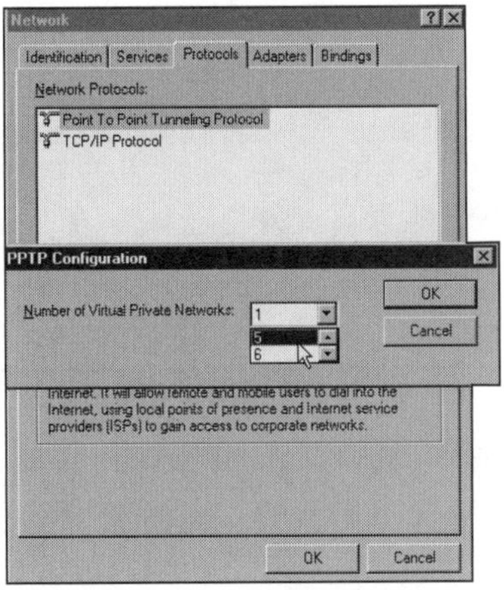

Figure 9.9 *PPTP Configuration panel.*

After you have selected the number of connections you want and select OK, you receive a prompt to configure the RAS devices associated with the new PPTP connectors. Click on the Add button (see Figure 9.10) and then select one of the new VPN devices (see Figure 9.11).

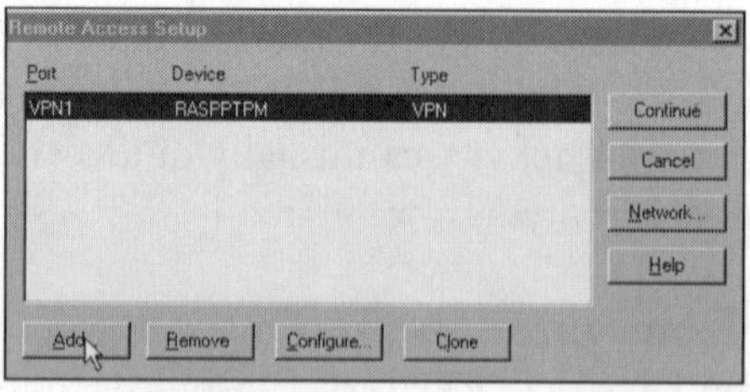

Figure 9.10 *Remote Access Setup panel showing Add button.*

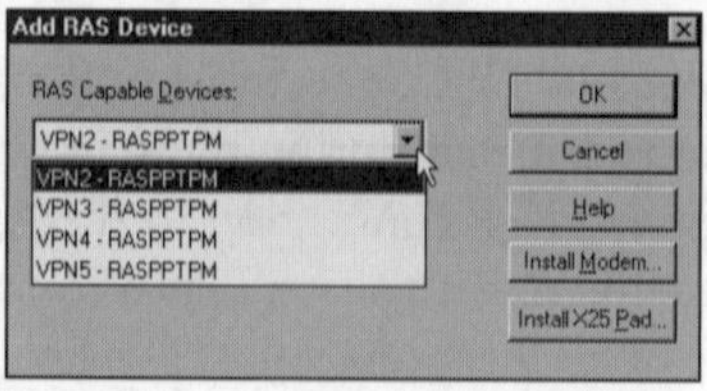

Figure 9.11 *Add RAS Device panel showing RAS Capable Devices.*

Do this for all the devices that you have added. After you have finished, the screen should look like the one in Figure 9.12.

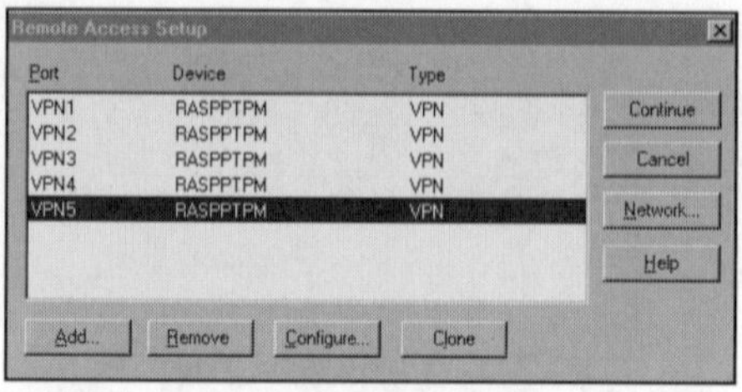

Figure 9.12 *Remote Access Setup panel showing a list of devices that have been added.*

Note that although you must *add* the devices to make them visible, you do not have to configure each of them. If you do not configure them, they use the configuration that the first VPN was configured with.
You can configure each VPN port to have different characteristics; one can accept and make calls, whereas another can just receive them.

As you use your PPTP server more, you may find a need to configure more simultaneous connections.

Configuring PPTP Filtering on the PPTP Server

This option provides the firewall function that is a part of VPN configurations. It can be used to configure a network adaptor to block all packets except PPTP packets. If you are using a multihomed (two or more network interface cards [NICs]) host, you can enable PPTP filtering on the public interface (the one that the PPTP client will connect to) and thus prevent any unwanted, non-VPN traffic from passing into your internal network. What this filter does is open port 1723 for protocol ID number 47 going in either direction. (Port 1723 is the port defined for PPTP traffic over TCP/IP connections.)

You can enable PPTP filtering in the Advanced button in the TCP/IP settings for the adaptor connected to the Internet (see Figure 9.13). You must check the PPTP Filtering option to enable it (see Figure 9.14).

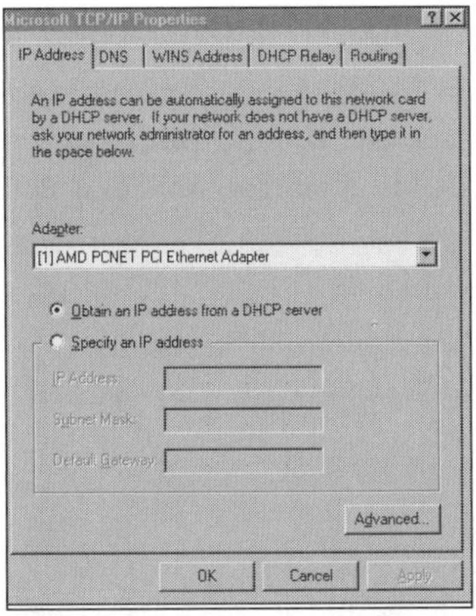

Figure 9.13 *Microsoft TCP/IP Properties Panel showing Advanced button.*

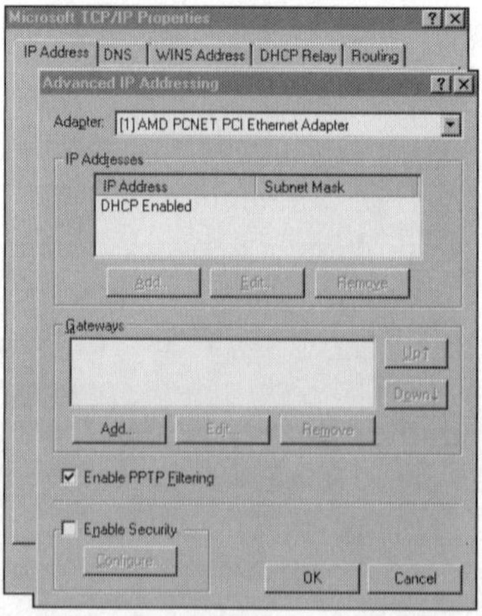

Figure 9.14 *Advanced IP Addressing panel showing PPTP Filtering option.*

Configuring LAN Routing

As described earlier, for PPTP clients to access the entire internal network, the PPTP server must act as a router (that is, forward packets, determine the route to forward them on, and so on). This configuration requires three configurations:

- Enable IP Forwarding
- Add Static Routes for Internal Networks
- Disable Adding of Default Gateway

Enable IP Forwarding

IP Forwarding is enabled in the Routing tab of the TCP/IP Properties in the Network Control Panel. Check the Enable IP Forwarding option (see Figure 9.15).

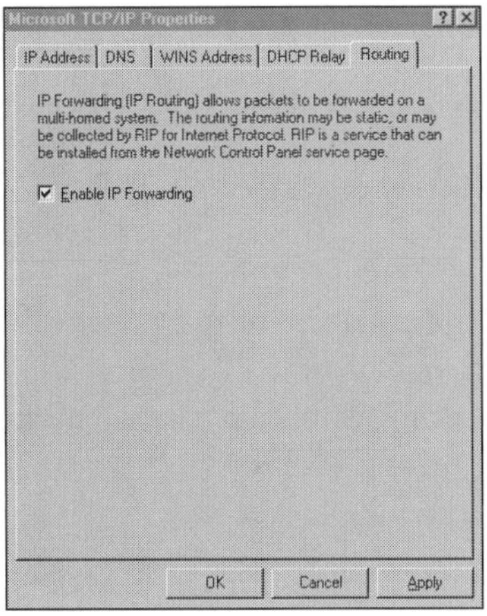

Figure 9.15 *Microsoft TCP/IP Properties panel showing Enable IP Forwarding option.*

Add Static Routes for Internal Networks

You need to add static routes[7] on your PPTP server to your private network. You can use the **route** command with the **–p** (persistent) option in the Command Prompt. This will ensure that routes to all internal subnets are known to the PPTP server. Without knowing these routes, the PPTP server instead broadcasts for every address requested by PPTP clients.

To add a static route for the `207.32.8` network, enter the following command:

```
C:\>route -p ADD 207.32.8.0 MASK 255.255.255.0 207.32.8.1 METRIC 1
```

These routes are very important, especially when you disable the addition of Default Routes (described next). If you don't add a route for a certain internal net, you cannot reach those hosts.

Disable Adding of Default Gateway

By default Windows NT adds a route for each network adaptor on the machine. On VPN servers, you don't want the machines to send route discovery requests for unknown IP addresses, so you can't have default routes. You need to disable automatic addition default routes on the PPTP server. You can do this by setting the following Registry value:

Hive: `HKEY_LOCAL_MACHINE`

Key: `\SYSTEM\CurrentControlSet\Services\<network adapter>\Parameters\Tcpip\`

[7] *What you are in effect doing is configuring a host to force use of a VPN.*

Value: `DontAddDefaultGateway`

Data: `0x1`

Type: `REG_DWORD`

Logging

The PPTP server logs information to the System Event Log. It logs events such as connection attempts to the PPTP server, when a user authenticated, the particular VPN port to which the user is connected, whether the encryption negotiation was "strong" (that is, 128 bit), and when the user disconnected. Figures 9.16 through 9.18 show a PPTP connection, disconnect, and summary.

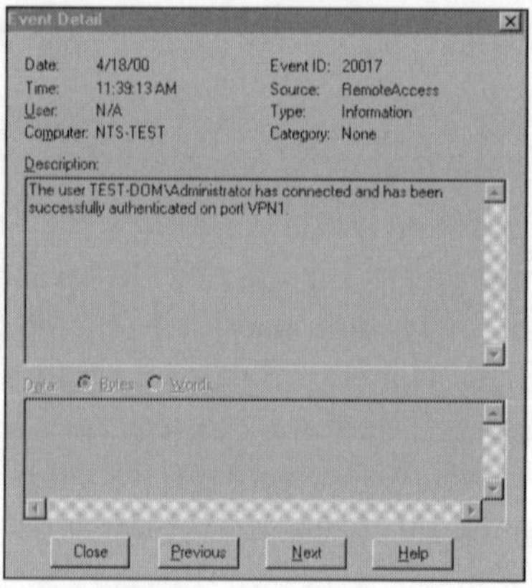

Figure 9.16 *Event Detail panel showing a PPTP connection.*

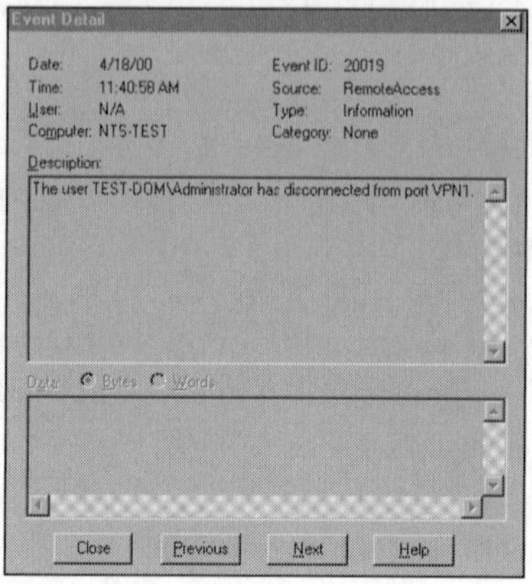

Figure 9.17 *Event Detail panel showing a PPTP disconnect.*

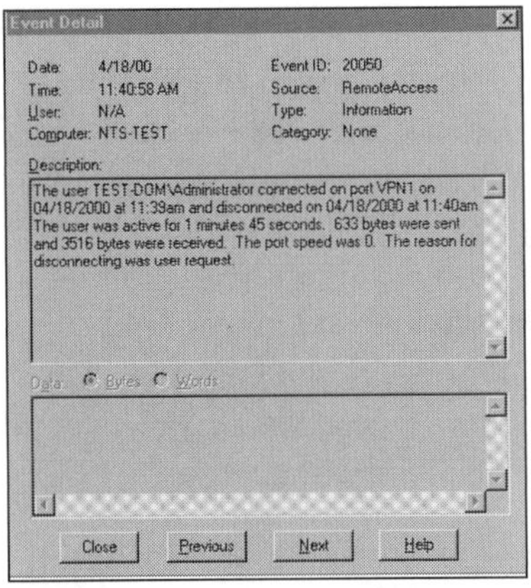

Figure 9.18 *Event Detail panel that displays summary information.*

Configuring PPTP on the Client

Now that you have set up the server, you must configure your clients. The client configuration consists of two steps:

- **Installing the PPTP protocol.** This is the same process as for the server. The only exception is that if you want only one VPN, you should choose Dial-Out Only (see Figure 9.19).
- **Configuring Dial-Up Networking to connect to the PPTP server.** The second step is to configure dial-up networking so that it will connect to the PPTP server. Do this by double clicking on *My Computer*, then *Dial-Up Networking* (DUN), then clicking on *New* below *Phonebook Entry to Dial.*

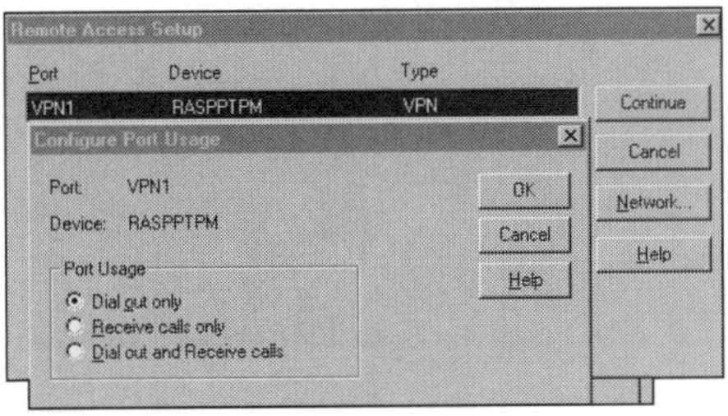

Figure 9.19 *Configure Port Usage panel.*

I assume that you have an existing IP connection to an ISP and therefore only discuss establishing a PPTP link over an existing IP connection.

Configuring a Dial-Up Networking RAS VPN Connection

Use *Dial-Up Networking* (DUN) to set up the PPTP client profile. The PPTP client "calls" the IP address of the PPTP server. The DUN profile you need to define specifies the VPN device (for example, a modem) and the host name (or IP address) of the PPTP server as the phone number. Let's now step through the Phonebook Entry settings that need to be configured. Figures 9.20 through 9.24 show these settings.

Under the Basic tab in the New Phonebook Entry panel, you need to define the entry name (see Figure 9.20). Make sure that you label it "PPTP" to identify it as the VPN connection.

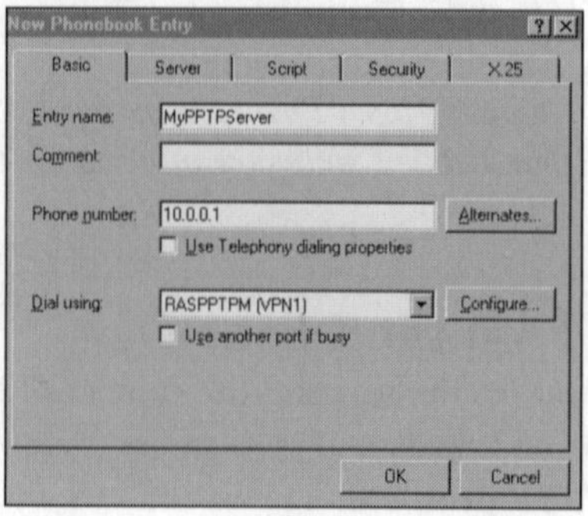

Figure 9.20 *New Phonebook Entry panel showing an entry in the Entry Name field.*

Enter the host name or IP address of the PPTP server to which you are connecting. You have the option of selecting more than one server. If you use the Alternates tab, you can specify a *list* of servers (see Figure 9.21). You need to also enter the VPN device that will be used to connect to that server.

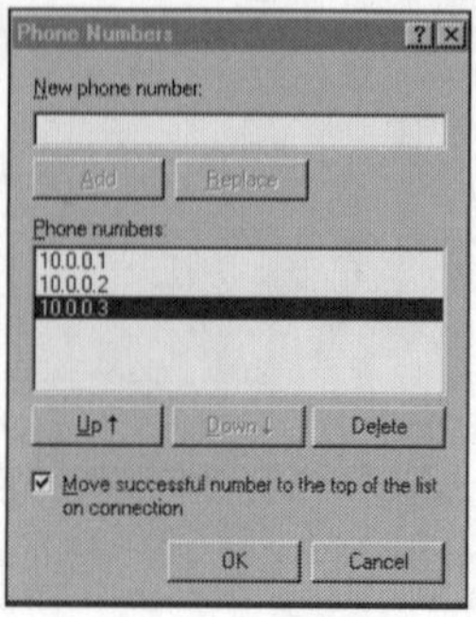

Figure 9.21 *Phone Numbers panel.*

Under the Server tab in the New Phonebook Entry panel, you need to choose the type of server to which you want to connect (see Figure 9.22). Using PPP to connect to a PPTP server is really the only viable alternative; other dial-in protocols are now obsolete. Also specify the networking protocols that will run over this connection. For VPN services, this should always be TCP/IP.

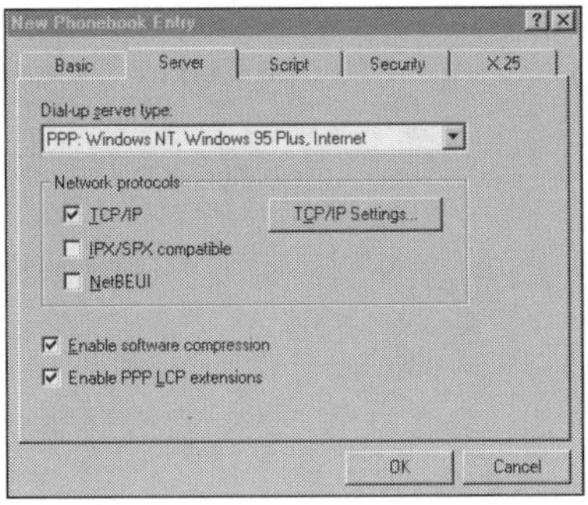

Figure 9.22 *New Phonebook Entry panel showing choice of Dial-Up server type.*

Configure the TPC/IP Settings (see Figure 9.23). The address assignment should be consistent with your server settings. Enable IP header compression. Compression lowers the bytes transmitted per second, which results in better network performance. On the other hand, the default gateway option is not relevant for PPTP because there is no default gateway defined on the PPTP server. You should then also enable compression.

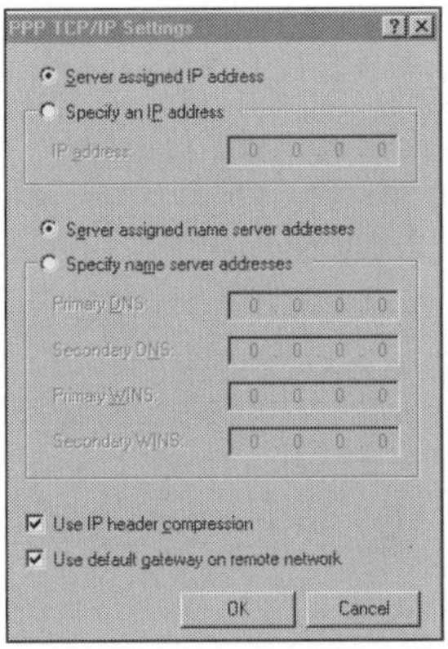

Figure 9.23 *PPP TCP/IP Settings panel.*

Under the Security tab in New Phonebook entry, you need to select the type of authentication you want to use to connect to the PPTP server (see Figure 9.24). Your selection must be consistent with your server. In the case of Windows NT Workstations (other Windows clients), you need to enable the MS-CHAP protocol (Microsoft's implementation of the DES protocol). Choose Accept Only Microsoft Encrypted Authentication in this case. You need also to choose the type of data encryption. Ensure that you select an option appropriate for your security needs. If your security needs are moderate to high, you should check Require Data Encryption.

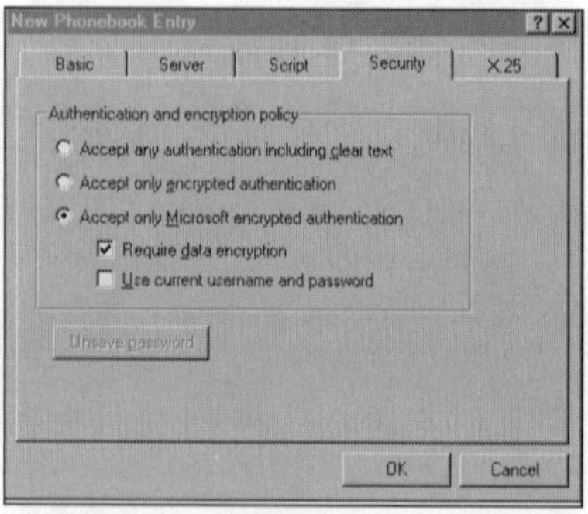

Figure 9.24 *New Phonebook Entry panel showing selection of authentication and data encryption.*

The option to use current username and password is dangerous. Your PPTP username and password should not be the same as your regular username and password. If the username and password are the same in both cases, an attacker who can authenticate as you on the PPTP server will also be able to access your internal resources as well.

What's New? PPTP and IPSec in Windows 2000

Windows 2000 offers two different PPTP implementations. The first is the PPTP protocol discussed in this chapter. This version allows for VPN interoperability between Windows 2000 and Windows NT 4.0 hosts. The second is a Windows 2000–specific PPTP protocol that allows VPN links between Windows 2000 but not Windows NT 4.0 hosts. Windows 2000 also supports the IPSec protocol, still another option for secure tunneling, as well as L2TP (the Layer Two Tunneling Protocol). IPSec potentially allows any Windows 2000 host to create a VPN link with any other host that supports this protocol. ♦

Routing and Remote Access Service

This section explores the Routing and Remote Access Service, its functions, and security-related considerations.

As you consider your options for creating encrypted network links, you are by no means limited to the client/server VPN capability that Windows NT RAS provides. You can also set up a PPTP VPN between networks using RRAS, or you can use an RRAS server to host connections from multiple RAS clients. The setup of the RRAS-based PPTP server is the same as the client/server setup. The main difference is that RRAS adds significantly more routing functionality. You would use this setup to configure secure routing between two networks, as shown in Figure 9.25.

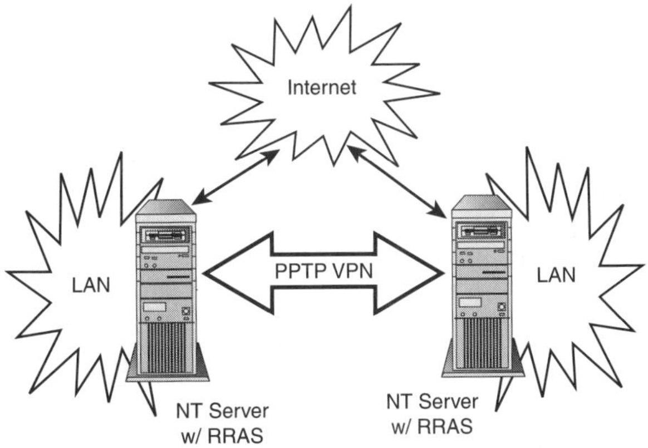

Figure 9.25 *Using RRAS for secure routing between networks.*

Some of the differences between RRAS and RAS are as follows:

- The graphical user interface (GUI) used to administer the RRAS service.
- You must use the Demand Dial Interfaces rather than Dial-up Networking (DUN) to configure the connections on the RAS server.
- You install RRAS/PPTP servers on both servers shown in Figure 9.25.
- Credentials are used to validate the two servers to each other (see Figure 9.25).

Why Use RRAS?

The Microsoft marketing literature promotes RRAS more on the basis of its integration capabilities than on anything else. IP-based networks are expanding rapidly, necessitating more remote access, increased routing capabilities, and VPNs. Microsoft contends that custom Application Programming Interfaces (APIs) must often be written to support many connectivity needs. RRAS provides a way for APIs to interface with a single host that provides a variety of functions, including routing, RAS, VPNs, and possibly also BackOffice applications.

Windows NT RRAS is not, however, just a service that provides integration capabilities. Other important functions include the following:

- Protocols such as RIP v2 for IP and IPX routing.
- Both a GUI and command-line interface. The latter can be used in connection with scripts developed for centrally managing a network.
- Packet-screening capability.
- API interfaces that work in connection with additional third-party routing protocols and management packages.
- Support for demand-dial routing.
- Support for RADIUS authentication server clients.
- VPN capabilities (the thrust of this chapter).

What's New? RRAS in Windows 2000

Windows 2000 RRAS offers a number of enhanced features and capabilities. For example, it provides built-in support for handling the Asynchronous Transport Mode (ATM) protocol as well as support for integrated Internet and conventional telephony. The Extensible Authentication Protocol (EAP) provides an interface capability with third-party authentication for RRAS PPP-based connections. The Bandwidth Allocation Protocol allows load management by adding or killing multilink connections on the basis of settings controlled by system administrators. Windows 2000 RRAS also features user profiles support through group profiles that enable system administrators to control ability to dial in as well as other security-related functions. ◆

Non-Microsoft PPTP Solutions

Many other VPN solutions not discussed in this chapter exist. Each solution has its own particular functionality, user interface, security advantages and liabilities, and so forth. The following is a list of non-Microsoft PPTP solutions; this list, however, is by no means exhaustive:

Cisco's PIX (`www.cisco.com/war[/public/cc/cisco/mktg/security/pix/`)

DSN's NetFortress (`www.fortresstech.com/`)

Brivida's Pirma One (`www.brivida.com/`)

Compaq's AltaVista Tunnel (`www.compac.com/info/issues/`)

InfoExpress VTCP/Secure (`www.infoexpress.com/`)

IBM's SecureWay (`www-4.ibm.com/software/secureway`)

Checkpoint's Firewall-1 SecuRemote (`www.checkpoint.com/svn`)

Computer Associates' etrust VPN
(`www.cai.com/solutions/enterprise/etrust/vpn/`)

Cylink's PrivateWire (`www.cylink.com/products/internetvpn/`)

Axent PowerVPN
(`www.axent.comAxent/Products/Framesection?ProductFamily=com.webridge.entity.Entity[OID[868C77278F5CD3118029009027856F18]]`)

NAI EagleRemote (`www.nai.com/nai_labs/asp_set/crypto/`)

Conclusion

Most people familiar with VPNs agree that despite a number of inherent vulnerabilities, Windows NT PPTP is an acceptable solution for limited VPN needs (provided, of course, that you install the latest fixes and updates). It is a very viable option for small companies and or for a small number of "road warriors," allowing a small business to realize the benefits of a wide area network (WAN), but necessitating that the business pay only for local ISP connectivity. Larger organizations that need a total VPN solution should look beyond the PPTP discussed in this chapter to third-party solutions such as the ones previously listed. In particular, commercial organizations such as banks should use a VPN product that does not present the limitations and introduce the vulnerabilities that the PPTP protocol discussed in this chapter does.

To further advance a theme promoted throughout this book, after you have installed and configured a PPTP solution, your work has only just begun. Maintaining PPTP security is every bit if not more important. At a minimum, ensure that you regularly check critical settings in PPTP clients and servers to verify that these settings have not been altered without authorization. Using a tripwire tool can be very useful in this respect.

Checklist for System Administrators

1. Determine whether Windows NT PPTP is suitable for your business and operational needs.
2. If you choose to go with Windows NT PPTP, and you decide that RAS is the best way to implement it, ensure that on the server side you do the following:
    - Enable the appropriate level of encryption for authentication. Remember that you can also encrypt data transmissions if you enable Microsoft encryption (MS-CHAP).
    - Choose the method of address assignment most suitable to your needs. In general, having a static pool is best.
    - Enable PPTP filtering.
    - Configure LAN routing and IP forwarding.

- Add static routes and disable adding a default gateway.
- Enable logging.
- At a minimum, ensure that SP4 is installed.

On the client side, do the following:

- Install PPTP.
- Configure the DUN RAS VPN connection.

3. Be sure to set up a set of procedures for security maintenance that include checking the integrity of critical security-related parameters.

10

Workstation Security

"Security of desktop machines is your newest worst nightmare."
–Marcus Ranum

What are you trying to accomplish when you implement Windows NT security control measures? If you are like most of us, you probably are most motivated to stop some Internet-based attacker or insider from breaking into your Windows NT Servers—especially your domain controllers. It is incredibly easy to overlook other kinds of threats that can sometimes be even more time-consuming and disruptive than break-ins. Workstation-related threats are perhaps the easiest to overlook because servers, not workstations, generally run business-critical applications, have greater storage capacity, and so forth. Servers can be domain controllers; workstations cannot. So what difference does it make if workstations are not secure?

Workstations that are not properly secured can cause widespread problems. Virus infections are a big case in point. Although not as dramatic as break-ins to systems, virus infections almost certainly occur more often and frequently cause extended down time and diversion of valuable resources to respond to the problem. If you are from a UNIX background and have recently introduced Windows NT into your computing environment, for all practical purposes you have not had to worry about viruses before—UNIX viruses "in the wild" are almost nonexistent.[1] This is not exactly the case with Windows NT, however, as you will see shortly. Viruses can attack virtually any machine, but workstations pose a particularly great threat because users can normally introduce new software and files by loading

[1] *UNIX systems have safeguards, such as the ld link editor, that not only prevent code relocation, but also permit only shared libraries to be used and require certain coding conventions. UNIX file permissions, in addition, provide protection against viruses. A source code virus could redefine* `main()` *to point to virus code, but other UNIX mechanisms would provide barriers against the virus' success.*

them into the desktop machines they use. Malicious executables (for example, ActiveX controls) loaded through browsers are another case in point. Some of these executables can access system and network resources without authorization. Once again the workstation becomes a special focus in Windows NT security. Finally, the Windows NT Workstations' relationships with Domain Controllers comprise still another reason to be concerned about workstation security.

After you have completed this chapter, you will have a genuine understanding of how to secure workstations to the degree that you need to. This understanding includes comprehending what viruses are and how they affect Windows NT systems, security-related problems with executables downloaded into browsers, and how clients can strengthen or reduce domain security. This chapter presents security-related solutions for each of these topics, presenting wherever possible the costs versus the benefits. The focus of this chapter once again is to enable you to achieve a *practical* understanding that you can apply to the workstation environment.

Viruses

Let's begin with the topic of viruses in the Windows NT environment by considering what a virus is, what the effects of virus infections are, the types of viruses, and why viruses flourish in certain environments.

Computer Virus Basics

A computer virus is a segment of unwanted, self-replicating code that spreads from one computer to another by attaching itself to and modifying an application program or other executable system component. Viruses generally disguise their presence temporarily for reasons to be discussed shortly, and may reside in a system and/or application for a considerable period of time until there are observable symptoms of the infection. In this respect, computer viruses mimic biological viruses for which they are named. After a period of dormancy, a virus can deliver its "payload," a manifest symptom, such as unusual graphic effects or reformatting a hard drive. Not all viruses deliver a payload, however. When viruses infect an application or some executable component, they modify the code in some way that compromises the integrity of the code, but may not affect the code integrity sufficiently to cause the program or system on which the program runs to crash or run incorrectly.

Effects of Virus Infections

The range of possible effects[2] of virus infections is wide. Some viruses cause virtually no manifest symptoms—these viruses just infect systems, and then spread. Other viruses cause damage to either systems (by reformatting hard drives, overwriting the File Allocation Table (FAT) or directory, deleting part of the system folder or system data files, and so on) or applications (by altering or erasing files). Non-damaging effects include reducing free memory, causing applications to quit for no apparent reason, displaying bizarre graphics (for example, a black box in the lower-right corner of a PC screen), bizarre or annoying messages, unusual pointer-input device mappings (for example, the pointer moves wildly whenever the pointer is in a corner of a display), an unexplained change in the system clock, failed warm boots, an increased number of disk sectors labeled "bad," and missing fonts.

Effects of virus infections are generally (but not always) caused by a virus's payload. *Logic bombs* are based on criteria, such as how many times the system has booted, how many infections the virus has caused, whether a certain file can be found, whether a particular character string can be found in a file, and even whether a particular number is generated by a random-number generator. *Time bombs*, on the other hand, deliver their payload when the system clock reaches a certain date/time, and/or afterwards or only during a particular interval of time (for example, any time during the month of October of any year, but not during any other month). Many time bombs, however, are not "true" time bombs, but rather are a combination of logic and time bombs. For example, most variants of the Michelangelo virus (a virus that infects the boot sector and can cause complete erasure of the hard drive) trigger after an MS-DOS system's first boot on or after March 6.

Virus infections can be costly. Viruses not only damage or completely destroy applications, data files, system software, and so forth, but a virus-infected machine cannot be used for its intended purpose while virus eradication efforts occur. This entails a compromise of mission for the infected system. It also requires effort on the part of users or technical support personnel to diagnose, contain, eradicate, and restore systems when virus infections occur. This, in addition to destruction of files that have not been backed up, can result in significant monetary loss.

---

[2] *Note that the effects of viruses are not necessarily planned by virus authors. Some virus algorithms work as planned, producing the intended payloads. A great number of known viruses, however, contain coding errors. Although some bugs do not produce any effects, some bugs produce unintentional damage. Bugs in virus code, therefore, are potentially a great threat to small systems, sometimes causing more damage than bug-free viruses were programmed to cause.*

Types of Viruses

Of the some 4,000 or more basic types of viruses in existence today (not counting, of course, the plethora of individual mutations), DOS viruses are by far the most prevalent. Although initially this may not seem relevant to Windows NT security, you will see shortly just how relevant it is. Several classes of viruses have emerged in the DOS arena, as explained here:

- **Boot infectors.** These attach themselves to the boot record or the *master boot record* (MBR). Some versions can even replace or displace either entirely. Because boot infectors infect systems during bootup, they virtually trigger automatic startup of a virus early in the boot sequence. The virus can monitor, trap, control system events, and can reside in memory to infect other programs. In addition, it is not difficult for boot infectors to defeat antivirus programs, because antivirus programs often execute relatively late in the bootup sequence.
- **System infectors.** These are programmed to infect a DOS executable, such as COMMAND.COM. These COM file infectors can also infect device drivers. Just as with boot infectors, system infectors can monitor system activity, search for new disks to infect, and even control all system events. Many viruses can infect system executables and/or device drivers, but few "true" system infectors exist. Most viruses that infect system executables and/or device drivers also infect applications, and, therefore, are really hybrids instead.
- **Application infectors.** These infect EXE files, gaining control of a system when the infected application is run. After application infectors have infected a host, they pass control to the application that is running. Some application infectors target only particular applications but do not infect others, whereas most other application infectors infect any application currently running. This type of virus then searches for additional applications to infect on floppy or hard disks.
- **Directory infectors.** These patch system directory entries to point to virus-infected code.
- **Hybrids.** These do not have all the characteristics of any one of the previously mentioned virus structures, but have characteristics common to two or more of these structures.
- **Macro viruses.** These infect macro code running within an application, such as MS-Word. These are a relatively new type of virus, which has been growing rapidly. Many of the recent, serious virus infections were Macro viruses that took advantage of the significant power imparted by the macro languages, especially in Microsoft's Office Suite.

Where Viruses Flourish

If you have seen a virus-infected system before, chances are that the infected system was a DOS-based system, or perhaps an older version of Macintosh. These types of systems are the most susceptible to viruses because these computers are single-state operating systems; each process continues to run until its completion or until an event (that is, a system interrupt or shutdown) occurs. A virus often takes control by generating an interrupt; the virus accomplishes what it is programmed to do, and then returns control back to the process counter. Memory-resident viruses have a major advantage in that they do not depend on other events (for example, interrupts) to become active, but instead lodge themselves into a memory block to stay active after the program they infect is done executing. Staying resident in memory, they can always maintain control and do whatever they are programmed to do (including reproducing themselves) at almost any time. Because a memory-resident virus remains active, it can capture system events, such as interrupt requests, thereby executing its own routines instead, and can also test for the presence of virus-detection software taking evasive measures if it finds such software running.

How Viruses Infect Windows NT Systems

Are viruses a real threat in the Windows NT environment or are they more "hype" than anything else, as in the UNIX environment? This section explores this issue.

Windows NT's Resistance to Virus Infections

Several features of Windows NT provide it with a certain degree of immunity to viruses, as explained here:

- As discussed in Chapter 2, "The Structure of Windows NT Security," Windows NT is a multi- rather than a single-state operating system. As such, the Process Manager determines how interrupts are handled; interrupts themselves do not therefore modify the execution stack. The Virtual Memory Manager also vigorously protects memory, determining which particular processes can stay resident in memory.
- Each of the Windows NT subsystems are resource independent, such that an abnormal condition that occurs in one should not be able to spread to or affect another subsystem.
- Windows NT–specific software drivers, rather than ROM BIOS disk drivers, govern low-level disk access. No virus of which we are currently aware can corrupt the NT-specific drivers, which run in Protected mode.

- The Windows *NT File System* (NTFS) also provides some protection against viruses. Viruses modify files; if set to prevent access, such as Write, Change, and Full Control access, NTFS permissions prevent unauthorized modification of files.
- Windows NT is a complex operating system. Making the proper set of system calls and coordinating events necessary for the successful execution of a virus is much more difficult in the Windows NT environment than in DOS.
- Windows NT does not allow User mode software access to the hardware. Furthermore, not even Kernel mode software is permitted to access certain portions of hardware, such as the MBR. This means that boot infectors cannot infect Windows NT directly. Boot infectors can only infect an NT system if that system is either booted from an infected DOS floppy disk, or dual-booted with a vulnerable operating system, such as Win9x.

In addition, a few non-technical factors have undoubtedly so far kept viruses out of the Windows NT arena. Purchasing a suitable hardware platform for the memory-hungry Windows NT operating system requires a significant cash expenditure—something that the culture of pranksters and disgruntled employees who have written so many DOS-based viruses is unlikely to be able afford. Additionally, it usually takes time for a body of knowledge that facilitates virus development for a given technology to develop—Windows NT was only first released in 1993.

Virus Infections in the Windows NT Environment

Just because Windows NT is structured in a manner not conducive to virus execution and because no successful viruses that target Windows NT alone exist does not mean that this platform is immune to virus infections. Windows NT is, in fact, vulnerable to viruses in several ways.

The boot sequence is vulnerable. When Intel, MIPS, and other platforms on which Windows NT runs boot, the first several stages of the boot process are independent of the particular operating system that has been installed; the hardware has no way of recognizing the operating system. Booting a Windows NT machine involves different types of boot drivers—BIOS boot drivers (which are invoked at first no matter what operating system is booted), as well as, Windows NT-specific boot drivers (see Figure 10.1). The former are susceptible to boot viruses because they cannot be protected by access permissions; if Windows NT is part of a dual-boot configuration, therefore, Windows NT can be affected by a boot virus. Boot viruses are programmed to infect a DOS partition—they are programmed to capitalize on functions, such as how DOS loads and how it controls interrupts. NT works differently, so some degree of mayhem is almost certainly bound to occur when a DOS virus infects a Windows NT system. In fact, one of the following several outcomes is likely:

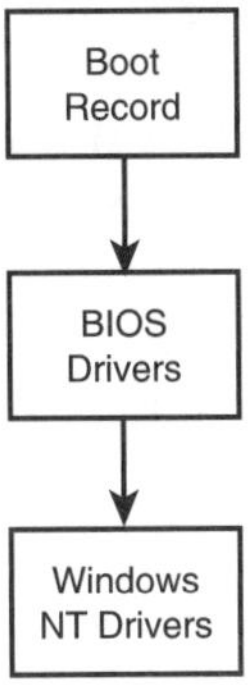

Figure 10.1 *The load sequence during the early part of the Windows NT boot process.*

1. As far as you can tell, the boot process proceeds normally and nothing else happens. The virus may replace a few instructions in the boot sector or may cause a few other changes, but it may not cause sufficient modification to result in detectable changes in the boot process. It may not deliver any payload.
2. The boot process proceeds normally (or, at least, *mostly* normally); the virus becomes noticeable only when it delivers its payload. An example is the One-Half virus, which does not prevent Windows NT from booting, but then encrypts data stored on hard drives.
3. The system boots repeatedly, but does not boot correctly. Many versions of the Monkey virus remove the pointers to the partition table, making Windows NT unable to boot properly because it cannot find the system's logical drives.
4. The boot process, for the most part, proceeds normally at first, but at some point (after a number of boots) the infected system cannot boot at all. If the virus infects the boot sector, but the boot sector code remains where it should; the impact on the boot process may initially be so small as to be virtually undetectable. Each boot is likely to make things worse, however, because more instructions are replaced, modified, and/or displaced with every boot. An example is most versions of the Form virus, which make Windows NT unable to boot after several successful boots.
5. The system begins to boot, but does not get very far before hanging catastrophically. It may even begin to do something bizarre (such as

internally mapping logical hard disk partitions to names of internal devices) first, and then suddenly freezes while displaying the Blue Screen of Death—a solid, Microsoft blue-colored screen. If you have ever seen the Blue Screen of Death, you are well aware that it is an indication of a worst-case scenario—a fatal error has occurred, as in the case in which the SCSI card has been configured incorrectly. Very often in such a case the virus will have infected the MBR, which, if corrupted very much at all, generally causes the boot process to fail. In this case, recovery is likely to be very difficult.

We do not currently completely understand the entire set of conditions that govern whether Windows NT can boot successfully despite an infection from a DOS boot infector and, if so, how many boots can occur before it can no longer boot. We do know, however, that MBR infections frequently spell major trouble. In all likelihood, additionally, the more the virus' assumptions about the DOS boot partition and MBR hold true in Windows NT, the more likely it is that viruses will not seriously damage or disrupt this operating system. Finally, although boot viruses can infect Windows NT, we have been unable to learn of any cases in which they could actually *reproduce* in the Windows NT environment. The viruses in existence at the time this book is being written are generally unable to accomplish functions, such as sending disk requests to corrupted BIOS disk drivers (because the Windows NT disk drivers, which run in Protected mode, are used instead). Replication to floppy disks and other media, therefore, has not been possible so far in Windows NT systems. To say it simply, boot viruses do not function well enough in the Windows NT environment to be able to complete the full virus life cycle—a cycle that includes self-reproduction. This in many ways is some kind of consolation, because although boot infectors may damage and disrupt Windows NT systems, at least the potential for boot viruses (the most prolific type of virus in the DOS arena) to *spread* in the Windows NT environment is limited.

CASE STUDY A Virus Infection in a Critical Network Host

A Fortune 100 company in the United States needed to install a firewall host to help protect one of its critical internal networks from unauthorized external access and other unacceptable security-related outcomes. After examining possible platforms on which to implement this firewall, security and network administrators determined that Windows NT provided a more secure environment than the other alternative they considered, UNIX. They designed, implemented, and installed a custom-built firewall. After it had been deployed, it worked properly at first, but then hung while booting several weeks later, stopping all incoming and outgoing traffic. They had a difficult time determining what was wrong, and finally after several days determined that a virus had damaged the boot partition, making the Windows NT system that housed the firewall unable to boot properly. Network administrators restored the infected system and installed a virus scanner to check for virus infections in the future. In discussing the incident some time later, an employee said that it had not even occurred to her that the firewall could get a virus infection because she was so used to working with UNIX systems. Furthermore, no one still is really sure how the virus was introduced in the first place or what specific virus had infected the Windows NT platform.

Applications running on Windows NT are also vulnerable to virus infections. This threat applies largely, but not exclusively, to DOS applications that run in Windows NT's DOS virtual environment because of the sheer number of application infectors in the DOS environment. If a virus should become memory-resident within the DOS virtual environment, the virus can potentially infect any program accessed and run if the permissions for the executable allow Write access.

As in the case of boot infector, viruses in the Windows NT environment, however, all may not go smoothly with a number of application infectors. First, the DOS Virtual Machine does not utilize DOS system service calls, causing a certain proportion of DOS applications to be unable to run within the Windows NT environment. This in turn in many instances justifies a dual-boot (DOS and Windows NT) configuration; now at least the DOS applications can run properly because they will have native DOS with all its system files and calls. If a certain percentage of DOS applications themselves do not run correctly in the Windows NT environment, application infectors will fare no better. Second, DOS application infectors, like other DOS viruses, make assumptions about how the application is loaded into memory and run, how interrupts are handled, which BIOS disk drivers are available and how to infect them, how graphics are generated, and so on. If Windows NT had a DOS-compatibility mode, it would be able to meet these assumptions; DOS application infector viruses would consistently work well in this mode. The fact that Windows NT has a *Virtual DOS Machine* (VDM) instead, however, often results in partial to complete failure of many of these application infectors to execute as programmed. One particular application infector, however, is so successful in the Windows NT environment that it merits separate discussion. Accordingly, the next section covers the topic of Word Macro viruses.

The Macro Virus Family

The viruses that have been most successful in the Windows NT environment to date are the Macro viruses that infect Microsoft Office files. Some of the better known viruses within this family include the Concept virus, WW6 Macro virus, Nuclear virus, Melissa, and others. Not at all hampered by the relatively limited environment that the VDM provides[3], these viruses can infect any Microsoft Word file by attaching themselves as an appended macro.

A macro is a set of commands used to manipulate files. Whenever an Office file with a macro attachment is exchanged, the macro is therefore also transmitted. An Office Macro virus replicates itself into other files when a user opens a file. Some of these viruses, such as the Concept virus, also modify the Save As routine within the Word executable. The main problem is that this virus is so proficient in reproducing that it is not uncommon to have hundreds or even thousands of infected files on workstations (if Word or Excel are run locally on workstations) or on servers within a matter of hours of the introduction of the virus via one file. This can make cleanup time-consuming, costly, and disruptive. Furthermore, although most versions of this virus do not damage anything, several versions (for example, Nuclear) are programmed to cause destruction of files.

Although prolific, the many variations of the Macro virus family are no cause for panic. As explained in the next section, with effective virus prevention and incident-response procedures, you can prevent outbreaks of these viruses and quickly eradicate any infections that may occur. The greatest concern is that these viruses provide several new infection vectors that were in many respects previously unprecedented (see Figure 10.2). A traditional vector through which most viruses have spread is through the "sneaker net," in which floppy disks containing infected files are inserted into machines. Web sites and electronic bulletin boards have also traditionally been responsible for spreading viruses.

More recently, infections have occurred with disproportional frequency as the result of users sending file enclosures over networks. More rarely, computer repair personnel introduce viruses or vendors ship viruses with releases of their products. Until last year, however, there had been a "catch"—the ability of viruses to spread depended on viruses' introduction to the proper operating system; DOS viruses were not able to infect

[3] *These viruses in almost every case infect 32-bit versions of Microsoft Office applications.*

Macintosh systems, nor were Windows 95 viruses able to infect Windows NT systems. The Macro virus family, however, is to a large degree platform independent. Any of these viruses can be transmitted from a large number of platforms—Win9x, Windows 3.1, Macintosh, Windows NT, and DOS-based systems to Windows NT and vice versa—because the Microsoft Office applications run on all of these platforms. Additionally, Windows NT provides a number of ways (for example, FTP and share access) to transfer files over networks; applications such as Microsoft Exchange, frequently found in Windows NT environments, further enhance file-transfer capabilities, as do most email packages. In addition, the fact that network connectivity has in general grown so much since viruses first emerged in the early 1980s allows many more opportunities to spread Macro viruses, as well as others.

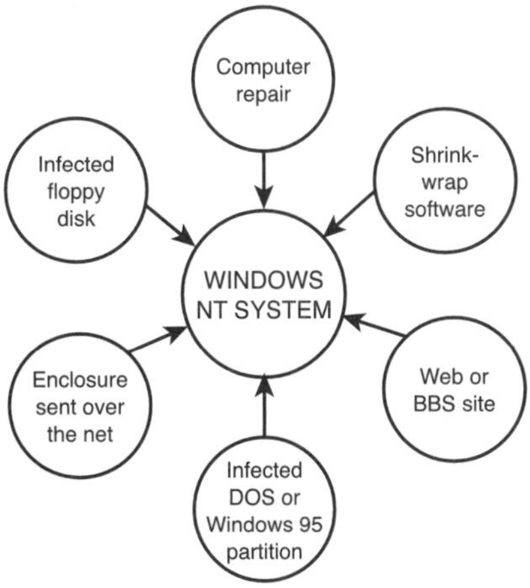

Figure 10.2 *Windows NT virus infection vectors.*

Practical Tips for Dealing with Viruses in the Windows NT Arena

Although virus infections in the Windows NT arena have not yet been prevalent (with the exception of the Macro viruses), the virus problem is likely to only get worse over time. The self-replicating property of viruses can make them extremely disruptive; when a virus has infected a Windows NT machine, it can rapidly spread to other servers and workstations until every system in a domain and also in related domains is infected. The fact that many viruses do not execute well in the Windows NT environment is in some ways an advantage, but it sometimes makes determining exactly what has happened and what steps of intervention to take more difficult. The first reasonable step in dealing with the Windows NT virus threat is learning how to the maximum degree possible to prevent Windows NT virus infections.

Preventing Virus Infections

Follow these guidelines for preventing virus infections:

- **Write-protect floppy disks.** The ideal solution for the Windows NT virus threat would be a software package that immunized all Windows NT systems against all virus infections. Unfortunately, such a package is not available; and even if it were, it would soon become obsolete as new viruses with increasingly sophisticated mechanisms emerged. You can, however, take a few practical precautions to minimize the likelihood of Windows NT systems becoming infected with viruses.

  Using *write-protect floppy disks* (including distribution disks) every time you insert a disk into one of your systems can help protect against virus infections. Normally, there is no reason to insert a write-enabled disk into your system when you are accomplishing tasks, such as copying files, to your hard disk. Write-protecting floppy disks can prevent spreading a virus from one Windows NT system to another. Write protection can also safeguard against virus reinfections if one or more machines have had a virus infection that has been eradicated, and you are reloading files from floppy disk. Locking up your disks when they are not being used (so that someone does not borrow your disks and possibly infect them with a virus before they are returned) is also important. Better yet is to avoid using floppy disks in the first place.

  In addition, you should take reasonable measures to protect your hard disk—software programs and electronic locking systems are available if needed. Finally, you should protect against the introduction of viruses from stray floppy disks by using the CMOS to disable default floppy boots.

- **Introducing new software.** This is another issue in the protection stage. Buying shrink-wrapped software from a trusted vendor is the best course of action; no matter how "clean" the software appears to be, however, a chance that it is virus infected always exists. Having a single central distribution point for all software, if practicable, is beneficial because it allows technical support personnel to first examine incoming software to determine whether the package appears to be legitimate. The new software package should ideally be run on an isolated machine to test whether a virus is present.

- **Backups.** Backups (covered in detail in Chapter 6, "Maintaining Windows NT Security") are an essential component of protecting systems: They prevent loss of data and programs, permit detailed analyses and comparisons (for example, when you suspect that someone has altered one of your files, or when you suspect that a new virus has infected a system), and provide a way to restore a system when all else fails. Be sure to keep backups, like any physical media, locked when they are not in use. In addition, regularly updating each system's *Emergency Repair Disk* (ERD) can prove extremely helpful when dealing with some kinds of virus infections, as discussed shortly.

- **Physical security.** Keeping server machines in a location where unauthorized users who might intentionally or unintentionally infect the system with a virus cannot access them is one of the most critical safeguards. Detaching external disk drives and keeping them locked when not in use is another good idea. Fortunately, Windows NT's mandatory authentication, screen saver, and the capability of limiting the Logon Locally right provide some sound controls against unauthorized physical access. Other possible physical security measures include circuit board authentication devices and programs that allow only predesignated software to run on a system.
- **Technical or small systems support center.** As mentioned previously, technical support personnel can check incoming software for viruses, and can distribute software when it is known to be virus free. These personnel can randomly check Windows NT servers and workstations for virus infections, thus preventing widespread outbreaks of viruses. Eradicating a virus is not often simple; technical support personnel can perform this function, as well as, coordinate site-wide efforts with computer security personnel. Finally, technical support personnel are critical in that they are likely to be up-to-date on virus-related issues.
- **Virus awareness and training.** At a minimum, inform users of required procedures, such as calling technical support if they think they may have a virus. (Idea: Place a sticker with the phone number of the appropriate technical support group on every computer, advise users against the use of software from untrusted sources (including Web and BBS sites), and also against responding to virus infections altogether, thereby risking worse damage and disruption (see the following sidebar). Users can prevent Word Macro virus infections by pressing the `Shift` key every time they open a Word file. Users can disable the Macro function altogether by choosing the Tools menu bar option, and then Macro options while running Microsoft Word. Having a policy (and possibly specific procedures) that embodies these and other, similar requirements is the most fundamental step in ensuring that users comply.

- **Avoid a dual-boot configuration.** You want to avoid a dual-boot configuration for the computers that run Windows NT. The dual-boot configuration can be a serious security liability in that it can allow viruses that target other operating systems to spread to infect the system partition which Windows NT also utilizes in addition to causing other problems. The Win32 viruses that target Win9x platforms are a good case in point. On the other hand, having a FAT partition may not only be necessary to enable certain DOS applications to run correctly, but in the case of infections by certain DOS boot infectors, this configuration may actually reduce or altogether prevent damage to the Windows NT partition. The reason is that some boot infectors can locate the FAT partition and then modify, delete, or displace instructions therein, leaving the Windows NT partition (which the virus might otherwise access and subsequently modify) untouched. The FAT partition may, in certain cases, act as a kind of virus "lightning rod." At any rate, the decision you make concerning whether to use a dual-boot configuration should depend on your particular business and operational needs.

Detecting Viruses

One of the major challenges in dealing with virus infections is determining whether a virus has really infected a system. Many anomalies, such as system crashes, failures of applications to run, and so forth, are not due to virus infections. They are instead often due to causes such as programming bugs in applications, software that does not run correctly (often due to faulty service packs or a non-standard system configuration), problems with media (for example, faulty disk drivers), and hard disks that approach capacity. Although there is a possibility that a system in which anomalies are observed is infected with a virus, many other possible causes exist. Consider these other possibilities before concluding that a virus is present (see the following sidebar).

What Is the Major Cause of Damage and Loss When Virus Infections Occur?

Statistics concerning estimated losses due to virus infections are almost invariably obtained in a less-than-credible, scientific manner. Worse yet, they also take the focus off what is the greatest source of loss in connection with computing systems: human error. *People faced with virus infections (as well as other incidents) do more damage to systems than viruses ever could! Panic-stricken users who think their systems are virus-infected all too frequently do foolish things, such as reformat their hard drives without first checking that a virus exists; or, if it does, reformatting their hard drives before ensuring that proper backups exist. If you are faced with a virus infection or possible symptoms of one, therefore,* avoid causing additional damage yourself! *The virus may or may not cause some damage, but ill-advised actions on the part of overzealous and/or frenzied users are likely to escalate any negative impact unnecessarily. If you are a system or network administrator, be sure to remove any ambiguity concerning what to do if your users observe possible symptoms of a virus infection by instructing and periodically reminding them to contact you and/or technical support instead of attempting to eradicate the virus themselves.*◆

If you suspect that one or more of your Windows NT systems has a virus infection, one of the easiest methods of exploring this possibility further is to run antivirus software. This software generally searches mounted media for indications of a virus infection, such as virus signatures (characteristic strings, directory modifications, a particular sequence of interrupt requests, and so forth). The best way to utilize this software is to run scans regularly—perhaps once every 24 hours in critical operational environments, and certainly every time any Windows NT workstation or server boots. You can easily schedule scans by using your antivirus program's scheduler by selecting the time the program is to run. Also be sure to regularly obtain, and then install signature updates for your virus-eradication program; otherwise, your antivirus package will fail to detect new viruses. Note also that virus-detection software which also scans every inserted floppy disk and/or downloaded file the very instant either is introduced to any system is also very useful.

Be careful. Detecting viruses in Windows NT systems is not quite the same as detecting viruses in other systems. Locating and identifying viruses that can infect Windows NT systems is not always very straightforward; the reason once again is that viruses often do not function as expected in the Windows NT environment. All a virus may be able to do in some instances is replace a few instructions and then hang the system, leaving minimal indication of its presence. The fact that some viruses have stealth mechanisms to hide their presence and that some are even polymorphic (that is, they can alter themselves to avoid detection) also makes the problem of detecting viruses in the Windows NT and other environments more difficult. Finally, be aware that not all virus-detection packages are equivalent with respect to capability to locate and eradicate viruses in the Windows NT environment. Be sure to consult sources such as *Virus Bulletin* (`www.virusbtn.com/`) to become familiar with the latest results of empirical tests of virus-scanner effectiveness.

Intervention

When you detect a virus in one or more of your Windows NT systems, the next step is to intervene. Normally, this means that you should contain and eradicate the virus, and then restore any infected system(s) to normal. In many cases, running an antivirus package that detects and automatically eradicates any virus that it finds is sufficient. As you might well guess by now, however, intervention in the Windows NT arena is not always straightforward. A boot virus infection, for example, may leave one or more NT machines altogether unable to boot. In another case, a boot virus may be able to replace only a very few instructions in the boot partition, hanging the Windows NT system it infected during the boot process without leaving any routines that can execute successfully in the system. Having a package that eradicates viruses will not help in these cases; you will have to go into troubleshooting mode. Furthermore, even if your antivirus package can eradicate a virus, you almost certainly still will have to restore some files that the virus has corrupted.

The level of intervention warranted depends on the type and severity of the infection. Consider the following possible scenarios and suggested intervention procedures:

- **The partition boot sector is corrupted.** If the partition boot sector is damaged, a good strategy is to boot from your Windows NT setup disks, choosing the Repair a Damaged Installation option (see Figure 10.3). *Deselect* all subsequent options except for Examine Boot Sectors. You may also be able to use the ERD to rebuild corrupted portions of this partition. Alternatively, you can boot from a DOS floppy disk, and then use a disk utilities tool to find where NTFS has copied the first logical sector of the partition.[4]

[4] *At a minimum, however, any virus adversely affects a system to some degree by modifying code and reducing available memory.*

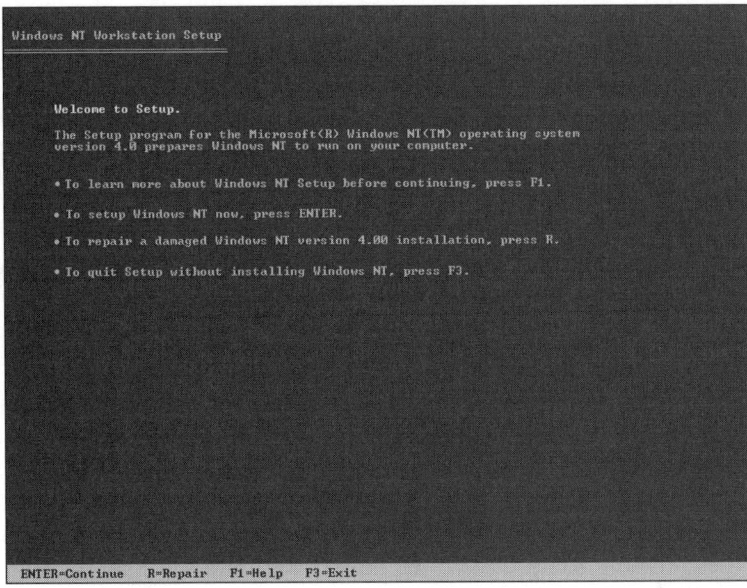

Figure 10.3 *Setup panel with Repair Damaged Installation option.*

- **The MBR is corrupted.** Using the Windows NT setup disks and/or the ERD may or may not work if the MBR is corrupted. A possible alternative approach, therefore, is booting the MBR-damaged system from a DOS boot disk and then restoring the MBR by running the FDISK utility. To involve this utility, enter the following command:

  ```
  C:\> FDISK/MBR
  ```

  There are some downsides to this approach, however, as indicated in Q121517, Q153973, and Q166454. One problem, for example, is that this command works only on hard drives that are within a 1024 cylinder limit. Some experts feel it is better, therefore, to use an antivirus package to rebuild a corrected MBR.
- **Part or all of your hard disk is erased or encrypted.** This is another worst-case scenario. The best overall course of action is probably to perform a complete restore from the last full backup before the infection occurred. (If you do a complete restore, be sure to scan the media from which the restore is to be made for viruses to avoid reinfecting your system!) There is, however, another, less radical strategy that may work if the entire hard disk is not corrupted or erased, or if data files are not involved. If you have another Windows NT installation on the same machine, you might try booting from this redundant installation and attempting to restore corrupted, missing, and other files from this second installation.

- **The system can boot, but one or more system file(s) is (are) corrupted.** Use the Windows NT Repair procedure to restore any corrupted files. If you do not have an ERD or have not updated it, restore from the last full backup before the infection occurred to restore these files.
- **The virus is in memory.** Use the Task Manager to view current processes; if a virus (or other malicious program) is running, you may see a bizarre process name that indicates that the process is not legitimate. If you are sure that the process is bogus, point to and click on the End Process option for each (see Figure 10.4). Because it may be difficult to determine exactly which processes the virus has spawned, you may instead want to first eradicate the virus (for example, by using an antivirus package), and then just reboot the infected system.
- **The system can boot, but one or more application(s) is corrupted.** Delete all executable files for the infected application and reinstall the application from virus-free installation media or from the last backup containing the application before the infection occurred. If the virus has possibly compromised the integrity of data files created by the application, use the last good backup to check data integrity and restore if appropriate.

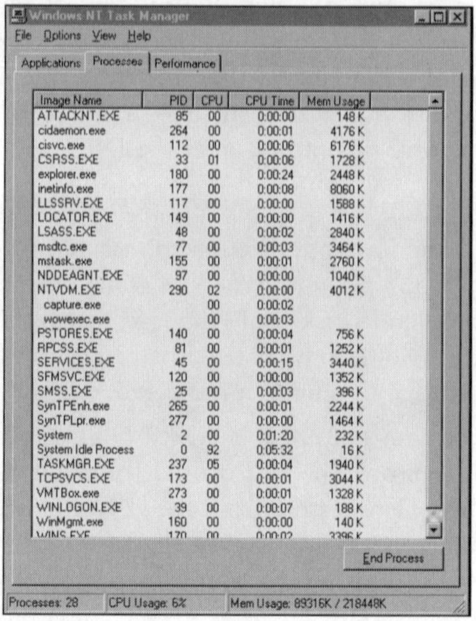

Figure 10.4 *Task Manager listing with a suspicious process name.*

The problem of containment is especially critical in the Windows NT arena because of the potential for self-reproducing code to rapidly spread from one networked Windows NT machine to another. If a machine is infected, a good move is to temporarily disconnect it from the network until the antivirus package you use gives an "all-clear" signal, especially in consideration of the way new types of malicious code, such as the Remote Explorer worm (see the following section). Remember, workstations are very often the point of origin of widespread virus infections throughout domains. Be sure to perform regular virus scans on all client workstations (as well as on all servers). And finally, be sure that whenever you restore files, you restore them from virus-free, write-protected backups or floppy disks. It is amazing how quickly a virus infection can once again spread through a domain because of only one restore operation in which a system administrator forgot to verify that the source media were virus-free.

New Malicious Codes in the Windows NT Arena: The Start of New Dimensions of Trouble?

Several new types of malicious code have surfaced recently in the Windows NT arena. One, Remote Explorer, generally installs itself as a service with the same name.[5] The path to the executable that is installed is generally `%systemroot%\system32\drivers\IE403R.SYS`, although mutations of this program , which work differently, have emerged. The Remote Explorer's effects depend both on the particular variant and the rights of the user account used to invoke it. If executed by someone with Local Administrator privileges, for example, it installs itself as a service, runs with Administrator privileges, and resides in memory. After it is installed, Remote Explorer checks the access permissions of the user who installs this code to locate targets to corrupt (usually by encrypting or compressing files to the point that they become unusable). When someone with Administrator rights logs on to an infected system, Remote Explorer attempts to infect other machines by starting itself as a service that connects to these machines. Its effects are markedly reduced if this rogue code is executed out of a non-privileged account. Not limited to the Windows NT environment, it can also infect Win9x systems, although it may have difficulty spreading itself across the network from these systems.

Many erroneous bulletins that have labeled Remote Explorer as a virus have been circulated. Remote Explorer is really more a worm than a virus. Worms are autonomous, self-replicating programs that do not require human intervention to succeed.

[5] *You can, in fact, find the process in the Services tab of the Windows NT Task Manager if a system is infected by this virus.*

The fact that Remote Explorer lodges itself in memory presents special complications. When this program first surfaced, in fact, Network Associates (an antivirus software vendor) recommended that if this executable is memory resident and has infected an NTFS partition, the proper intervention method is to disconnect the infected machine from the network, and then reformat the partition and perform a complete restore. Most major antivirus products now include routines that locate and eradicate this executable.

A new type of virus in the Windows NT arena is the Scripting virus family. This type of virus can infect IIS servers or Windows Scripting Hosts (but not clients, at least so far) through self-reproducing scripts written in VBScript and JScript (Microsoft's version of Java Script). The problem is that these scripting languages can access file systems on the machines on which the scripts execute to run any arbitrary code. The unsuspecting user needs to upload one or more *Active Server Pages* (ASPs) containing a virus written in one of these languages. The virus must only be stored and run locally on the platform that houses the Web browser to be activated. At this time this book is being written, no specific detection packages that locate Scripting viruses are available. The current best solutions for dealing with Scripting viruses, therefore, are solutions for dealing with other malicious, downloadable, browser-based executables. These solutions are presented in the next section of this chapter, "Executable Content Languages."

The fact that new classes of malicious code affecting Windows NT systems are emerging is anything but good news. The best overall solution is usually not just buying good antivirus software because this software usually cannot recognize new types of viruses. The best overall solution, therefore, is to keep abreast of the latest malicious code discoveries and solutions, and then employ what appear to be the best solutions after first testing them in a non-production environment.

After all your efforts, if you are still not completely convinced that all copies of any virus-related executables have been removed from one or more servers and that all files are back to their pre-infection condition, you may consider performing a disk reformat and complete restore. Reformatting normally requires a major expenditure of time and effort, however; you should take this course of action only if all else fails.

Executable Content Languages

Viruses are by no means the only threat to Windows NT Workstations. Web browsers and workstations go hand-in-hand today; malicious code (including, but by no means limited to, viruses) that can be downloaded via browsers has proliferated in recent years. This threat traces to a large degree to the increased popularity of executable content languages (XCL). These languages provide environments that allow executables to be downloaded into Web browsers and run automatically, either within the browser or separately. ActiveX[6] and Java, both of which are discussed shortly, are currently the two most popular XCLs. Others (not specifically discussed in this book) are *Dynamic HTML* (DHTML)[7], JavaScript, and VBScript.

XCLs have grown in popularity in connection with the increasingly greater sophistication of the *World Wide Web* (WWW). When the WWW first emerged, it generally enabled users to do little more than link to sites, and then to read static Web pages. Current Web technology now routinely enables users to enter input, view animated display sequences, hear unusual sound effects, play games within the browser, and so forth. The Web browser has in many respects become the embodiment of the network computing platform, and very sophisticated software is now either being developed or sold that uses the browser platform (for example, Web-based productivity software, such as many email packages, and collaboration software, such as Microsoft Exchange Server 2000). XCLs deliver this kind of functionality. The executables can run on servers, although they most commonly run on client machines, such as Windows NT and Win9x workstations. The major security-related threat is the possibility of downloading a malicious executable; the workstation therefore once again emerges as a source of security concern in the Windows NT environment.

Java

Java, a language based on C++, is presently the most popular XCL. Its main advantage is portability; it also offers other features, such as flexibility and reliability. Java runs on nearly any type of platform because of the *Java Virtual Machine* (JVM), an interpreter designed for multiple operating systems. Java offers two different types of executables, applets and applications. The primary difference is that applets are executables that run inside a browser. Java applications, on the other hand, can run completely independently of browsers and networks.

---

6 *ActiveX is not actually a language, but rather a collection of technologies used to deliver dynamic content. Strictly speaking, an ActiveX object is any object which implements the IUnknown interface. This includes a surprising number of things, such as Microsoft Word, Excel, and PowerPoint, in addition to a number of much smaller things. ActiveX is primarily a marketing term for a collection of technologies centered on DCOM. Many languages can be used to develop ActiveX objects, such as C++, Java, and Visual Basic.*

7 *DHTML is a Hypertext Markup Language (HTML) extension designed to work in connection with a Web scripting language. The main use of DHTML is to modify Web pages.*

Any time users download code from untrusted sources, security-related problems begin. Java, fortunately, incorporates a number of reasonable security control measures, the most fundamental of which is providing a limited execution environment ("the sandbox" environment) during runtime. Limitations include restrictions against reading or writing files on the computer that houses the browser, executing other executables on that computer, and connecting to any remote computer except the one from which the applet was downloaded in the first place. Java's limited environment, however, applies only to applets that have been downloaded from remote computers, not to ones that have been locally installed and then run on a machine.

Java security mechanisms depend to some degree on the particular release of Java. Version 1.1, for example, supports digital signatures for applets; users can expand or restrict the execution environment for each applet on the basis of the applet's signature. Version 1.2 works differently by allowing system administrators to determine the level of restriction (if any) of the applet execution environment on the basis of individual users or groups of users.

Although Java's security features might convince you that Java applets are inherently safe, this assumption is not all that true for the following reasons:

- Java's limited environment *does not* restrict the capability of applets to transmit data stored on the computer that houses the Web browser.
- A signed applet or even an unsigned one from a trusted source could be modified as it is sent over the network to the destination browser.
- A signed applet or one from a trusted source could have coding errors, resulting in unintentional damage or disruption.
- Contrary to a widely-held misconception, there is no such thing as one JVM for Java. Each JVM varies to some degree from one operating system to another and may therefore have its own particular set of vulnerabilities.
- Different browsers work differently in connection with Java security. Later versions of Netscape Navigator, for example, display a dialog box whenever an applet tries to run in a manner that is not permitted by the restrictions on the execution environment, or when the applet is executing inside its own console window. Other browsers do not have this capability.
- Java's constraints on the execution environment (the sandbox) can be defeated by clever programmers. Numerous vulnerabilities of this nature have emerged over the past few years.

- Java is not conducive to auditability. It would be nice to know at a minimum what particular applets a browser has downloaded.

ActiveX

ActiveX executables are called "controls." ActiveX, like Java, also supports impressive functionality, although ActiveX controls execute mostly on Intel platforms. ActiveX is therefore not as portable as Java.[8] It is also limited with respect to the browsers (mostly, but not exclusively, versions 3.x and beyond of the Internet Explorer). ActiveX can only run on Netscape browsers by means of a special plug-in.

Security in ActiveX is based on limiting whether controls can be downloaded on the basis of their origin. To allow a user to know where an ActiveX control came from, programs can be digitally signed using Microsoft's Authenticode technology. This enables developers to include a digital certificate with each control. Users or system administrators can set their browsers to accept or reject each control on the basis of characteristics, such as the particular user or organization from which the control originated (as indicated by the digital signature). These signatures potentially also allow someone to identify the origin of controls. ActiveX does not, however, provide the kinds of restrictions that can be enforced in the Java environment. Therefore, security in the ActiveX environment is weak for the following several reasons:

- ActiveX controls are executed without being subject to the restrictions that an interpreter imposes. A malicious ActiveX control could, therefore, not only read files on the machine that houses an ActiveX-enabled browser, but (depending, of course on NTFS permissions) could write to those files and/or potentially connect to virtually any remote Windows NT or other machine. The potential for damage is even higher on Win9x systems, which do not offer most of the security capabilities that Windows NT does. Needless to say, however, this vulnerability constitutes a serious security concern no matter which type of operating system is involved.

[8] *One of the major advantages of ActiveX, however, is that development of Web applications using this XCL is generally rapid and straightforward.*

CASE STUDY

Malicious ActiveX Controls

Several malicious ActiveX controls that have surfaced in the past few years illustrate just how vulnerable Windows systems are to attacks in which malicious controls are downloaded. An example is the malicious control named Explorer. Anyone reaching a certain HTML page on a widely-accessible Web site downloaded this control. Explorer appeared to be safe in that it included an Authenticode-based digital signature. If downloaded to an IE browser (versions 3 or 4), however, Explorer shut down the computer that housed it if the computer was a Win9x system. Verisign, which issued the certificate used in the digital signature, learned that Explorer was malicious and rescinded the certificate. Meanwhile, the developer proved the point he wanted to make, namely that Authenticode-based digital signatures are by no means any guarantee of the trustworthiness of ActiveX controls.

The good news about Explorer is that all it does is shut down Win9x systems; some ActiveX controls accomplish even more undesirable results. The notorious *Chaos Computer Club* (CCC) developed an ActiveX control that, once downloaded, invoked a financial transaction application (Quicken) on the computer with the browser that downloaded it. Someone who downloaded this control had a bogus payment initiated by this application. Fortunately, CCC nullified this transaction shortly afterwards, but they once again proved the point that ActiveX is fundamentally insecure.

- Just as in the case of Java applets, a signed ActiveX control or even an unsigned one from a trusted source could be modified as it is sent over the network to the destination browser.
- Again as in the case of Java applets, an apparently trusted ActiveX control could be programmed incorrectly, resulting in accidental damage or disruption.
- Certificates used in digital signatures can be issued to perpetrators. It is only *after* an ActiveX control is found to be malicious that one realizes that a signature needs to be revoked. The fact that a control has a signature does not in and of itself make that control safe. The signature just verifies the identity of the developer, not that person's intentions!
- Users generally experience great difficulty in determining how to set their browsers to limit the ActiveX controls that can be downloaded. Users, consequently, usually do not set any limitations whatsoever.

Furthermore, the default permissions on ActiveX controls in Microsoft's Internet Explorer are extremely lax from a security perspective. Internet Explorer needs considerable hardening to have some measure of security.

- Like Java, ActiveX is not conducive to auditability.

Security Control Measures

The logical beginning point for controlling Java-related security risk is incorporating into an organization's InfoSec policy appropriate provisions concerning use of Java, ActiveX, JavaScript, and similar executable languages. One solution, for instance, is to prohibit all use of Java, ActiveX, and JavaScript. The resulting technical security control would be blocking all incoming applets and controls at each gateway and routing point and disabling Java and ActiveX entirely via an option provided in Web browsers. Disablement and blocking are not, however, likely to be either popular or cost effective. The fact is that Java, ActiveX, and other similar technologies are becoming mainstream technologies in business and other environments—especially scripting technologies, which Microsoft calls "Active Scripting." (This term includes both JavaScript and VBScript.) These are extremely pervasive, and a number of Web sites (such as `http://www.microsoft.com`) just do not function if your browser does not allow scripts to be executed. Your best bet, therefore, is to employ one or more of the following measures, depending, of course, on the results of your particular cost-benefit analysis:

- Applets and controls from sources outside an organization's internal network can be partially blocked according to perceived level of trust. You can, for example, block all incoming applets and controls from all sources except trusted vendors and third-party business affiliates.
- Users with a legitimate need to download applets and controls can be restricted to using Web browser–installed hosts within an isolated portion of a network—a part that is well segregated from high-security zones. Keeping these machines apart from the rest of the network limits the potential for widespread damage if one or more hosts downloads a malicious applet or control. The major disadvantage is that users are likely to complain because of the inconvenience involved in accessing the isolated workstations.
- Netscape 4.x offers "extensions" that work in connection with the Java sandbox. Extensions are really nothing more than access control lists that limit applets from doing things such as accessing critical sys-

tem resources on the machines in which they execute. Relying on extensions is unwise, however, because they constitute a relatively new, mostly untested approach.

- Signatures, another method for controlling Java and ActiveX security, have already been discussed in connection with ActiveX security. Java also allows the use of signatures; Java-enabled browsers can be configured to selectively download certain classes of applets based on the JAR file format signature. Limitations with this approach have been presented previously. In the case of Java signatures, the complex JAR file formats and the susceptibility of JAR servers to intrusions may also enable perpetrators to attach false signatures to malicious applets.
- Secure channels based on protocols such as SSL, HTTP-S, PCT, and others offer yet another approach for Java (and potentially ActiveX) security. Having an encrypted channel between clients and servers protects the data sent over this channel from threats, such as unauthorized capture. It also limits the possibility of forming a connection between a rogue host and a workstation somewhat by restricting the set of machines that can exchange applets and controls—the host from which applets or controls are to be downloaded must first present the correct certificate. Some of the main limitations include certificate management and the vulnerability of certificate servers to break-ins that lead to issuance of false certificates.

All things considered, it is better to be more restrictive with respect to ActiveX controls than with Java applets. Note that more of the previously discussed solutions apply to Java applets than to ActiveX controls—that is, you have a broader set of security control alternatives with Java. In many business environments (for example, banking environments), in fact, ActiveX poses too much security risk to justify any approach other than significantly restricting its usage. Many corporations do not allow any ActiveX controls from external sources, but allow controls to be downloaded within the corporate intranet. Some organizations go even further by blocking all incoming applets, regardless of their origin. In organizations with lower security needs, fewer restrictions on ActiveX controls are appropriate. Finally, note that securing Java requires paying close attention to vendor and other alerts about new vulnerabilities; this is particularly important because Java's basic security model revolves around restricting the Java execution environment. Any bug that enables an executable to break out of this environment renders Java no safer than ActiveX. Several such bugs have been discovered in popular browsers. Microsoft has issued a number of updates to their virtual machines. These updates can usually be obtained

from http://www.microsoft.com/security. The most recent patch was issued in February 2000, and can be obtained from
http://www.microsoft.com/technet/security/bulletin/ms00-011.asp.

Workstation Considerations in Domain Security

So far, this chapter has covered both viruses and executable content languages, and how to control against security-related threats involving both. Workstation-related security considerations are, however, broader than malicious code. This last section of the chapter covers security-related issues involving workstations and, in particular, the relationship between client workstations and domain servers.

Types of Client Workstations

A variety of different operating systems can be client workstations in a Windows NT domain. Some of these operating systems include Windows NT Workstation, Windows 95, Windows 98, a LAN Manager Workstation (although you won't see many of these around anymore!), and even MS-DOS boxes that run Windows 3.1. Additionally, applications installed on workstations can enable these workstations to be clients in Windows NT domains. For example, SAMBA Client can allow UNIX workstations to become clients.

The type of client workstation used makes a huge difference in the type and strength of domain authentication. MSV1_0 authentication (discussed in Chapter 2) is not always the same. Its strength depends on the context of authentication, namely the type of client used. Here are the major contexts in which MSV1_0 authentication transpires:

- The strongest authentication occurs when the client is a Windows NT Workstation. In this case, the NT version of challenge-response authentication occurs in which the client returns a 24-byte encrypted version of an 8-byte nonce to the domain controller with which it has formed a secure channel. Encrypted passwords do not cross the network in this context of authentication. Password hashes used in the authentication sequence are derived from case-sensitive.
- The next strongest form of authentication occurs when the client is a Win9x or LAN Manager workstation. In this context, the LM version of challenge-response authentication is used. Encrypted passwords do not cross the network in this context of authentication. Password hashes in this context have been created from all uppercase passwords.
- Other types of clients can also authenticate via the MSV1_0 package, but normally only in the context of connecting to shares. By default, a

user can enter a **net use** command using a command prompt on the client. This command can include in its arguments a username and password. If users do not include both when they enter this command, they are prompted for both. No nonce is ever sent if the client is not a Microsoft client, such as Windows NT Workstation, Win9x, and so forth; passwords are thus in some access contexts sent across the network in clear text in this version of MSV1_0 authentication.

- If another application, such as NDS for NT or SAMBA Client is used to access Windows NT, each application has its own particular authentication method. Some applications utilize the LAN Manager (LM) version of MSV1_0 authentication; others do not and just send a clear-text password to the server.

By now it should be apparent that using Windows NT Workstations as domain clients is inherently best for the sake of the strength of authentication. The NT side of NTLM authentication is the best from a security perspective.

Security Vulnerabilities in Workstations

Workstations have a number of inherent security vulnerabilities. The following are some of the most notable:

- In Windows NT Workstation versions 3.1 through 3.51, the Guest account is by default enabled. As mentioned previously in this book, the Guest account provides a convenient conduit of unauthorized access to perpetrators. Only in Windows NT Workstation 4.0 is the Guest account disabled by default.
- If the Guest account on a Windows NT Workstation that is a domain client is enabled and unpassworded, a user who attempts a domain logon using that workstation may attempt a domain logon, but may reach the criterion number of bad logons for locking an account. If the user has attempted to log on to a non-existent account (possibly because the user did not know how to spell the name of the account correctly), the workstation will grant Guest access on the workstation (but not the domain). This can lead to unauthorized access to workstation resources, denial of service, and a variety of other undesirable outcomes. The vulnerability once again applies only to versions 3.1 through 3.51 of Windows NT Workstation.[9]
- If a user of a Windows NT Workstation (versions 3.1 through 3.51 only) attempts to log on to the workstation itself and the Guest account on that workstation is once again enabled and unpassworded, the user is given Guest access on that workstation after reaching the bad logon limit.

- RAS running on Windows NT Workstations introduces a potentially serious security threat. Unfortunately, the RAS server can be installed on both Windows NT Servers and Workstations. If Remote Access Service (RAS) is installed on workstations, users can obtain RAS access to that workstation, and can then invoke scripts that automatically connect that user to domain shares or do other, potentially dangerous things. Therefore, RAS on workstations is a perfect backdoor access mechanism that can bypass even the strongest of firewall-based restrictions!
- Workstation users, even those with only User-level privileges, are by default allowed quite a bit of access to their own workstations. One of the biggest problems is User-level access to the Control Panel and Task Manager on workstations. This increases the likelihood of denial-of-service attacks. A user could, for example, reset the communications baud rate using the workstation's Control Panel. A user could also use the Task Manager to kill a process, causing the workstation to crash.
- One of the default groups in Windows NT Workstation is the Power Users group. This group has what amounts to a combination of Server Operator, Account Operator, and Print Operator rights and abilities. In many operational contexts, the combination of all three privilege levels is inappropriate because it is too powerful. The particular apportionment of default rights in Windows NT Workstation also invites overassignment of privileges because the Power User level of privileges is for all practical purposes the only level of privileges between Administrator- and User-level privileges.
- As discussed at the start of this chapter, workstations can serve as a springboard for the introduction of malicious code.
- Central administration of workstations using conventional Windows NT remote access methods is difficult for system administrators. Workstation security, therefore, is likely to suffer (in that it ends up being inconsistent from workstation-to-workstation or just lax).
- The previously discussed problem of password caching in workstations is a serious one. Anyone with local access to a workstation could retrieve and then crack password hashes stored in with the PWL extension files on Win9x worksations. These machines offer very little in terms of security. To obtain password hashes from Windows 95 machines, for example, just use the File Manager's Find function to locate *.

[9] *It applies also to the FTP server in IIS. If you allow both authenticated and anonymous ftp, and you try to log on but give the wrong password, it will log you on as anonymous, without telling you that the password was incorrect.*

PWL files.[10] Privilege level is not even a consideration here because there is no tiering of privileges in Win9x machines. The major point here is that unauthorized access to *workstations* can result in unauthorized *domain* access. A secondary point is that cached logons on workstations also result in a certain amount of access to workstation resources—this access could be unauthorized and undesirable.

Solutions for Protecting Workstations

The starting point of workstation security is realizing that every client workstation is really part of the domain itself. Therefore, protecting each workstation adequately is more important than one might think! Suitable solutions for the types of workstation-level vulnerabilities that surface in Windows NT include the following:

- Use Windows NT rather than other types of workstations. Windows NT is not only superior in that it enables strong authentication to occur, but also because it offers capabilities such as privilege tiering and NTFS, capabilities that Win9x and Windows for Workgroups do not offer.
- Create an InfoSec policy that discourages or (better yet) prohibits users from storing extremely sensitive and valuable files and applications on their workstations. Such files and applications should be stored on servers (where they are likely to be better protected) instead.
- Run virus-detection and eradication software on every workstation. After reading the contents of this chapter, this solution should make a great deal of sense.
- Limit privilege levels according to the principle of least privilege. If you allow everyday users too high a level of privilege, they may be able to plant and execute software on workstations that has negative consequences for security. Running certain cracking tools requires Administrative-level privileges. These tools (such as Netcat, a port listener) can threaten the security of servers within a given local network, and sometimes within an entire wide area network (WAN). Similarly, privilege escalation can result in subversion of systems and/or denial of service. Users have also been known to plant Trojan horses that execute when an administrator logs on to the workstation, thereby elevating the privileges of the user.
- Limit cached logons. In general, users with desktop machines that connect to domain servers within the same local network do not need cached authentication. Users who connect remotely within a WAN are

[10] *Note that going through all this trouble is not even necessary in Windows95 workstations that run earlier versions of VNETSUP.VXD and several other files.*

more likely to need this capability. Limiting the number of authentication contexts in which cache logons occur can be very beneficial for security because of the potential for retrieving password hashes used in domain access from workstations.

- Do not allow RAS to run on workstations in critical operational environments because RAS may serve as a means of backdoor access.
- Enable security auditing on workstations and inspect log entries regularly. Sometimes the best way to discover an attack on servers is to examine the logs of *workstations* used to perpetrate attacks.
- Include workstations in your backup strategy. It is so easy to overlook workstations in a backup strategy. Yet if hard drives on workstations become corrupted or users accidentally delete files on workstations, the consequences can be catastrophic.
- Administer workstations from a central console, but first carefully think through what you want to do and how you want to do it. It is possible to make a mistake in remotely administrating any machine that causes considerable disruption. An example is modifying user profiles on workstations—objects that determine what desktop each user sees after that user has logged on locally. Changing a profile may disrupt a user's ability to use a workstation.

Conclusion

Although servers constitute the main focus of security-related attention in Windows NT, client workstations are also a significant concern. Viruses, for example, constitute a significant security threat in the Windows NT environment. Although Windows NT has a number of features and capabilities that effectively address this threat, this operating system is nevertheless very vulnerable to virus infections. Viruses that target Win9x, DOS, Windows 3.1, and specific applications (for example, Microsoft Word) can infect Windows NT Servers and Workstations. Responding to virus infections requires a strategy that involves steps such as protection, detection, containment, and eradication. Virus containment is especially important in the Windows NT network environment, where viruses can spread rapidly and critical systems, such as domain controllers, can be disabled by the actions of viruses.

Another major workstation-related concern is Java applets and ActiveX controls in the Windows NT environment. Malicious applets and controls can cause a wide range of undesirable outcomes, although the likelihood of catastrophic consequences is considerably less with Java applets because of the constraints built in to the applet execution environment. Many potential security control solutions exist for Java and ActiveX; the right one for you depends on your organization's needs in terms of cost versus benefit. Allowing ActiveX only within one's internal network(s) is a reasonable and widely adopted solution for controlling ActiveX security.

Finally, Windows NT Servers can interface with a variety of client workstations. The workstation used makes a major difference in terms of the potential for security. The best overall solution from a security standpoint is to always use Windows NT Workstations as domain clients because they support the strongest version of MSV1_0 authentication, allow NTFS-based access control, offer reasonably granular privilege assignment, and so forth.

Checklist for System Administrators

1. Ensure that you take appropriate actions to minimize the risk of virus infections in workstations. The most important steps are obtaining, installing and updating adequate antivirus software. Also consider using supplemental methods, such as physical security measures, using caution when introducing new software, making backups, limited access to the floppy drive, and avoiding a dual-boot configuration.
2. Develop procedures for virus recovery. Update them as appropriate.
3. Adopt measures that minimize risk due to malicious XCLs. Consider selectively filtering incoming XCL traffic at the external gateway, isolating browsers that download XCLs from unknown sources from the rest of the internal network, using extensions and signatures that limit the potential for malicious XCLs to be downloaded, and/or setting up encrypted sessions between browsers and web servers.
4. Ensure that workstations do not create a weak link in your Windows NT domains. If you can do nothing else, when practicable use Windows NT rather than other clients. Consider additional measures such as exercising the least privilege principle, disabling cached logons, ensuring that RAS is not enabled, and making backups.

11

Security Considerations for Windows 2000

"Windows 2000 is the most important software release ever."
–An anonymous Microsoft sales representative

As stated early in this book, the primary direction has been to describe the major kinds of security-related threats in Windows NT systems and networks that are most likely to impact you and your organization's goals, and then to present practical solutions. At this point, it should be clear to you that securing Windows NT is not an easy task; it requires a systematic plan of attack if you are going to succeed in this endeavor. Even if you follow all the security control measures recommended in this book, your Windows NT networks will nevertheless be vulnerable to new exploitation methods. The likelihood of continuous, new, efficient exploitation techniques is, in fact, high because of several of Windows NT's festering problems, such as implementation immaturity.

Although it is important to invest considerable effort in securing your Windows NT 4.0 environment, it is also very important to devote some of your time in looking ahead. Windows NT is anything but a slowly changing product; many new features have been added with each new release. But the newest release of Windows NT (originally called Windows NT 5.0 but renamed Windows 2000) introduces many *major* changes from current and past Windows NT functionality. Because these changes differ so profoundly, it is important to start familiarizing yourself with the features of this release and planning for an eventual migration to Windows 2000. You need to not only discover how Windows 2000 works and what features it offers, but also what its security capabilities are and potential security-related exposures. This chapter describes the functionality of Windows 2000 and how it affects security for the good and sometimes for the bad. It evaluates the probable impact of the security weaknesses in this product that are likely to emerge, and suggests ways to begin the process of planning for system and network security in the new and substantially different system and networking environment that Windows 2000 supports.

About Windows 2000

One of the most notable limitations in Windows NT to date has been the absence of capabilities for efficiently locating and then accessing resources on the network. Windows NT's browser and other IPC[1]-based services have not, for example, evoked a great deal of enthusiasm within the user community. In my own experience, I have found that remote resources and even hosts are visible sometimes, but then at other times are unexplainably nowhere to be found. The browser service appears to fail for reasons unknown. Domains, as good as they are in many ways (in that they define a security perimeter with central security-related settings), also provide somewhat of an obstacle to users. Because access tokens are domain specific, they do not provide a very suitable vehicle for enterprise networking because access tokens for one domain are not interchangeable in other domains. Passthrough authentication can, of course, be used to allow users to access resources in other domains, but setting up trust properly can require considerable work. Equally problematic is the fact that trust in and of itself does not solve the problem of locating and accessing remote resources and services on the network.

Novell NetWare, in contrast, offers an efficient implementation of directory services in its 4.x and 5.0 releases. These services, implemented as the *NetWare Directory Services* (NDS), store information about accessible objects, hosts, users, and so forth, and use this information to enable users and applications to easily locate and then reach them. Microsoft is "following suit" with the introduction of *Active Directory*, the Windows 2000 directory services. In addition, Windows 2000 offers many new capabilities.

What Is Windows 2000?

Windows 2000 consists of four new products:

- **Windows 2000 Professional.** This is the workstation product.
- **Windows 2000 Server.** This is the "standard" server product. It provides multiprocessor support for up to four processors.
- **Windows 2000 Advanced Server.** This product is higher ended than Windows 2000 Server, with features such as support for very

[1] *Interprocess communication.*

large memory capacity, clustering, and load balancing. It provides multiprocessor support for up to eight processors.

- **Windows 2000 Data Center.** Windows 2000 Data Center provides support for large hosts that need high amounts of fault tolerance, RAM, and multiprocessor support beyond that available in the other server products. Windows 2000 Data Center Server has not been released at the time of this writing, but it will likely support 32 processors.

Deployment Options

Windows 2000 Active Directory can be deployed in two modes: Mixed mode and Native mode. Mixed mode consists of NT 4.0 and Windows 2000 machines running within the same domain. In this case Windows 2000 domain controllers do not behave as Windows 2000 domain controllers, but rather as Windows NT 4.0 domain controllers. All security mechanisms used are Windows NT 4.0 security mechanisms. In Native mode, all servers are Windows 2000 machines and, as expected, security functionality is based on Windows 2000 mechanisms. Most of the discussion of Windows 2000 security in this chapter presupposes a Native mode deployment.

New Features

Windows 2000 introduces numerous additional features, including (but not limited to) the following:

- **Active Directory.** Active Directory is explained in more detail later in this chapter.
- **Kerberos.** This tool is well established and is widely accepted as one of the best solutions for authenticating users and their access to services. This tool is discussed in more detail later in this chapter.
- **Zero Administration for Windows (ZAW) Initiative.** This initiative, which goes hand-in-hand with the Microsoft Management Console (MMC), represents an attempt to reduce the total cost and effort of system administration through automated software installation capabilities, configuration management, and other functions.
- **The Microsoft Management Console (MMC).** The MMC consists of a set of tools and a common, consistent user interface for performing system administration. The *Security Configuration Manager* (SCM), of which the previously discussed SCE is a part, goes hand-in-hand with the MMC.
- **Terminal Services.** Terminal Services supports the capability for thin clients running on a reasonably wide range of different hardware

platforms. Terminal Services can also be used for remote administration of Windows 2000, marking the first time that it is possible to run a truly headless Windows system.

- **Distributed File System (DFS).** DFS provides mechanisms that support remote access to files; these mechanisms work in connection with directory services.
- **Encrypted File System (EFS).** EFS allows files to be transparently encrypted, protecting them against unauthorized disclosure or possession.
- **Smart card support.** Windows 2000 provides an architecture that supports smart cards for authentication and for other functions, such as validating access to applications.
- **Certificate capabilities.** Active Directory can validate, store, and retrieve certificates that can be used for functions such as *Public Key Infrastructures* (PKIs) and validation of access to applications.
- **Miscrosoft Clustering Services (MCS)** Scalability has always been an issue with Windows NT. MCS (Microsoft Clustering Services); Windows 2000 provides the ability to form Windows 2000 server clusters to attain better runtime performance with complex applications.
- **Windows Driver Model drivers.** Another problem with Windows NT 4.0 and earlier versions has been dealing with the different drivers (Windows-based drivers, Intel-based drivers, and so on). Windows 2000 offers a set of Windows drivers along with a Windows driver model.
- **Disk quotas.** You can now set user quotas on each partition if you want to. This enables you to specify, by object, how much disk space is allocated to each.
- **Dynamic disk allocation.** Another current problem with Windows NT, so far, is that disk space allocation is largely fixed. Windows 2000 changes this by supporting dynamic disk allocation. This is designed to (a) support resizing of partitions without (b) rebooting the computer, as was necessary in Windows NT 4.0
- **Plug and Play.** Plug and Play is a feature in which services can be started by just inserting the appropriate network card.
- **Universal Serial Bus (USB) Support.** This works like a peripheral chain that enables users to freely plug in different peripherals
- **IntelliMirror.** This feature provides a type of steady-state environment in which workstation-specific settings are cached on domain controllers. If a user's workstation is replaced with another, IntelliMirror automatically adjusts the settings on the new workstation to coincide with the old workstation. Another capability of IntelliMirror is keeping

a cache of the files that users access most frequently to increase access efficiency and to enable access to these files even when the file server is unavailable.

- **Power management.** Windows 2000 has built-in support for two different power management technologies: *Advanced Configuration and Power Interface* (ACPI), and the older *Advanced Power Management* (APM) standard. ACPI is supported on all platforms, whereas APM is supported only for legacy systems running Windows 2000 Professional. Both come with various security features, such as the capability to lock the system automatically when it goes into Standby or Hibernation mode.

To say that Windows 2000 is a very ambitious release is an understatement. Let's examine the features of Windows 2000 that most affect security.

Security Architecture

Figure 11.1 below depicts the security architecture for Windows 2000. Note that this architecture is largely the same as Windows NT 4.0's (see Figure 2.1). Just like Windows NT 4.0, Windows 2000's architecture is divided into two modes: User Mode and Kernel Mode.

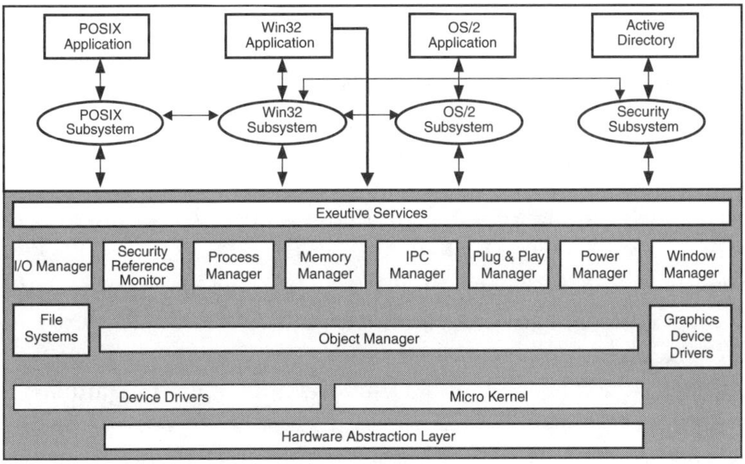

Figure 11.1 *Windows 2000 Security Architecture.*

User Mode

User Mode is for user interaction and applications, as well as, many subsystems (including the subsystems used for emulation of other operating system environments). The Security Subsystem (Local Security Authority

[LSA]) still validates logons, but it functions somewhat differently in that it now initiates the Active Directory (to be discussed in detail shortly) whenever a logon request occurs. Note also the absence of Winlogon in the Windows 2000 architecture (although the Winlogon Utility is still "alive and well" in Windows 2000).

Kernel Mode

Kernel Mode once again is for privileged operations that can access hardware and memory. The Security Reference Monitor (SRM) not only determines whether requests for access to Kernel Mode are allowed, but it also validates accesses to objects and controls the audit policy. New Executive Services, such as the Plug and Play Manager, Power Manager, and Window Manager are included in Kernel Mode. Both Device Drivers and Graphics Device Drivers are now also built into Kernel Mode, as are File Systems Services.

Vulnerabilities in Windows 2000—Already!

Numerous vulnerabilities in Windows 2000 have already been identified. One of the earliest identified vulnerabilities concerns administrative shares such as the `C$` share (to `c:\`) and the `ADMIN$` share (to `%systemroot%`). Although passwords protect against unauthorized access to these shares, both shares are remotely accessible when Windows 2000 is being installed if someone tries to connect to them before the Administrator account is passworded. Unauthorized access to administrative shares could result in catastrophic outcomes, including unauthorized changes to the Administrator account password that result in the legitimate administrator being locked out.

Unattended installation tools in Windows 2000 do not properly deal with passwords that start with an asterisk (`*`). These tools assume that such passwords are blank, leaving a null password. The best solution for this problem is to avoid choosing passwords that start with an asterisk during unattended setup.

Another vulnerability is in the Windows 2000 window station. The window station contains objects, such as a clipboard, keyboard, pointing device, and so forth. A non-privileged, non-interactive user can access the window station and obtain data, such as keyboard input from other users who are currently logged on interactively on the same host.

Windows 2000 users may be able to exceed assigned disk quotas by adding a small amount of content to a large number of existing files. This vulnerability is exploitable only if a small amount of content is added.

Microsoft has released "updates" for most of these and other vulnerabilities in Windows 2000. See the Windows Update at `http://windowsupdate.microsoft.com`.

Active Directory

In Windows 2000, Active Directory is in many respects "the center of the universe." This section explores Active Directory and how it works.

Active Directory is a directory service that serves as Windows 2000's primary basis for storing and disseminating critical information within one or more domains. This information includes data about accounts, *organizational units* (OUs)[2], security policies, files, directories, printers, services, domains, Active Directory itself, inheritance rules, and so forth. Active Directory services disseminate the information held within to users and applications, as well as, to every domain controller within a domain. It also performs management services to ensure not only that its information is available, but that the information is accurate and up-to-date. Based on X.500 specifications (but actually accessed through the *Lightweight Directory Access Protocol*, [LDAP]), Active Directory is in a few respects conceptually similar to the *Security Account Manager* (SAM) database in Windows NT 4.0 and earlier releases. Active Directory, however, contains a vastly greater amount of data and is based on considerably more complex functionality. Consider, for example, Windows NT 4.0's limitation of 40,000 authentication objects per domain. The Windows 2000 Active Directory can in contrast hold up to 10 million authentication objects, a vast increase

Active Directory is not limited in scope to single domains. Multiple domains can share a common Active Directory. Every machine within a local area network (LAN) (or perhaps even a wide area network [WAN]) can have a common Active Directory. Each domain has its own set of security policies, trust relationships, and so forth that may be similar to or entirely different from those in another domain. The policies and relationships are defined by Active Directory in which they are stored.

Groups

Windows 2000 has two types of groups and three scopes of relevance for each group within the types. The types are as follows:

- **Security groups.** These groups can be assigned security policies and rights.
- **Distribution groups.** These groups can only be used for dissemination of information, such as email lists, and simple administrative groupings. They are not security enabled.

---

[2] *OUs provide a way of dividing domains into smaller units of users, groups, shares, policies, and so forth for management purposes; OUs and groups are somewhat conceptually similar in that they provide a way to assign rights and access permissions to multiple users, but OUs are broader.*

The scope of relevance governs where the group can be used, as follows:

- **Domain local.** Domain local groups in Windows 2000 are very much equivalent to local groups in Windows NT 4.0. Global groups can be included in domain local groups. They are designed to be assigned access to non-Active Directory resources within a domain, such as file system objects, and shares. They should not be assigned permissions to Active Directory resources because Active Directory is often replicated beyond the domain where these groups are defined and domain local groups cannot be evaluated beyond the domain where they are defined.
- **Global.** Global groups are somewhat equivalent to the global groups in Windows NT 4.0. However, they can only be assigned access to resources in the domain where they are defined. In a Native-mode domain, global groups can be made members of other global groups.
- **Universal.** Universal groups are a new type of group in Windows 2000. They are available only in a Native-mode Active Directory, and they can contain users and groups from every domain in linked trees of domains called "forest," thus cutting across domain boundaries. They therefore provide the most flexible way of forming groups and providing access to them.

Organizational Units

The OUs in Windows 2000 hold information about users, groups, individual accounts, policies, shares, applications, and so forth. The main value of the OUs is to provide hierarchical (and thus more efficient) organization to Active Directory namespace, as well as, to allow finer, more individually precise assignment of rights, management, and access permissions within a domain. The Windows 2000 OUs should not, however, be equated with true X.500 OUs. OUs by default apply to only one domain at a time, although administrators who have sufficient rights can extend OUs over multiple domains. Inheritance of rights and permissions can be set up on the basis of OUs.

Wire Protocols

Windows 2000 provides a set of protocols called "wire protocols" to support access to Active Directory. These protocols specify the formats of messages and the interactions needed for the various types of access. Also included are numerous APIs to provide an interface to the protocols themselves.

How the Domain Name Service Fits In

The DNS is closely intertwined with Active Directory. DNS continues to perform name resolution within TCP/IP-based networking (as it has in

Windows 4.0). Windows NT 4.0 and previous versions, however, have required an additional service, the *Windows Internet Naming Service* (WINS), to provide an interface between IP addresses and the naming conventions used in, for example, Network Basic Input Output System (NetBIOS). In Windows 2000, WINS is not necessary because Microsoft intends to abandon the NBT protocol in favor of a native TCP/IP stack, where SMB runs directly on top of TCP/IP. Therefore, name resolution is done based on fully qualified domain names (FQDNs) rather than on NetBIOS names. The information each Active Directory holds about objects enables DNS to resolve names (for example, host names) but also to obtain information, such as naming contexts, about those objects. This design has several implications, including the following:

- Each domain in effect constitutes a unique "namespace" that defines a kind of virtual territory within which names of hosts and objects can be resolved.
- Windows 2000 domain names coincide with DNS domain names. Domain names therefore take the form `globalintegrity.com`.
- DNS holds service *resource records* (RRs) that link together the names of services with the IP addresses of servers that deliver them. This allows clients to discover desired services through the knowledge and use of domain names.

DNS alone is not, however, in and of itself sufficient to deal with Active Directory. Microsoft therefore has introduced a new service, *Dynamic DNS* (DDNS), to enable each client to register its existence on a network when it becomes connected to that network, and to verify and update its network registration if necessary. Any Remote Procedure Call (RPC)-compliant version of Dynamic Host Configuration Protocol (DHCP) should also be capable of assigning addresses to hosts.

Domains

Even a superficial look at the planned changes in Windows 2000 should reveal that domains are still very much a part of Windows 2000, but their implementation differs substantially from Windows NT 4.0 and earlier. In versions before Windows 2000, domains were a fairly self-contained set of computers whose security and other properties were defined to a large degree by Registry settings, profiles, and so forth. Domains in Windows 2000 comprise, for all practical purposes, a *namespace*.[3] Every Windows 2000 system still (like Windows NT 4.0) has a Registry that holds many critical parameters.

[3]*A namespace is the basis of a naming structure for domains.*

Windows 2000 domains are not intended to exist in isolation. To implement Windows 2000 in the context of largescale enterprise networking, in fact, makes creating multiple domains likely. These domains can be linked together in a tree structure of objects, something that Microsoft calls a "named object hierarchy." Linking domains together entails trust between the domains that have a common Active Directory that provides a continuity of Active Directory services among them. The Active Directory store of information concerning objects includes names, unique *object identifiers* (OIDs), object properties, class of objects in which each object is included, definitions of higher-level and similar objects, and so forth. All this information is held in a variety of "containers," which are special kinds of objects that include other objects. What linking domains together does is to form a hierarchical tree structure of objects (see Figure 11.2). The top nodes of every branch are containers; the endpoints are "leaf objects." Parent directories are, of course, higher up in the tree structure than the files and subdirectories they hold. Another way to view Active Directory is just as a group of one or more of these trees.

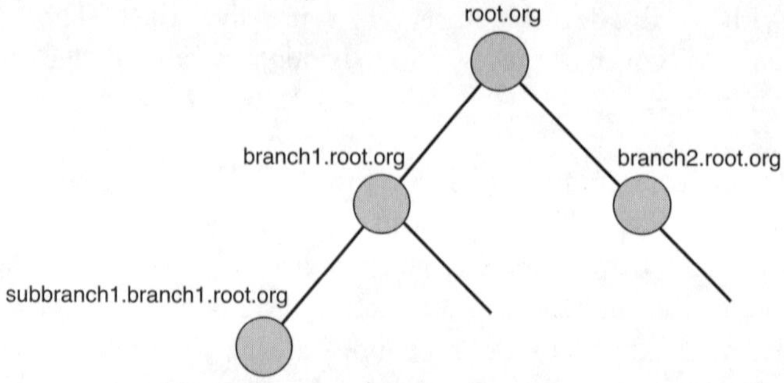

Figure 11.2 *Schematic of a Windows 2000 tree showing levels and naming conventions.*

One of the major advantages of a continuous tree structure is that user- and program-initiated searches for objects and services can be performed recursively from a particular node in the tree structure all the way down to particular leaf objects. This kind of arrangement is called a contiguous subtree—that is, one in which a *continuous* path within a tree exists. This arrangement also allows continuity in name resolution between different domains within the tree and produces more efficient utilization of namespace in and of itself. It is also possible to use trust to link trees that *do not* share the same Active Directory, resulting in a "forest." One of the major functional differences between a tree and forest is that recursive searches in a forest are not necessarily fully recursive—they stop at the point at which trust (rather than a common Active Directory) links the tree structures together. Another result is a discontinuity in DNS's capability to resolve names.

Trees have a root domain that is the basis for naming the entire tree. So, for example, in Figure 11.1 the tree depicted would be named `root.org`. Forests are *not* assigned names. The implicit name of the forest is the name of the first domain installed, the root domain.

Domain Controllers

A Windows 2000 domain does not have *primary domain controllers* (PDCs) or even *backup domain controllers* (BDCs); only *domain controllers* (DC) exist. Windows 2000 uses a multiple master distributed database architecture for Active Directory, as opposed to the primary copy distributed database architecture used under NT 4.0 for the SAM. Another major difference between the functionality of Windows NT 4.0 (and earlier versions) and Windows 2000 domains, in fact, is that the latter now use a "peer controller" model. A client does *not* have to connect to a PDC to send updates and changes to the SAM database, as in the case of Windows NT 4.0 and earlier, because BDCs no longer exist. All DCs are just DCs, not PDCs and BDCs. The client can instead contact *any* DC within the same domain. That DC then records the appropriate changes in Active Directory and subsequently replicates the data to the other DCs within the domain. The resulting effect is less dependence on one server within a domain (in contrast to the undue dependence on the PDC that exists in Windows NT 4.0 and earlier domains).

Schemas

Another critical concept in Windows 2000 is "schemas," which define object properties and include information about object class memberships. Schemas not only determine the kind of data held within Active Directory, but also serve as a mechanism to allow Active Directory to update itself by doing things such as creating new object classes. At the same time, schemas enable user applications to efficiently discover the particular objects, classes (for example, group), and attributes (for example group names) that can be accessed.

One of the most obvious potential hurdles is locating objects in what will be, in most deployments, massive tree structures. Windows 2000 enables users to browse through a list of trees using a feature called the Global Catalog. The Global Catalog performs the previously discussed recursive searches, helping users locate objects not only in their own home domain, but also in other domains. Figure 11.3 shows the organization of the Global

Catalog—it searches for objects in the highest domain in a tree, and then the next highest, and so forth.

Note also that when Windows 2000 domains have a contiguous namespace, they by necessity have a Global Catalog and common schema.

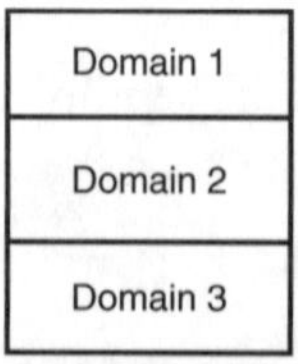

Figure 11.3 *Structure of Global Catalog searches.*

Kerberos

As mentioned earlier, Kerberos is integrated into Windows 2000. Kerberos provides both strong network authentication and ensures that all authentication credentials are encrypted. In Kerberos, each user authenticates through a prescribed set of steps. First, the user sends an authentication request that includes the appropriate username. The authentication server (also known as the *Key Distribution Center*, KDC, or Kerberos server or Windows 2000 DC) sends a *Ticket Granting Ticket* (TGT) and session key back to the client; both are now used in communications between the client and KDC from this point on. The user then enters a password on the client. If the password is correct, the client requests and receives a Service Ticket from a *Ticket Granting Server* (TGS). The Service Ticket enables the client to reach services and objects throughout the domain. Figure 11.4 depicts this sequence of events.

Kerberos is an established security solution frequently used in high-risk environments, such as in the banking arena. A fairly significant concern in Windows 2000, however, concerns the interoperability of Microsoft's particular implementation of this software. Kerberos is based on RFCs 1510 and 1964. Microsoft has implemented RFC-compliant Kerberos version 5 in Windows 2000. Several differences between Microsoft's and MIT's implementation exist by design; they have different Kerberos extensions, for example. The Windows 2000 Kerberos is therefore *not* by default completely compatible with other Kerberos implementations, the practical implication of which is that work and resources are necessary to produce any needed compatibility between both.

As good as it is, MIT Kerberos is by no means perfect either. Bugs in candidate releases of this product have emerged that have allowed perpetrators to successfully attack via mechanisms, such as predicting the Kerberos key (because of a faulty key-generation algorithm), replaying Kerberos requests, and spoofing Kerberos servers. In addition, if an attacker gains physical access to a Kerberos server, that person can engage in actions, such as reinstalling the server software to gain Administrator privileges.

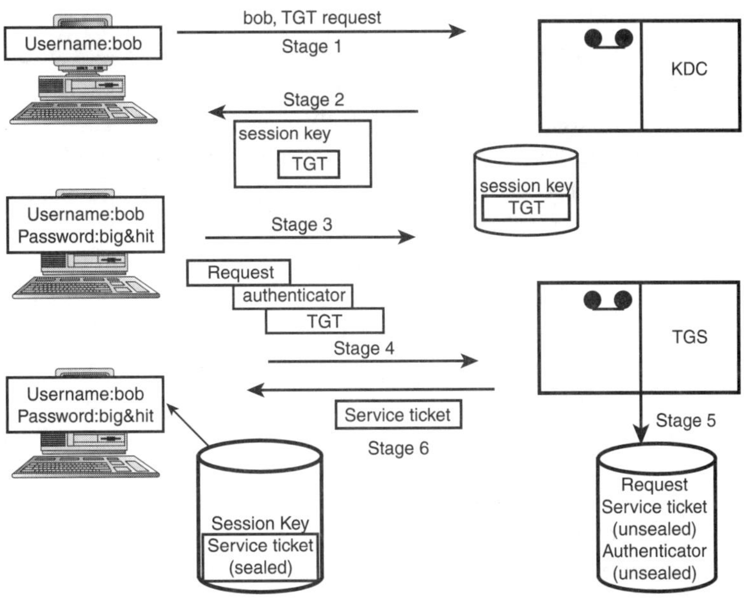

Figure 11.4 *A simplified view of Kerberos functionality.*

Delegation

One of the major features in Windows 2000 is "delegation" of rights and capabilities. Recall that in Windows NT 4.0 and earlier default rights are assigned reasonably (all things considered), but that some of the rights and abilities are too all-encompassing for many of today's business and other environments. The greatest privilege-related problem in Windows NT 4.0 is with Administrator privileges; Administrators are all-powerful in every domain (regardless of the particular domain model used).

Windows 2000 differs from the previous releases of Windows NT in that it allows more granular, individual assignment of rights. In Windows 2000, a low-level right, such as the right to change a password, for example, may or may not be assigned to individual users. Equally important, delegation supports the capability of limiting rights according to the particular OU within a domain. Default Administrators receive the full set of rights. The set of rights given to a top-level OU could be the same as Administrators, or they could be less. Lower-level OUs within the same domain can be given the same set of rights as their parent OU, or the rights for these lower-level OUs can be attenuated. If attenuated, the rights given to the OU below the parent cannot be higher than in the parent; in other words, the set of rights assigned to an OU cannot increase from a higher- to a lower-level OU within a domain.

Delegation is potentially extremely important as a security feature. The chief prize, so to speak, for a perpetrator is unauthorized Enterprise Administrator access. This allows virtually unrestricted access to virtually every object within every domain within a tree. If the perpetrator cannot gain this level of access, the second-best strategy from an attacker's perspective is to gain Administrator access to a domain. Remember, lower-tier domains share the same Active Directory as the root domain within the same tree, so the attacker can attempt to read and/or modify Active Directory after gaining unauthorized access to a site (that is, a group of Active Directory–capable hosts within a domain). If, on the other hand, administration is performed through delegation of rights to OUs that receive progressively fewer rights as one goes from the parent to the child to the grandchild, there is less chance that an attacker will be able to gain full Administrator privileges. Delegation thus provides an important method of not only enforcing the least-privilege principle, but also of potentially minimizing widespread unauthorized privileged access. In contrast, if delegation is not utilized, the result can very easily be widespread catastrophe.

Trust

Windows 2000 also defines and utilizes trust differently from the way Windows NT 4.0 and earlier versions do. One of the previously discussed advantages in Windows NT 4.0 trust, in fact, is that it must be set up one way at a time and is never *transitive* between domains (see Chapter 6, "Maintaining Windows NT Security"). In Windows 2000, trust is based on sharing Kerberos keys across domains. Whenever you establish trust between domains, trust is by default bidirectional, as well as transitive. Within a tree, trust is present among *all* domains, from the lowest-tier domains all the way to the root domain. The now quite familiar trust models of Windows NT 4.0 are superceded by the Windows 2000 trees designed to support efficient location of and access to objects within this structure.

Trust in Windows 2000 *does not*, however, necessarily have to be all pervasive. Anyone with sufficient rights can disable any trust created between domains by default. Disabling trust can and will, of course, have negative consequences for functions, such as locating and resolving objects. Forests rather than tree structures may provide a suitable solution if you want to limit trust but maximize the efficiency that trust affords within certain domains. In Mixed (sometimes called Hybrid) mode, furthermore, Kerberos-based trust is not possible between the different types of domains; tree structures between both cannot be established. It is possible, however, to have Windows NT 4.0–style trust between Windows NT 4.0 and Windows 2000 domains. Therefore, trust in mixed environments is in effect based on the "lowest common denominator."

Authentication

In Windows 2000, DCs provide authentication services to users and clients. Windows 2000, as previously discussed, uses Kerberos as the default authentication method. When a user or client is authenticated, the authenticating DC creates a ticket; afterwards, a TGS creates still another one. The DCs store the tickets of all clients and users within the domain. If all domains within a tree structure are Windows 2000 domains, Kerberos authentication prevails; the Kerberos tickets given to users are proxyable, precluding the need for reauthentication every time the user needs access to another machine within this tree structure.

Using MD-4 Versus MD-5 in NTLM: What Difference Does It Make for Security?

MD-4 is the Message Digest version 4 hashing algorithm that creates password hashes used in NTLM authentication for Windows NT 4.0 and earlier. Developed by RSA in 1990, MD-4 is an asymmetric key algorithm; two different keys exist. The initial string to be hashed is padded with characters so that the length of the padded string plus 448 is divisible by 512 with no remainder (modulus). A 64-bit binary string that indicates the length of the string is then added to the string, and then finally the string is hashed three times.

The MD-4 algorithm may superficially seem strong from the standpoint of security, but cryptologists would disagree. Cracking programs that break MD-4 are now widely available; worse yet, the amount of effort needed to break MD-4 is much less than one might expect for a 128-bit hashing algorithm. Microsoft's solution to this problem in Windows 2000 is utilizing MD-5 rather than MD-4 in the context of Windows NT 4.0 authentication. MD-5, widely considered a much stronger algorithm than MD-4, should increase the strength of password hashing considerably.◆

In addition to providing Kerberos in Windows 2000, Microsoft also provides the *Security Support Provider Interface* (SSPI). SSPI is a type of generic API for accessing security services in connection with authentication, ensuring that message content has been read without authorization or altered, and other similar functions.

Authentication of trusted access between older Windows NT 4.0 domains and Windows 2000 domains is via Windows NT 4.0's NTLM authentication package (see sidebar). Windows 98 clients can interface with Windows 2000 domains, and interact with these domains as if the Windows 2000 domains are Windows NT 4.0 domains. The NTLM authentication package is also used to authenticate Windows 98 clients. Note, however, that there is also an Active Directory client on the Windows 2000 Server disk that can be installed on these machines to enable them to interface with the Active Directory.

Windows 2000 support a customizable logon screen through a more readily modifiable *graphical identification and authentication* (GINA) DLL than in Windows NT 4.0 and earlier. Windows 2000 also supports TLS to allow use of protocols, such as SSL. As in Windows NT 4.0, Windows 2000 provides CryptoAPI for interfacing with third-party authentication products such as smart cards.

Another related and potentially beneficial feature in Windows 2000 is `RunAs`. `RunAs` provides the ability to launch a process with a different user context from the one for the currently logged on user. Someone who has already logged on to one account can use a command line to bring up a command window by entering the following in the Run Window:

```
RUNAS /user:STRIDE@domain command
```

You can also simply right-click on a program or a shortcut and select Run As from the Context Menu. One of the main advantages of RunAs is that it allows privileged users to execute programs in a non-privileged contexts, thereby reducing the dangers of activities such as web browsing and executing unknown programs.

Authorization

The main basis of authorization to access objects and services in Windows 2000 is Kerberos. As covered earlier in this chapter, DCs issue "proxyable tickets" to clients. These tickets enable servers to remotely connect to other servers to process client requests without requiring that the client reauthenticate.

As in the case of Windows NT 4.0 and earlier, objects, schemas, and so on in Windows 2000 have *access control lists* (ACLs) with *access control entries* (ACEs). Access by users and programs is allowed or denied on the basis of the ACEs. The SRM validates attempted access to objects, data in Active Directory, and so forth by determining whether the rights and permissions assigned to the user match the ACE requirements. Within every domain, the same logic that applies to accumulation of NTFS permissions on the basis of membership in multiple OUs also applies in Windows 2000. Windows 2000's new version of NTFS (NTFS-5), however, works somewhat differently from the previous version of this file system. In NTFS-5 it is possible to assign a group or user in a domain or individual host and Allow or Deny for each of a number of permissions (listed below) that allow access to a given object. By default, domain permissions take precedence over permissions for individual hosts; and noninherited permissions take precedence over inherited permissions.

NTFS-5

Windows 2000 also features the latest release of the NTFS file system, NTFS 5. One of the new challenges is getting accustomed to the new permissions. New "base" (individual) permissions include the following:

- **Traverse Folder/Execute File.** Determines whether someone can go from one folder to another that is below it as well as to run executables.
- **List Folder/Read Data.** Determines the ability to list the contents of a folder or read a file.
- **Read Attributes.** Determines the ability to read "normal" file attributes—that is, those created by the file system.
- **Read Extended Attributes.** Determines the ability to read extended file attributes—that is, those created by applications.
- **Create Files/Write Data.** Determines the ability to create new files and add new data to them.
- **Create Folders/Append Data.** Determines the ability to create new folders within a particular fold and append data to files.
- **Write Attributes.** Determines the ability to modify file attributes.
- **Write Extended Attributes.** Determines the ability to modify extended file attributes.
- **Delete Subfolders and Files.** Determines the ability to delete subfolders and files, regardless of whether a specific Delete permission has been assigned.
- **Delete.** Delete allows the person who has this permission to delete an object, such as a file or directory.
- **Read Permissions.** Determines the ability to inspect file permissions.

- **Change Permissions.** Change Permissions allows someone to modify current permissions of someone else with respect to a particular object.
- **Take Ownership.** With this permission someone can take ownership of an object.

Encrypted File System

Another new feature in Windows 2000 is the *Encrypted File System* (EFS)[4], the main function of which is to encrypt files written to disk media. The actions of EFS in encrypting and decrypting files is done automatically based on a unique key that exists for every user and a key for each particular file. If a user accesses an EFS-encrypted file, EFS applies this key from its repository of keys to convert the file to its plain-text representation. Users, fortunately, are not aware of any of the encryption and decryption of files. The interface to the key repository is through Microsoft's CryptoAPI routine. Therefore, a major additional advantage is the ability to embed keys on physical devices (for example, smart cards).

Several misconceptions about Windows 2000 integration of EFS have already been circulating. Consider the following corrections to these misconceptions:

- Contrary to some of information on Windows 2000 that is circulating, EFS is not new. Its *integration* into Windows 2000 is new, however.
- EFS does not encrypt *not* files sent over a network or files held in memory. It protects only *stored* files.
- EFS *does not* enhance performance of file storage and retrieval. It causes at least a modest degree of performance degradation.
- The implementation of EFS in Windows 2000 actually utilizes both *secret* key and *public* key encryption. Secret key encryption is used to encrypt each file, but public key encryption is used in a key escrow[5] or data recovery function to keep an additional copy of the secret key in case it is destroyed or becomes corrupted. This enables an authorized recovery agent to recover EFS keys, which in turn enables people to decrypt stored data when necessary.
- EFS does not entail "all-or-none" encryption in which EFS is either enabled or disabled on a given Windows 2000 system. It is possible to

---

4 *Note that EFS is actually part of NTFS-5.*

5 *In the broadest sense, key escrow involves making an additional copy of a key and storing it independently of where the original key is stored.*

enable EFS on a per-user basis, such that all of one user's stored files are EFS-encrypted, but another user's files are all stored in plain text.

- EFS cannot always be deployed. EFS encryption *is not* possible when files are accessible by *multiple* users.

IPSec

As discussed earlier in this book, Microsoft's own rendition of PPTP in Windows NT 4.0 did not really work out as well as many security professionals had hoped. Fortunately, Microsoft decided to jump on the proverbial IPSec bandwagon in its Windows 2000 release. IPSec (referenced in RFCs 1825 through 1829 as well as numerous IETF drafts with higher RFC numbers) is actually a set of specifications for a more security-conducive IP protocol, as implemented either in IPv6 or an expanded version of the older IPv4 protocol. IPSec implementation is via two protocols: the *Authenticating Header* (AH) protocol and the *Encapsulating Security Payload* (ESP) protocol:

- The AH protocol, shown in Figure 11.5, ensures data integrity by authenticating packets' IP headers and payloads (that is, data sent in the packet). AH informs the destination host whether any changes to the packet have been made while the packet was being sent over the work. The authenticating header itself is designed to be tamper resistant in and of itself.

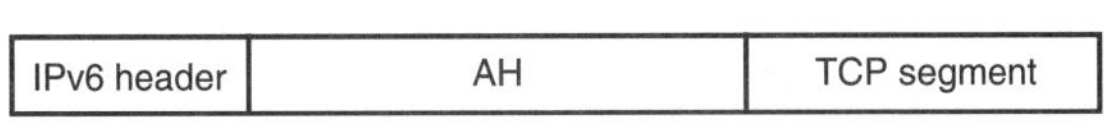

Figure 11.5 *The AH protocol.*

- The ESP protocol, shown in Figure 11.6, has as its primary purpose the encryption of data transmitted over the network so that someone who captures packets cannot read the plain-text contents of packets because data therein is in ciphertext. In IPSec, ESP encryption is automatically done to keep clear-text data transmissions off the network altogether. Because a perpetrator who wants to modify ESP data needs to have the key used to encrypt the data payload to decode that data, ESP can also help ensure the integrity of data content sent over the network. ESP, unlike AH, is not an authenticating protocol, however.

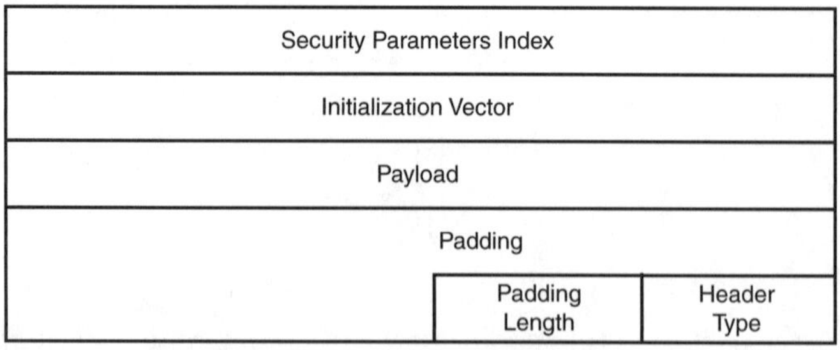

Figure 11.6 *The ESP protocol.*

IPSec specifications describe a series of steps in which communication conventions between the sending and receiving host are established. Initially the sending and receiving machines must negotiate a set of security parameters (called *Security Association* [SA]) that include the shared session key, method of host and data authentication, and the encryption method to be used. The Internet Security Association and Key Management Protocol/Oakley protocol is used during this negotiation process. The latter half (that is, Oakley) of this protocol is used in determining the actual keys to be exchanged. One of two SAs is used, depending on whether Phase I or Phase II negotiation transpires. Table 11.1 compares both phases.

Table 11.1 A Comparison of Phase I and II SA Negotiation

	Phase I	**Phase II**
Name	**Main mode**	**Quick mode**
Type of SA	ISAKMP/Oakley (bidirectional)	IPSec (one-way)[6]
Type of Authentication	Kerberos, preshared key, or certificates	
Protocol for Creating and Exchanging Keys	Diffie-Hellman	Negotiated (Key can be derived from Main mode key.)
Context of Use	Getting an initial SA in place	Protecting data secrecy *after* the initial SA is in place
Default Key Lifetime	One hour	Five minutes

[6] *Because IPSec is one-way, a two-way negotiation between machines requires that two one-way links be created for the IPSec SA.*

Configuring IPSec

From the superficial appearance of IPSec, it might seem that IPSec-related protocols automatically do everything for you while you go about doing something else without having to worry about security. This is just not true; you must configure how IPSec works through an IPSec security policy in Windows 2000. You have options for setting attributes of this policy that control the following:

- **IP filters.** Chapter 7, "Basic Network Security Measures," examined how the packet filter built in to Windows NT 4.0 can limit the machines that can communicate with one another on the basis of TCP, UDP, or IP port destinations. Windows 2000 offers IP filters as part of its IPSec support. These filters are similar to the Windows NT 4.0's packet filter in that they allow traffic blocking on the basis of type of protocol and port numbers (both of the sending and receiving machines). The IP filters are, however, not subject to the types of limitations inherent in the Windows NT 4.0 packet filter. The Windows 2000 IP filters enable system administrators to specify ranges of addresses, as well as, individual addresses in the filter rules. Additionally, more than one IP filter can be part of a single security policy; to be able to communicate with each other, however, both the sending and receiving machine must set up mutual IP security attributes and methods. Machine 1, for example, may allow all outgoing traffic destined for TCP port 80. Machine 2 must not, therefore, block incoming traffic bound for TCP port 80 from Machine 1 if these machines are to communicate through these ports.
- **Negotiation policies.** Another set of policy settings in Windows 2000 IPSec involves the particular encryption algorithms that reach a consensus on the SA to be used when two machines are to engage in IPSec-based communications. It is possible to employ one type of encryption (for example, Triple Data Encryption Standard [3DES]) for confidentiality and a completely different one (for example, DES) for integrity. System administrators can even set up an ordered list of algorithms to be used so that the highest one common to both lists (that is, the list in the sending machine and the other in the receiving machines) is used. Table 11.2 presents a list of the various algorithms that Windows 2000 supports.

Table 11.2 Encryption Algorithms in Windows 2000

Algorithm	Description
Diffie-Hellman	An asymmetric (public key) cryptography algorithm that has two entities that combine each other's public information along with each other's own secret information to produce a shared-secret value.
Hash Message Authentication Code (HMAC)	A symmetric (secret) key algorithm for integrity and authentication (used to produce digital signatures).
HMAC-MD5 Message Digest Function 95	A hash function that produces a 128-bit value.
HMAC-SHA Secure Hash Algorithm (SHA)	A hash function that produces a 160-bit value.
Data Encryption Standard (DES)	A symmetric key algorithm used for secrecy of data—starts with a random number, which is used with the secret key to encrypt data.
Triple-DES (3DES)	A variant on DES which uses two symmetric keys. The payload is first encrypted with the first key, and then decrypted with the second key, and then encrypted again with the first key. This produces an effective key length of 112 bits rather than the 56 bits used by DES.
Internet Security Association and Key Management Protocol (ISAKMP)/Oakley	Key determination, key recovery.

- **The authentication method used.** As indicated in Table 11.1, IPSec in Windows 2000 can employ any of three authentication methods—Kerberos (the default method), certificates, and preshared keys—for authenticating computers to each other. No "mix-and-match" logic is allowed; both machines must use the same method if authentication is to be successful. Kerberos authentication is very strong from a security perspective, but it is not suitable for authenticating machines outside of one's internal network because of all the communications involved. Certificate-based authentication can be used for authenticating machines in far apart networks. Certificates are validated by a trusted *Certificate Authority* (CA). The third and final method is the preshared key authentication method. Machines in this case share a common key.

The major weaknesses with this method include having to share a common key (which you must create using the security policy) and then having to transmit it over the network (where it can be copied or altered).

- **How IPSec tunneling works.** You can set up secure tunnels by naming a particular server as an IPSec tunnel server in the negotiation policy. Doing so causes all IPSec communications from the machine in which this setting is chosen to use the tunnel server as the destination point for tunneled communications.
- **The type of network connection.** You can also specify the type of network connection (LAN and dial-up) allowed by each security policy. You can, for example, prevent dial-up connections into individual machines, requiring instead that only LAN connections be allowed.

Advantages of IPSec

One of the greatest advantages of Windows 2000 IPSec is that it is, in effect, an add-on capability which does not by all appearances require retrofitting applications to interface with it. Policies can be set on the basis of individual users, OUs, machines, and so forth. IPSec in Windows 2000 increases network security capabilities considerably.

IPSec does, however, have one significant drawback concerning its use as a *virtual private network* (VPN) implementation. One of the primary uses of VPNs today is to connect employees who have fast Internet connections (such as cable modems or DSL) to the internal company network. Previously, this kind of access was typically granted using dial-up. With the proliferation of fast Internet access, however, many employees want to be able to access the corporate network at faster speeds. Corporations frequently want their employees to protect their home computers from unauthorized access, however, by using a personal firewall. These are implemented in several forms. Users can obtain a minimal Linux build that has this functionality, or they can purchase a prepackaged solution, typically bundled with an Ethernet hub or switch, from third-party vendors. All these solutions have one thing in common: They use *Network Address Translation* (NAT). The problem is that whereas PPTP works across a NAT router, IPSec does not. Therefore, the two goals—fast, secure access to the corporate network, and security for the users home network (which may well have corporate secrets stored on it)—are at odds when IPSec is being used. This significantly limits the value of IPSec as a VPN technology to enable organizational network access from employees' homes.

Smart Card Support

Reliance on nothing more than entry of a username-password combination for authentication constitutes what many security professionals now label incompetence. Third-party authentication is not only the wave of the future, it is a necessary component of system and network security *now*. Accordingly, Windows 2000 has built-in support for smart cards. In fact, smart cards can be used not only in connection with authentication, but also for any application aware of smart cards. The scalability of the Windows 2000 smart card interface capabilities is one of the greatest advantages of migrating to Windows 2000. Figure 11.7 illustrates the new CryptoAPI architecture that Windows 2000 provides for smart card support.

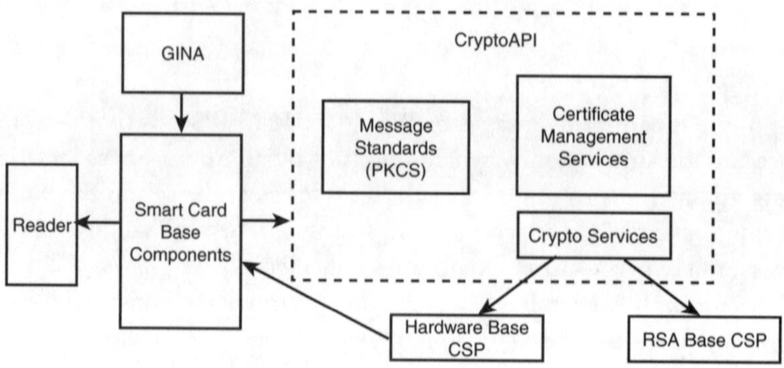

Figure 11.7 *The Windows 2000 CryptoAPI architecture.*

Migrating a user community to the use of smart cards is anything but an easy issue; it is one that requires careful planning and gradual phase-in of smart cards (rather than a sudden leap to smart card technology). Other issues dramatically affect the suitability of smart card solutions and the degree of acceptance of the user community. These issues include such things as fault tolerance (that is, what happens when smart card readers fail or smart cards wear out or are lost), whether other types of third-party authentication (for example, biometric authentication, such as fingerprint-based authentication) might be more appropriate for some kinds of users and applications, and the particular applications most in need of the additional security that smart card–based access can provide.

One of the potential security-related flaws in Windows 2000's smart card support is reliance on DLLs for smart card–related functionality. Earlier chapters have described how DLLs are easy targets. How can the DLLs used in smart card as well as other functionality in Windows 2000 be adequately protected, if at all? The answer remains yet to be seen.

Basic Security Model

The Windows 2000 security model is in many respects parallel to the security model for Windows NT 4.0 and earlier. Active Directory is part of a *Trusted Computing Base* (TCB) that serves as the basis for Windows 2000 security. ACLs (and the ACEs within) are the grounds for permitting or denying access to all objects in Active Directory. No access to any object or property in Active Directory is allowed unless the SRM has determined that the credentials of the user or process requesting access match or exceed those required in the appropriate ACE. Even Administrator-level access to Active Directory is allowed or denied on the same basis—administrators cannot override ACEs purely on the basis of their privilege level.[7]

Recommendations

Based on the analyses presented earlier in this chapter, you should seriously consider the following recommendations for planning and implementing Windows 2000 security. Issues that require attention include domain structure, deployment, protecting Active Directory, managing trusts, and maintaining group security.

Determining a Domain Structure[8]

One of the areas in Windows 2000 that affects security the most is domain structure. Assuming that your organization will develop and use trees, it is extremely important to plan the tree structure well in advance of rolling out Windows 2000. You should determine what the namespace will be, assign meaningful names to domains (including domains not now implemented, but which will be implemented in the future), and which particular domain will be the root domain. In cases of very large organizations, multiple namespaces are appropriate.

The breadth versus depth of trees is also a very important security-related consideration. Too deep (that is, in terms of too many levels) a tree may make controlling access and privileges at the lower levels too difficult; Enterprise Administrators are likely to overlook lower-level domains. Remember, too, trust between domains is by default both bidirectional and transitive. Because affording Administrator rights at lower levels of a tree is not likely to be scrutinized, as well as in higher levels, (for example, the root domain), obtaining administrator privileges at a lower level can poten-

7 *They can, however, replace the ACEs and grant themselves the permissions they desire. They must only be Administrators of the particular object in question.*

8 *This property of Windows 2000 is advantageous from a security perspective in that it helps protect against "domain spoofing" (connecting bogus domains to a tree).*

tially be catastrophic for the entire tree, depending on the specific accesses and privileges allowed. From a security perspective, therefore, having no more than, say, three levels within each tree is in general more conducive to security than having many levels. Interestingly, many analysts also propound that too many levels hurt performance.

Considering Deployment Issues

If at all possible, run only Windows 2000 servers. Don't intermingle Windows 2000 servers with Windows NT 4.0 Servers without a compelling business-related rationale. To the degree that you have both Windows NT 4.0 and Windows 2000 services within the same domain, Windows 2000 security will necessarily be reduced to the least common denominator, namely Windows NT 4.0 security. Windows 2000 Kerberos does not work in Mixed mode! Remember, too, that you *cannot* add Mixed-mode domains to a Native-mode tree.

Protecting Active Directory Adequately

Because Active Directory is the "center of the universe" in Windows 2000 and because security also depends on the integrity of Active Directory, it is important to ensure that Active Directory is adequately protected. The best strategy in this regard is to ensure that only authorized system administrators can access Active Directory. Severely limiting the number of Enterprise administrators and instead using OUs to delegate subsets of administrative powers is a very appropriate strategy in this regard. Alternatively, if determining the particular subset of administrative powers is too cumbersome, you can assign full Administrator-level rights—but only directly to OUs. You should also ensure that ACLs allow only the necessary level of access to OU objects. If you invoke Active Directory Users and Computers, you can view and modify ACLs for Active Directory objects. Be especially stingy with permissions that allow modification, deletion, and/or ownership of Active Directory objects.

Managing Trust

Be careful about assigning trust between domains too freely. Because of the practical advantages of having trust between domains, system administrators may by default just link in all domains into a single tree. From a network security perspective, doing so could be dangerous. Establishing security zones (logical areas within networks in which a uniform level of security exists) is a currently accepted way of designing network security; having domains from different zones linked by trust could comprise an implicit violation of zone-based security (for example, when a domain in one zone is more secure than a domain in another, yet the two domains trust each other).

Establishing Appropriate Group Security

Based on business and operational needs, set up local, global and universal groups and meaningful criteria for membership in each. Establishing appropriate levels of privileges and access is one important additional step, but it is not the only challenge with respect to group security. It is also important to set appropriate Group Policies. Group Policies are sets of settings that control properties, such as failed logon limits, minimum password length, user environment, versions of software that can be run, and so forth. One major advantage of Windows 2000 Group Policies is that they can be layered, meaning that different group of settings can be applied to different OUs and groups. Consider, for example, the value of having more stringent failed logon limits for Administrators than for others.

Managing Delegation

Develop a delegation scheme now. Address questions such as these:

- Who will be the Enterprise administrators and what qualifications will they need?
- Who will be domain administrators, and how many such administrators will you need?
- To what degree will Administrator rights be attenuated from one OU level to the next within a given domain?

Also consider your use of third-party applications, EFS, and IPSec security policies.

Controlling Inheritance

In Windows 2000, inheritance by default flows from higher-level domains, OUs, etc. to lower levels. It is possible to block inheritance at lower levels with the “Block Inheritance” setting—although the “No Override” setting at higher levels takes precedence. Developing a suitable set of inheritance settings is a major challange in Windows 2000.

Using Third-Party Authentication

Just as in Windows NT 4.0, integrate third-party authentication with Windows 2000 authentication to the maximum degree possible. Although Windows 2000 authentication appears to be stronger than ever before, it is extremely likely that a number of vulnerabilities in Windows 2000 authentication will emerge in time. Third-party authentication will at least to some degree, if not entirely, compensate for these vulnerabilities. The fact that Windows 2000 has built-in support for smart cards is a drawing point to be seriously considered.

Utilizing EFS

Determine whether you need EFS, and, if so, for which particular users and groups. Enable EFS appropriately and determine who will get access to the recovery agent function, ensuring that you apply the least-privilege principle.

Utilizing IPSec

Determine the IPSec security policies you will use as soon as possible. The settings you choose determine, to a large degree, the effectiveness of your deployment of IPSec. Unfortunately, they also affect system and network performance. Learning your options and the tradeoffs they involve will be critical in guiding you to making good IPSec-related decisions.

Maintaining Security

Be especially vigilant concerning hot fixes, service packs, and other solutions that affect security. Windows 2000 represents a major escalation in the number of lines of code used to implement this product. The sheer increase in the number of lines of code is certain to produce an unprecedented number of security-related, as well as other, bugs.◆

Conclusion

Security in Windows NT 4.0 is by no means easy, but dealing with security in Windows 2000 is likely to be even more complicated. Windows 2000 offers many security capabilities; to deny this is to fail to understand what this release has to offer. Perhaps best of all, Windows 2000 out-of-the-box is considerably more secure than Windows NT out-of-the-box. But Windows 2000 at the same time presents a big dilemma. It offers more security-related features (many of which are considerably stronger than in Windows NT 4.0). Yet because of the potential for creating massive domain trees structures and the fact that trust is potentially all pervasive by default in Windows 2000 makes this release, in many ways, the most difficult to deal with from a security viewpoint. Worse yet, the fact that DCs are by default authoritative (making it necessary to compromise any DC or spoof a DC), and that Active Directory is shared across different domains within the same tree, make Windows NT extremely vulnerable to "weak-link" attacks.

The good news is that because Windows 2000 is so complex and more expensive, it is not likely to become the mainstay operating system at many sites in the very near future. This at least affords you, as well as the rest of the IT and security communities, some time to analyze and plan for this very intriguing next release of Windows NT. Being somewhat conservative at this time with respect to the timing and extent of any Windows 2000 migration is, in fact, the smartest strategy of all.

A

Port-Assignment Conventions

This appendix contains a list of the port numbers and associated functions used in Windows NT. Any Microsoft networking alias is also listed. Note that many of the indicated ports are "not assigned," that is, Microsoft does not consider them to be well-known ports. This appendix can be useful in setting up a port-filtering scheme for your network(s).

Port Number	Function	Microsoft Networking Alias
7 TCP and UDP	Echo	
9 TCP and UDP	Discard	
13 TCP and UDP	Daytime	
17 TCP and UDP	Qotd	
19 TCP and UDP	Chargen	
20 TCP	File Transfer Protocol (default data)	
21 TCP	File Transfer Protocol (control)	
22TCP and UDP	Not assigned (but often used for secure shell)	
23 TCP	Telnet	
24 TCP and UDP	Private Mail System	
25 TCP	Simple Mail Transfer Protocol	Mail
26 TCP and UDP	Not assigned	
27 TCP and UDP	NSW User System FE	
28 TCP and UDP	Not assigned	
29 TCP and UDP	MSG ICP	
30 TCP and UDP	Not assigned	

Port Number	Function	Microsoft Networking Alias
31 TCP and UDP	MSG authentication	
32 TCP and UDP	Not assigned	
33 TCP and UDP	Display support protocol	
34 TCP and UDP	Unassigned	
35 TCP and UDP	Private printer server	
36 TCP and UDP	Not assigned	
37 TCP and UDP	Time	Timeserver
38 TCP and UDP	Not assigned	
39 UDP	Resource Location Protocol	Resource
40 TCP and UDP	Not assigned	
41 TCP and UDP	Graphics	
42 TCP and UDP	Host name server	Nameserver
43 TCP	Whois	Nicname
44 TCP and UDP	MPM Flags Protocol	
45 TCP and UDP	Message Processing Module	
46 TCP and UDP	MPM (default send)	
47 TCP and UDP	NI FTP	
48 TCP and UDP	Not assigned	
49 TCP and UDP	Logon Host Protocol	
50 TCP and UDP	Remote Mail Checking Protocol	
51 TCP and UDP	IMP Logical Address Maintenance	
52 TCP and UDP	XNS Time Protocol	
53 TCP and UDP	Domain Name Server	DNS
54 TCP and UDP	XNS Clearinghouse	
55 TCP and UDP	ISI Graphics Language	
56 TCP and UDP	XNS authentication	
57 TCP and UDP	Private Terminal Access	
58 TCP and UDP	XNS Mail	
59 TCP and UDP	Private File Service	

Port Number	Function	Microsoft Networking Alias
60 TCP and UDP	Not assigned	
61 TCP and UDP	NI Mail	
62 TCP and UDP	ACA Services	
63 TCP and UDP	VIA Systems FTP	
64 TCP and UDP	Communications Integrator	
65 TCP and UDP	TACACS Database Service	
66 TCP and UDP	Oracle SQL*NET	
67 UDP	DCHP/bootp	
68 UDP	DHCP/bootp	
69 UDP	Trivial File Transfer	
70 TCP	Gopher	
71 TCP and UDP	Remote Job Service	
72 TCP and UDP	Remote Job Service	
73 TCP and UDP	Remote Job Service	
74 TCP and UDP	Remote Job Service	
75 TCP and UDP	Private Dial-out service	
76 TCP and UDP	Not assigned	
77 TCP and UDP	Private RJA service	
78 TCP and UDP	Vettcp	
79 TCP	Finger	
80 TCP	Hypertext transfer	
81 TCP and UDP	HOSTS name server	
82 TCP and UDP	XFER utility	
83 TCP and UDP	MIT ML device	
84 TCP and UDP	Common trace facility	
85 TCP and UDP	MIT ML device	
86 TCP and UDP	Micro Focus Cobol	
87 TCP and UDP	Private Terminal Link	ttylink
88 TCP and UDP	Kerberos	Kerberos
89 TCP and UDP	SU/MIT Telnet Gateway	

Port Number	Function	Microsoft Networking Alias
90 TCP and UDP	Default WINS Name Server Destination	
91 TCP and UDP	MIT Dover Spooler	
92 TCP and UDP	Network Printing Protocol	
93 TCP and UDP	Device Control Protocol	
94 TCP and UDP	Tivoli Object Dispatcher	
95 TCP and UDP	SUPDUP	
96 TCP and UDP	DIXIE Protocol Specification	
97 TCP and UDP	Swift Remote Virtual Protocol	
98 TCP and UDP	TAC News	
99 TCP and UDP	Metagram Relay	
100 TCP and UDP	New Account	
101 TCP	NIC Host Nameserver	Hostname
102 TCP	ISO-TSAP	
103 TCP and UDP	Genesis Point-to-Point Transnet	Webster
104 TCP and UDP	ACR-NEMA Digital Image and Communication 300	
105 TCP and UDP	Mailbox Name Nameserver	
106 TCP and UDP	3COM-TSMUX	
107 TCP	Remote Telnet Service	
108 TCP and UDP	SNA Gateway Access Server	
109 TCP	Post Office Protocol, version 2 (POP2)	Postoffice
110 TCP	Post Office Protocol, version 3 (POP3)	Postoffice
111 TCP and UDP	Sun Remote Procedure Call	
112 TCP and UDP	McIDAS Remote Transmission	

Port Number	Function	Microsoft Networking Alias
113 TCP	Authentication Service	Authentication
114 TCP and UDP	Audio News Multicast	
115 TCP and UDP	Simple File Transfer Protocol	
116 TCP and UDP	ANSA REX Notify	
117 TCP	UUCP Path Service	
118 TCP and UDP	SQL Services	
119 TCP	Network News Transfer	Usenet
120 TCP and UDP	CFDPTKT	
121 TCP and UDP	Encore Expedited Remote Pro.Call	
122 TCP and UDP	SMAKYNET	
123 UDP	Network Time Protocol	ntpd ntp
124 TCP and UDP	ANSA REX Trader	
125 TCP and UDP	Locus PC-Interface Net Map Server	
126 TCP and UDP	Unisys Unitary Login	
127 TCP and UDP	Locus PC-Interface Conn Server	
128 TCP and UDP	GSS X License Verification	
129 TCP and UDP	Password Generator Protocol	
130 TCP and UDP	Cisco FNATIVE	
131 TCP and UDP	Cisco TNATIVE	
132 TCP and UDP	Cisco SYSMAINT	
133 TCP and UDP	Statistics Service	
134 TCP and UDP	INGRES NET Service	
135 TCP and UDP	Location Service	
136 TCP and UDP	PROFILE Naming System	
137 TCP and UDP	NetBIOS Name Service (nbname)	
138 UDP	NetBIOS Datagram Service (nbdatagram)	
139 TCP	NetBIOS Session Service (nbsession)	
140 TCP and UDP	EMFIS Data Service	
141 TCP and UDP	EMFIS Control Service	

Port Number	Function	Microsoft Networking Alias
142 TCP and UDP	Britton-Lee IDM	
143 TCP	Interim Mail Access Protocol (v.2) (IMAP2)	
144 TCP and UDP	NewS	news
145 TCP and UDP	UAAC Protocol	
146 TCP and UDP	ISO-IPO	
147 TCP and UDP	ISP-IP	
148 TCP and UDP	CRONUS SUPPORT	
149 TCP and UDP	AED 512 Emulation Service	
150 TCP and UDP	SQLNET	
151 TCP and UDP	HEMS	
152 TCP and UDP	Background File Transfer Program	
153 TCP and UDP	Simple Gateway Management Protocol	sgmp
154 TCP and UDP	NETSC	
155 TCP and UDP	NETSC	
156 TCP and UDP	SQL Service	
157 TCP and UDP	KNET/VM Command/ Message Protocol	
158 TCP	PCMail Server	repository
159 TCP and UDP	NSS Routing	
160 TCP and UDP	SGMP-TRAPS	
161 TCP and UDP	Simple Network Management Protocol	snmp
162 TCP and UDP	SNMPTRAP	
163 TCP and UDP	CMIP/TCP Manager	
164 TCP and UDP	CMIP/TCP Agent	
165 TCP and UDP	Xerox Name Service	xns
166 TCP and UDP	Sirius Systems Net	s-net
167 TCP and UDP	NAMP	
168 TCP and UDP	RSVD	
169 TCP and UDP	SEND	
170 TCP	Network PostScript	
171 TCP and UDP	Network Innovations Multiplex	
172 TCP and UDP	Network Innovations CL/1	

Port Number	Function	Microsoft Networking Alias
173 TCP and UDP	Xyplex-MUX	
174 TCP and UDP	MAILQ	
175 TCP and UDP	VMNET	
176 TCP and UDP	GENRAD-MUX	
177 TCP and UDP	X Display Manager Control Protocol	
178 TCP and UDP	NextStep Windows Server	
179 TCP	Border Gateway Protocol	
180 TCP and UDP	Intergraph RIS	
181 TCP and UDP	Unify	
182 TCP and UDP	Unisys Audit SITP	
183 TCP and UDP	OCBinder	
184 TCP and UDP	OCServer	
185 TCP and UDP	REMOTE KIS	
186 TCP and UDP	KIS Protocol	
187 TCP and UDP	Application Communication Interface	
188 TCP and UDP	Plus Five MUMPS	
189 TCP and UDP	Queued File Transport	
190 TCP and UDP	Gateway Access Control Protocol	
191 TCP and UDP	Prospero	
192 TCP and UDP	OSU Network Monitoring Protocol	
193 TCP and UDP	Spider Remote Monitoring Protocol	
194 TCP	Internet Relay Chat Protocol	
195 TCP and UDP	DNSIX Network Level Module Audit	
196 TCP and UDP	DNSIX Session Management Module Audit Redir	
197 TCP and UDP	Directory Location Service	

Port Number	Function	Microsoft Networking Alias
198 TCP and UDP	Directory Location Service Monitor	
199 TCP and UDP	SMUX	
200 TCP and UDP	IBM System Resource Controller	
201 TCP and UDP	AppleTalk Routing Maintenance	
202 TCP and UDP	AppleTalk Name Binding	
203 TCP and UDP	AppleTalk (Not assigned)	
204 TCP and UDP	AppleTalk Echo	
205 TCP and UDP	AppleTalk (Not assigned)	
206 TCP and UDP	AppleTalk Zone Information	
207 TCP and UDP	AppleTalk (Not assigned)	
208 TCP and UDP	AppleTalk (Not assigned)	
209 TCP and UDP	Trivial Authenticated Mail Protocol	
210 TCP and UDP	ANSI Z39.50	
211TCP and UDP	Texas Instruments 914C/G Terminal	
212 TCP and UDP	ATEXSSTR	
213 UDP	IPX	
214 TCP and UDP	VM PWSCS	
215 TCP and UDP	Insignia Solutions softpc	
216 TCP and UDP	Access Technology License Server	
217 TCP and UDP	dbase UNIX	
218 TCP and UDP	Netix Message Posting Protocol	
219 TCP and UDP	Unisys ARPs	
220 TCP and UDP	Interactive Mail Access Protocol (v.3) (IMAP3)	

Port Number	Function	Microsoft Networking Alias
221 TCP and UDP	Berkeley rlogind with SPX authentication	
222 TCP and UDP	Berkeley rshd with SPX authentication	
223 TCP and UDP	Certificate Distribution Center	
243 TCP and UDP	Survey Measurement	
245 TCP and UDP	LINK	
246 TCP and UDP	Display Systems Protocol	
345 TCP and UDP	Performance Analysis Workbench	
346 TCP and UDP	Zebra server	
347 TCP and UDP	Fatmen Server	
371 TCP and UDP	Clearcase	
372 TCP and UDP	UNIX Listserver	
373 TCP and UDP	Legent Corporation (v.1)	
374 TCP and UDP	Legent Corporation (v.2)	
389 TCP	ldap	
443 TCP	Secure Hypertext Transfer Protocol (HTTP-S)	
445 TCP and UDP	Microsoft CIFS	
464 TCP and UDP	kpasswd (Kerberos v.5)	
500 UDP	ISAKMP	
512 TCP	Remote Process Execution (exec)	
512 UDP	biff mail notification	comsat
513 TCP	Remote login	
513 UDP	Who	whod
514 TCP	Remote Command	
514 UDP	Syslog	
515 TCP	Print Spooler	spooler
517 UDP	Talk	
518 UDP	Ntalk	

Port Number	Function	Microsoft Networking Alias
519 TCP and UDP	UNIX Time	
520 TCP	Extended File Name Server	
520 UDP	Local Routing Process	router routed
525 UDP	Timeserver	
526 TCP	Newdate	
530 TCP and UDP	RPC Courier	
531 TCP	Chat	
531 UDP	MIT Disk	
532 TCP	Readnews	
533 UDP	Emergency Broadcasts	
540 TCP	UNIX-to-UNIX Copy Protocol	
543 TCP	Kshell login	
544 TCP	Kshell command	cmd
550 UDP	New-who	
555 TCP and UDP	DSF	
556 TCP	Remote File Service	rfs_server
560 UDP	Remote Monitor	
561 UDP	Monitor	
562 TCP and UDP	Ch command	
564 TCP and UDP	Plan 9 File Service	
565 TCP and UDP	Whoami	
570 TCP and UDP	Meter Daemon	
571 TCP and UDP	Meter Udaemon	
600 TCP and UDP	Sun Interprocess Communication (IPC) Server	
607 TCP and UDP	Nqs	
636 TCP	ldaps (LDAP over TLS/SSL)	
666 TCP and UDP	Mdqs	
704 TCP and UDP	Errlog Copy/Server Daemon	
740 TCP and UDP	NETscout Control Protocol	
741 TCP and UDP	NetGW	
742 TCP and UDP	Network Revision Control System	

Port Number	Function	Microsoft Networking Alias
744 TCP and UDP	Flexible License Manager	
747 TCP and UDP	Fujitsu Device Control	
748 TCP and UDP	Russell Information Science Calendar Manager	
749 TCP and UDP	Kerberos administration	
750 TCP	Kerberos authentication	kdc
750 UDP	loadav	
751 TCP and UDP	Kerberos authentication	
752 TCP and UDP	Kerberos password server	
753 TCP and UDP	Kerberos userreg server	
754 TCP and UDP	Kerberos slave	
758 TCP and UDP	nlogin	
759 TCP and UDP	con	
760 TCP and UDP	ns	
761 TCP and UDP:	rxe	
762 TCP and UDP	Quota daemon	
763 TCP and UDP	cycleserve	
764 TCP and UDP	omserv	
765 TCP and UDP	webser	
767 TCP and UDP	Phone	
769 TCP and UDP	vid	
770 TCP and UDP	Cadlock	
771 TCP and UDP	rtip	
772 TCP and UDP	cycleserve2	
773 TCP	submit	
773 UDP	notify	
774 TCP	rpasswd	
774 UDP	acmaint-dbd	
775 TCP	entomb	
775 UDP	acmaint_transd	
776 TCP and UDP	wpages	

Port Number	Function	Microsoft Networking Alias
780 TCP and UDP	wpgs	
781 TCP and UDP	HP Performance Data Collector	
782 TCP and UDP	HP Performance Data Managed Mode	
783 TCP and UDP	HP Performance Data Alarm Manager	
800 TCP and UDP	mdbs_doesmon	
801 TCP and UDP	device	
888 TCP	Login and environment passing	
996 TCP and UDP	XTREE License Server	
997 TCP and UDP	maitrd	
998 TCP	busboy	
998 UDP	puparp	
999 TCP and UDP	puprouter	
999 TCP	garcon	
999 UDP	Applix AC	
1000 TCP	cadlock	
1000 UDP	ock	

B

RFCs Supported by the Windows NT Implementation of TCP/IP

Requests for Comments (RFCs) by the Internet Engineering Task Force (IETF). For more information go to `http://www.ietf.org/rfcs/` for a complete listing of current RFCs. This appendix is a listing of RFCs implemented in Windows NT 4.0, as well as several implemented in Windows 2000. This appendix does not include draft RFCs that may apply to the Windows NT TCP/IP implementation. This list also may not include additional RFCs that have been added in service packs.

RFC	Protocol or Service	Abbreviation
768	User Datagram Protocol	UDP
783	Trivial File Transfer Protocol	TFTP
791	Internet Protocol	IP
792	Internet Control Message Protocol	ICMP
793	Transmission Control Protocol	TCP
	Fault Isolation and Recovery	
826	Address Resolution Protocol	ARP
854	Telnet protocol	Telnet
862	Echo protocol	Echo
863	Discard protocol	Discard
864	Character Generator protocol	Chargen
865	Quote of the Day protocol	Quote
867	Daytime protocol	Daytime
	IP over Ethernet	

RFC	Protocol or Service	Abbreviation
919, 922	IP Broadcast Datagrams	
	Internet Standard Subnetting Procedure	
959	File Transfer Protocol	FTP
1001, 1002	NetBIOS Service Protocols	
	Requirements for Internet Gateways (Windows 2000 Only)	
1034, 1035	Domain Name Service	DNS
	IP over Token Ring	
1055	Transmission of IP over Serial Lines	IP-SLIP
	Internet Gateway Multicast Protocol	IGMP
1122, 1123	Host Requirements (Communications and Applications)	
1134	Point-to-Point Protocol	PPP[1]
	Compressing TCP/IP Headers for Low-Speed Serial Links	
1157	Simple Network Management Protocol	SNMP
	Line Printer Daemon Protocol	
	IP over FDDI	
	Path MTU Discovery	
	IP over ARCnet	
1231	IEEE 802.5 Token Ring MIB	MIB-II (support removed in Windows 2000)
	ICMP Router Discovery Messages (Windows 2000 Only)	
1323	TCP Extensions for High Performance (Windows 2000 Only)	
1332	PPP Internet Protocol Control Protocol	IPCP
	PPP Authentication Protocols	
	Architecture for IP Address Allocation with CIDR	
	Classless Inter-Domain Routing	CIDR

[1] *Supported in Windows NT 4.0. In Windows 2000, this RFC is not supported; it has been made obsolete by RFC 1661.*

RFC	Protocol or Service	Abbreviation
	DHCP Options and BOOTP Vendor Extensions	
	Interoperation Between DHCP and BOOTP	
	Dynamic Host Configuration Protocol	DHCP[2]
	Clarifications and Extensions for the Bootstrap Protocol[3]	
1547	Requirements for Point-to-Point Protocol	PPP[4]
1548	Point-to-Point Protocol	PPP[5]
	PPP in High-Level Data-Link Control Framing[6]	
1552	PPP Internetwork Packet Exchange Control Protocol	IPXCP
	IPX Header Compression (Windows NT 4.0 only)	
	Link Control Protocol Extensions	
	Point-to-Point Protocol (PPP) (Windows 2000 Only)	
	PPP in HDLC-Like Framing	
1748	IEEE 802.5 MIB using SMIv2 (Windows 2000 only)	
1749	IEEE 802.5 Station Source Routing MIB using SMIv2 (Windows 2000 only)	
1812	Requirements for IP Version 4 Routers (Windows 2000 only)	
1828	IP Authentication Using Keyed MD5 (Windows 2000 only)	
1829	ESP DES-CBC Transform (Windows 2000 only)	

[2] *Made obsolete by RFC 2131. Hence 1541 is supported in NT 4.0, and 2131 is supported in Windows 2000*

[3] *Made obsolete by RFC 2132. Hence 1542 is supported in NT 4.0, and 2132 is supported in Windows 2000*

[4] *Informational RFC only. Not technically supported by Windows 2000.*

[5] *Made obsolete by RFC 1661. Hence 1548 is supported in NT 4.0, and 1661 is supported in Windows 2000.*

[6] *Made obsolete by RFC 1662. Hence 1549 is supported in NT 4.0, and 1662 is supported in Windows 2000.*

RFC	Protocol or Service	Abbreviation
1851	ESP Triple DES-CBC Transform (Windows 2000 only)	
1852	IP Authentication Using Keyed SHA (Windows 2000 only)	
1878	Variable Length Subnet Table for IPv4 (Windows 2000 only)	
1994	PPP Challenge Handshake Authentication Protocol (CHAP) (Windows 2000 only)	
2018	TCP Selective Acknowledgment Options (Windows 2000 only)	
2085	HMAC-MD5 IP Authentication with Replay Prevention (Windows 2000 only)	
2104	HMAC: Keyed Hashing for Message Authentication (Windows 2000 only)	
2131	Dynamic Host Configuration Protocol (DHCP) (Windows 2000 only)	
2132	Clarifications and Extensions for the Bootstrap Protocol (Windows 2000 only)	
2136	Dynamic Updates in the Domain Name System (DNS Update) (Windows 2000 only)	
2205	Resource Reservation Protocol (RSVP), Version 1 Functional Specification (Windows 2000 only)	
2236	Internet Group Management Protocol, Version 2 (Windows 2000 only)	
2401	Security Architecture for the Internet Protocol (Windows 2000 only)	
2402	IP Authentication Header (AH) (Windows 2000 only)	
2406	IP Encapsulating Security Payload (ESP) (Windows 2000 only)	
2637	Point-to-Point Tunneling Protocol (PPTP) (Windows 2000 only)	

2661	Layer Two Tunneling Protocol (L2TP) (Windows 2000 only)

Draft RFCs Supported by Windows NT 4.0

NetBIOS Frame Control Protocol (NBFCP)

PPP over ISDN

PPP over X.25

Compression Control Protocol

C

Significant Security-Related Features of Service Packs 3–6a for Windows NT 4.0

This appendix covers the security-related service packs most relevant to current deployments of Windows NT 4.0. The TechNet reference, the nature of each vulnerability that the service packs address, and the major threat that each vulnerability entails are listed for each service pack. Additional features (such as security enhancements that do not address specific vulnerabilities) are also included. Vulnerabilities in IIS are excluded because they are not generic to Windows NT.

To obtain additional information about each issue, go to the Microsoft support site. As of this writing, articles can be retrieved by modifying this URL:

```
http://support.microsoft.com/support/kb/articles/QXYZ/A/BC.ASP
```

XYZABC is the number of the article. You may also receive KBase articles via email by sending an email to `mshelp@microsoft.com`. Just put the article number in the subject of the email. If you need a copy of article Q135707, for example, send an email with Q135707 as the subject. Of course, all these articles are also available on the TechNet CD/DVD.

Table C.1 discusses Service Pack 3. For a complete list of fixes in SP3, see Q147798.

Table C.1 Service Pack 3

TechNet Reference	Nature of Problem	Threat
Q135707	Process Manager can accept bogus priority parameter.	System crashes.
Q143470	Synchronous execution of logon scripts not applied to new users.	Logon script failures.
Q143474	Anonymous users can remotely discover shares and accounts.	Facilitates unauthorized share access and break-ins to accounts.
Q143475	Passwords can easily be cracked.	Unauthorized access to accounts.
Q151082	Passwords that are short or contain part of username or full name are easier to crack.	Break-ins to accounts.
Q160990	DHCP server can assign identical IP addresses to different clients.	Address spoofing, disruption of networking.
Q161372	Bogus clients can become "man-in-the middle" to steal sessions.	Unauthorized access to data and programs.
Q161830	Inability to properly handle message from UNIX Smbclient.	System crashes client when long username is sent.
Q162567	Telnet to port 135 can cause massive CPU overallocation; 100% CPU utilization.	System hangs.
Q162927	Telnet to port 53 can flood DNS with input.	Denial of service.
Q163196	Specially constructed Ping packets can hang TCP/IP stack.	System crashes.
Q164938	Heavy logging can freeze event logging.	Lack of user accountability.
Q166478	Use of logon rights are excluded from Audit log.	Lack of user accountability.

Additional features of SP3 include the following:

- Improves default installation.
- Tightens security through measures such as deleting an unused Registry key that contains a password.

- Restricting anonymous users from obtaining access to the Registry is possible
- Creates Authenticated Users group, which excludes anonymous users (that is, null session users).
- Registry setting must be made to send clear-text passwords to other SMB-capable hosts, such as UNIX systems.
- Provides enhanced cryptographic functionality for Crypto API.
- Provides password filtering based on simple criteria.
- Limited support of MD5-CHAP over PPP.

Table C.2 discusses Service Pack 4. For a complete list of fixes available in SP4, see Q150734, Q194834, and Q224793.

Table C.2 Service Pack 4

TechNet Reference	Nature of Problem	Threat
Q129457	Anonymous users can discover password policy settings. (RestrictAnonymous in SP3 did not work.)	Facilitates break-ins to accounts.
Q142615	Event Logger Service excludes access to Security log.	Lack of user accountability.
Q143478	Out-of-band input can stop TCPIP.SYS.	Denial of service.
Q143484	IIS services stop with large client requests.	Denial of service.
Q146965	GetAdmin Trojan horse utility causes unauthorized rights escalation.	Unauthorized local Administrator-level access.
Q147706	LM authentication allows dangerous connections from low-ended clients. (`LMCompatibilityLevel` introduced.)	Unauthorized access to resources or systems.
Q154087	Client can send wrong buffer size to LSASS.	No local logons; tools that depend on LSASS will not work.
Q154174	Fragmented ICMP packets can hang systems.	Denial of service ("Teardrop").
Q154460	Simple TCP/IP services are vulnerable to attack.	Denial of service.

continues ▸

Table C.2 Continued

TechNet Reference	Nature of Problem	Threat
Q154990	A different user's password can be changed using SETPASS.	Break-ins to accounts; denial of access to legitimate users.
Q155701	WINS quits if it receives invalid UDP packets.	Denial of service.
Q162230	Certain input can cause PPTP server to crash.	Denial of service.
Q165005	Attack on TCP/IP stack can cause systems to slow down (LAND attack)	Performance degradation.
Q167629	Query IDs guessing can lead to compromise of DNS servers.	Integrity of service compromise.
Q169461	Piped output to DNS can crash systems.	Denial of service.
Q173059	Failure to record security events.	Lack of accountability.
Q174205	Memory overutilization by LSASS on domain controllers.	Denial of service.
Q174929	ARP bug can result in duplicate IP address assignment.	Invalid addressing, disruption of networking.
Q177670	Weak encryption for dial-up clients in RRAS.	Confidentiality compromise.
Q178381	SNMP memory leaks.	Performance degradation.
Q179129	System halt due to IP packet-fragmentation attack (Teardrop attack).	Denial of service.
Q180963	Unauthorized users can restart systems by corrupting SMB requests.	Denial of service.
Q183054	Take Ownership right remotely can cause wrong ownership of object.	Unauthorized Read, Change, and so on.
Q183859	Secure channels with domain controllers are subject to compromise.	Unauthorized reading of network traffic.

TechNet Reference	Nature of Problem	Threat
Q184017	Service account password can be displayed.	Unauthorized access to services.
Q186473	A bug in SNMP allows deletion of records on WINS server.	Denial of service.
Q186494	Purging of Audit log by non-system administrator is not recorded.	Lack of accountability.
Q188700	Screen saver password works for locked-out account.	Unauthorized access to systems.
Q188806	`::$DATA` request returns source code of files over Web.	Disclosure of sensitive and other information.
Q189595	PPTP transmissions are subject to compromise.	Unauthorized reading of network traffic.
Q190288	SecHole Trojan horse program can allow escalation of privileges.	Unauthorized local Administrator access.
Q193233	RPC spoofing can cause overallocation of CPU.	Denial of service.
Q194341	Flaws in simple TCP/IP services can cause CPU overallocation.	Denial of service.
Q194431	Applications may listen on TCP or UDP ports.	Disclosure of sensitive and other information.
Q194465	PPTP connections are denied under certain conditions.	Denial of service.

Additional features of SP4 include the following:

- **Quota for user profiles.** If the size of a user profile exceeds the quota, the user is not permitted to log off.
- **Security Configuration Manager (SCM).** This utility enables administrators to evaluate, compare, and set security settings on a single host (multiple hosts can be evaluated and configured using a command line tool).
- **Access restrictions for the Event log.** This requires anyone (including an Administrator) who wants to access the Security (Audit) Log to have the Manage Auditing and Security Log right.

- **DHCP auditing (and other) enhancements.** SP4 also enables DHCP auditing. The IP addresses assigned to DHCP clients in addition to the time of address assignment are written into log files that are added to the System32 directory daily. Each DHCP log file is named with a unique date and time.

Note that Microsoft describes the DCOM/HTTP tunneling capability that allows DCOM traffic between clients and servers to go through firewalls over TCP 80 as having security-related benefits. This capability, introduced by Service Pack 4, is in most respects a security *liability*, however, not an advantage. DCOM itself is considerably less than ideal from a security viewpoint (see Chapter 7, "Basic Network Security Measures," in this book).

Table C.3 discusses Service Pack 5. For a complete list of fixes in SP5, see Q225037 and Q244974.

Table C.3 Service Pack 5

TechNet Reference	Nature of Problem	Threat
Q188348	Especially malformed FTP requests can cause denial of service.	Denial of service.
Q193361	MSGINA.DLL does not clear passwords.	Unauthorized access to systems.
Q193793	`::$DATA` can return source code of file on Web server.	Disclosure of sensitive and other Information.
Q195733	Bugs in applications that use RPC over named pipes.	Denial of service.
Q196270	SNMP agent memory leaks.	Performance degradation.
Q214802	Unauthorized user can paste text into unlocked workstation dialog boxes.	Disclosure of sensitive and other information.
Q214840	MSV1_0 bug allows network connections to certain accounts.	Unauthorized access.
Q215367	`GetEffectiveRightsFromAcl()` may produce wrong access mask.	Inappropriate access or denial Of service.

TechNet Reference	Nature of Problem	Threat
Q217336	Source routing (this fix disables source routing).	Increased susceptibility to certain types of network attacks.
Q218473	Trojan DLL can escalate privileges.	Unauthorized Privilege escalation.

Table C.4 discusses Service Packs 6 and 6a. For a complete list of bugs fixed by these service packs, see Q241211 and Q244690.[1]

Table C.4 Service Packs 6 and 6a

TechNet Reference	Nature of Problem	Threat
Q218934	Flaws in Security Configuration Manager MMC snap-in.	Incorrect permissions may be applied.
Q223408	Scheduled logoff may not occur on locked workstation with Active Screen Saver.	Increased susceptibility to unauthorized access.
Q224547	RRAS memory leak.	Performance degradation.
Q225503	MD-5 CHAP authentication incompatibility with SP4.	Denial of service to RAS clients.
Q230677	Malformed phonebook data in RAS client.	Unauthorized access.
Q230681	DUN credentials can be cached under certain conditions. (This article discusses the same issue as Q233303, but applies to RAS rather than RRAS.)	Unauthorized access with RAS.
Q231457	LSA service can become unresponsive after malformed request.	Denial of service.
Q233303	DUN credentials can be cached under certain conditions. (This article discusses the same issue as Q230681, but applies to RRAS rather than RAS.)	Unauthorized access with RRAS.

continues ▸

1 *Service Pack 6 had numerous problems that could cause systems to not function properly. Therefore Microsoft recalled Service Pack 6 and reissued it as Service Pack 6a. I highly discourage you from deploying the original Service Pack 6 to any system.*

Table C.4 Continued

TechNet Reference	Nature of Problem	Threat
Q233323	Exceeding `MaxRequestThreads` can cause the system to freeze.	Denial of service.
Q236359	Unprotected IOCTL function call.	Denial of service.
Q237849	FIPS 140-1 Validation for Cryptographic Service Providers.	
Q238453	Disabling of source routing may not work if certain data is in Route Pointer field.	Increased susceptibility to certain kinds of network attacks.
Q241189	SNMP memory leak.	Performance degradation.
Q241549	RAS callback may not work right when accessing an IAS server running on Windows 2000.	Lack of callback verification.
Q242009	Malformed packets can halt TCP/IP.SYS on an FTP server.	Denial of service.
Q242033	Smbtorture can result in access violation in SERVICES.EXE.	Access violation.

D

Useful Security-Related Tools from the Windows NT 4.0 Resource Kit

This Appendix briefly describes tools in the Windows NT Resource Kit that are useful in securing systems and networks. This is not an exhaustive listing of security-related tools in the Resource Kit. Instead, this information will help in the potentially overwhelming task of combing through the many Resource Kit tools trying to find and test those relevant to security.

Tool Name	Description	Notes
ADDUSERS.EXEC	Creates and removes user accounts.	The documented syntax for this tool is incorrect. The NET USERS tool, which is built in, provides the same functionality.
DELSRV.EXE	Deletes services.	Unregisters a service with the service control manager.
DISKMAP.EXE	Reports information about disk configuration by reading the Registry.	
DISKUSE.EXE	Dumps information about how much disk space each user is using.	
DUMPEL.EXE	Dumps log data to a text file, enabling to the administrator to selectively choose among the log data.	
FINDGRP.EXE	Reports all group memberships for each user within a domain.	

Tool Name	Description	Notes
FLOPLOCK.EXE	Uses ACLs to protect against unauthorized access to the floppy drive.	
GETSID.EXE	Compares SIDs for different accounts on different machines.	Used primarily for checking for corruption of the user account database on a backup domain controller.
GLOBAL.EXE	Shows global group memberships on remote servers/domains.	
LOCAL.EXE	Similar to GLOBAL.EXE, but shows local group members.	
MONITOR.EXE	Records log and alert data on remote machines.	The Performance Monitor service. Enables performance monitoring without being logged on.[1]
NETDOM.EXE	Provides a command line for managing domains.	
NETSVC.EXE	Enables the administrator to remotely start and stop services as well as to determine their status.	
NLMON.EXE	Shows trust relationships between domains.	
NLTEST.EXE	Used to test and monitor various parameters with regards to domains, trust relationships, and so on.	Provides a plethora of options and output. For example, can be used to determine when the last time a user changed a password, how long a machine has been running, and what a user's password hashes are.
NTRIGHTS.EXE	For managing user rights.	

1 *Not available in recent versions of the Resource Kit.*

Tool Name	Description	Notes
PASSPROP.EXE	For preventing remote Registry access by non-administrators, restricting remote shutdowns, simple password filtering, and so forth. Used to configure simple password requirements and whether the Administrator account can be locked out from network logons.	This is the only method forenabling Administrator account lockout.
PERMS.EXE	For displaying permissions assigned to any given user.	
PVIEWER.EXE	Lists all processes.	Shows information about a specific process.
PULIST.EXE	Process list.	Also works to list processes on remote computers.
RASLIST.EXE	Displays the names of all hosts within a domain network that are running RAS.	
RASUSERS.EXE	Shows all users who have RAS access within a server or domain.	
REG.EXE	Enables the administrator to edit the Registry.	Used for editing the Registry remotely and/or from the command line.
REGDUMP.EXE	Enables the administrator to get a dump of the Registry on both local and remote machines.	
REGINI.EXE	Can take output from REGDMP.EXE and enter it into a Registry.	
REGFIND.EXE	Enables the administrator to find and edit Registry keys.	
RKILL.EXE	Enables the administrator to find and kill processes on remote hosts.	

Tool Name	Description	Notes
SCANREG.EXE	Enables the administrator to search to specific keys and entries in Registries of remote hosts.	
SCLIST.EXE	Shows all services on both local and remote hosts.	
SECADD.EXE	Enables the administrator to modify ACLs for Registry keys.	
SOON.EXE	Enables the administrator to schedule commands and programs to run in a very short time on both local and remote hosts.	Note: SOON.EXE does not work on systems that have the MS Task Scheduler that comes with IE 4.x installed.
SU.EXE	For switching to another user account.	
SUBINACL.EXE	Shows permissions, Registry settings, services, and enables the administrator to duplicate settings locally and remotely (even across domain boundaries).	
TLIST.EXE	Provides PID listing for all background processes, the state of each process, and the dependencies (executables, DLLs, and so forth).	Only works on local system.
XCACLS.EXE	Displays permissions and enables the administrator to modify them.[2]	

[2] *This tool is better than CACLS.EXE in that it is more reliable in producing the ACL changes specified by commands that are entered.*

E

A Script for Securing Windows NT Systems

This script, written by Mad Dog, is a security cleanup procedure. It tightens permissions on critical directories, makes Registry changes that fix vulnerabilities, and so forth. Be sure to read the comments in the script first; the one about running the script as a .BAT file is particularly important. You may also want to modify some of the commands according to your particular needs. Finally, note that the script is intended primarily for use on servers; not on workstations.

```
echo This script was written by Mad Dog on Dec. 8, 1999.
echo Last edited Dec. 8, 1999.
echo Version 1.0
echo.
pause
echo.
echo Note that the following NT Resource Kit utilities MUST be
echo in the same directory as this batch file for the
echo batch file to work!
echo.
echo XCACLS.EXE, REQ.EXE, NTRIGHTS.EXE, PASSPROP.EXE
echo.
pause
echo.
echo.
echo Note that you must reboot after running this script for the
echo changes to take effect.
echo.
echo The script will run after this pause.
echo.
echo. pause
rem
rem Sets necessary permissions on c:\winnt\repair
```

```
rem
rem The following section changes the Windows NT user rights on the computer.
ntrights -r SeNetworkLogonRight -u Everyone
ntrights -r SeNetworkLogonRight -u "Power Users"
ntrights +r SeNetworkLogonRight -u "Authenticated Users"
ntrights -r SeInteractiveLogonRight -u Users
ntrights -r SeInteractiveLogonRight -u Guests
ntrights -r SeInteractiveLogonRight -u "Power Users"1
ntrights -r SeShutdownPrivilege -u "Backup Operators"
ntrights -r SeShutdownPrivilege -u "Server Operators"
ntrights -r SeShutdownPrivilege -u "Users"
ntrights -r SeShutdownPrivilege -u "Power Users"
ntrights -r SeRemoteShutdownPrivilege -u "Power Users"
rem
rem This part of the script deletes the OS/2 and POSIX subsystem files.
del %systemroot%\system32\posix.exe
del %systemroot%\system32\psxss.exe
del %systemroot%\system32\psxdll.dll
rem
rem This sets SOME of the account policy stuff. (Some stuff must be done in the GUI.)
net accounts /minpwlen:7
net accounts /uniquepw:10
passprop /complex
passprop /adminlockout
rem
rem Hides the last user who logged on.
reg add "HKLM\Software\Microsoft\Windows
➥NT\CurrentVersion\Winlogon\DontDisplayLastUserName"=1
rem
rem Disables 8.3 filename generation on NTFS partitions.  This will break 16-bit
➥programs,
rem including many software installations. This change is essential on IIS Web
➥servers.
reg update
HKLM\System\CurrentControlSet\Control\FileSystem\NtfsDisable8dot3NameCreation=1
rem
rem Disables DCOM. Will break DCOM-based applications.
reg update "HKLM\Software\Microsoft\Ole\EnableDCOM"=N
rem
rem Deletes the Registry entries for the OS/2 and POSIX subsystems.
reg delete "HKLM\System\CurrentControlSet\Control\Session Manager\Subsystems\Os2"
➥/FORCE
reg delete "HKLM\System\CurrentControlSet\Control\Session Manager\Subsystems\Posix"
➥/FORCE
reg delete "HKLM\System\CurrentControlSet\Control\Session Manager\Subsystems\Optional"
➥=
reg delete "HKLM\Software\Microsoft\Os/2 Subsystem for NT" /FORCE
rem
rem Restrict anonymous connections to the computer.
reg add "HKLM\System\CurrentControlSet\Control\LSA\RestrictAnonymous"=1 REG_DWORD
```

[1] *If this command runs on workstations, however, it results in denial of access to Users and Power Users—a highly undesirable outcome.*

```
rem
rem Sets the number of logon credentials Windows NT will cache to zero.
reg add "HKLM\Software\Microsoft\Windows
➥NT\CurrentVersion\Winlogon\CachedLogonsCount"=0 REG_DWORD
rem
rem Clears the page file at system shutdown. Not recommended due to tremendous
➥increase
rem in the time it takes to reboot.  Seriously, who is gonna steal your hard drive and
rem read the page file?
rem reg update "HKLM\System\CurrentControlSet\Control\Session Manager\Memory
➥Management\ClearPageFileATShutdown"=1
rem
rem Removes unnecessary named pipes and named shares (anonymous connection methods).
reg update "HKLM\System\CurrentControlSet\Services\LanManServer\Parameters\
➥NullSessionShares"=
reg update "HKLM\System\CurrentControlSet\Services\LanManServer\Parameters\
➥NullSessionPipes"=EPMAPPER;LOCATOR
rem
rem Enables (does not require) SMB packet signing both when the computer is acting
rem as a server (sharing files) and as a workstation (using files on the network).
reg add "HKLM\System\CurrentControlSet\Services\LanManServer\Parameters\EnableSecurity
➥Signature"=1 REG_DWORD
reg add "HKLM\System\CurrentControlSet\Services\Rdr\Parameters\EnableSecurity
➥Signature"=1 REG_DWORD
rem
rem Secures base system objects.
reg update "HKLM\System\CurrentControlSet\Control\Session Manager\ProtectionMode"=1
rem
rem Allow (not force) better encryption of passwords sent over the network.
reg add "HKLM\System\CurrentControlSet\Control\LSA\LMCompatibilityLevel"=1 REG_DWORD
rem
rem Restrict guest access to the Event logs.
reg add "HKLM\System\CurrentControlSet\Services\Eventlog\Application\Restrict
➥GuestAccess"=1 REG_DWORD
reg add "HKLM\System\CurrentControlSet\Services\Eventlog\Security\RestrictGuestAccess"
➥=1 REG_DWORD
reg add "HKLM\System\CurrentControlSet\Services\Eventlog\System\RestrictGuestAccess"=1
➥REG_DWORD
rem
rem Allocate floppy and CD-ROM drives.
reg add "HKLM\Software\Microsoft\Windows
➥NT\CurrentVersion\Winlogon\AllocateFloppies"=1 REG_SZ
reg add "HKLM\Software\Microsoft\Windows NT\CurrentVersion\Winlogon\AllocateCDRoms"=1
➥REG_SZ
```

F

Manual Clean-Up Procedures for Tightening Security after Script Execution

The following set of manual procedures accompanies the security script listed in Appendix E, "A Script for Securing Windows NT Systems." After you have run the script on a system, you may want to tighten security by making the recommended changes listed here. Mad Dog originally wrote these procedures.

1. Open User Manager.
2. Go to User, Select Domain and enter *servername*; *servername* is the name of the server on which you are working.
3. Go to the Policies menu and select Audit.
4. Enable auditing for Logon/Logoff Failure.
5. Enable auditing for Restart, Shutdown and System, Success and Failure.
6. Go to the Policies menu and select Account.
7. Set the following parameters. (Some, but not all, may be set already—the exact values you choose will, of course, depend on your particular security needs.)
    - Minimum Password Length: 7 characters
    - Account Lockout After: 5 bad logon attempts
    - Reset Count: 60 minutes
    - Duration: 60 minutes
    - Password Uniqueness: 10
    - Minimum Password Age: 2 days

8. Set security on `C:\WINNT` as follows:
    - Administrators: FULL CONTROL
    - Creator Owner: FULL CONTROL
    - SYSTEM: FULL CONTROL
    - Everyone: Read
9. Open `C:\WINNT` and select all folders except Repair and Profiles.
10. Do a properties on them. Go to the Security tab and click Permissions. You will be asked whether you want to reset security information. Click Yes.
11. Be sure to check the Apply Permissions to Subdirectories option.
12. Set the permissions as follows:
    - Everyone: Read
    - Administrators: FULL CONTROL
    - SYSTEM: FULL CONTROL
    - Creator Owner: FULL CONTROL[1]
13. Set permissions on these directories as follows:
    - In `C:\WINNT\Repair`, give FULL CONTROL to Administrators.
    - In `C:\WINNT\Profiles\Administrator`, remove the Read permission from Everyone.
    - In `C:\WINNT\System32\Config`, change the Read permission to the List permission for Everyone.
14. Set the permissions of `C:\BOOT.INI`, `C:\NTLDR`, and `C:\NTDETECT.COM` as follows:
    - Administrators: FULL CONTROL
    - SYSTEM: FULL CONTROL
15. Set permissions on CONFIG.SYS and AUTOEXEC.BAT as follows:
    - Administrators: FULL CONTROL
    - Everyone: Read
16. Open REGEDT32 (*not* REGEDIT).
17. Set permissions on the following keys, as specified here:

    Go to `HKLM\Software\Microsoft\Windows\CurrentVersion` and set security on the following subkeys:

---

1 *The Read-Only access to Everyone propagated down the directory tree is risky in that it may cause a number of processes to break. You may therefore also want to consider propagating Add and Read to Everyone instead.*

Run

RunOnce

RunOnceEx

Uninstall

To Administrators, give FULL CONTROL. To SYSTEM, give FULL CONTROL. To Everyone, Read. (Remove all other permissions.)

Do the same thing to these keys:

Go to `HKLM\Software\Microsoft\Windows NT\CurrentVersion`, and set security on the following subkeys:

AeDebug

WinLogon

These keys can be used to initiate the execution of Trojan horses by non-administrators if they are not properly secured.

Go to `HKEY_LOCAL_MACHINE\System\CurrentControlSet\Control\SecurePipeServers\Winreg`.

Verify that only Administrators have write access or greater to the Winreg key, because such access determines who can edit the Registry over the network.

Go to `HKEY_LOCAL_MACHINE\Software\Microsoft\WindowsNT\CurrentVersion\Perflib`.

Set the permissions on the key so that only Administrators and SYSTEM have access. This prevents any random person from using Perfmon (the Performance monitor) to learn what services are installed on the server.

Go to `HKEY_LOCAL_MACHINE\System\CurrentControlSet\Services\Schedule`.

Set permissions so that only Administrators and SYSTEM have access. This prevents Server Operators from running stuff in the context of LocalSystem, and also prevents random people from looking at the task list.

Go to `HKEY_LOCAL_MACHINE\Software` and remove the permission for Everyone. Set permission for Users to Read. Give Administrators, SYSTEM, and Creator Owner FULL CONTROL. Optionally, give Power Users Special Access to have everything except Create Link, Write DAC, and Write Owner.

Index

Symbols

A

B

C

D

E

F

G

H

I

J-K

L

M

N

O

P

Q-R

S

T

U

V

W

X-Z

Windows 2000 Answers

Selected Windows 2000 Titles from New Riders Publishing

This is the updated edition of New Riders' best-selling *Inside Windows NT Server 4*. New Riders proudly offers something unique for Windows 2000 administrators—an interesting and discriminating book on Windows 2000 Server, written by someone in the trenches who can anticipate your situation and provide answers you can trust.

ISBN: 1-56205-929-7

ISBN: 0-56205-886-X

Managing the user and the user's desktop environment is a critical component in administering Windows 2000. *Windows 2000 User Management* provides you with the real-world tips and examples you need to get the job done.

Windows 2000 Active Directory is just one of several new Windows 2000 titles from New Riders' acclaimed *Landmark Series*. Perfect for network architects and administrators, this book describes the intricacies of Active Directory to help you plan, deploy, and manage Active Directory in an enterprise setting.

ISBN: 0-7357-0870-3

Advanced Information on Networking Technologies

New Riders Books Offer Advice and Experience

LANDMARK

Rethinking Computer Books

We know how important it is to have access to detailed, solution-oriented information on core technologies. *Landmark Series* books contain the essential information you need to solve technical problems. Written by experts and subjected to rigorous peer and technical reviews, our *Landmark* books are hard-core resources for practitioners like you.

ESSENTIAL REFERENCE

Smart, Like You

The *Essential Reference* series from New Riders provides answers when you know what you want to do but need to know how to do it. Each title skips extraneous material and assumes a strong base of knowledge. These are indispensable books for the practitioner who wants to find specific features of a technology quickly. Avoiding fluff and basic material, these books present solutions in an innovative, clean format—and at a great value.

MCSE CERTIFICATION

Engineered for Test Success

New Riders offers a complete line of test preparation materials to help you achieve your certification. With books like the *MCSE Training Guide*, and software like the acclaimed *MCSE Complete* and the revolutionary *ExamGear*, New Riders offers comprehensive products built by experienced professionals who have passed the exams and instructed hundreds of candidates.

Other Titles of Interest from New Riders...

Windows 2000 Professional
By Jerry Honeycutt
1st Edition
450 pages, $49.99
ISBN: 0-7357-0950-0

Windows 2000 DNS
By Roger Abell, Herman Knief, Andrew Daniels, and Jeffrey A. Graham
2nd Edition
500 pages, $39.99
ISBN: 0-7357-0973-4

Windows 2000 Deployment and Desktop Management
By Jeffrey Ferris
1st Edition
400 pages, $34.99
ISBN: 0-7357-0975-0

Windows 2000 Routing and Remote Access Service
By Kackie Charles
1st Edition
400 pages, $34.99
ISBN: 0-7357-0951-3

Windows 2000 Thin Client Solutions
By Todd Mathers
2nd Edition
600 pages, $45.00
ISBN: 1-57870-239-9

MCSE Training Guide: Windows 2000 Professional (70-210)
By Gordon Barker
1st Edition, June 2000
ISBN: 0-7357-0965-3

MCSE Training Guide: Windows 2000 Server (70-215)
By Dennis Maione
1st Edition, June 2000
ISBN: 0-7357-0968-8

MCSE Training Guide: Windows 2000 Network Security Design (70-220)
By Roberta Bragg
1st Edition, July 2000
ISBN: 0-7257-0984-X

MCSE Training Guide: Windows 2000 Network Infrastructure Design (70-221)
By Dale Holmes and Bill Matsoukas
1st Edition, July 2000
ISBN: 0-7357-0982-3

MCSE Training Guide: Installing and Administering a Windows 2000 Directory (70-217)
By Damir Bersinic and Rob Scrimger
1st Edition, July 2000
ISBN: 0-7357-0976-9